WOMEN AMONG MARGINALISED COMMUNITIES OF INDIA

WOMEN AMONG MARGINALISED COMMUNITIES OF INDIA: ISSUES AND CHALLENGES

Edited by

General Editor

Dr. GNANAPRAGASAM LAZAR

Working Editor

Prof. Sudhakar Rao

GYAN

Published, 2020

Published by

Gyan Publishing House
5, Ansari Road
Daryaganj, New Delhi-110002
Phone: 011-47034999, 9811692060
www.gyanbooks.com
E-mail: books@gyanbooks.com

Printed at: G. Print Process, Delhi.

Cataloging in Publication Data—DK
Courtesy: D.K. Agencies (P) Ltd. <docinfo@dkagencies.com>

Women among marginalised communities of India : issues and challenges / [edited] by Dr. Gnanapragasm Lazar.
pages cm
"... National Seminar on 'Women Among Marginalised Communities of India: Issues and Challenges' held on 1st and 2nd of February 2019"—Message.
ISBN 9788121219747

1. Women—India—Social conditions—Congresses. 2. Tribes—India—Social conditions—Congresses. 3. Marginality, Social—India—Congresses. 4. Women in development—India—Congresses.
I. Lazar, G., editor.

LCC HQ1742.W66 2019 | DDC 305.420954 23

Contents

Acknowledgements

The awakening of marginalized segment of Indian society has been the focus of the past six national seminars conducted by SANSKRUTI – the Institute of Dravidian Culture and Research, Hyderabad. According to the Population Research Institute, at least 12.7 million sex-selective abortions were conducted in India between 2000 and 2014. The 2011 census showed that the female child population in the age group of 0-6 years declined from 78.83 million in 2001 to 75.84 million in 2011.

Women's emancipation and gender equality has been a movement for over a century and still continues. India's future is interlinked with the lives of the girls and women of the country. Women from the marginalized communities form half our population and cannot in today's age be denied their fundamental freedoms. There are several glass ceilings that keep women out of the social fabric in India.

This volume on, ***Women Among Marginalised Communities of India: Issues and Challenges*** discovers the contemporary issues connected with the women of marginalized communities. While literature has contributed a great deal towards transforming society and empowering women, the world continues to grapple with pernicious phenomenon – Gender issues. Can the present world help bridge the divide?

In this issue galaxy of eminent professors, scholars, and social activists have closely looked at the issue of women among marginalized communities. Throughout the process of conducting the seminar and editing this volume, many distinguished personalities have taken time to help us out. At the outset we thank Fr. Antony Joseph SVD, the Provincial Superior of India Hyderabad Province (INH) who is also the President of SANSKRUTI has been the chief motivating force in this endeavour.

It is my bounden duty, to place on record, my immense gratitude to Fr. Xavier Alangaram SVD, the Missionsprokur, St. Augustin, Germany, for having readily come forward with the grant for the seminar. May I express my profound gratefulness to all at the Mission Office at St. Augustin, Germany with a due sense of gratitude!

SANSKRUTI is grateful to Padmashree Prof. Smt. Shantha Sinha, former Chairperson, National Commission for Protection of Child Rights, India

Recipient of Magsaysay Award – 2003, Prof. Dasari Sreenivasulu, IAS (Rtd) Member, Executive Council of University of Hyderabad and Smt. Tejdeep Kaur Menon, IPS, Director General of Police, Telangana Special Protection Force – TSSPF and Fr. Prof. S. Maria Michael from Mumbai University who added academic and social framework to the seminar during inaugural and valedictory functions.

SANSKRUTI is immensely indebted to Prof. Dr. Malli Gandhi, Professor and Head, Dept. of Social Sciences and Humanities, Regional Institute of Education, NCERT, Mysuru. Understanding the nuances of the current social and political situation of India he worked out the concept-note for this seminar. Deriving benefit from his fruitful interactions by way of time-bound progress in research, and acquisition of clarity in research he properly streamlined the nuances of the seminar. At this juncture, my heart goes forth in gratitude to Prof. Midatala Rani, Director, UGC, HRD, University of Mysore, a perceptive intellectual person for proposing the theme for the seminar. We thank her for her forward-looking and praxis-oriented contribution for the publication of this book.

We recall with gratitude, the dynamic vision and guidance of Prof. Srinivasa Rao from University of Hyderabad – Centre for Regional Studies, who helped the Institute to invite the chief guests and scholars for the national seminar. We place on record our profound gratitude to Prof. Sudhakar Rao, from University of Hyderabad (Rtd), (South Asian Social Systems, Indian Society and Ideology, Anthropology of Communication, Political Anthropology), for offering incisive and insightful comments towards the improvement from the perspective of the contemporary reach of the people. SANSKRUTI is indebted to Prof. Sudhakar Rao for having proof-read the final version of the manuscript, at short notice.

SANSKRUTI is grateful to Prof. Dr. Kamal K. Misra, the Vice-Chancellor, Utkal University of Culture, Bhubaneshwar who has been rendering constant support to our publication every year.

Big thanks to all our collaborators, the staff and students of St. Francis Women's College, Little Flower College, St. Pious-X College and Kasturba Women's College for their active participation and intellectual contribution.

SANSKRUTI thanks Dr. Savari Rayan SVD, Dr. Victor Sagayam SVD, and (DR) Wilson SVD, who had been supportively solicitous in the dynamics of the seminar. It is my duty to place on record, my immense gratitude to Gyan Publishers, New Delhi for their collaboration, unflinching support, qualitative printing with proficient touch and excellence. We gratefully acknowledge the intellectual contribution of the eminent professors, scholars and other social activists who helped shape this volume.

This is the time of the "flowering of the backward" – to borrow a phrase from U.R. Anantha Murthy in Indian Writing. The papers contained in this volume are not just confined to literature. It is a reflection of the democratic aspirations of the subaltern sections of the Indian population, a collective step towards fuller freedom of the women among the marginalized communities. These papers will inspire Indian people and the policy makers' final battle against the tyranny of communal, capitalist and authoritarian dehumanizing forces.

Dr. Gnanapragasam Lazar,
Director, SANSKRUTI - Institute of
Dravidian Culture and Research,
Hyderabad, T. S. INDIA

Foreword

I am extremely pleased to write a foreword to this book, devoted to a comparative understanding of women in different types of society in India. Scholars from different disciplines have contributed their respective papers to this book. Whilst some of them are rich empirical accounts, the others are theoretical, which, however, do not lose their relationship with field data. Read as a whole, the book tells us that women are far being a homogenous category. Not only do the social and economic conditions differentiate women, but also in most societies, the progression of age increases their prestige in their households, giving them larger control over economic and human resources. My observation is that the elderly women (grandmothers, mothers, mothers-in-law) wield robust control over their men (husbands, husband's younger brothers, sons and sons-in-law). The life of a woman, therefore, graduates on a continuum from 'minus power' to 'plus power'. Surprisingly, in the studies of gender relations, the dimension of time is forgotten, what is called 'time in social structure'. It will be interesting to analyze how age, though debilitating physical capacity to work, thus reducing one's abilities to produce (and reproduce), empowers the individual (particularly, women) in social terms.

The papers in the book also reiterate the point that the economic situation of a community conditions the relative status and power of gender category. One of the major reasons for the lower status of upper caste women is that they are 'non-producing, consuming members' of the society, whereas their counterparts in lower castes, who have a higher status, are 'producing' – they work in fields, augmenting family income. In some cases, it is seen that while the husbands take to alcohol, to which they sacrifice a substantial portion of their meager daily wages, the women take up, knowingly but grudgingly, the arduous responsibility of running their household, taking care of children and family resources. They may even plough their cultivating land and supervise agricultural operations, notwithstanding a battery of taboos that may be imposed upon them. Although the society may have patrilineal and patriarchal style of kinship, in reality such households are matrifocal, or 'mother or female-centred'. These types of households are not rare. Many societies in the world have reported the absence of a 'functional male', or dimunition of the male role. Consider these cases: men are away on grazing expeditions with their herds of animals, or are employed in armies, or are on business tours lasting for months, or have been incarcerated, or may have deserted their wives for other relationships, or may lead the life of a peregrinator or mendicant. In all these cases the women are the heads of their households – these households are called 'female-headed' or 'male-absent'.

Economy plays a crucial role in affecting the interpersonal ties. Those elderly, the newspaper reports inform us, who have parted their wealth in favour of their progeny, are languished to lead the life of a destitute. Well known are the heart-rending cases of the widows in the sacred towns of Mathura and Vrindavana, who have been left uncared and 'lost' in places far away from homes, to eventually find a refuge in hospices that the philanthropists have built. The state of many of these 'residential homes' is so despicable that their description will fill the reader with loathe. Not unknown are the cases of those senior-citizens who suffer indignation silently in their own households at the hands of their children, rather than knocking at the door of the court, or any informal institution that is expected to render help, for they do not want the world to know they gave birth to un-filial offspring. One of the pieces of advice for middle classes given in websites titled 'Age Gracefully' is 'never part with your money and property during your lifetime'; in fact, it is tacitly telling its readers that 'your children, so fond of you now, will leave you like the baby birds on growing up fly in the firmament to explore their future, and may have scant concern for you. Mobile phones will replace interpersonal conversations; short message service (sms) will replace post cards.' The old people are advised to learn to fend for themselves, demanding no attention or favour from anyone except the state. This is graceful ageing!

Essays in this book, in one way or the other, make us face the stark reality of gender disparity. Women should be economically empowered; laws especially enacted for protecting the rights of women should be strictly enforced; and the sensitization programmes aiming to create gender equality and respect should be intensified, are some of the suggestions the book offers. Of great significance is the attention paid to the women of the most vulnerable of the vulnerable groups (such as de-notified, nomadic and semi-nomadic communities). Documenting the cases of the marginalization of women, a forceful argument of the book is that the traditional distinction between 'public' and 'private' spaces needs to be reworked for gender relations. No more are women confined to the four walls of the household (the 'familial domain'), and no more are men only concerned with the outside world, what the anthropologists call, the 'politico-jural domain'. Gender roles are reversing; new role sets are being added to each of them. Forces that attempt to justify the golden past, the pristine gender roles, are also rising, and so are the attempts to put them to rest, for the forces of development and change are unstoppable.

I am sure the book has many more points for mulling and discussion. Kudos to the editors!

Vinay Kumar Srivastava

Director, Anthropological Survey of India.

Message

Padmashree Prof. Shrimati Shantha Sinha
Magsaysay Award winner (2003)

I am honored to be associated with the National Seminar on 'Women among Marginalised Communities of India: Issues and Challenges held on 1st and 2nd of February 2019.

This gives us an occasion to congratulate women who made many advancements against all odds in the fields of education, medicine, environment, and agriculture, combating gender discrimination or violence. We also celebrate the gains made by women movements to bring about radical laws towards gender equality. We applaud the efforts of Ritu Karidhal and M Vanitha for leading the mission Chandrayan-2. We also commend the sprinter, Hima Das, who recently won her fifth gold medal of the season in 400m race, Dutee Chand who won the 100m and 200m silver at the 2018 Asian Games and boldly announced that she was gay and that 'everybody should have the freedom to love', India is also home to Vinesh, Babita and Geeta Phogat—award-winning wrestlers and sisters—and Poorna Mallavath, who broke world records when she climbed Mt. Everest at the tender age of thirteen. This is also an occasion to celebrate the female *sarpanches* in our country who are changing the landscape of village India. It is also a moment to recognise the radical laws in India in favour of women's empowerment which was possible due to the women's movement in our country.

At the same time, it is necessary to see how difficult the battle against patriarchy and for gender justice has been. We are witness to increasing crimes against women that show an upward trend. This is especially true for violent crimes such as rapes, dowry deaths, and honour killings. Also troubling is a very skewed sex ratio that persists in several states. While there is evidence of economic growth it shows that it *does not* automatically foster gender equality. The male female wage gap has been stagnant at 50%, though this narrows to a 27% pay gap. We have experienced a significant seven points drop in female labour force participation.

It is true that patriarchy cuts across all classes, castes, religious and ethnic groups, states and nations. However, it gets further compounded in the face of poverty, economic exploitation and oppression, illiteracy, caste discrimination and so on. Poor women from and marginalised communities have little control or right over themselves and find it difficult protecting their bodily integrity against violence, sexual assault, abuse - domestic as well as in work place. They need support of the State as well as civil society.

The battle for gender equality is not a women's issue alone. In this endeavor, men and women have equal and shared responsibility. Indeed, the process of rendering gender equality goes beyond binaries of male and female. We band together as human beings with new imaginations and ways of thinking and doing things, bringing about transformation of all humankind.

Shanta Sinha is an academician with Hyderabad Central University. She gained the internationally renowned 2003 Ramon Magsaysay award for community leadership. She has also been awarded with Hyderabad Women of the Decade Achievers Award for Social Service by ASSOCHAM Ladies League. She is also the Founder Secretary Trustee and Chief Programme Advisor MVF. It is a rights based grass root level NGO operating in and out of Hyderabad.

Introduction

"India's future is interlinked with the lives and empowerment of the marginalised women of the country" is the focus of this particular volume. The papers published in this book is the proceedings of the the 6th Annual National Seminar conducted by SANSKRUTI – Institute of Dravidian Culture and Research at Arnold Bhavan, Hyderabad on February 1 and 2, 2019. The main theme of the Seminar was on: **"Women among Marginalised Communities of India: Issues and Challenges."**

In the web of alternate realities women's studies have been a landmark in a united drive by scholars, students, social activists, and allies of the women's movement in India to advance the agenda of gender equality. Many conferences have provided an important platform for studies, debates, and clarification of perspectives on a wide range of issues and questions that impact the lives of women. The present National Seminar constituted one more step in this journey of ideas.

In the mid and late – 1800s, social movements in Europe for equal rights for women threw up the word 'feminism', which traces its origins to French. The suffrage movement in Britain in the early part of the 20th century was another component of women's fight for equality across the world. Over the years, this fight has gained momentum, often with varying goals depending on the cultural traditions and the degree of prevalence of patriarchy in different societies. Various instances have inspired women to collectively get together and assert their rights – to create a combined voice that strongly advocates the impending need to view them. In the current world, there are strong stances that women are taking to support causes, such as the #MeToo movement that started in the U.S. and took down power players like Harvey Weinstein and Roy Price and is now a force to reckon with in India (Damini Chopra, THE HINDU, July 11, 2019, p. 9).

The central theme of the book reflects the current context of a rapidly changing economy and society that is simultaneously and increasingly mired in a lived experience of uncertainty, volatility, insecurity, and conflict. There is accumulating evidence that far from being an equalizing or liberating force, the nature of contemporary change and continued restructuring of the State and the economy by neo-liberalism and globalization has expanded the range of inequalities, modes of discrimination, and forms of violence against women in general and women among marginalised groups in particular.

In the midst of a significantly more complicated terrain of inequality, assertions and resistance by women across several new sites of public action have also come to the fore, even as some others may have become less visible. The intricately intertwined multiplicity of issues, questions, and debates that confronts any student of women's studies today can indeed appear like a confusing medley of situations.

A popular recognition of and widespread hunger for education as the way forward, has indeed led to significant increases in enrolment ratios among girls, including in higher education. This surge in women's involvement with education as students and teachers has also been reflected in a heightened presence of girl students and women teachers in debates and movements in colleges and universities across India.

Gender issues, feminist perspectives, and resistance against inequality and discrimination have emerged as important components of campus discourse. Even as ascendant privatization is transforming and restructuring the political economy and role of education in India, it appears that public institutions have become important sites of renewed questioning by an increasingly diversified community of students and teachers. At the same time, the academic institutional space seems more fraught, restricted, and subject to new uncertainties at various levels. Nowhere is this uncertainty more directly apparent than in the case of the more than 150 Women's Studies Centres that have been established by the UGC, whose continued existence is still not assured. Debates around quality, interdisciplinary, employability, accountability in education, thus necessarily intermingle with concerns regarding increasing contractualisation, adhocism, and discontinuities experienced by students, teachers, and practitioners of women's studies, as well as other new and old disciplines. This book provides a platform to review, document, debate, and develop collective thinking and strategizing on all these issues to face the challenges ahead.

For quite some time, the hyper-visibility of some new forms of employment for women, particularly in urban services, had masked the crisis in women's employment. After a quarter century of entrenchment of the neo-liberal policy framework, we now know that it has resulted in female employment rates having actually dropped to the lowest levels in the history of independent India. Paradoxically, the sharpest fall in women's employment took place during the period that saw the highest rates of economic growth. 21st century rural India has also witnessed widespread agrarian crisis marked by increasing non-viability of agricultural livelihoods. Its consequence has been a dramatic reduction in self-cultivation, with a greater fall in the number of women cultivators. The number of agricultural labourers, on the other hand, continued to increase to record levels. Declining workdays in agriculture suggests that significant proportions of even those counted as employed in agriculture have little work. Interconnected to these processes are the issues of sustainability, environmental degradation, reduction of rights over common property resources, and the impact of climate change.

Once criticized for ignoring the divergent experiences and articulations of women of socially oppressed Adivasi, Dalit and Minority castes/communities, women's studies and the women's movement in India have become significant contributors to contemporary Adivasi/Dalit/Minority assertion against caste based discrimination, stigma, inequality, and for affirmative action. Varied positions and arguments have emerged from within women's studies on Adivasi/Dalit/Minority women's unique experience and issues including one argument, advocating for feminists who may not be Adivasi/Dalits/minority groups to reinvent themselves as 'Adivasi/Dalit/Minority feminists' to enable a more 'emancipatory standpoint'. At the same time, diverse forms of Adivasi/Dalit/Minority women's organizations are also increasingly allying their anti-caste/anti-patriarchy assertions with the broader women's movement. Social perceptions of women's 'honour' being linked to caste identity and endogamy have of course long been accepted as oppressive for women, and the women's movement has indeed stood steadfast beside young couples who cross such boundaries. Yet, in such cases, vulnerability to assaults, degrading forms of public humiliation, and even killings, remain a continuing reality, particularly when a Adivasi/Dalit/Minority is involved.

This book provides a rich and long history of anti-caste social movements and ideas that have been ideologically linked with an agenda for women's emancipation. It provides us with a special opportunity for collective learning about this heritage, and also for debating its place and relevance for women located within restructured correlations of caste domination and countercurrents of resistance that define the contemporary Indian context.

New issues have also emerged from the recent experience of organized attempts to brutally suppress Adivasi/Dalit/Minority ferment intersecting with organized attempts at communal polarization and promotion of communal hatred. Recurrent practices of 'dishonouring' women in the name of community honour, and the virulent attacks on inter-faith marriages, do indeed appear to share features in common with violence against inter-caste marriages, albeit on a stridently political and communal register. Women's studies has from its inception, been committed to peace and communal amity as a basic condition for progression towards equality and emancipation. The adverse effects of politicization of religion on the advance of equality for women, the dangers of majoritarianism, as well as contemporary articulations of women's rights from within minority communities, are all important issues before this Conference.

There are other minorities whose movements for democratic rights and equality have come to the fore in recent years. The disability rights movement has expanded in scope and scale in recent years, and this volume makes space for integrating their location within the broader themes of the conference, while also providing a platform for articulation of their special issues. This issue also includes voices of sexual minorities, and discuss their key concerns, including but not restricted to discrimination, prejudice, stigma, violence, as well the articulation and assertion of their right to dignity and equality.

Of special significance of the of this book is the upsurge of different forms of militarization, and the immediate impact on women's rights, external as well as internal to their existence and location in the societal structures and regions. Issues of conflict and peace thus form an essential component of this book, in order not only to debate and discuss, but also to develop theoretical research in tandem with women's strategies and movements for peace and security by focusing on the most important area like marginalised groups and sections in India.

Dr. G. Lazar

Prof. N. Sudhakar Rao

Chapter - 1

Role of Women among Nomadic and Denotified Tribes: Issues and Challenges

Prof. Malli Gandhi[1]

Introduction

Environmental orientation and adaptive strategies of indigenous communities in India reflect harmonious bonds with their ecological set ups. Some of them are wandering, nomadic and semi-nomadic groups (NT/DNTs) Some of them are living as hunter-gatherers and inhabiting uplands and lowlands, while few of them are riverine fishing communities. Some of them are following traditional occupations but several have changed them and diversified into other occupations. Some of them are living by means of cattle breading, menial casual labour, and dealing with works related to forest, and agricultural. In addition they make baskets, mats, ropes, brooms and brushes. Most of them are acrobats, following different types of occupations such as monkey trapping, bird snaring, singing, snake charming, fortune telling, and collecting forest plant parts, fruits, nuts, seeds, berries, leaf and roots, vegetables, yams, mushrooms etc. They have developed institutionalized culture and their indigenous knowledge, includes a way of information processing and storing it. A mechanism in situating different social groups within the changing social environment has also been developed by them. In these societies women play significant role.

Traditional means of livelihood

Independent India envisaged to build an egalitarian society in which people with diverse socio-cultural and economic background can have equal opportunities in various fields with dignity and honour. In order to achieve a cohesive society, some sort of social engineering is imperative for bringing the historically neglected people on par with privileged sections of the society. Positive discrimination along with developmental interventions and capacity building were considered essential for social engineering. In order to achieve a state of social and economic equality, builders of modern India had undertaken certain measures right from the beginning of independence. The communities that are historically disadvantaged are classified into categories such as Scheduled Castes (SCs), Scheduled Tribes (STs) and Other Backward Classes (OBCs). Certain Privileges are given to them to overcome socio-economic disabilities. As a part of the categorization, communities who have been wandering, nomadic, and semi-nomadic, criminal tribes are excluded from the lists of SC,ST and OBC categories. However, their categorization has not been not logical and uniform. A large number of communities are not included in any category of SC/ST/OBCS. They are placed on par with the general sections of population. These communities have a long history of marginalisation. They are neglected and oppressed during the colonial and post-colonial independent India. The development schemes designed for SC/ ST categories have not benefited the DT/DNT communities. They are denied, segregated and pushed to the walls on account of stigma of nomadic and gypsy way of living. They are identified as wanders, following customs such as earth diggers, fisher men, salt sellers, shepherds, scavengers and basket makers, furriers and tanners, landless agricultural laborers, waterman, toddy tapers, pig breeders, collectors of forest produce, hinderers and beggars. In India there are 192 NT/DNT communities comprising around nine percent of the tribal population.

NT/DNT communities in Andhra Pradesh and Telangana are Poosala (bead sellers), Woddera (earth diggers), Pamula (snake charmers), Uppara (salt manufacturers), Dudekula (cotton cleaners), Pichiguntala (genealogists), Lambadis or Sugalis (carriers of salt and grain), Chenchu (hunting and gathering tribe), Nakkala, Boya, Nirshikari (trappers of birds and animals), Dasari, Bogam, Satanis (temple attendants), Piriki Muggalas, Koracha, Yerukula, (professing tattoing, fortune telling). Further, Dasaris, Parayas, Korawas, Dommaras, Jogis, Konda Doras, Rellis, Paidis, Gollas, Malas, Madigas, were also declared as NT/DNs in Andhra Pradesh. In the State of Hyderabd there 7 denotified tribes are identified. In the erstwhile Madras Presidency 43 denotified tribes were listed. Andhra Pradesh government declared 56 communities as NT/DNT communities in the state. NT/DNTs are very poor and economically backward. Most of them are living with meagre income. Their habitations are usually a cluster of thatched huts or settlements. A few of them are well off and they are engaged in petty business and government jobs. Among the NT/DNTs family is considered as the basic unit. Males go out for manual labour works. Women take care of children and participate in household work and indoor activities.

The *Kulapanchayat* (the hereditary council of the caste elders) constitutes the primary political organization. Its primary responsibility is settling various disputes, overseeing the observance of community norms relating to marriage, divorce, inheritance of property if any, economic transactions, inter-family, intra-community and inter-community disputes etc. The *Kulapanchayat* system that prevailed among these communities has degraded their positions due to various ordeals conducted on them. Society among nomadic, semi-nomadic and denotified communities is based on patriarchal system. However, women occupy a relatively important position. The decision making power is entirely vested with males. Men, women and children of NT/DNTs received their livelihood as small traders, in various districts in Madras presidency in 18-19th centuries. These tribes moved from district to district, carrying salt, food items, and household materials from the plain areas to inland districts. They used animals such as donkeys, oxen, and bullocks to carry their trade. Thus, these communities once upon a time were nomadic. Nowadays, they are settled and earning their livelihood by following different occupations. Trading activities are predominantly their means of livelihood.

Social Practices of NT/DNT Women

Social practices among denotified tribes inform us about the general position of women among these communities. A system of bride price existed among these communities during the 19th century. Bride price *(voli)* was very high among Yerukulas. During the year 1871 bride price among the Yerukulas was rupees 70. Bride price was paid in the form of donkeys, bullocks, rather than in the form of cash. The degree of bride price implied high economic status of women among these communities. With the destruction of their economic foundations bride price also disappeared among them. Selling, mortgaging of women and prostituting them to moneylenders and the local landlords replaced bride price. In the past, both men and women used to practice polygamy and polyandry. Widows were allowed to remarry. Their women could get divorce very easily. Girls were married only after their puberty. It was observed that: "Women formed an important factor in the settlements of the NT/DNTs. They generally come and go as they liked and acted as spies and informants to their leaders. They used to go out on the pretext of selling *Karipak* leaves but really to spy out the land and keep themselves in touch with absconding members. The women have now been formally placed in the criminal settlements. Many of the wandering women have been registered under various sections. It is hoped that this step will further tend to put down crime in the Madras Presidency. The chief employment provided for them is agriculture. Besides agriculture, the women in the settlements were also provided with the employment in weaving, silk production, making of ropes and baskets. They were provided with sheep and goats"

There were a number of ways in which women were described in the literary texts. Missionaries like American Baptist Telugu Mission, Canadian Mission, London Mission and Salvation Army described them as "thievish raw materials "Anthropological, sociological, historical studies of the colonial and post-colonial era described these people with different appellations and tags. The high caste Hindus and administrative authorities weakened their position in the society. The different laws of colonial government weakened the position of women. Parents make merchandise of children. The police raid their houses, molest them and drive them away from village. Sometimes they were forced to commit crimes and pay bribes to the police and village authorities. They go for rag picking in order to eke out their livelihood. The types of crime committed on them are peculiar and their photographs were kept in railway stations, bus-stands, and cinema theaters for chain snatching, pick pocketing and other crimes. Poverty-stricken conditions, lack of alternative avenues for livelihoods, lack of work, living in the ex-settlement areas are some of the reasons for their misery and the state of affairs. Government should provide suitable opportunities for their development. Women enjoy lower status than men. They did not have the right to inherit property of their parents. Women worked in fields and go to collect fuel and fodder. No important role was assigned to women in social functions. Women were assigned only household work. They were listed as a criminal tribes under the provisions of the Criminal Tribes Act, 1911. The *Kulakattu* (a traditional community council) contrived the activities of women. Some women go round the villages begging and foretelling events. Some women among these communities were aware of black magic and sing *Burrakathalu* (folk story singing) and folk music. Some of them took to agricultural labor, masonry work and petty trade for their livelihood.

Colonial Economic policies and NT/DNTs

In the early part of the 19th century trading practices of these communities were destroyed by the economic policies of the British government. The introduction of railways, metalled roads, establishment of police constabulary, repeated famines in 1823, 1866, 1876, 1895 and the forest policy of colonial government crippled the traditional occupations of a number of communities. Cattle possessed by them died in large numbers. Forest officers did not allow them to depend on forest produce. The police and forest officials prevented their business, cattle and trading possibilities. The worst affected people out of these policies were women and children among these communities. For example, Dasari women were traditionally employed as village watchers. They used to collect roots, tubers, vegetables etc. They used to work as domestic laborers, village servants and engage in cattle rearing activities. Dasari women used to sell fancy goods, cosmetics, wigs, and trinkets. They accompanied their males when they go round villages for begging. Performing magic was the traditional occupation of Pedditi Gollas. They were experts in tattooing. Jogis were experts in indigenous medical care. They were aware of many varieties of herbs and shrubs. They used to carry antidote for snake venom. Traditionally they were mendicants. Katipapala women in addition to household work used to sell combs, beads, and aluminium wear in the surrounding villages. Konda Dora women used to participate in agricultural operations like thrashing, animal husbandry and collection of minor forest products. Koracha women participated in agricultural activities like sowing, transplantation, weeding, harvesting and other activities. They used to collect palmyrah leaves, bamboo and made mats, ropes and toys. They used to collect minor forest produce like tamarind, soap nut and sold their items in market. They were experts in fortune-telling and collecting food grains. They maintained close relationship with their customers. *Banjara* women were very colorful. They were experts in colorful prints and embroidery work. They supplied their products, transported grain, salt and other items from plains to the inland areas. Likewise, Mandula women used to collect herbs and roots to prepare herbal medicine. Manggarudi women used to sing folk songs and folk tales. Muttarasi women worked as contractors, mill workers and manufacturers. Nakkala women assisted their males in making snares, stuffed animals and colorful necklaces. They were treated as expert sales women. They derive income from selling bangles, mirrors, combs, safety pins, needles etc. Parika Muggala women were experts in sorcery and black magic and fortune-telling. Pitchiguntala women were traditional bards, folk singers, genealogists and wandering mendicants. Veera Mushti women used to work as casual laborers. They used to prepare artificial pigtails (*savaralu*) to supplement their family income. Yata women were experts in toddy-tapping, making umbrellas and other house articles. With the enactment of Criminal Tribes Act of 1911 the local police authorities showed reasons for their alleged involvement in different kinds of crimes in the Madras province and declared them as criminal tribes under section 10 and 12 of the CT Act. Since then, they lost their traditional occupations and led a poverty stricken life.

Disintegration of Tribes into communities and family units

With the enactment of the CT Act 1911, many tribes in the country were declared as criminal tribes. They were kept in agricultural, reformatory, penal and voluntary settlements opened by the colonial government. Men, women and children were placed in the settlements. In reality, they were not criminals. The local moneylenders demanded free labor from women and children. Prejudices of the British administrators also played an important role for the suppression of these communities. It was stated that "the women and children of these communities have the lust for wandering. The women possessed loose sexual morality. Women took on as many husbands as they liked, return on as many husbands as they liked, return the former husband with their children farthered by the new husband, that easy divorce was permitted and that the women as well as men drank toddy on all social occasions". Women possessed slack moral code in the eyes of colonial administrative authorities.

Women as wives, mothers, daughters, and sisters worked hard for the development of their families. It was noted that: "in Guntur the Yerukula women were confined in large numbers. The Stuartpuram settlement was actually started with the women folk whose men were expected to be released from the jails within a year or two. The Salvation Army specified different tasks to be performed in the settlements at various levels. Land was allotted to the women, *pattas* were provided to the individual women, a woman has to work within and outside the family for the welfare of her husband, children and the family members. She used to collect the date palm leaves, and weave the mats, ropes, and baskets for the sale. They used to furnish their houses with the material. They kept their houses and environment very clean. They showed the skills of knitting, sewing, physical labor, agricultural and quarry work". They were asked to pay attention towards their appearance. They strove hard to stop the practice of drinking toddy by males. Thus, the contribution of women for the family welfare and survival among these communities is very critical.

Women and grown-up girls who were very averse to manual labor, were being taught how to make mats. Salvation Army introduced lace and other domestic industries in order to discipline the women folk. The government had stated that in Godavari, Kistna, Kurnool, Bellary, Anantapur and Cuddapah and the other districts in Madras presidency women members of these communities were confined to various kinds of settlements due to their operations. There was an increase in crime rate under dacoities, robberies and house breakings in the Godavari and Krishna districts, which was attributed to women and children of criminal gangs viz, Pamulas, Kondadoras, Donga Waddars etc. who were not settled and who escaped from the settlements. The increase of crime in Kurnool was attributed to Chenchu women who had been declared as a criminal tribe and Yerukulas who have not been settled yet. The employment of Donga Waddar women had prevented crime on their part. There was a slight increase of dacoities in Bellary district for which women of Yerukulas and the out-of-view members of Rudrapad Korchas were said to be responsible. The increase in dacoities in Anantapur district was attributed to the escaped women members from Bhumannagadda settlement, while the marked decrease of crime in Cuddapah district was due to the settlement of women members of Korachas in Chittoor and Nellore districts.

Administrative policies of the Colonial government

Women among these communities had a chequered life. The police used to investigate and detect ordinary, non-professional crime of women among criminal classes in the Madras Presidency. The government had a great hope on women and children in the settlements as a means of reducing crime, as an instrument of reformation, rehabilitation and reclamation of criminals. The chief thing government had adopted was providing them education to bring them up in a proper atmosphere, to disassociate themselves from criminal associations, teach them to lead an honest life and earn their livelihood through honest means. Reformation of adult males and females was more difficult. Reformation work carried in many of the settlements was of a high order.

In industrial settlements women used to carry various forms of employment which the settlement managers allotted to them. The rate of payment for women's work was very low as far as possible. The works which they were engaged included silk worm rearing, silk reeling, spinning and weaving, wool spinning or weaving, cotton weaving and warping, carpet and *durrie* making, black smithy, shoe-making, tailoring, mat and basket-making, coir-picking, pottery-making, metal work, stone-breaking, dressing, quarrying, mining, gardening, building and repairing the buildings, making of treasure bags and boxes, tending poultry and livestock, scavenging, sugar-manufacturing and other duties connected with the upkeep of settlements. In agricultural settlements women actively participated in agricultural activities along with male members. They participated in tasks such as reclamation of lands, growing crops, weeding, and working as agricultural laborers. Their role in obtaining, developing and preserving land was remarkable. They used to work 10 hours daily in order to bring land under cultivation with works such as watering, manuring, levelling, removing bent grass, thrashing floor, processing crop etc.

Women also played significant role in protecting their family members from the strict supervision and control of the police force in settlements, obeying the orders of managers, assistant managers and protected them from various penalties such as warning, additional work, arduous work, reduction of wages, cancellation or withholding of passes, loss of other privileges, daily roll call, restriction of movements to particular areas, fines, prosecution, discipline inside and outside the settlements. It was stated that: "the Waddar women are as criminals as the men. They take part in the commission of heinous crime. They are however, clever at poultry and other petty thefts. They are very daring and immoral and are adepts in the art of spying and concealing and disposing of the stolen property and also in collecting the information useful to the males in the commission of crime. Should any of the males be accused of crime, the women are most troublesome and there are some instances in which they have even rescued the males from lawful custody. The children are equally clever at petty theft. Many of the women and children are convicted".

Repercussions of Women

Women who were working among these communities were removed from settlements with the orders of the Commissioner of Labour Department. Their males were incorrigible. Under these circumstances women members of the family had to prove the good behavior of their husbands, their sincerity and honesty, uniformity of good conduct and behavior despite the fact that males were cruel in treating women. The management, control and supervision of the settlements were vested with settlement managers, assistant managers and police authorities by virtue of their office. But they used to harass women and grown-up girls in settlements in the name of well-being and proper upbringing of members of the tribe. They were allowed to go out with a pass. Women who went beyond settlement limits for fodder, palmyra leaves, date leaves, or women having received the pass overstay outside the limits of settlements for a longer time than specified time in the pass were imposed penalties. Women were expected to take-up regular and daily employment in and outside their settlements in order to eke out livelihood.

Some of the women were appointed as daily wage workers by the Public Works Department in order to take-up works such as road repairs, construction work, cultivation of their lands and also works like ploughing, weeding, reploughing the land after harvest, clearing lands, cutting fuel, and selling in head loads, cutting grass, and selling it as fodder, cutting *tangedu* wood, and removing its bark, repairs to buildings, building revetment, contract works, repair works to buildings etc. It was an interesting factor that the managers of the settlements were instructed by the government to keep a record of women members of settlements with a brief note on their history, associations, avocations, movements, conduct, behavior, with a view to help the police as well as the management to have proper control and watch over them. The sub-divisional officers of police used to watch settlements periodically and inspect them annually. Police constables and head constables from the police outpost used to go round settlements in the nights regularly and check men, children and women. Whenever there was a chance they used to commit crimes on women and children. This was with the pretext to find out whether they go out in nights for committing prostitution or crime.

Women used to get substantial income from weaving, knitting, basket-making, mat- making, and rope-making to run their families. Managers stated that: "in agricultural settlements there was no provision for them to provide employment for the women". They used to provide employment for women somehow. They used to provide continuous work only to male members. Women and children started making mats, baskets very fast in their houses. It paid them better. Some women forced their males to join them in making the items. In order to protect their males from the influences of arrack, punishments from the local police, and other criminal influences women used to encourage males to work at home in household industries.

There were a number of ways in which Salvation Army fashioned women. Women were initially trained in feminine virtues. They were expected to sew, embroider and cook for their families. Mat-making which was a traditional activity of Yerukula men and women was handed over exclusively to women as an indoor activity. Women were taught to pay attention to their appearances. Salvation Army even helped women with periodic parades. The most neatly dressed women and most neatly kept houses were awarded prizes. Women were not allowed to go outside the settlements frequently on passes. The before and after photographs of women were taken by Salvation Army and given to the office. Records show the after version with a completely changed Hinduised appearance, with neatly tied saris, oiled hair, with the flowers and vermilion marks on their fore-heads. Their appearance in the settlement was in fact modified according to the opinions of outside people.

The Changed Roles and Responsibilities of NT/DNT Women

In 1920s Missionaries played an important role in the development of poor women in the presidency. They attracted a large number of poor women and converted them into Christianity. They encouraged moral education to women and children in the settlements. They recommended to the government to provide agriculture as a means of employment. Women were encouraged to work in sugar factories, cement factories, tea gardens, tobacco company, quarry industry, rail industry etc. Income for women from their traditional work soon replaced with industrial wages. They became wageworkers in companies. The materials prepared in these companies were exported to foreign countries. For instance, tobacco processed by Yerukula women was neatly packed in wooden crates and exported to England for cigarette manufacture. Mats and baskets prepared by them were in great demand for the company. Women provided excellent and profitable labor work. Women became factory workers and household workers. They combined the two operations as a single worker. Women used to demand company authorities for extra hours in factories in order to earn more to support their family income. The Labor Department and companies demanded longer hours of work. It was an advantage for the company if the whole family works in the factory. Companies lowered the wages of women's labor. They often used to threaten women workers to lose their jobs if they fail to bring their males to work along with them. Sometimes women used to plead with the managers of company not to handover their wages to their males. Salvation Army in the settlements used to take personal decisions with regard to the matters pertaining to women and children. Thus, missionaries curbed the choices of women in settlements. They played an arbitrary role with regard to women and children.

In connection with the employment of women at the Indian Leaf Tobacco company (ILTD) factory, a nursery or crèche for infant children was also provided. Mothers carried their babies to the company. They left their children in the shed outside the factory gates under the charge of old women. Women who had more children had no one to take care of them. The managers and Forest Department officials attracted children to collect date leaves and hence used to take children along with them. There were lapses and fighting amongst settlers themselves. This was largely due to the sale of toddy in neighboring villages. Whenever, toddy was obtainable, feuds were inevitable. Women used to face severe stress and strain with the drunkard males in settlements. Women often requested to ban the sale of liquor in the settlements. Women used to regularly attend the company's work walking 20 kilometers every day. Women in settlements used to receive subsistence allowance under two main categories: 1. Widows with children and 2. women whose husbands absconded or in the jail. Women used to suffer without food. Food and clothes were distributed to women in settlements.

Patterns of Earning Livelihood

The materials produced by these communities did not directly enter the markets. The companies looked after manufacturing process. For example, the Indian Leaf tobacco Company used to process tobacco prepared by Yerukulas. The materials developed by other communities were taken over by the Public Works and Labor Department authorities and handed them to cooperative societies. Men, women and children were always hired to labor contract works in mines, quarries, as factory workers outside their settlements. They employed them to do multiple jobs at a time and exploited them due to their innocence. Thus, a large number of women among these communities became workers in the factories and labor contract workers. Land was distributed to some of the communities. Agriculture became the chief means of livelihood. Women did not seek employment on their own. Missionaries played an important role in obtaining employment to these communities. The families wanted to self support themselves. But they remained as low wage paid laborers in their work places. The factory management found these people less troublesome to pocket profits.

The role of women as the principal contributors to family income continued among these communities. Men also requested the company management to absorb them into factories. The company always demanded more works for cheap labor. With the distribution of land and development of agriculture, some of the communities depended on agricultural and other related activities. Water resources were provided. Government provided sole ownership of land to some of the communities. For example, Yerukulas demanded *pattas* for their lands. Government discharged a large number of them from the settlements and company's work. The company demanded as many hours of work as possible from them. The Labor Department used to find new employment for these people in times of need. A large number of communities were shifted to other places in order to provide suitable employment for them. In settlement areas the whole family members used to work for the company. Wages were given to family members. Companies lowered the wages of women and children. They interfered with the domestic and personal life of workers. Sometimes women due to the harassment of their husbands wanted to desert them or demand companies to give salaries of their males directly to them. Companies used to put pressure on males and females for more work. These companies threatened the workers with loss of employment in case they did not obey their demands. They, however, pleaded with the companies not to send them out from work. These companies never conceded the personal demands of these people. The division of the community into families curbed women's own choices in matters of position. The government wanted to mould characters of these people under the management of missionaries and philosophic agencies.

It can be observed that whole families of these communities started working on different kinds of avocations and occupations. Women organized as workers in 1930s. They developed rapidly due to the influence of other sections of people. They consolidated themselves as strong communities. They used to select works very near to their habitations. They formed as unions. Women achieved substantial success. They participated in the strikes and understood the spirit of national movement. W.J. Hatch wrote about Yerukulas: "trade unionists of the most thoroughgoing kind and united action was a necessity in the tribal existence. Group thinking and belied in group action, they formed themselves into a close brotherhood and would on no account betray their fellow class men. They were free masons and helped each other to the end".

These communities had lost their traditional occupations due to the laws of government, protection of environment, wildlife protection, prevention of cruelty to animals and other such acts. They were driven away from their traditional habitats and occupations. Their women have no other option than to accept petty trade to eke out their livelihood. There are many communities eking their livelihood by street performances of the bears, monkeys, parrots, snakes, oxen etc. Women assist their males in traditional occupations. They are suffering to a great extent due to the implementation of Forest Protection Act, Wild Life Protection Act, banning exhibition of animals in streets and public. Many communities became jobless as a consequence. They are unable to locate themselves in an alternative means of livelihood. The anti-social elements frequently visited their habitats luring their males to carry crime as a means of livelihood and exploited their women by various means. Since their life support system was lost they were allegedly involved in petty offences.

In places like Maharastra women from these communities were used as bar dancing girls. They are traditionally from dancing communities and entertainers. As dancers and entertainers, they received patronage from feudal classes. However, in due course of time, with the introduction of television, cinemas their performances were not entertained. These dancers and entertainers took to street performances. There was no other alternative for these women to eke out their livelihood. They are forced to send their grown-up girls to dance in bars. In the bars they were subjected to exploitation and abuse. These women bore the brunt of exploitation. They had no support to run their families. Their males were often left out without any work. There were two important issues to be noted here. 1. With the loss of traditional livelihood, their skills and occupations were lost. In distress women among these communities were forced to accept certain other professions. 2. Due to globalization and the affect of modern industries, competition entered into their life. They need money to lead a comfortable life. These were pull and push factors for women of these communities to accept any kind of profession. They were deprived of their traditional livelihood. Studies point out that a large number of women among NT/DNTs, Dalit and Muslim communities in Maharastra, Andhra Pradesh, Karnataka, TamilNadu, West Bengal, Uttarpra-desh, Delhi, and Rajasthan the women were subjected to various kinds of ill treatment. When the bars were closed down in Maharastra, they were arrested and kept behind bars.

Dommara women in Andhra Pradesh labeled as prostitutes. It was stated that prostitution was their profession. It was also believed that the entire community was involved in the practice of prostitution. Thus, irreparable damage was done to the social life of Dommaras in the state. The media, newspapers carried special articles, with misleading titles stigmatizing the community. Clients visited their houses for women. They forced women to take to prostitution. Law enforcing agencies started troubling them. It might be true that some women of these communities had taken to prostitution due to the poverty-stricken conditions and lack of employment opportunities, lack of skills for pursuing jobs in cities. But women from the other communities even if they were indulged in these activities they were never treated as prostitutes. Many women among Dommaras were hard working and law abiding. They constantly engaged themselves in street performances, agricultural labor and petty business.

Problems and Challenges of NT/DNT Women

1. Dishonor to NT/DNT women

Women among these communities are facing various kinds of dishonor in society even today. Due to poverty some of the women are allegedly involved in illegal brewing of liquor. Some are following witchcraft. Some are involved in the *rapu* (replacing original gold in the place of artificial gold) practice. Many stereotypes are wrongly attached to these communities. It is very unfortunate that for the activities of a few individuals and deviant persons, the entire community is branded negatively. The whole community is brought to public discourse. However, the worst affected people are women among these communities. The vulnerable conditions of women are due to their backward position. Community members looked down upon women members. Their women often go outside in search of employment. Males often suspect the reputation of females. Many a time, petty quarrels in the house often lead to divorce and second marriages. Women are the victims of their customs and institutional practices. The *Kulapanchayats* (caste councils) play a negative role as far as the issues of women are concerned. Women are subject to virginity tests. If they fail to prove their virginity they were levied with different kinds of punishment and fines such as dipping their hands in burning oil, lifting crow bars. Women are forced to name illicit relations before the members of caste council. Kulapanchayats treat women very badly.

Nowadays changes are taking place in the society of NT/DNTs. They are following traditions, customs, language and habits of the mainstream society. There is a lot of change in their dress pattern, material goods, language, dialects, customs, ceremonies etc. They are imitating others in this respect. Communities which are better off are not allowing their women folk to work outside. They are particularly confined to the four walls of their household work. The custom of demanding dowry in the form of gold, silver, money, vehicles, land and other items at the time of marriage is taking place. This is replacing their custom of bride wealth. In the earlier days they used to fully recognize abilities of their women. Their productive and reproductive systems were totally respected. They worked in paddy fields, and contributed to their household works through various economic pursuits. They also supplemented greatly the income for the development of their households. Some of these communities adopted dowry system. Position of the women has drastically changed. Nowadays, women among NT/DNTs are seen as an economic liability. Two important points need to be considered seriously. There is a need to promote their economic conditions, education and health. The literacy rate among girls and women among these communities is almost zero. Women are treated as bread-winners for their families. Their women are exposed to many kinds of violence and stigma from outside world. The government should take care of the problems of NT/DNT women with special packages. The policies initiated by government should be gender-specific.

Gender discrimination

The important aspect of inequality among NT/DNTs is gender discrimination. Indian society is patriarchal and patrilineal and male-dominated. Women among these communities are denied several basic rights. They are discriminated in society and suffer from several social cultural and economic handicaps. Women are the victims of discrimination and their material conditions are immeasurably pathetic and pitiable in their localities. They lead a very poor life and social exclusion and exploited due to their precarious conditions. Poverty increased due to loss of their traditional means of livelihood. Their natural habitations were destroyed and nor pro – active measures are being undertaken for their gainful employment. Women are greatly oppressed in sharing of power, voting rights, education, health, nutrition and political process. Nobody comes to their rescue when the need arises. They are unable to take their representations to government and fight for their basic rights. Women among these communities are subjected to exploitation, suppression and oppression. The sufferings of women among these communities are several times higher than that of women of other communities. They are the victims of cumulative inequality. Under these circumstances, they deserve immediate policy intervention. The government should take serious note of the cases of atrocities on women. Atrocities are reported in the media, public pronouncements and radio. People were petitioned to the commissions and government authorities about their grievances several times. Enquiries are pending. Memoranda were also submitted. Many women among these people are homeless. They are leading a wandering life even after 65 years of independence. The administration is totally indifferent to their problems. Speedy justice has to be made to the victims of these poor communities to provide safety and dignity for them. For instance, in a recent incident it was reported in a local newspaper that a girl from the denotified tribe settlement was forcibly carried away by a group of miscreants in a car. She was dumped at the same place from where she was picked up the following day. Her family did not even approach the police authorities with a complaint because it was committed by people of the dominant sections and affluent persons in society. Since the victim is from a denotified tribal family the police did not register case. She was not paid compensation for the problem she had faced.

There were a large number of cases of this type that can be collected from newspapers every month. There are also many representations from members of communities, NGOs at the village, district and state level. Women were specifically targeted for sexual abuse, and the attacks of the male members in society. The pathetic situation is that neither the administration nor the police take serious note of the problems of women. Women are beaten severely in police stations and public roads. They were subjected to severe atrocities, violence, rape and custodial deaths. In a recent incident, a twenty year young woman was brutally beaten to death due to severe beatings. In the settlements women and children narrate their owes and experiences with the administrative authorities and police. The police invariably round them up for petty offences, confine them to police stations, and beat them up, torture them and release them when the police were bribed. In the police stations women police constables are not available to deal with women's cases. Women are the victims of oppression. Many women members are leading their life as rag pickers and by some tertiary occupations of selling beads, herbs, plastic items, medicines etc.

Police Harassment

Some of the women in settlements said that their children couldn't get jobs. They have to work with bread-winners of the family having a criminal record and serving a prison sentence. Women folk in the colonies are compelled to work along with their children to eke out a living in the absence of any assistance from the government. There is nobody to see the plight of women and come forward to provide help for them. According to police records eighty percent of women in NT/DNT colonies are hard core criminals who live by committing pick pocketing, chain snatching, and other offences in busy centers. The state government had provided bank loans, and self-employment schemes. They did not reach them properly. The distressing factor with regard to women is that whenever their men folk are sent to jail for minor or major offences, some women folk either work as coolies or take illegal means of livelihood practices in order to keep their families going. Women ex-criminals in settlement colonies confess that after taking all the risks and tensions in committing offences they are left with nothing but police harassment and imprisonment. Women in these colonies feel that the government shall provide some gainful employment opportunities and jobs for their children in railways, postal, telecommunications, public works department, police department etc. Government officials from revenue, home, education, social welfare, women and child development, Ppanchayat Raj and other Departments should formulate a long range of policies to solve the problems of women among these communities.

Better future for children

In most of the settlements women demand a better future for their children. The government should provide an opportunity to develop bright future of the tribal children. Women are leading a life of frustration and fear. Women are living in the perpetual fear of police and want to lead a normal life. They are afraid of police when male members are caught by police. The police convicted some poor women who were not at all involved in theft cases. Society, however, looks at them with suspicion and the stigma of a women offender. Above all the police haunt them to keep a track of their activities.

Freedom from fear and inferiority complex

Another problem that the women among these communities are facing today is fear and inferiority complex. Narrating their problems the Woddar women in Siddhapuram settlement said, "no one wanted to lead a criminal life. Even after 65 years of Independence and identification of the tribes we are still discriminated against our daily life. People treat us with suspicion and as outcastes here".

Rational and humane approach to the problems of NT/DNT women

Many women members in the colonies poured out that their tale of misfortune being wrought upon them even after they changed their ways of past life. They lamented and narrated that their plight, particularly in the hands of brutal attacks of the rich, zamindars, local upper caste communities and the police. They say that "the police stand in our way of leading a respectable and honorable life. They are steeped in corruption. The police are instigating us to commit crimes. The police should adopt a rationale and humane approach to our problems and help us to eke out our livelihood through labor contract work and agricultural activities". A reformed woman criminal blamed the police squarely for trying to condemn them forever to criminal life style. She had observed that reformed criminals were forced to replace into criminal life by the indifference displayed by society towards them. The district administration should help them launch self-employment projects to remove the injustice imposed upon the settlement. They crticised discrimination people show every day.

Participatory Approach

Women should participate and discuss their problems, issues, concerns regarding their social, economic problems, human rights, protection, integration, development etc. Co-operative societies must be opened in the settlements. Women in these settlements and outside the settlements should be influenced through development activities through the distribution of bank loans, livestock, sewing and knitting machines, and job oriented skills and vocational training centers. There are many hurdles coming in the way of their development programmes. The illiterate women are exploited due to multiple handicaps. There is an urgent need to create social awareness with regard to health issues like HIV/AIDs and other communicable diseases among women. Whatever the materials prepared by them in the form of the handicrafts and other materials should have marketing facilities. The government should also provide materials for women for the preparation of household articles. The experiences of women in these settlements should be taken to the women ministers in the Parliament and they should take serious note of their problems. Heinous practices on women should be curbed. The government should provide them proper guidance and encouragement for their overall development.

Persuasion Method

Efforts should be made by the government to educate them and orient them in order make them realize the importance of the programmes initiated for their development by the state and central government organizations. They must be pursued to make use of these programes for speedy development. Several schemes are initiated for the development of women among Scheduled Tribes and Scheduled Castes. These schemes must be initiated for the development of tribal girl child and women. Corrupt officials and middlemen should be punished. There should be strict monitoring on the implementation strategies, time for implementation process of government schemes, utilization, advantages and disadvantages of the programmes. The village committees and Panchayats have to be empowered. Government should design new programmes and policies for the development of women. The village councils, Gram sabhas should act as nodal centers in order to implement welfare schemes initiated for women. Proper recommendations and guidelines must be provided to the government in order to implement these schemes. The government should provide them employment guarantee schemes, at least 180 days of employment through National Rural Employment Guarantee Scheme (NREGA) of the central government and state government. They should be brought on par with upper middle classes within a time span of ten years. Women members are alienated from decision-making, political representation and economic empowerment. Therefore, women among these communities must be brought to the mainstream society. Factories which will promote small scale industries, home-based agro -based, forest-based, flora and fauna based occupations may be introduced in the settlements as employment guarantee schemes for women. They should be mixed up the industrial trainers. The present legal system with regard to protection of women is lopsided. Effective law and judicial help must be provided to women and children of these communities. Their problems must be understood with and solved on war footing.

Non-Government organizations and self help groups

The problems of women among these communities should be handed over to non-governmental organizations. Women and child welfare projects have to be launched in order to protect them. There is every chance that women and children becoming more vulnerable if the government doesn't come to the rescue of their problems. They should be provided with quality education, life skills, vocational skills, training, and nutrition. The non-governmental organizations should make sincere efforts to promote their well-being. The constitutional obligations failed with regard to the welfare of these sections of people. The enforcement authorities are not performing their responsibilities. Moral education has taken a backseat. The state and central government organizations are not seriously concerned with the problems of women. Primary education system had created a lot of differences in the country. Quality primary education in the settlement schools for children is not provided so far. There are no residential and tribal welfare schools for tribal girl children of NT/DNT communities. They should be treated specially due to their segregation and isolation in society. They must be provided with hostel and scholarships without any delay. Children of rich go to reputed schools, others who cannot afford good education languish in government schools, where there are no proper facilities, teachers, curriculum and environment. Women and children have to compete with limited resources and with those who had all facilities at their disposal. Education authorities have to achieve 100 percent enrolment and literacy among women and children in the NT/DNT colonies. Proper efforts have to be made to provide some sort of comfort to them. They should be made as responsible citizens of tomorrow. Every year the government should target 10000 women and children under the NT/DNT projects. Counselling centers needs to be opened in all the ex-settlement colonies to provide proper guidance to eke out their social, cultural, economic rights and needful employment opportunities. In this connection, efforts made by *Samskar,* a voluntary organization in Betapudi, Stuartpuram is noteworthy. They are providing skills, guidance and councilling, moral enlistment, removal of stigma and protection from the police and public for these communities. Similarly Asmita, another important organization is very actively working with the problems of women among Scheduled Castes, Scheduled Tribes and Minorities with regard to protection of the girl child, women's education, land rights, protection of women, research and training opportunities with committed workers in the field. Similar organizations have to be brought to the common platform in order to exchange and share experiences and speed up the process of development in the state. The contribution of NT/DNT women to domestic labor, labor market and the people has been neglected by our society. They played variety of roles in the country. They formed into distinct communities like peasants, workers, laborers etc. They are hard working than the women of other communities. They played important role in the socialization, lifecycles, daily work, domestic labor, childcare, financial, business transactions, investments, daily trade and customer relations.

Participation of Women in Economic Activities

There is an increase in the percentage of the female population among NT/DNT communities in rural and urban areas. However, they are unable to get 180 days of work in a year. The position of women is gradually changing in the settlement colonies. Women workers are increasing every year. The percentage of women workforce is gradually increasing. At the same time, the problem of unemployment is very high among them. Women among NT/DNTs have acknowledged the fact that they are unemployed. Males are willing to send women to work outside their colonies for various kinds of employment. Employment opportunities are very few for them. The government must tackle the problem of chronic unemployment problems among these people. Many communities among NT/DNTs are becoming seasonal migrants. They are migrating to urban centers in search of employment opportunities and facing severe financial crisis. Women members are working as marginal workers. Child labor is rampant among these communities.

Women and girl children from Nomadic and Denotified Communities have to sweat it out to earn their bread for the day. They wander braving scorching sun on the streets to sell their products for cheaper rates.

Avenues of Employment

There is an increase in the role of women with regard to economic development in the settlements of NT/DNTs. Their women possess good amount of skills. They are concentrating on various activities other than agriculture. Poverty is the main hindrance for their development. If they are employed properly, their poverty-stricken conditions can be easily eliminated. They can be employed in avocations like plantation work, preservation of medicinal plants, mining work, quarrying, industrial establishments, manufacturing industries, protection and preservation of meat, manufacturing of food, manufacturing of edible oil, fats, coffee-curing, roasting, cashew nut processing, manufacturing of tobacco products, processing of cotton, roots, tubers, vegetables, flowers, traditional plants, livestock, forestry, fishing, manufacturing of wool, silk, synthetic fibres, manufacture of jute, paper products etc. Qualified women should be employed in public and administrative services, educational serves, medical and health serves and laundry services. Women should be encouraged towards technical and vocational education. They can be appointed as wage laborers.

Conclusion and Recommendations

Even after 65 years of Independence the Adivasi, NT/DNT women and children are confined to certain unclean and vulnerable occupations in the agricultural and non-agricultural sectors. Their involvement in self-employment is very much lacking (not even 10 percent). They are lacking primary education and vocational training skills. They are not having any political, bureaucratic and people's support to fight for their constitutional rights and assert themselves. Public employment opportunities are inaccessible to them. Women among NT/DNTs are very poorly represented in the high paid and high skilled jobs. Their percentage in the police, judicial, educational, medical, sectors is very insignificant. They are mainly concentrated in the low paid, minimum skilled, labor incentive, traditional, unproductive, menial, and low paid jobs. They are seen in the highest numbers as housemaids, rag pickers, earth diggers, fortune-tellers, acrobats, agricultural and other types of labor works. Therefore, self-employment and credit facilities must be extended to NT/DNT women. Local self help groups, banking institutions and credit organizations must be encouraged to develop these communities. There are many challenges and hindrances, coming in the way of development of NT/DNT women. First of all, the union and state governments should allocate resources in order to tackle problems of these communities. The budgetary provisions are not considering the problems of NT/DNT communities in the five-year plans and budgetary allocations. The central and state governments' programmes reinforce caste, class and gender discrimination and implementing them. Education is an important tool for their development. Most of these communities have no access to primary, secondary, technical, vocational and medical education. They do not have any economic and physical assets with them to fight their cases. They do not come under tribal sub-plans and special composite plans etc. The government should take immediate steps to include all NT/DNTs under the tribal sub-plans or create a separate NT/DNT sub plan for their development. Positive discrimination is very much necessary for development of women. Their accessibility to employment, land, and credit facilities needs to be improved. The wages they are earning are so meager that they are unable to run their families. Their wages under the national wage policy must be improved. They should be provided employment under the National Rural Employment Guarantee scheme. Their labor market needs to be strengthened. The state governments should make a policy for the protection of NT/DNT women from exploitation, discrimination, police and public harassment. Social security mechanisms such as Rastriya Swasth Bheema Yojana and Rashtriya Vimuktajati Mahila Yojana must be initiated.

The educated youth among NT/DNTs must be supported with supplementary coaching facilities for clearing competitive examinations, entrance examinations and enter into professional courses. Study of English must be made compulsory. Infrastructural facilities like community halls, Information and communication technology and other fast growing sectors must be strengthened. Micro-finance initiates, bank loans with no interest or very simple interest (25 paise interest) must be provided. The government must also promote self-help groups, vocational, industrial schemes, and self-employment opportunities. Development schemes under the special component plant and ICDS must be strengthened. There is a need to ensure gender perspective and gender budgeting programmes in all policy matters of government. Private sector institutions should come forward to tap the skills possessed by women. There is also an urgent need to study and review the existing conditions of NT/DNT women in India and also the policies and schemes implementation strategies by independent bodies for ensuring speedy and quality delivery of government programmes and schemes. The voice and opinions of women and educated members of these communities must be heard and understood what kind of developmental peogrammes are urgently required needs to be identified. Results of the findings of the state and central government programmes must be widely publicized in the websites, newspapers and media. Periodic surveys must be conducted to understand the effectiveness of government programmes, policies, problems of these communities and specific needs by the government. What is urgently required with regard to the speedy development of these communities is that of social empowerment including education, health and nutrition; economic empowerment including right to land, resources, forests, water, housing, sanitation, occupations, agriculture, industrial development, attractive wages for their labour etc; political empowerment including protection from atrocities, discrimination, harassment from the police, forest official, revenue officials and the public, participation in elections, Panchayat, municipalities, wards and decision-making bodies; cultural empowerment including preservation of their culture, languages, cultural sites etc. for the empowerment of women and children.

The development of socially backward classes particularly, women sections of these communities is an integral part of the national development. The central and state governments are given equal responsibilities to execute constitutional guarantees given to SCs and STs. Commissioner at the central level and social welfare director at the state level are the two functionaries who deal with these guarantees. At the state level, programmes designed for the welfare of these sections of people often overlap. As a result, many of the needs of these communities are not fulfilled. The government officials say that there are no specific funds for the welfare of these poorer sections of society. Such a tendency culminates in discontentment among these sections of society. Important questions today that needs to be debated and understood with regard to the development of NT/DNTs and their women are: should women among NT/Dents in the settlement colonies be treated as habitual criminals? What is the fate of women and children whose male and breadwinners are sentenced to life imprisonment? Should women in NT/DNT colonies be left destitute and fend for themselves? What measures the state and the central government organizations had taken so far for the development of women and girl child? What are the gaps and what needs to be done in order to improve the conditions of women among these communities? Attempts made by government in this sphere have only touched the fringes of problem leaving the large area of the problems of NT/DNTs unattended so far.

References

Banerjee, Nirmala, "Trends in Women's Employment, 1971-81, Some Micro Level Observations", *Economic and Political Weekly, Vol. XXIV, No. 17, April 29, 1989.*

Booth Tucker, Frederick, *Mukti Fauj or 40 Years with the Salvation Army in India and Ceylon,* Marshall Brothers, London, nd.

Deccan Chronicle, Cops driving them to crime, *Vijayawada Edition, dated 19.6.1984.*

Gandhi, Malli and Lalitha V., *Tribes Under stigma: Problems of Identity,* Serials publishers, New Delhi, 2009.

Gandhi, Malli, *and Development of Denotified Tribes: Policy and Practice*, Sarup and Sons, New Delhi, 2006.

Gandhi, Malli, *Denotified Tribes: Dimensions of Change,* Kanishka Publishers, New Delhi, 2008.

Ghani, Muhammad Abdul, *Note on the Criminal Tribes of Madras Presidency,* Provincial Police Training School, Vellore, 1915.

Government Of Andhra Pradesh, Tribal Cultural Research and Training Institute, Hyderabad, Report on Denotified tribes of Andhra Pradesh, Hyderabad, 1964, pp 1-10(un published Report).

Government of India, *Report on National Commission for Denotified, Nomadic and Semi-NOMADIC tribes, Ministry of Social Justice and Empowerment, Vol. I,* (un published Report), GOI, New Delhi, June 30th 2008.

Government of India, *Report on National Commission for Denotified, Nomadic and Semi-NOMADIC tribes, Ministry of Social Justice and Empowerment, Vol. II,* (un published Report), GOI, New Delhi, June 30th 2008.

Government of Madras, *Administration Report of the Forest Department (Southern and Northern Circles), Madras Presidency for 1889-1890,* Madras, 1890, PP. 23-27. Also, *Government of Madras, Report of the Forrest Committee, Madras, 1912, Vol.2.*

Government of Madras, *Administration Report of the Labor department, 1925-1928,* Madras. Also see, Public Works Labor Department, *GO.NO. 2338L, dated 19.8.1930* and *Public Works Labor Department, GO. NO. 1313L.,* dated 17.6.1932.

Government of Madras, *Administration Report of the Labor department for 1927-28,* Madras, 1928.

Government Of Madras, *Administration Report of the Labor department for the year's 1927-28, 1929-1930 and 1930-1931,* Madras, 1932, PP7.

Government of Madras, *Development Department, GO.NO. 1315, dated 27.10.1933, Commissioner of labor letter to Secretary to Government of Madras, dated 1.10.1933.*

Government of Madras, *Home Department, GO.NO. 1544, dated 20.3.1939.*

Government Of Madras, *Home Judicial Department, GO. NO. 1534 14.6.1916, PP12.*

Government Of Madras, *Judicial Department, GO. NO. 110, dated 27th April 1921,* P.3, APSA.

Government Of Madras, *Judicial Department, GO. NO. 1161 dated 12th June 1913.* Also see, *Home Judicial Department, GO. NO. 1140 dated 1st May 1920.* Also see, *Home Judicial Department, GO. NO. 1649, dated 19th July 1919* PP.1-4 and *Home Judicial Department, GO. NO. 2497, dated 29th October 1919.*

Government of Madras, *Madras Criminal Tribes Manual, Criminal Tribes Act VI of 1924, Brought up to 31st March 1927,* Superintendent Government Press, Madras, 1927.

Government of Madras, *Memorandum on Donga Yerukulas by the Deputy Inspector General of Police and Criminal Investigation Department,* Madras, 1918. Also see, Government of Madras, *Judicial Department, GO. NO. 917, dated 10.5.1913* (Mis).

Government Of Madras, *Note Showing the Progress Made in the Settlement of Criminal Tribes in the Madras Presidency up to January 1925,* Madras, 1927.

Government of Madras, *Public Works Labor Department, GO. NO. 1313L., dated 17.6.1932.*

Government of Madras, *Public Works Labor Department, GO. NO.1654L., dated 6.7.1928.*

Government of Madras, *Public Works Labor Department, GO.NO. 2671L., dated 6.12.1934.*

Government of Madras, *Public Works Labor Department, GO.NO. 2726L., dated 17.12.1935.*

Government Of Madras, *Stuartpuram Administration Report 1920-21,* Tamil Nadu Archives.

Lalitha, V., *Making of Criminal Tribes: Patterns and Transition,* New era Publications, Madras, 1995.

Lavanam and Hemalatha Lavanam, *Notes on Reformation of Criminal Tribes people,* Atheist center, Vijayawada, February 1976.

News Time, Reformed criminals to take part in the meeting, *dated 12.6.1984.*

NT/DNT Rag, *Technical Advisory Group Report 2005.*

Radha Krishna Meena, *Dishonored by History, 'Criminal Tribes and British Colonial policy',* Orient Longman, Hyderabad, 2001.

Radha, Krishna Meena, "From Tribal Community to working Class Consciousness: A case of Yerukula Women", *Economic and Political Weekly, Vol. XXIV, No. 17, April 29, 1989.*

Raw deal to Residents of Settlement Colonies, *Indian Express, June 16th 1984, Vijayawada, Edition.*

The Hindu dated 19th June 1984, A Change For the Better, *Vijayavada edition.*

The Hindu, High Court Judge Fours sending Juvenile Offenders to NGOs, *Hyderabad Edition, October 3rd 2001.*

The Hindu, Reform Process a pace at Stuartpuram, *Hyderabad edition, Saturday, March 13, 1999.*

The Hindu, Reformed criminals want the Government to lift ban on employment, *Wednesday, June 20th, 1884.* Vijayawada Edition.

The Hindu, Thirteen Criminals Surrender, *March 1999.*

The New Indian Express, Twenty fife hard core dacoits of Guntur Surrender, *Hyderabad, Tuesday, march 30th 1999.*

Tucker Booth Frederick, *Criminocurology or the Indian Crim and What to do with him-A Report of the work of the Salvation Army among the Criminal Tribes, Habituals and Released Prisoners* in India, London, n.d.

Unni, Jeemol, "Changes in Women's Employment in Rural areas, 1961-63", *Economic and Political Weekly, Vol. XXIV, No.17, April, 29, 1989.*

Notes

1. Malli Gandhi, Head, Department of DESSH, Regional Institute of Education, NCERT, Mysore, Karnataka. Govt. India.

Chapter - 2

Power, Marginalisation and Tribal Women: The Northeast Perspective

Prof. M.C. Behera[1]

Introduction

The present paper is based on the premise that the phenomenon of marginalisation is symptomatic of unequal power relations operating in human society at its various spatial dimensions. A society may exist, for example, in a small space as an ***isolate*** like Jarwas, Onges, Sentinelese of Andaman and Nicobar Islands or many other tribes a few decades ago; or as a ***connect*** through progressive integration at different levels-local, regional and national. A contemporary tribal society no more presents a picture of isolation; rather it reflects the process of integration in different degrees; particularly, through State sponsored development interventions.

It is axiomatic that unequal power relations have intra- and inter-community dimensions existing within the community and between communities, and drawing on inequality based on gender, sex, race, wealth, education, caste, creed, participation in governance and on other things of the sort. The inequality becomes the source of constructing dichotomy of power relations in terms of powerful and powerless, dominant and subordinate, strong and weak, rich and poor, upper caste and lower caste, ruler and ruled, central and marginal, chief and commoner, privileged and underprivileged, barbarous and civilised, and so on.

The dichotomous construct of *tribe* and *non-tribe* is based on unequal power relations drawing on diverse factors across race, ethnicity, technology, mode of production, concept of purity, socio-political structure and so on (see Dube, 1977:2). In this binary social construct tribe is situated at the lower end on the scale of power relations as compared with non-tribe, and thus bears the epithet *marginal*.

But a tribe in itself is a construct of dichotomous power relations along sex divide. The dominant axis of power is male centric, woven into the fabric of patriarchy and reinforced through the cultural construct *gender* (Zhimo, 2018:158 and Patnaik, 1993). Gender is the instrument at the hand of the patriarch which sustains through the norms and values of the tradition, and is used to determine the role of man and woman in the community (see Jackson,1998 and Wittig, 1981). Woman is placed at the lower end on the scale of status-role constructed drawing on the ethics of patriarchy. Obviously, women constitute the marginal section within the tribe[2].

It follows that the tribe is a marginal section of the Indian society and women in a tribe constitutes marginal section due to patriarchal power relations.

In independent India Constitutional safeguards and welfare commitment of the government are directed to remove all sorts of social discrimination and provide for equal opportunities to raise the status of weaker sections like the tribes and women at par other societies. The objective is to ensure status of all irrespective of caste, creed, class, sex, etc. and raise their socio-economic and political status at par national standard through affirmative action and positive discrimination wherever necessary. As a result, tribes are expected to enjoy status equal to other sections of Indian society and women at par their male counterparts.

But still tribes constitute marginal communities of the nation and tribal women as marginal section within the tribe. Forces, such as patriarchy and/or dominant development agenda operate which not only create marginal position but perpetuates it. Tribal women undoubtedly present a situation of marginalisation in double sense-being women in general and being women in tribal patriarchy.

So the issue of marginalisation of tribal women offers a crucial area of critical investigation of the phenomenon. In view of this, tribal women of the Northeast India have been considered as a case in point. The issue of marginalisation is explored within the theoretical background that difference in power relations and power holder's natural instinct to resist power delegation are responsible for operating the process of marginalisation (see Coser,1996; Stewart, 2011 and Richards,2010).

The study draws on field observation spread over a period of more than three decades and secondary sources as well. The study presents an overview of tribal situation in the Northeast for the background knowledge and examines the phenomenon of marginalisation along the axes of *property rights and inheritance* and *political participation* both in the tradition and changing context with reference to patrilineal and matrilineal tribal communities. Besides, the emerging trend of interface between patriarchy and assertion of female rights has been presented briefly.

Tribal Situation in the Northeast

The North-Eastern Region (NER) of India, also known as the Northeast, consists of eight states, namely Assam, Arunachal Pradesh, Manipur,

Meghalaya, Mizoram, Nagaland, Sikkim and Tripura and covers an area of 262476 square kilometres and 8% of total land area of the country. The region lies between 21^0 57' to $29^0$30' North latitude and $88^0$3' to $97^0$45' East longitude.

Before the inclusion of Sikkim in 2002 as a member of North-Eastern Council (NEC) for development purpose, according to the provision of the NEC Reorganisation Act, which was passed in Decembe,2002, the Northeast, also popularly known as 'Seven Sisters', comprised seven states. The seven political units were created following the North-East Reorganisation Act, 1971 and is a contiguous territory covering an area of 2, 55,134 square kilometres. The contiguous territory lies between 21^0 57' to $29^0$30' North latitude and $89^0$46' to $97^0$45' East longitude.

The NER is known as predominantly tribal dominated area; it shares 12.4 per cent (12.2% in case of *seven sisters*) of total tribal population (Census, 2011) and 8 % of total geographical area of the country. Despite small percentage of total tribal population as compared to non-tribal population in the region, some states are designated as tribal states with high concentration of tribal population. According to Census 2011, Mizoram has highest concentration of tribal population (94.43%) followed by Nagaland (86.43%), Meghalaya (86.15%) and Arunachal Pradesh (68.79%). Among other states, Manipur has 35.12 % followed by Sikkim (33.80%), Tripura (31.76%) and Assam (12.45%).

The sex ratio among the tribes of the NER, according to the Census 2011, is comparatively favourable; it is 994:100 as against the national ratio of 990:100 for tribes and 943:1000 for general population. The ratio is lowest in Sikkim (960:1000) and highest in Arunachal Pradesh (1032:1000). In Mizoram and Meghalaya it is 1007:1000 and 1013:1000 respectively. Similarly, tribes of the NER show higher female literacy rate. ST female literacy rate in the region is 59.97% as compared to 41.59% of their national female counter parts. ST literacy rates range between 49.01% in Arunachal Pradesh and 75.85% in Mizoram.

According to the Census of reference, work participation of ST women is recorded 45% as against 59% of their male counter parts. This indicates that female participation in formal sector activities is still lagging behind, though tribal women are known for their hard work in traditional sector of activities.

There are more than 300 tribal communities in the NER-both scheduled and non-scheduled, which belong to Mongoloid stock. There are tribes mostly specific to a state and there are also tribes who are found in a number of states. Adi, Apatani, Galo, Mishmi for example are glued to Arunachal Pradesh while Bodos and Rabhas are found in Assam and Meghalaya. A number of Naga group, Kuki group and Mizo group of tribes are found in Nagaland, Manipur, and Meghalaya and even in Assam.

Further, the tribes can be divided into matrilineal communities like Khasi, Jaintia, Garo of Meghalaya and patrilineal tribes like Naga, Mizo, Tani and

Kuki group of tribes, Khampti, Nocte, etc. Patriarchy is predominant in patrilineal communities, though it is not altogether absent in matrilineal ones as we shall see in subsequent discussions. There is another dimension of tribal power dynamics in patriarchy as the tribes are divided into cephalous (chieftain type- Naga tribes, Khamptis, Singhphos, etc., and acephalous (democratic or non-centralised power- Adis, Nyishis, Jamatia, Monpa, Chamkma, etc.). The line of divide between domination and subordination along gender line is not two-fold in cephalous tribes like the one in acephalous tribes. The society is divided between chief and marginalised commoners. The subordination of women of commoner group happens at two stages: one at tribe level power structure and the other at patriarchy power structure of the commoner. In addition, the women of chief social category display another dimension of marginalisation relating to patriarchy in chieftain power structure. In a similar sense, the women in Puroik tribe, (earlier known as slave tribe) has an element of marginalisation in patriarchal power structure within the community and with the Nyishi and the Miji tribes with whom the tribe entered into a subordinated clientele relationship (see Behera,2004). Study of marginalisation of tribal women in the Northeast context provides several possibilities depending on patrilineality, matrilineality, cephalous and acephalous power structure, and religious denominations as well. But in this study a preliminary investigation is presented with reference to patrilineality and matrilineality..

Perspective of Marginalisation in Patriarchy

Marginalisation of women is an inherent feature in patriarchy. It reflects in patriarchal thinking and translates into various practices. In this section the nature of woman marginalisation is examined along the axes of rights to own property, inheritance rights and participation in traditional body politics. A brief reference to changes in these fields has also been alluded.

Right to ownership and Inheritance

As the name suggests, in all patrilineal communities of the NER- whether *cephalous* or *acephalous*, rights to ownership of property and inheritance are defined along the male line (Zhimo, 2018:160 and Walling, 2014:248), often following the rule of primogeniture in different degrees. Even when a man does not have a male child, the ownership right goes to nearest male relatives, or to adopted son, but not to the wife or daughters (Dzuvich, 2012:84; Also see Zhimo, 2018:158; Mitkong, 2002&2006; Roy, 1960; Elwin, 1965 &1988 and Sitlhou, 2015). A clarification is due. A woman can rear a pig, own it and sell it as long as she is the member of the family. She can also cultivate a portion of land and sell its products for own use. But when she leaves the family she cannot claim ownership over it. If she remains unmarried she gets a plot from bother's share as long as she lives (see Norbu, 1997 and Sitlhou, 2015:100-101). Usufructuary rights, therefore, shall be distinguished from ownership rights.

Absence of ownership rights in women reflects in the absence of inheritance rights. The concept of inheritance has a broader meaning in two senses. In the first sense she does not have the right to inherit ancestral property. But she herself is customarily the property of the family, and particularly of the husband. Being a property she has the potentiality of being inherited which is instituted in the practice of widow inheritance or marriage by any of the fraternal brothers of the deceased husband (Riddi, 2006:64; see Roy,1960: 202; Elwin,1965:94 and Riddi, 2006).

In recent years, however, the practice of giving daughters a portion of father's self-acquired property is in vogue (Dzuvichy,2012:86-87 and Sitlhou,2015:100-101). The crucial point to note is that the practice is like giving a gift, but not transferring rights over property (Sitlhou, 2015:100). Such gifts also go to wife(ves) which she may own legally; but she cannot claim rights over deceased husband's property; her inheritance rights are limited to gifted property.

However, a change in the incidence of widow inheritance, particularly in elite families, is observed; for the widow is not insecure with the ownership over gifts or rights over property which she can also procure. Moreover, self-acquired property of the husband does not follow traditional line of ownership and inheritance (see Dzuvichu, 2012:84).

Political participation

The patrilineal tribes of the NER have two major types of traditional body politics, namely, chiefdom and a type of democratic organisation. The body politics, primarily councils, exist among some tribes-both cephalous and acephalous, at different levels- village, territory and at tribe level. In the chiefdom, the chief has his council with members from higher clans[3]. In democratic types, village councils vary from elected representative (s) (Tsorgen of the Monpa), representation of clan heads on the basis of seniority and wisdom (Kebang/Keba members of the Adi/Galo), representation of hereditary members (Bulinags - members) of Apatani Bulinag (council), members of Thong clans[4] to Sherdukpen Jung) to an ad-hoc gathering of male members of family, lineage, clan (Nyishi Nyele, Tagnis's Dupam or Mishmi's Paharia). Among the Apatanis the eldest son of a Buliang inherits his position and rank, but in case of Shredukpen, the members normally come from the families of the previous members.

The councils in acephalous or cephalous communities, existing at different levels, are exclusively male affairs (Karlo, 2005:125; Walling, 2014: 247-248; Roy,1960:279, Elwin 1965/2007; Zhimo:2018 Dzuvichu, 2012, Sitlouh, 2015 and Kani 1993). Women are not allowed to participate in the process of deliberations or decision-making of the council[5] except as witness or providers of food and drinks to members and other participants (ibid). Among the Nyishi and Tagin tribes the institution of *Gingdung* (go-between) plays a crucial role in the arbitration of disputes, the *Gingdung* is always a male person.

Since colonial period, the Government appoints village heads as its representatives, who are usually clan heads in democratic types of councils (of the Adi, Galo, the Nyishi, etc.) or the chiefs (as among the Khamptis, Noctes, Tangsas or other Naga tribes). They are designated as *Gaon burhas*, meaning village head and are members of traditional councils. The word *burha* is an elder male member in Assamese vernacular. Obviously the institution is male centric. In recent years the Government appoints female village head (*Gaon burhis*), though their numbers shall be around 20 in the NER. By virtue of their status, these female village heads participate in village councils (Riddi, 2006, and Mitkong, 2002 &2006 and Sitlouh, 2015). As their presence is just ceremonial because of their absence or less numbers, the councils still remain male dominated. Needless to say, other councils are exclusively male affairs.

Perspective of Marginalisation in Matriliny

Matriliny in Meghalaya among the Khasis and the Garos, for example, does not represent matriarchal power relations as binary opposite of patriarchy in patrilineal tribes in the Northeast. Ancestral landed property along with residential house and ritualistic role of mother is practically inherited by the youngest daughter, *Khadduh/Khatuh* among the Khasis and *Nokna* among the Garos. *Khadduh/Khatuh* (Lyngdoh and Nongkynrih, 2015) or *Nokna* (Bose,1980) is a position that entitles the girl, but not her other sisters, to inherit family property and status-role from the mother. The *nokna* is referred to *aongipa méchik* – the girl kept for home (Majumdar,1985:xv) Evidently, daughters other than the heiress form the marginalised section in matrilineal tribes of Meghalaya so far as inheritance of family property is concerned. Self acquired property of these daughters before marriage while living in the family house goes to the family (Bose,198:148) which ultimately belongs to *nokna*. These other daughters may build their own houses, or purchase land with their husbands, but do not enjoy the same status and power in mother's family as that of the heiress sister.

However, the rights and power of the heiress are not same as those of her counterpart in a patriarchy. She owns the land; but the authority of management, the decision making power rests on her brother. Lyngdoh and Nongkynrih (2015) portray mother's brother as the centre of authority in the family. Amongst his diverse roles, he controls property in sister's household, takes decision on all family issues, assists in the management of ancestral property and performs several customary roles (see Lyngdoh and Nongkynrih, 2015:40). However, ordinarily, the *nokrom*, the husband of *nokna*, becomes the manager of the whole property (Bose,1980:121).

Though the position of women in matrilineal tribes is not like the one in patriarchy, yet it does not reflect female domination. A critical look will show that the women are also marginalised in different degrees as the control, management and decision making power rests on mother's brother. The power of would-be heiress to inherit ancestral property is not absolute; she can be deprived of it if she marries on her own to someone other than from among mother's brother's son (see Bose, 1980:121). Even her freedom to choose any one of the mother's brother's son is limited by customary prescriptions. For example, *Machong*-the social institution of a clan denomination, is the central decision making and regulatory body relating to issues of marriage (see Bose,1980). The heiress position is also an arrangement where girl's opinion does not figure. It is not always the youngest daughter, but the suitable one (ibid.) which places her in the glorified position of *nokna,* behind which male authority in *machong* plays a crucial role.

The heiress-would-be does not enjoy the same position in all occasions. In case of the death of father of the would-be heiress, her husband (*nokram* in Gaor-husband of *nokna*) marries the widowed mother-in-law (mother of the heiress)[6]. The mother, now the step-wife of the *nokan*, occupies the position of *Jit mamung* (principal wife and actual family head) and the *nokna*- i.e. the would -heiress, takes the position of the second wife, called *Jit gite* - slave wife (see Bose:1980:133-34 and 137).

The status of *Jit gite* is attached with second wife. Polygyny is not altogether absent in matrilineal society. Second wife is taken when the first one does not have a female issue (ibid.;129) or the husband wants to go for a second marriage. The position of second wife is subordinate to that of the first wife (ibid.: 133) even though she comes from the *machong* of the first wife. If she comes from other *machong*, her status is still lower. The practice of a type of polygyny is also reported by Majumdar. He informs that the second or subsequent wives enjoy the status of *kanki* (concubine) and are kept at different places (Majumdar, 1985:xvii).

As development process brings in forces of modernity, the authority of mother's brother is being gradually replaced by father's growing authority in the family (Lyngdoh and Nongkynrih, 2015:44). Marginalisation of women in matrilineal communities is perhaps following the path of patriarchy[7]. This statement may be corroborated with Roy's (2018) findings in the field of occupational trend. He reports that though female workforce has mostly established a foothold in the low profile economic activities, the male workforce is found dominating such economic activities as associated with higher social status.

Political marginalisation of women is quite visible. Roy (2018) states that in Khasi matrilineality the role of women relegates in politics and governance. Similarly, Kahrkhongor (2018) reaffirms discrimination of tribal women in Meghalaya in political arena (also see Nongsiej, 2018). From 1972 to 2018, out of 10 Assembly elections, there were 1(one) woman member in four elections, 2 (two) in two elections, 3 (three) in two elections and 04 (four) in one election who were elected to the Assembly. In one Assembly Election there was no woman member in the Assembly.

Data available with Election Commission of India reveal that in Assembly elections held in February, 2018, only 29 out of contesting 307 ST candidates were women, constituting 9.4 per cent. But only three candidates were elected. At present there are two ST women members (3.5%) against 57 ST male members in 60 member Meghalaya Assembly after the resignation of Agatha K. Sangma to pave way for her brother, present CM Mr. Conrad Sangma, to contest the by poll from her constituency.

Women participation in Autonomous District Council also does not present an encouraging picture. Nongsiej (2018) lists a total of 11 women members elected/nominated to Khasi Hills Autonomous District Council (KHADC) from 1952-57 to 2014-18. Out of them three members were elected twice, reducing actual participation to 8 (eight) women. It is to be mentioned that Khasi Hills Autonomous District Council and Jaintia Hills Autonomous District Council were together till 1972 under the label of United Khasi-Jaintia Hills Autonomous District Council. Nongsiej (2018) has reported only one women member in the combined council in 1952-57[8]. The next women representation has been recorded with two members during 1972-78.

Emerging Trend

The emerging trend presents the changing dimension of women's position relating to traditional space and the space beyond tradition. Participation in ballot-box politics, empowerment through SHGs and occupation in formal sectors and formation of pressure groups are women's space outside tradition. While working in non-traditional space they often encounter opposition from patriarchy in different forms. A conflict between tradition (the patriarchal mind set) and women's struggle to inherit property in Sumi Naga community is well documented by Zhimo (2018:160-163).

On the other hand, tribal women have been able to raise their voices against social evils and successful in fighting against some evil practices. Unfortunately in this non-traditional women's space, a new dimension of women marginalisation has emerged.

Interface of conflict between ethos of patriarchy and assertion of rights by women has different dynamics. The cause of conflict is apparent around traditional ethics of land ownership, but beneath the surface the attitude of male dominance is driving force. In this regard a recent event merits mention. Tribal organisations in Nagaland went on protest against the government decision to conduct election for urban Local Bodies on 1 February, 2017 with 33 per cent reservation for women according to the provisions of the Nagaland Municipal Act, 2001 amended up to 2006 on the ground that the decision infringes the rights of Naga people guaranteed under Article 371 (A) of the Indian Constitution with regard to customary property rights. But feminists see it as male design to perpetuate gender inequality (Behera, 2018; 30, Fn.17, see Sitlouh, 2015:107). This is a direct confrontation. There are movements on emerging social issues which are related to land rights, but underneath male chauvinism is the driving force (see Zhimo, 2018 and Sitlouh, 2015).

In recent years, tribal organisations in the Northeast, particularly students' unions have been organising movements against tribal status to girls of their communities marrying to non-tribals. In Manipur, Nagaland, Mizoram and Meghalaya the protest movements are very frequent and pressing. In Arunachal Pradesh social media provides an active platform on the issue in recent years. Several tribal organisations in the state openly have been opposing tribal girls marrying non-Arunachalees. The protest is around the issue of tribal status, rights and privileges, reservation in educational institutions, jobs and right to purchase of land and such other privileges which a tribal girl is entitled to.

Karlsson (2018:74) reports the stand of the Khasi Students' Union (KSU) on the issue in the context 'of recognition of tribal membership, eventually barring children of mixed marriages (especially if the father is non-Khasi) from recognition as Khasi' and hence also from the right to purchase land or trading licenses. Even the KHADC has passed a bill to this effect. The Khasi Hills Autonomous District (Khasi Social Custom of Lineage) (Second Amendment) Bill, 2018, declares the children of a Khasi woman married to a non-Khasi man as non-Khasi. Understandably, patriarchy places systematic or institutionalised barriers to maintain statuesque of traditional power structure.

The movement in its core contains male attitude of domination over female by depriving them right to chose a life partner in the plea of the problem of land alienation. But the issue is more delicate and sensitive, for the phenomenon of educated or other liberal minded girls married to outsider amounts to rejection of potential grooms of the community and a challenge to male chauvinism.

As girls marry outside, male ego gets hurt; and this is not unusual in a patriarchy and in tribal communities where group identity is based on ethnocentrism defined within the boundary of tradition. No doubt, traditional norms and practices are invoked when there is an apparent breach. Marrying outside is a challenge to traditional practices of MBD (mother's brother's daughter) and FZD (father's sister's son) types or tribe endogamy. Tribal status to the children of the woman marrying outside but retaining the tribal surname, which the children follow, interferes in the traditional practice of land rights and privileges constitutionally guaranteed to ST category. Obviously, the protest to outside marriage of tribal girls and tribal status to their children who take the clan name is a complex issue. Apparently, patriarchy seems reinforced affecting female decision in selecting a partner.

Educated girls often do not find a suitable match in the tribe and in Arunachal Pradesh several instances are found where educated girls prefer polygyny to marrying a 'mismatch'. A few educated girls being career conscious fall into late marriage bracket and so do not find match for their age. Career consciousness and pursuance of education in a non-traditional atmosphere in residential schools within and outside the sate make them familiar with non-traditional life ways so much so that they do not want to fall back into traditional role set by marrying in the community where they would be expected to perform traditional role along with newly acquired status. There are a number of cases in Khampti, Galo and Adi tribes, in fact in almost all tribes, where girls have married to non-Arunachalees. A few cases are there where traditional marriage is broken up in favour of someone to promote professional career. In contrast, marriage with non-Arunachalee is also broken up in favour of a partner from own community. These cases are observed with women of high status and average educated ones as well.

The trend apparently shows women empowerment. But theoretically, status inconsistency, as Lenisk would like us to believe (see Behera, 2015), also explains the emerging situation. Women empowered in the process of modernity do not belong to the group of marginalised ones; they live a life in an intersecting space of tradition and modernity, a few of them search for an identity that leads them to a situation of status inconsistency.

An interesting trend has emerged. There are cases of separation and divorce of married women as a mark of protest to the practice of polygyny. Such women, independent though, do not have good reputation in the community, especially in the lineage or clan of the separated or divorced husbands. On the other hand, there are several cases of educated and even well employed women married to already married politicians, contractors, government officers, etc., as second, third or even as fourth wife, thereby strengthening the traditional polygyny practice.

Marginalisation has different manifestations in the development process. The crucial aspect of it is class formation in an active and passive binarity which has been reported in some tribes like the Mogs of Tripura. In the active side there are landlords who depend on the families of passive landless class to meet labour demand for agricultural activities. The active-passive dichotomy is constructed drawing on Das Gupta's (2012) study of Mogs in which landlords are presented as a conscious class and landless wage labourers without it. Members of the latter group take pride from the fact that 'they worked for a particular big land owner' (ibid.:107). The sense of pride attached with the status subordination indicates to the stage where the subordinates have surrendered both their body and mind to the power of dominance. The landless labourers without class consciousness, without any doubt, certainly form a marginalised section that has emerged in the process of class formation. In this marginalised group, women form another marginalised section of comparatively low paid wage labourers, the rate of their wage being half of their male counterparts (ibid.: 102). These working Mog women did not have any education or political affiliation (ibid.:107), another area of their marginal position in the community.

So marginalisation in the process of development is a situation of 'adverse inclusion', to use the phrase from Dev Nathan and Xaxa (2012). Mog women are engaged in money income, but the inclusion renders a marginalised status. Adverse inclusion has an implicit dimension. Basar (2011) in her study among the Galos finds that to avail Indira Awas Yojana (IAY), required area of land is registered in the name of the woman beneficiary. This serves the procedural requirement of availing the scheme. The ownership given, however, is contextual and notional from community point of view as the woman cannot transfer the land in any way to any members even within the community.

The nature of marginalisation of women, as is the case of the Mogs, in the process of development is different from the one in traditional patriarchy. These women are placed on the scale of an intersecting marginal identity in tribal patriarchy. Development process often brings in elite-non-elite divide in women group itself.

Women are conscious about their rights; it is reflected in their participation in non-traditional activities- jobs in government and private sectors, professional occupation, self-employment, formation of SHGs (self-help groups), participation in Panchayatiraj[9] institutions, and most significantly by organising into different bodies to assert their rights. [10]

Evidently, an elite section has emerged from among what once was a marginalised section in patriarchy. Unfortunately a few of them have become responsible in creating a new dimension of marginalisation. Patriarchy demands household role of women, looking after family members, entertaining guests, etc., to which elite women do not have time due to their non-traditional life ways and engagement in various activities. So, they engage house helps, particularly poor women and girl children from the community or from tea garden communities and other tribal communities of Assam like Bodo-Kachari, Hajong, Mishing, etc. Even in villages, when tribal girls attend schools domestic helps are engaged in their place for babysitting and attending to other household chores.

In tradition, tribal women are repository of indigenous knowledge. The knowledge in general does not have a market use in the absence of promotional organisations and obviously, such knowledge gets competition from the market and thus is in the threshold of vanishing. Tribal women empowered with such traditional knowledge in some contexts do not find its use in the development process. On the other hand, a few women using one or other type of such knowledge creates a structure of dominance and subordination. The weaving knowledge is shifted to the factory, the production being organised by an elite woman. In such weaving centres tribal women work as wage earners, but the difference between the elite woman and the workers do not present a situation of equal status. Moreover, the factory production affects household production which was used for self consumption and sometimes for exchange purpose. Village women are deprived of an income source due to factory production of traditional clothes and that too under the community banner.

An important issue concerned with tribal women in recent years is infection with HIV/AIDS. Alcohol related deaths among young women are on the rise (Dzuvicy, 2012:87-88). Indian Council of Medical Research (ICMR) and National AIDS Control Organisation (NACO) report that Mizoram, Manipur and Nagaland were accounted as states with adult (15-49 years) HIV prevalence is above the national average. Mizoram, Manipur and Nagaland each reported 2.04, 1.43 and 1.15 per cent respectively. Percentage for affected men and women is almost same. Meghalaya state reported according to NACO, 191 new HIV infections in 2017 with a 10 per cent increase and 42 per cent new HIV infections among women.

Resistance to national integration is seen in Nagaland's armed struggle for autonomy. In this struggle women are the worst sufferer (Dzuvichu, 2012:82). The agony, torture, violence, incidents of rape, killings, substance abuse and the quest for peace resound in the voices of female poets of Nagaland (see Sebastian, 2019). The helplessness against violence gets expressed in poetic emotions and sense of resistance.

The phenomenon of marginalisation in recent years is not tribe-specific across gender divide. It reflects in both specific and general contexts. Undifferentiated marginal status of tribal women in patriarchy shows power differences in the group with the rise in elite section among tribal women. In addition, similarity of marginal status related to political participation, human trafficking, substance abuse, etc., reflects beyond-tribe problem in the process of integration and interaction. As new areas of marginalising forces emerge, women have been resisting to patriarchy for assertion of identity. The resistance has counter move, though women have been able to make their identity feel. The emerging situation of marginalisation of tribal women reflects a multiple status complex, and needs further investigation for objective analysis and comprehensive understanding.

Acknowledgments: I am grateful to Dr. Bhaskar Kumar Kakati and Ms. Jombi Riba for sharing information used in this paper.

References

Basar, J. 2011. 'A Study of Indigenous Knowledge System in Development Policies and Programmes with Special reference to Resource Management by the Galo of Arunachal Pradesh'. *Unpublished Ph.D. Thesis*, Itanagar: AITS, Rajiv Gandhi University.

Behera, M.C. 2004. 'Slavery or Institutionalising Efforts at Perpetuating the Source of Labour?: The case of the Nyishi-Sulung Relationship'. *Man and Life*, Vol. 30, Nos. (1-2) , January-June, 2004, pp. 27- 40.

———2015. 'Contemporary status of tribal women: A Critique of 'Lenski's Status Inconsistency''. In S.N.Chaudhary (ed) Tribal *Women: Yesterday, Today and Tomorrow*, , Jaipur: Rawat, pp. 77-85.

Bose, J.K. 1980. *Glimpses of Tribal Life in North-east India*. Calcutta: Institute of Social Research and Applied Anthropology.

——.1985. *Culture Change among the Garos*. Calcutta: Institute of Social Research and Applied Anthropology.

Coser, L.A.1996. *Masters of Sociological Thought.* Jaipur/New Delhi: Rawat.

Das Gupta, Malabika 2012. 'Class Formation among the Tribals:A Case Study of the Mogs of Tripura". In Dev Nathan and V.Xaxa (eds.), *Social Exclusion and Adverse Inclusion- Development and Deprivation of Adivasis in India*, New Delhi: Oxford University Press

Dev Nathan and V.Xaxa (eds.),2012. *Social Exclusion and Adverse Inclusion-Development and Deprivation of Adivasis in India*, New Delhi: Oxford University Press.

Dube, S.C.1977. 'Introduction'. In S.C.Dube (ed.), *Tribal Heritage of India*, New Delhi: Vikas Publishing House, Pvt. Ltd., pp. 1-7.

Dzuvichu, Rosemary 2012. 'Development and Women: The Discourse in Nagaland'. In Dev Nathan and V.Xaxa (eds.), op.cit. pp. 81.-93.

Elwin, Verrier 1965. *Democracy in NEFA*. Itanagar: Directorate of Research.

———— 1988. *A Philosophy for NEFA*. Itanagar: Directorate of Research. (First published in 1957).

Jackson, S. 1998. 'Theorizing Gender and Sexuality'. In S.Jackson and J.Jones (eds.) *Contemporary Feminist Theories*. Edinburgh: Edinburgh University Press. In S.Jackson and J.Jones (eds.) *Contemporary Feminist Theories*. Edinburgh: Edinburgh University Press. pp. 131-143.

Kakati, Bhaskar Kumar 2018. *Tribal Women of North East Inid and Empowerment: Tiwa Women's Participation in Panchayati Raj Institutions.* New Delhi: Nation Press.

Kani,Takhe 1993. *Advancing Apatanis of Arunachal Pradesh. Itanagar*: Mrs. Takhe Omang.

Karlo, Rejir 2005. *Emerging Pattern of Tribal Leadership in Arunahcl Pradesh*. New Delhi: Commonwealth.

Kharkongor, Elizabeth 2018. 'Role of Women in Politics in Meghalaya'. *IOSR Journal of Humanities and Social Science,* Volume 23, Issue 4, Ver. 7 (April. 2018), pp. 01-03. www.iosrjournals.org

Lyngdoh, Angelica Queenie and A.K.Nongkynrih 2015. 'Mother's Brother in Matrilineal Societies: A Study of Khasi Matriliny'. *The NEHU Journal, Vol. XIII, No. 1*, pp. 33-46

Majumdar, D.N. 1985. 'Introduction'. In Bose, J.K.1985. *Culture Change among the Garos*. Calcutta: Institute of Social Research and Applied Anthropology, pp. vii-xix.

Nongsiej, E. Plieladdalin 2018. 'Women and Political Participation in Meghalaya'. *International Journal of Research in Social Sciences,* Vol. 8 Issue 5, May 2018, http://www.ijmra.us

Mitkong, N. 2002. *Customary Laws of the Adis of Arunachal Pradesh*. Itanagar: Director of Research.

———— 2006. *The Customary Laws of the Tagins*. Itanagar: Director of Research.

Norbu, T. 1997. 'Status of Women:Gallong'. In B.B.Pandey (chief ed.) Status of Women in Tribal Society-Arunachal Pradesh, Itanagar: Directorate of Research, pp. 112-132.

Parwez, M. 2012. 'Customary Laws and Practices in North East India: Records and Reports Preserved in law Research Institute (LRI), Gauhati'. *Indian Journal of Applied Research*, Vol. 2 (3), pp. 81-83.

Patnaik, S.M. 1993. 'Patriarchy among the Paraja: Innocuous Tradition or Invisible Violence'. *Indian Anthropologist*, Vol. 23 (1), pp. 65-71.

Richards, Peter 2010. Herbert Spencer: Social Darwinist or Libertarian Prophet? Auburn/Alabama, United States: Mises Institute.

Riddi, Ashan 2006. *The Tagins of Arunachal Pradesh-A Study of Continuity and Change*. Delhi: Abhijeet Publications.

Roy, Animesh 2018. 'Discord in Matrilineality: Insight into the Khasi Society in Meghalaya'. *Society and Culture in South Asia*, Vol. 4, 2: pp. 278-297. https://doi.org/10.1177/2393861718767238

Roy, Sachin 1960. *Aspects of Padam Minyong Culture*. Itanagar: Director of Research.

Sebastian, A.J. 2019. 'Voices of Poets on Contemporary Maladies in Naga Society'. In M.C.Behera (ed.), *Tribal Language, Literature and Folklore*, Jaipur: Rawat, pp. 201-215.

Sitlhou, Hoineilhing 2015. 'Patriarchal Bargains and Paradoxical Emancipation: Issues in the Politics of Land Rights of Kuki Women'. *Indian Journal of Gender Studies*, 22(1) 92–115, DOI: 10.1177/0971521514556949, SAGE Publications. Downloaded from ijg.sagepub.com by guest on June 6, 2016.

Stewart, Iain 2011. 'Commandeering Time: The Ideological Status of Time in the Social Darwinism of Herbert Spencer'. Australian Journal of Politics and History, 57 (3): 389–402. doi:10.1111/j.1467-8497.2011.01604.

Walling, A.Wati. 2014. Customary Land Owning Practices: The Norm Practitioners, Land Bearers and the Commoner's identity in a Tribal Community in Nagaland'. In M.C.Behera and Jumyir Basar (eds.), 2014. *Resources, Tribes and Development*, Jaipur:Rawat, pp. 242-255.

Wittig, M. 1981. 'One is not Born a Woman'. *Feminist Issues*, Vol. 1(1), pp. 47-54.

Zhimo, Avitoli G. 2018. 'Customary Laws, Patriarchy and Gender relations in Contemporary Sumi Naga Society'. In M.C. Behera (ed.), *Revisiting Tribal Studies: A Glimpse after Hundred Years*. Jaipur: Rawat Publicaitons, pp. 154-172.

Notes

1. Prof. M.C. Behera, Arunachal Institute of Tribal Studies, Rajiv Gandhi University, Itanagar-791112. *Email:mcbehera1959@gmail.com.*
2. This is applicable to non-tribes also. But as the scope of the paper involves tribal women, the reference is made to the tribal context.
3. For example, the Khamti tribe is divided into *chowpha* (royal) clans, *paklung* (commoner) clans and *phan-e-on* (lower division) clans. Members to *Mukchum*, the Khampti council is taken from royal and *paklung* clans. Those families having matrimonial alliance with royal clans are preferred.
4. The Sherdupen tribe is divided into Thong and Chao groups in social hierarchy where Thong clans belong to upper division.

5. Most villages in Nagaland have reserved 25% of Village Development Board (VDB) seats for women, but the quota exists in paper, in reality traditional norms prevail.
6. Majumdar (1985:xvi) also reports the two different status of *nokna* on the occasion of her husband marrying her widowed mother.
7. Parwez (2012:82) maintains with reference to Dimasa tribe that the traditional institutions are transforming in a manner to strengthen patriarchy.
8. In 2005 Tokheli Kikon became only woman village council chairperson. Till 2017 she continues to be the only woman village council head in Nagaland despite high female literacy in the State.
9. Kakati (2018) finds the presence of Tiwa women in Gram Sabha only at the time of selection of beneficiaries. They never take part in any decision making.
10. Mention may be made of State organisations like *Mizo Hmeichhe Insuihkhawm Pawl*, *Arunachal Pradesh Women Welfare Association*, *Naga Mothers Association*; issue based NOGs and society like *Impulse NGO Network* and *Civil Society Women's Organisation* of Shillong; and other village societies/ associations like *Adi Bane Kebang Women Wing in Pasighat*, *Centre Village Pyndensohsaw Women Social Welfare Association* (village based Khasi women organisation), *Bugakol Mahila Samity* (village based Khasi women organisation), *Women Welfare Society of Higi Bagra* (village based Galo women organisation) and many others.

Chapter - 3

Empowerment of *Savara* Tribal Women among the Marginalized communities of India: An Ethnographic profile

***Dr. M. Gnana Selvin Raj*[1]**

Introduction

The state of Andhra Pradesh (including Telengana) stands in seventh position with regard to density of tribal population in India consisting of 33 tribal groups. Among them 8 groups are primitive tribal group (PTG) namely *Chenchu, Kolam, Thoti, Konda Reddi, Khond, Porja, Savara* and *Gadaba.*

The *Savara* are mostly found in Southern Odisha and in north coastal Andhra Pradesh. According to 2011 Census the *Savara*, numbering 1, 37, 613 (5.23% of the total tribal population of 495, 75, 771) are one of the most populous tribes in the state. They are also a prominent tribal community in Rayagada district of Odisha and specific pockets of Koraput and Gajapati districts. In Andhra Pradesh they are mainly found in the Palakonda hill ranges (part of Eastern Ghats) of Srikakulam, Vijayanagaram and Visakhapatnam districts. Besides the *Savara*, three other important tribal communities, namely *Jatapu, Kondadora* and *Gadaba* inhabit the districts.

Origin

Etymologically, in Sanskrit, *Savara* or *Sabara* means a mountaineer, since they are experts in climbing and hunting in the mountainous forest area. It is believed that *Savara* were one of the indigenous tribes of pre-historic India. H.D. Sankalia was of the opinion that the bearers of the Nevasa – Nevadatoli culture as well as of the copper hoard belong to indigenous tribes, such as *Nishads, Pulindas* and *Savara.* Those primitives might have made 3000-4000 years ago beautiful painted pottery and even copper tools and weapons (Swararao Delli et al: 2016).

The *Savara* were the first tribal groups mentioned in the Hindu epics like the Ramayana and the Mahabharata. Lord Rama, when he was in search of Sita, is said to have met an aryanised *Savara* woman known as *Sabari.* She was known as the descendant of sage Viswamitra, who lived around 800 BC. During Mahabharata, Sahithya Darpana mentioned that the *Sabari* and *Ahiri* dialects were spoken by the leaf-gathering and wood-cutting people, the *Sabaras.*

Family set up

In *Savara* tribal community father is the head of the family. Descent is patrilineal. Inheritance of property is also through father's line. All sons share the property of their father equally among themselves (i.e. male equigeniture). The rule of residence is patrilocal. Neolocal residence is also common among them after marriage. However, when a man acquires his mate through marriage by service (*Kinarsung or Illarikam*), he agrees to stay either forever or for a fixed period in his father-in-law's house. Usually, this practice is confined in families having no male children. In such families women have a say in all economic activities. She is respected and regarded.

Extended families are common in a traditional *Savara* community, yet nuclear families are predominant among the *Savara*. Monogamy is a rule but polygyny is also practiced occasionally. So, these days we can notice polygynous family along with monogamous families in the *Savara* community. In a polygynous family all the women have equal role to play with regard to their dealings with the male members in the house. Family is the basic unit of the *Savara* community. This single unit of their social structure constitutes the nucleus of their social life. The women play an educative role in a *Savara* family in bringing up their children in personal, social and community values.

Savara family is in transition now-a-days. When a conflict occur between a father and his son or between a mother and her daughter the maternal uncle no longer comes to the scene to counsel the family and to give strong advice to them, as it was earlier days. Even the parents keep away themselves when their married son begins to strike his wife or mistreat his children. The consequence of this indifference was loss of protection against suicide and incest and domestic violence. As a result the social safety net for the young women and children was torn apart in *Savara* family structure. At present the *Savara* family is vulnerable to problems from which it had been protected by the larger kin group in the past. That's why the women's role in a family becomes more important. She not only begets the child but also brings up the child in human and societal values that protect and safeguard the integrity of family life in a *Savara* community.

When the family, the foundational social structure of a society is shaken, the whole edifice of family structure crumbles. When the well integrated family system begins to collapse, the tremors are felt throughout the *Savara* culture.

Thus empowerment of *Savara* women in their socio-economic and political aspects of life deserves paramount importance now.

Kinship

The *Savara* kinship terminology is mostly classificatory and a few of their kinship terms are descriptive. The terms of kinship applicable to relatives, consanguineous and affinal, are strikingly the same. All the male grandparents of the speaker both from the maternal and paternal side are classified by the only term '*Jojong*'. All the female relatives of the third generation above the speaker are indicated by the term '*Yoyong*'. The collateral and the lineal relatives are not kept distinct, but they are merged together and a single kinship term expresses the relationship.

Kinship Terms

English term	*Savara* Term
Father	*vang*
Mother	*Yeng*
Grand father (M/P)	*Jojong*
Grand Mother (M/P)	*Yoyong*
Elder brother	*Kakun*
Elder Brother's wife	*Boning/Kakin*
Younger brother	*Uba*
Younger Brother's wife	*Koyeng*
Elder sister	*Kaking*
Younger sister	*Aie*
Wife	*Dokkiri*
Husband	*Gaman*
Father's elder brother	*Thatha*
Father elder/ younger brother's son	*Kakun/Uba*
Father's younger brother	*Dadan*
Mother's elder sister	*Anthalai*
Mother's younger sister	*Yayan*
Wife's sister's husband	*Saddu*
Elder brother's wife	*Bonni*
Younger brother's wife	*Koina*
Wife's elder sister	*Kinar*
Wife's younger sister	*Erriboi*
Sister's husband	*Baun*

Kinship behavior which is universal in many societies such as avoidance and joking relationship are also very common among *Savara*. They observe avoidance relation towards daughter-in-law, mother-in-law, father-in-law, younger brother's wife etc. There is a strict distance maintained between elder brother-in-law (husband's elder brother) and younger sister-in-law (wife's younger sister). Similarly, avoidance is observed between son-in-law and his mother-in-law also.

Joking relationship also is very common among the *Savara* families. An extreme degree of familiarity expressed through joking relationship between certain kin relation by way of cracking a satire, taunt, ridicule, exchange of abuse, obscene and vulgar references to sex etc. They observe joking relationship between consanguine groups such as grandchildren and grandparents, younger brother-in-law and elder sister-in-law (elder brother's wife), wife and husband. Radcliffe Brown (1940) regards the joking relationship as having a symbolic meaning. Joking relations may be only a kind of friendliness expressed by a show of hostility. Such relationship smoothens the tension arise in family members. Women play a catalytic role of human solidarity in a family.

Marriage

Savara people have widespread kinship networks. The kinship relations between villages are established through affinal relations i.e., marriage links. Marriage plays a very important role in kinship networks of *Savara.* They follow strict endogamy at community level. The village endogamy is commonly approved and sanctioned by the *Savara* community. The breach of which is considered to be the breach of law and the sanctions may range from excommunication from the tribe or from the village community. The tribal council or tribal head (*Sabhabadi)* will impose sanctions and order others not to talk, associate, exchange things, maintain relations with those who are excommunicated. The *Savara* in rare case do observe village exogamy, where only one *birinda* is inhabited in the entire village. In big villages having more than one *birinda* marriage are often arranged within the village.

Marriages are possible between a man and woman of his maternal side but not with maternal uncle's daughter. Only those who fail to arrange girls for their sons elsewhere select one of maternal cross-cousins for marriage (mother's brother's daughter). The father's sister being a member of the same *birinda* there is little scope for marriage with her children.

Serial monogamy is practiced by *Savara* and limits themselves to one wife at a place. In case of divorce or death of wife, a *Savara* marries again and remains to be monogamous. Polygyny exists in two ways, sororal polygyny and non-sororal polygyny. In sororal polygyny the multiple wives of a *Savara* man are sisters. In non-sororal polygyny the multiple wives of a Savara man are not sisters.

When a *Savara* woman is unable to bear a child or she does not want her ancestral property to be divided among others, she encourages her husband to marry her own sister. This sororal- polygyny happens only when all the siblings are females without a single male to inherit the family property. Though property belongs to girls in a family where there is no male sibling, at the time of marriage of the girl, they look for a man (would be husband) of the girl, who can look after the girl's property. Consanguineous marriages between parallel cousins i.e. among brother's children or among sister's children are prohibited. Cross cousin marriages (FZD and MBD) are more common among the Savara.

Three types of prominent tribal marriages among *Savara*:

Dube (1969) classifies tribal marriages into three types (a) the ideal or general or regular marriage. The ideal marriage ceremony is arranged according to their religious norms and social customs by parents of both the boy and the girl. This is the most preferred method of acquiring a mate among the *Savara.* This type of marriage by negotiation and mutual agreement (*Penkui*) which involves long procedure depending upon the talks between both parties takes place in every tribal family. (b) The non-ideal yet socially approved marriages are by elopement (*Dingdengboi* or *Dandaboi*), marriage by service (*Kinarsung* or *Illarikam*) and marriage by exchange (*Ulaiboi*). The non-ideal marriage like elopement and capture find certain social prestige. (c) The disrespectful marriage category has the lowest prestige and effected through force, intrusion, and so on. It is very interesting to note that among these primitive people, marriage by capture involves the elements of surprise and brute to some extent but not force and violence! Such marriage process leads to dispute between the families of the boy and the girl, but eventually they get reconciled through the intervention of elders of the village.

Economic consideration determines mostly for the less number of marriages through negotiations. Because the marriage by negotiation is very costly involving considerable expenditure on gifts, liquor, community meals etc., In marriage by elopement besides bride-price, liquor is served only on one occasion, when both families reconcile to their marriage; the couple is allowed to settle down in their village. Marriage by elopement is comparatively less expensive.

Even though *Savara* understand the relationship between conception and sexual inter-intercourse, still they believe that human effort should be complemented by divine intervention. So they seek blessings of gods for the proper conception and safe delivery of the child. During the period of her pregnancy, she invariably avoids passing through burial grounds and other places of evil spirits since they tend to believe to face the wrath of abortion or still-birth.

In some remote villages, delivery is always conducted outside the main house, either in the verandah or in their cattle shed. An enclosure is made by using *saris* or bamboo reeds closing all the sides of the cattle shed to provide privacy for conducting delivery. As soon as the woman feels labour pain, she comes out of the house to sit on a stone in the delivery enclosure, holding a strong rope sling that is hanging from the roof with her legs stretched wide apart. The *"Kudanboi"* (mid-wife) or any other elderly woman of the village conducts the delivery. But now-a-days the Government appointed nurses take the pregnant women to hospitals by the ambulance for pre-natal, delivery and post-natal care. Since there are many interior villages without proper road, people are unable to get ambulance facilities even at the time of emergency.

Concept of Purity and Pollution

After delivery both mother and child are given a ceremonial bath with hot water mixed with turmeric powder. The woman who delivered her child, is considered to be under 'birth – pollution' till she is given purification bath. Until that time the woman is not allowed to touch anything in the house, and she continues to stay in the enclosure in the verandah. After the purification bath she is allowed to enter into the house. But she should not touch any of the household articles. She is permitted to sleep on a cot confined to one corner of the house. She avoids shaking hands with their guests and the outsiders as a sign of welcome among them. Similarly the woman in menstruation period also avoids shaking hands with others. During the days of her period she avoids going to the hills and forest for work or collecting fire wood. Moreover after the death of a person in a family, all the household members are considered polluted for a period of time. They do not hold or attend any functions or celebrations and avoid associating with others.

Dress Pattern

Savara's traditional dress pattern has been changed drastically now-a-days. Men mostly wear *dhoti* and cover their upper part with towel. The women wear *sari* leaving it up to their ankle. The same *sari* covers their upper part as well as their head. But the younger generation put on blouse and ties their *sari* as any other non-tribal woman. The *Savara* women wear simple ornament to adorn themselves. A few necklaces of beads, round wooden plugs, spiral rings made of grass, bell metal or aluminum in the fingers and toes, little rings in the nose, metal anklets and colorful plastic bangles are worn by them. Garland made of colorful beads is preferred by them to be worn around the neck. The *Savara* women known for not accumulate gold ornaments as valuable things are not the same today. These days they also use ornaments made of gold.

Food Habits

In general the *Savara* people are non-vegetarians and eat fowl, pork, beef, goat, fish, dry fish, wild boar, wild sheep, rabbit etc. They also consume potato, tubers like *savadi dhumpa, donda dhumpa, adavi dhumpa* found in the forest. Their staple food is rice and jowar. They used to consume millets in the past, but now they take rice since subsidized supply of rice is available to them through Public Distribution System (PDS). *Savara* live in the plains cultivate paddy in their lands for their consumption. They consume a variety of pulses, green leaves, edible wild fruits etc. They rarely consume dairy products, and not much interested in maintaining vegetable gardens, because most of them buy vegetables from the weekly markets *(Santha).* They drink country liquor brewed from *vippa* flowers commonly found in the forest. When they go to weekly markets to Palakonda and Kothuru towns they do buy alcoholic beverages i.e. beer, whiskey, gin and brandy. They are also fond of fermented liquor (*kallu*) extracted from palm trees. Till today we do not find any liquor shop existing in any of the interior tribal villages around Seethampeta. By and large liquor consumption among the Christian tribal is uncommon to a great extent. Habit of smoking is drastically reduced among the *Savara* people, except a few elderly men and women continue the habit of smoking.

Work Culture as an indigenous knowledge

Agriculture, especially *podu* or shifting cultivation is the mainstay of the *Savara* people. Every family member works in the field or mountainous forest, despite their unstable physical condition.

Mostly they depend on "slash and burn cultivation" (*swidden*) which does not require any sophisticated technological input. The forest on the hills is considered a common property of the people though the divided portions of the land are looked after by many families. The members make a collective decision in selecting *podu* lands according to a number of criteria - some ecological and some social. With regard to ecological criteria, they restrict site selection by excluding too rocky or too steep mountain range as it is not fit for cultivation. In some places a village occupies the entire hill slop. Others do not intrude into the land that belongs to a particular village. *Podu* plots are difficult to irrigate since one has to depend on rainfall to cultivate. Failure in rainfall results in failure of crops. So generally now-a-days, they prefer settled cultivable land near hill streams than cultivation in *podu* plots. Terraced cultivation is mainly practiced by those living along the foothill of Palakonda and Kotthuru or near the plains of hill streams.

Most of the *Savara* people living around Seethampeta do posses small plots of land on the hill as well as hill terrain. They cultivate paddy, cashew, turmeric, zinger, pineapple, custard-apple, plantain, mangoes, tamarind, red gram and maize. The minor forest produce such as *adda* leaves for leaf plates, yams like *adavi vaimu, savadi dhumpa, donda dhumpa, sheekai,* soap nuts, hill brooms and honey are gathered and taken to the weekly markets *(Santha)* for sale. They do not cultivate in large quantity to sell them in market to make more money. They cultivate what they really need for their consumption throughout the year. Notwithstanding their hard labour their land does not produce as much as they want because of uncertainty of rain, unfertile soil added to poor irrigation facility. The land is full of rocks, stones, thorns and thistles. However, an individual family members work hard in their portion of land throughout the year, still they find difficult to clear the thorny bushes from the land completely and make it cultivable. Most portion of their land is left fallow.

Gutthi pani (Group work), a kind of work culture among the *Savara,* is one of the indigenous knowledge systems prevalent even today. In many villages they do practice *Gutthi pani.* The *Savara's* economy is not market oriented; neither is it aimed at making more money nor to gain maximum profit. Rather it is 'subsistence' economy, oriented towards the survival of the household members. Their system of production, distribution and consumption cater to day-to-day needs of the people for their continual sustenance and survival.

The practice of *Gutthi pani* in *Savara* tribal community enables them to attend to their fallow land and make it fit for cultivation with the help of other people in the same tribal community. *Gutthi pani* means "group work". A family is helped by the other community members. The elders of the Adivasi community assign number of people to work in the land of a particular family. In some tribal hamlets, the one who seeks help, goes to each house and requests them to come to his aid. The family which gets the help of the labour force from the community has to provide a meal for all of them and at the end of the day each labourer is given Rs. 100 which is a nominal wage for one day. Thus, the community supports the individual family by extending collective labour force. Actually many *Adivasi* families are very poor and they could not afford to give a meal and Rs. 100 each, their land remains fallow for many years.

The work culture of *Gutthi pani* is "other centered" – involves cooperation and collaboration of every individual member in the community. The process of decision making is more democratic which fosters communal solidarity. The views of the elders are respected and followed up. Ultimately it strengthens their unity and fellowship with one another. A tangible expression of compassion and solidarity intertwined in this indigenous practice of group work (*Gutthi pani*) among the *Savara* is in fact praise worthy. The "helper-therapy principle" postulated by Riessman (1965) pointed to the process by which helping others has a therapeutic effect on the helper.

Caste percolates in tribal society

Though the *Savara* tribe constitutes an egalitarian society, there is a social cleavage among the people of *Savara, Kondadora, Gadaba* and *Jathapu* in this locality. Since the *Jathapu* who reside in the plains and mostly live in nearby towns having access to education, employment, transport, communication and other modern facilities, consider the *Savara* a socially backward and economically impoverished community. There is a tendency that the *Jathapu* somewhat look down upon the *Savara* who still remain illiterate. As far as the *Savara* people are concerned they possess land and cultivate them on their own. There may not be any threat to their dignity and tribal identity in their egalitarian community. But if they mortgage or sell away or lose their land and start working in the fields of others for daily wage, then their landlessness will lead to imbibe a mentality of caste hierarchy. So caste discrimination is sure to percolate in tribal way of life in a more deceptive manner!

Prevalence of Untouchability

Now, if we think of the origin of the practice of untouchability, we find that in ancient India, as people took to different professions, they were classified according to their association and allegiance to work. If some one's work was of a clean and pure in nature, he/she was regarded as 'high'; if it were dirty and unclean, such person was looked down upon by others as 'low'.

Dr. Ambedkar propounded a unique thesis to explain how some are treated as untouchables or as a separate class. He writes that in the beginning, people led a nomadic life. Later on, some settled down. There were always fights and battles between the nomads and the settled people. The defeated people came to be known as the 'Broken Men'. These Broken people did not know where to go for shelter or whom to approach for protection. Simultaneously the settled people had to constantly face the challenge of watching and guarding their dwelling places from the attacks of the outsiders. The work of guarding the locality of the settled people was assigned to the 'Broken Men' who were desperately on look out for shelter and protection. They were made to live outside the village as guards. Later on these 'Broken Men' came to be regarded as outcastes and untouchables. Dr. Ambedkar says that they were not the people who were first declared as untouchables and then deported out of the villages but they were the people who from the very beginning lived outside the village and were subsequently declared as untouchables (Dr. B. R. Ambedkar: 2017).

Caste practices can easily percolate in *Savara* tribal culture when they are in close contact with the non tribal Hindu population by adopting Hindu way of life and worship at the cost of discarding the tribal way of life and worship. This situation will arise once they dispose their lands and take up menial jobs for their continual survival.

Religious beliefs

The *Savara* are highly religious with each and every natural phenomenon attributed to the works of some Gods, deities or spirits of folk religion. The Savara religion is very elaborate and deep rooted. The *Savara* still continue shamanic practices in many places. They are polytheists and believe in a large number of deities and ancestral spirits. Therefore, the customary laws, values, norms are highly respected by all members of the society for the fear of inviting wrath of these divine being on personal or community levels.

A shaman, usually a woman, serves as an intermediary between the two worlds. During a trance, her soul is said to climb down to the underworld, leaving her body for the dead to use as their vehicle for communication. People crowd around the shaman, arguing vehemently with the dead, laughing at their jokes, or weeping at their accusations. According to *Savara* thinking, death is not the end of life, but merely another phase. After death one becomes a powerful spirit. The *Savara* believe in many supernatural powers. To ensure their protection and success in their lives, various deities are propitiated. These deities and supernatural beings are classified into benevolent and malevolent ones. The benevolent deities are revered and propitiated to secure their favors and sustained blessings while the malevolent deities are feared and offered bloody sacrifices to appease them in order to escape from their wrath. Sickness, bad luck and other difficulties are attributed to the work of malevolent deities. Diagnosis and treatment of sickness involve a series of magico-religious practices besides administering herbal medicine. The native doctor is known as *vejjodu*.

Hinduism and animism are two separate faiths

Delliswararao (2016) observes that now-a-days a move by Hindu groups to convert the *Savara* to Hinduism is taking place leading to conflict and tension in certain areas. The religion of *Savara* is understood in two different ways. There is one school of thought that speaks of *Savaras* as not Hindu but there is a superficial imposition of Hinduism on them. The other school believes that they are Hindus. A *Savara* makes offerings to certain Hindu deities and calls himself a Hindu for no better reason than that he believes. His/her allegiance to Hinduism improves his social status and elevates him/her in the social ladder. The following reasons are generally given in order to argue that the *Savara* are not Hindus:

- They do not perform rituals and worship before Hindu idols.
- They do not enter Hindu temples.
- They do not have idols in their houses.
- They do not employ Brahmin priests for any of the ceremonies such as birth, marriage, and death but employ their own "*Vajjodu*"
- They live in great fear of evil spirits and most of their religious practices are endeavors to propitiate these spirits which always seem bent upon harming them.

The *Savara* who adopted Christianity approach the Parish Priest (in case of Catholics) or the Pastors (in case of Protestant) for blessings and keep vigil in the churches for healing. According to them death is not the end of existence, but merely another phase of life on this earth. After death one becomes a powerful spirit. The Christian belief in resurrection (life after death) also synchronizes with theirs.

Presence of Christianity

In the recent past, their traditional beliefs have undergone change due to

Christianity and teachings of missionaries. In many areas the shamanic and animist beliefs are only distant memories. The presence of Christianity in this region also goes back to more than hundred years of its existence. A small church dedicated to mother Mary situated on a small hillock near the village Goidhi symbolizes the presence of their Christian faith. The surrounding villages which adopted Christian faith regularly visit this Marian shrine on the Goidhi hillock. Talking to the Parish priest Fr. N. Kishore SJ, a Jesuit working among the *Savara* tribe (in the year 2016) narrates, "The Story of Goidhi Fatima Mata Tribal Shrine goes back to century old story when the Christian missionaries from the Vizag MSFS province used to work in the bordering areas of Andhra and Orissa. Their Missions were located at the nearby places namely Palakonda, Palavalasa, Kothuru, Battili and Nallarayaguda. The missionaries chose Goidhi hill as a place to build a church as it is accessible by the road. The hillock was partially leveled. They built a church that stood on the hill for more than hundred years. Beside this church they built a small house with two rooms. One for the priest to stay and the other room where the priest used to shelter his horse on which he used to travel to reach the remote tribal villages in those days. The house was strongly built to resist heavy wind and it was strong enough to protect them from wild animals. The missionary work brought a few *Jatapu* and *Savara* tribal families to embrace Christian faith. The *Savara* men, women with their children visit this Marian shrine regularly to pray. Occasionally as a community they render *sramadan* (free service) to clean the surrounding of the church located on the hill top.

Possibilities of women empowerment among *Savara*

1. *Active participation of members:* The primary challenge facing women today is to increase their participation and become actively involved in decision making (Chandra, 1997). Given the patriarchal notions of the Indian society, in general women are perceived with contempt and suspicion. They are not easily trusted by the rest of the community. Yet the women need to be mobilized, trained and taught to take up leadership role in their community. Participation has two dimensions – quantitative and qualitative. People's participation in terms of numbers has no meaning. Today there is a need for change from quantitative to qualitative. Promotion of active participation in social, economic and political spheres would help enhancing process of decisions making and empowerment. It will also give women the desired self-respect and social dignity which are the pre-requisites of empowerment.
2. *Uniqueness of Tribal community:* The socio-economic structure in tribal communities is markedly different from that of the non-

tribal or advanced groups of people. The tribal community has a very simple technology, which fits well with their ecological surroundings. The varied needs of the people and their diverse culture need to be considered seriously, lest resulting into success in one place and failure in another place. Moreover their economy can be said to be of subsistence type. They practice different types of occupations to sustain themselves and live on 'marginal economy'. Hence, projects and programmes should aim at involving women in economic activities apart from their role in family maintenance. A serious scrutiny and understanding of the tribal community should precede development initiatives. It is important to know which gender among different tribal community is the working force and who can be entrepreneur and decision maker. Promoting entrepreneurial spirit among them is very important. It enables to push them up the economic ladder.

3. *Saving dimension among the tribe:* A tribe is usually considered an economically independent group of people having their own specific economy. Most of them do not think for tomorrow as they are more concerned with their day-today needs. So saving is not at all a part of their life. But as a matter of fact, Micro-Credit Union (MCU) is started with the purpose of savings only. So during the initial stage of formation of MCU, the real problem arises in motivating them to save and to regularize the savings. The *Savara* women have little financial independence at home. This makes banks reluctant to finance the projects and programmes. NGOs and other stakeholders should come forward to assist them financially.

4. *Promotion of literacy*: Low literacy level among the rural poor especially among the rural tribal women proves to be a major barrier. Adult education and skill training has to be implemented in order to empower them. Hardly we find the projects and programmes focus on investment potential and improvement of their skills. Freebies should be avoided and subsidies should be given if necessary. Help from the Government and NGOs doesn't come often following the need. This leads to improper utilization of funds. Thus, wider consultation with the local people has to be initiated and the decision should be evolved from the people.

5. *Free them from exploitation:* Usually the poor people at the time of emergency run to the landlords and money lenders (*Shavukarlu*) for their credit needs. They borrow money usually at a very high

interest. Eventually the women become vulnerable to exploitation by the middle men. To alleviate this situation, community corpus fund has to be created by every member of the tribal household. Failure to develop proper audit mechanism leads to widespread corruption. So, they should be taught to be transparent and accountable to the community regarding their financial management. Every development project and programme has been emerged with the tremendous support from the Government of India and state governments. As a result in many cases it gave the ruling party a political mileage.

Indicators of Women Empowerment:

Empowerment has been defined broadly as the expansion of assets and capabilities of poor people to participate in, negotiate with, influence, control, and hold accountable the institutions that affect their lives (Narayan, 2003).

The 4th World Conference on women held at Beijing in 1995 proposed the following qualitative and quantitative indicators for evaluating women's empowerment.

Qualitative Indicators

- Increase in self-esteem
- Increase in knowledge and awareness levels on issues affecting the community, such as women's health, nutrition, reproductive rights, legal rights, literacy, etc.
- Change in the women's role and responsibility in the family and community.
- Visible increase or decrease in levels of domestic violence perpetrated on women and girl child.
- Change in social and other customs e.g. Child marriage, dowry, discrimination against widows, etc.
- Visible changes in women's participation in attending public meetings, training programmes.
- Increase in bargaining/negotiating power of women as an individual as well as in collectives.
- Formation of cohesive women's groups at village, district and state levels.
- Recognition of women's economic contribution within and outside the household.
- Women's decision- making over her work, income and expenditure.

Quantitative Indicators

- Demographic trends like – maternal mortality rates, fertility rates, sex ratio, life expectancy at birth, and average age of marriage.
- Increase in the number of women participating in different development programmes.
- Greater access and control over community resources and governmental schemes.
- Visible changes in health, nutritional status and increased level of literacy.
- Increase in the participation level of women in political process at the local level.

Women Empowerment through Micro–Credit Unions

Micro-Credit Unions (MCUs) or Self Help Groups (SHGs) enhance the status of women as participants, decision-makers and beneficiaries in the democratic, economic social and cultural spheres of life. In all stages of social and economic activities, involvement of women becomes essential. MCUs bring out the supremacy of women in molding the community in right perspective and explore the initiative of women in taking up entrepreneurial ventures. This model relies on development through empowerment and not subsidies. Repayment procedure is also flexible and it proclaims 'Self Help through mutual help for common good'. It is an ideal combination of one's rights and responsibilities.

Rathidevi (2009) comments that SHG is mainly concerned with the poor. SHG is for the people, by the people and of the people. It focuses on the weaker sections, particularly women, for their social defense and contains great potential to create awareness on day-to-day affairs. It promotes saving habit, develops self and community assets. It enables them to increase the income level, social power. It generates in them confidence, self-scrutiny and self-reliance. Thus, it is a mechanism to extend mutual help and support through sharing ideas, experiences, information, resources and other services. The groups may be viewed as a process or an institution for socio economic transformation leading to empowerment of women. She says that empowerment means, becoming powerful. Women empowerment is a process whereby women are able to organize themselves to increase their own self-reliance, to assert their independent right to make choices and control resources, which will assist in challenging and eliminating their own subordination.

Margaret (1949) described three levels of empowerment. The first is the awakening of individual consciousness; the second is development of collective consciousness; and the third is at the level of translating collective skills and resources into political and legal action, ultimately leading to women's empowerment.

Mohini (1998) defines empowerment as a process whereby women become enlightened, and thus, increase their own self-reliance to assert their independent right to make choice and control resources that assist in challenging and eliminating the factors that subjugate them. Thus the concept of SHGs is that of helping oneself for development through one another. SHGs enable women to look at old problems in new ways, analyze their environment and situations, recognize their strength, and alter their self image.

Sohoni (1994) asserts empowerment to be a process that starts with awareness from individual consciousness, grows with action and broadens at the collective level. Individually poor rural women cannot overcome powerlessness; collectively they can. Their strength is in organization. The members gain a feeling of confidence by being a member of a women's group that is working on the problems of the poor.

Suguna (2001) defines that empowerment is a process of awareness and capacity building leading to greater participation to greater decision-making power and control, and transformation action. Empowerment of women means leading them to socially developed, politically active, and economically productive. Empowerment makes them independent and enables them to make informed choices and intelligent decisions in matters that affect them and their nation.

Actually empowerment is an active, multi-dimensional process, which enables women to realize their full potential and powers in all spheres of life. Power is not a commodity to be transacted, nor can it be given away as alms. Power has to be acquired and once acquired it needs to be exercised, sustained and preserved (Pillai, 1995). Empowerment literally means 'becoming powerful'. In short, empowerment is a process of challenging existing power relations and of gaining greater control over the sources of power.

Conclusion

Any community that stands at the threshold of development and progress has to concentrate more on the empowerment of women. The *Savara* tribal community which is still considered as Primitive Tribal Group (PTG) deserves all our attention. Special focus on their economic development will certainly lead them to all other developments. A study on development of SHGs in India undertaken by V.M. Rao (2002) reveals that the existing formal financial institutions have failed to provide finances to landless marginalized and disadvantaged groups. SHGs encourage savings and promote income-generating activities through small loans. The experiences available in the country and elsewhere suggest that SHGs are sustainable, have explicability, stimulate savings, and in the process help borrowers to come out of vicious circle of poverty (V.M. Rao, 2002). Thus starting Self Help Groups (SHGs) or Micro-Credit Unions (MCUs) are the potential pathway to their empowerment and their overall development.

References

1. Ambedkar B R (2017). The Untouchables : Who were they and why they Became Untouchables, Kalpaz Publications (2017) ISBN-10: 9351282643 ISBN-13: 978-9351282648
2. Chandra (1997), "Women and Empowerment", Indian Journal of Public Administration, Vol. XLIII, No. 3.
3. Delliswararao K (2016). *Ethnographic Analysis of Savara Tribe in India,* Imperial Journal of Interdisciplinary Research (IJIR) Vol. 2, Issue-4, 2016
4. Dube S.C (1992). Understanding Change - Anthropological &Sociological Perspectives, Vikas Publishing House Pvt Ltd, New Delhi -14.
5. Margaret EG (1949). In Elaine Murphy editor, Reproductive health rights – Reaching the hardly reached. Pp. 129-137.
6. Mohini GV (1998). Emancipation and Empowerment of Women. Gyan Publishing House, New Delhi.
7. Narayan, P. (2003). "Empowerment through participation. How effective is this approach?" Economic and Political Weekly, June 21, pp. 2484-2486.
8. Pillai, J.K. (1995). Women and Empowerment, Gyan Publishing House, New Delhi, 1995.
9. Radcliffe-Brown, A. R. (1940). *"On Joking Relationships"*. Journal of the International African Institute. 13 (3): 195–210. Doi: 10.2307/1156093. JSTOR 1156093.
10. Rathidevi, R. (2009). *A study on women empowerment through the management of Self Help Groups with respect to Dharmapuri District*. Salem: Periyar University.
11. Rao V.M. (2002). *"Women Self Help Groups; Profiles from Andhra Pradesh & Karnataka",* Kurukshetra, Vol. 50, No.6, April 2002.
12. *Riessman, Frank (1965),* "The helper therapy principle". *Social Work. 10 (2):27–32.* ISSN 0037-8046
13. Sohoni NK (1994). Status of Girls in Development Strategies, Har Anand Publications, New Delhi
14. Suguna, B. (2001). *"Women's Empowerment: Concept and Framework"*, Social Welfare, Vol. 48, No. 9.
15. Interview (2016): - An interview with a Jesuit Parish priest Fr. N. Kishore SJ at Seethampeta.
16. Census of India, 2011.
17. Fourth World Conference on Women: Action for Equality, Development and Peace, the United Nations during 4–15 September 1995 in Beijing, China.

Notes

1. M. Gnana Selvin Raj. SJ. Dept. Anthropology, University of Madras. Specialist in Tribal welfare and promoting Micro-Credit Unions among the tribes.

Chapter - 4

Victims of State Frame: Women Prisoners from the Marginalised Communities of India

Dr. (Mrs.). Tinku Paul[1]

Introduction

Let us start with the basic premise that all humans are born equal and free. Impositions of restrictions in form of duties complement to ensure the rights of others. The ideal condition wherein the rights of humans are ensured decides the ideal of governance. To ensure proper governance deprivation of liberty by incarceration is consequential upon real or perceived misdemeanors. This role of punishing for misdemeanors is of the state in a democratic set up. How far the judicial system has been able to address this idea of justice is questioned in this research paper. The paper also tries to delve into the causal and consequential repercussions of such detentions with empirical understanding[2].

1. Positioning Women Prisoners from the Marginalized Sections

A general question that I encountered while seeking people's perceptions about criminals and what should be done to better their prison life, was "Why should you at all question about these people? They need to be punished. The very thought of jail and its captives sends me chills.... criminals, murderers and hard core drug addicts. The society needs to be shielded from them"[3]. This individual perception that bears the consequential reflections on the social exclusion of prisoners and their further mainstreaming in the society after release may be generalized with marginal aberrations.

Though the Constitution of India grants equal rights to women and various laws have been enacted to protect and empower women. While some women have definitely benefited from these provisions and have occupied highest positions in political system but for majority of poor and illiterate women especially belonging to the lower strata of social hierarchy, life still remains a continuous struggle in a very traditional, patriarchal and feudal society. Customs, practices and prejudices position against women in our society. Thus, Indian society harbours a clear bias against women but the situation worsens if women happen to be in prison either as convicts or as under trials. They are branded as bad women who deserve bad treatment. This predicament is often combined with their total dependence of prison officials, corruption, lack of resources and lack of work culture further worsens their condition. The jeopardy of the women prisoners from the lowest order of the social hierarchy becomes even more pertinent because the justice framework as well as the operational framework of justice are both skewed against women. So it becomes all the more important to understand the state of women from Dalit or other marginalized communities who become victims of the Indian judicial system. The present paper attempts to picture the condition of women prisoners from the marginalized sections of the society in India in the context of their human rights.

2. Languishing Incarceration: Dalit Women, A Misfit in the State Made Frame

There are many crimes (issues) of the criminal justice system that have led languishing incarceration of many poor and innocent people. The major issue that the paper addresses to is of the problem of inability of poor prisoners to pay surety amount for bail resulting to their prolonged and even life time imprisonment.

But did you know justice bears a cost? There are around 3.81 lakh prisoners in the country out of which around 2.54 lakh are undertrials. The SC of India in its landmark judgment asked the trial court judges to allow undertrial prisoners to be released on personal bond with or without any surety[4]. But the lacuna of the criminal justice system with its indifference is responsible languishing imprisonment of lakhs of poor prisoners.

When I met these prisoners I was not with neutral feelings but, I was taken aback by their plight. Though the prison statistics speak of rising numbers of under trial prisoners, yet there are also considerable numbers behind bars languishing in Indian jails even after their bail. Intrigued by their plight I tried to probe into the causal factors. Most of these prisoners who had been bailed out but were still in prisons were from very poor background. They were unable to pay surety amount. Like Gagrai[5], Gudunnu imprisoned in 1994 on false charges of murder shares his ordeal saying, "I was released on bail for a surety amount of Rs. 1 lakh in the year 1996, but since then I have been waiting all his life to be released. I am dying each day hopelessly ending my life in dungeon. Gudunu who is now in his fifties has lost all his youth in punishment of confinement and tears. The slow and whimsical Indian judiciary has notoriously been responsible for incarceration of poor and needy". Similar was the case of one Piyush Sharma, a third stage cancer patient who got bail but due to impoverishment failed to pay back the surety bonds. He only pleads with folded hands to let him die at home his family.

Table 1: Status of Imprisoned by Sex

Imprisonment Status	***Total***	***Male***	***Female***
Convicts	1,27,789 (33.2% of total inmates)	1,22,776 (96.1% of total convicts)	5,013 (3.9% of total convicts)
Under Trials	2,54,857 (66.2% of total inmates)	2,43,055 (95.4% of total undertrials)	11,802 (4.6% of total undertrials)
Detenues	1,922 (0.5% of total inmates)	1,832 (95.3% of total detenues)	90 (4.7% of total detenues)
Others	567 (0.1% of total inmates)	521 (91.9% of total others)	46 (8.1% of total others)

Source: NCRB Report 2012

3. Theorizing the State of Marginalized Community Women Prisoners: The Central Jail of Naini

When a woman commits a crime or an act not agreed upon in the state frame she is deemed unfit for the society and its rules and dislocated in the prisons. The state takes charge of the aberrant and deviant behavior of the woman meticulously through phases of languishing and slow paced criminal justice system. This pace could end a woman's life in jail as an under trial without even terming her as a convict in the legal process.

Table 2: Educational Status of the Cases of Women Inmates and their Crime Records

Educational Status	***Educational Status of the Cases of Women Inmates and their Crime Records***															
	Murder		***Child Murder***		***NDPS***		***Kidnapping***		***POSCO***		***DPA***		***Prostitution***		***Total***	
Illiterate	19	41.3	3	6.5	2	4.3	1	2.2	3	8.7	14	30.4	3	6.5	45 83.3	100.0
Literate	1	33.3	0	0.0	1	33.3	0	0.0	0	0.0	0	0.0	1	33.3	3 5.6	100.0
Educated	3	60	2	40.0	0	0.0	0	0.0	1	20.0	0	0.0	0	0.0	6 11.0	100.0
Total	23	100.0	5	100.0	3	100.0	1	100.0	4	0.0	14	100.0	4	100.0	54 100.0	100.0100.0

Source: *Field Survey 2017* NDPS = EXPAND POSCO= EXPAND DPA = EXPAND

Total Of The Percentages Shown For Educated Under Murder, Child Murder, Ndps, Kindnaping, Posco And Dpa Is Not Correct I.e., It Can Not Be 120.

In 83.3 per cent of all crimes illiterate women were convicted of which highest number of women were in the murder category comprising of 41.3 per cent of total illiterate women followed by 30.4 per cent women in the DPA category. What is even more interesting is the fact that all the educated women were booked for murder cases except for one case of Suman Srivastava[6], the Superintendent of Nari Bandi Niketan, who was booked under POSCO Act.

Table 3: Social Status of the Women Inmates and their Crime Records

Caste Category	*Social Status of the Women Inmates and their Crime Records*															
	Murder		*Child Murder*		*NDPS*		*Kidnapping*		*POSCO*		*DPA*		*Prostitution*		*Total*	
·SC	17	50.0	4	11.8	1	2.9	1	2.9	2	5.9	7	20.6	2	5.9	34 63.0	100.0
OBC	2	40.0	0	0.0	0	0.0	0	0.0	0	0.0	3	60.0	0	0.0	5 9.3	100.0
General	2	28.6	0	0.0	1	14.3	0	0.0	1	14.3	2	28.6	1	14.3	7 13.0	100.0
Minority	2	25.0	1	12.5	1	12.5	0	0.0	1	12.5	2	25.0	1	12.5	8 14.8	100.01 4.8
Total	23	42.6	5	9.3	3	5.6	1	1.9	4	7.4	14	25.9	4	7.4	54 100.0	100.0 100.0

Source: *Field Survey 2017*

The Table 3 shows murder (including murder of children) was the major crime committed by the sample women prisoners (51.9 per cent). Dowry Prohibition Act was the next important category which was most visible among the SC caste category followed by the OBC and equally by the General and Minority communities (14 per cent). 63 per cent of the total sample comprised of the SC followed by 15 per cent Minorities and 13 per cent General category. Among the SC category 61.8 per cent women had committed murders. Among the Minorities the major activity of crime was murders committed by 37.5 per cent of the women.

Table 4: Categorized Years in Jail by Crime Committed and Economic Status of the Women Prisoners

Economic Status	*Crime Committed*	*Categorized Years in Jail*								
		0-5 years %		*5-10 years %*		*10-15 years %*		*More than 15 %*		*Total*
Poor	Murder	4	25.0	7	43.8	2	12.5	3	18.8	16
	Child Mur der	1	50.0	0	0.0	0	0.0	1	50.0	2
	NDPS	0	0.0	0	0.0	1	100.0	0	0.0	1
	Kidnapping	1	100.0	0	0.0	0	0.0	0	0.0	1
	POSCO	3	100.0	0	0.0	0	0.0	0	0.0	3
	DPA	2	50.0	0	0.0	1	25.0	1	25.0	4
	Total	11	40.7	7	25.9	4	14.8	5	18.5	27
	DPA	0	0.0	1	50.0	1	50.0	0	0.0	2
	Total	0	0.0	1	50.0	1	50.0	0	0.0	2
	DPA	2	66.7	1	33.3	0	0.0	0	0.0	3
	Total	2	66.7	1	33.3	0	0.0	0	0.0	3
	Murder	5	71.4	2	28.6	0	0.0	0	0.0	7

(Contd...)

Middle	Child Murder	2	66.7	0	0.0	1	33.3	0	0.0	3
	NDPS	0	0.0	0	0.0	1	100.0	0	0.0	1
	POSCO	0	0.0	1	100.0	0	0.0	0	0.0	1
	DPA	2	40.0	3	60.0	0	0.0	0	0.0	5
	Prostitution	4	100.0	0	0.0	0	0.0	0	0.0	4
	Total	13	61.9	6	28.6	2	9.5	0	0.0	21
Well-off	NDPS	1	100.0	0	0.0	0	0.0	0	0.0	1
	Total	1	100.0	0	0.0	0	0.0	0	0.0	1

Source: *Field Survey 2017*

Table 5.15 (A): Categorized Years in Jail by Social Status of the Women Prisoners

Caste	*Categorized Years in Jail*								*Total*
	0-5 years %		*5-10 years %*		*10-15 years %*		*more than 15 years %*		
SC	16	59.0	7	47.0	5	71.0	5	100.0	33
OBC	2	7.0	3	20.0	0	0.0	0	0.0	5
General	5	19.0	3	20.0	0	0.0	0	0.0	8
Minority	4	15.0	2	13.0	2	29.0	0	0.0	8
Total	27	100.0	15	100.0	7	100.0	5	100.0	54

Source: *Field Survey 2017*

Incarceration as treatment to crime fails to meets the standards when examined under the lens of social status of the prisoners. As is evident in the Table 3 the representation of SC in all crimes has been higher than the other castes. They had been booked for 78 per cent of all murders cases and 29.4 per cent of the SC women convicted and imprisoned for various crimes had served sentence term 'more than 10 years' in comparison to General and OBC caste women prisoners who had served term less than 10 years.

4. Empirical Cases of Some Dalit women Prisoners of Central Jail of Naini

In this pathway we locate the commitment of crime as a consequence of past life outcomes at various transition stages. These transitions could be from childhood to adulthood, adulthood to married life etc. That is, the pre-conditions set in one's lives frames his/her life outcomes as consequences of the conditions. Thus, the aggressive, volatile nature of the person could be attributed to the self security mechanisms developed as stimulus to outside hostile environment. The crime pathways of women as extensively researched bears its roots from the women's past experiences, at different stages of life cycle. This could be childhood abuse or trauma where a conventionally understood safe and secure haven for a girl turns hell shaping and reshaping her attitude and outlook towards the outer world and society at large. These experiences could breed at adulthood with changing social ambience and exposures. Also included are the experiences that women face after marriage. Time and age form prime phases of women experiences that cultivate and nurture women's life experiences that show reflections in their perceived notion and behavior towards the society. Within the frame of socially backward or marginalized class we present the different pathways that frame women's approach and orientation towards life and people degenerating them as socially deviant or criminals.

4.1 Case of Childhood Trauma and Battered Experience

The very positioning of a girl in an abusive or torturous childhood ambience and her relocation in her marital home or dislocation in an orphanage or shelter home may either nurture her negative experiences of childhood positively or even negatively further aggravating her deviation from normal course. This making of a 'criminal women', *per se*, could be very much in absence of her conscious level so that it could be checked. Thus, the outcome of such adversities is a '***harmed and harming women* woman'**. These were women who had suffered neglect, physical and/or sexual abuse as children, and who were labelled violent or troublesome as youths and acted in ways consistent with those appraisals. Harmed and harming women experienced a chaotic home life and began using and abusing drugs and alcohol as a teen. Generally, these women showed symptoms of emotional and psychological damage as adults and demonstrated an inability to cope with difficult situations. Therefore, due to hostility shown to her she becomes hostile in her behaviour and this behaviour becomes a routine nature of her life actions. When such actions go beyond the socially decided rules and laws she lands up in jail!!!

Case No.: Under Trial no. 15

Aarti daughter of Ram Murat belongs to a poor SC joint family and her father works as a mason. She has two brothers, one younger and one elder. She also has two sisters and both are younger. The trial in her case has not yet initiated. Mother is a housewife. Aarti who is convicted under 302 IPC, at the time of committing the crime was a juvenile and hardly had any idea of the gravity of crime she had committed.

The family members went for *Nishaani* and asked me to stay home to take care of cattle. Parents fought with other neighbouring family when both the families were in fight over a petty issue regarding children in-fights, the other lady slapped Aarti's brother hard on his face. Aarti got furious and silently carried the lady's son who was hardly four years old to a nearby field where lot of grass (dry) was laid to make a *Machaan.* She tied the boy's hands and strangulated him to death. Later she ran back to her home panting to narrate the whole story to her family members who asked her to run away. She did the same and ran away from her home. For 24 hours she was absconding and the police were trying hard to nab her.

But the body was soon traced and boy's dead body was recovered as some passer's by noticed tiny legs peeping out of the covered grass. The local police on the tiff given by locals and the family of the boy nabbed Aarti. Her trail in this case is to initiate from the 23rd of September 2017. Needless to say these trials are a uniform customary ritual followed religiously as a routine more than a judicial intervention. Nothing is heard and only thumb impressions are collected for records and the trials are over on paper. At times it is the police officials who direct the prisoner to speak as directed. Therefore, it is only a one sided affair.

Aarti seems to be slightly mentally challenged though not medically tested and declared. She has been a renounced by her poor parents. For a few days her father used to come to see her but then stopped. She does work for other inmates like washing clothes and cleaning for which she is given small tokens.[7] When asked what do you do the whole day if you do not find interest in studies, she says shyly, "Sunita didi ka kaam karte hai". There is a visible hierarchy within the inmates. This hierarchy is not directly relational to the social and economic strata of the inmate but depends on the age, type of crime, attitude of the inmate etc. Age of the inmate has directly proportional relation to the power of the inmate to dominate others in the group, i.e., more the age of the inmate along with her gravity of crime committed, higher is her dominating capacity. But this does not mean that old and feeble inmates have power over capacity.

Her case is in doldrums. Her parents produced her age certificate proving her as a juvenile at the time of crime committed. But it falls short of two months. But if the school administration takes interest and takes the matter as human error and revises the certificate she could be released. But because no personal interest of parents takes place the correct certificate is not produced in the court of law. She is registered as 18 years at the time of crime. If proper advocacy is done she could be released. The jail authorities took personal interest and pursued her family (father) but he fails to contribute.

4.2 Case of Misfit in the State Made Frame

The understanding of women as interviewed for the study brings to light that these women in question were mostly from poor socio-economic background and had least knowledge of the legal procedures and rights they possessed. More so the laws specifically made by the state for the welfare of women at times pose a threat for women in general. For example, in the Indian context, the avowed objective of the Dowry Prohibition Act has been to combat the menace of dowry deaths and cruelty but it has fallen very much against women with more of misuse rather than use of the act. In response the Supreme Court had directed the State governments to instruct police "not to automatically arrest when a case under section 498 A of IPC (dowry harassment) is registered but to satisfy themselves about the necessity for arrest under the parameters laid down flowing from Section 41 of the Criminal Procedure Code" . Of the various types of crimes committed by women in the sample of 54 women in the study at least 14 cases under Dowry Prohibition Act were captured. That is 26 per cent of the cases taken up were of those women who were sentenced under this Act. These high rates of incarceration under such laws made for the protection of women often pose a threat to their peaceful existence.

The cases of Kusum, Anju, Geeta, Haseena Begam, Kaushalya, Kusum, Priyanka, Saroj, Shanti, Shyamkali, Sudha, booked under Dowry Prohibition Act and Nanhi, Noori, Kamla Devi booked under section 302 of IPC show how poor illiterate women with no knowledge of the laws living in pre-Newtonian rural ambience fall prey to the law of the land. These women reflect the similar docile and calm behaviour in the jail also. Most of these women still fail to understand their crime.

Case Released Prisoner No. 2

Kamla Devi wife of Lt. Vishwanath is an illiterate Paasi woman released from jail after completion of sentenced punishment under sections 304/34, 498 A'3/4, IPC of Dowry Prohibition Act. Kamla Devi now in her early 70s released from jail had been a victim of Dowry Prohibition Act which was used against her and her son. Because this case was a case of a released prisoner she was interviewed along with informal discussions with her neighbours, relatives, daughters etc., who readily informed that she was gone to the dairy when her daughter-in-law committed suicide. The intervening night she had returned from her maternal home in Delhi. The whole locality accepted that she was a fine lady and had been framed under this Act. Kamla now works in a local school as a Dai.

My son works as a Carpenter nearby. My daughter-in-law though was from Delhi but her maternal home was in Pratappur. We were supposed to visit her maternal home in Pratappur on Bhaiya Duj. Her mother was also convinced. But on the second day after Diwali she committed suicide hanging her-self on the fan. My fault was that I barged open the locked door (from inside) and tried to save her life as I saw her staggering for breath, her legs were shaking and still could feel her nerves. I yelled out to my neighbours who came running for my help. I had gone to take milk from a nearby dairy when someone informed me that look "*Mami ka kar lihe hai*", (go look… what aunty has done!!) At the outset we though she was electrocuted when people were shouting "*Bhauji dulhahin k current mar dees*". But when we reached on the scene we found her hanging. We pulled her down and then rushed her to hospital at Rajapur where she died. "*Delli wale hoshiyaar to hotai hai*". While we were in the hospital fighting for her life, some of her relatives who live in Chaowfatka Mahila Gram went and filed case against me and my son. They went to the extent of bribing a Bailey Hospital doctor to frame a false report against us. The charge on me was that I murdered her on purpose strangulating her to death. Once when the report was made against us in the police station we were trapped. My daughter –in-law was very fair, look at her daughter... We never did any kind of physical assault on her. The police made a good strong report in our favour but the doctor's report went against us.

I was put in jail along with my son. I also carried my granddaughter along with me. For this, reason I was soon bailed out in a month as the child was only one and half months old then. I have got bail in this year in January. In jail I was not allowed to do any work as I was old. I just had to sit the whole day and remain quiet. When I was arrested and put in jail for the first time I carried my granddaughter. The second time I was not allowed by the judge to carry her.

Within the jail barrack women follow the strict routine and do only the daily routine work assigned to them. Women do fight amongst themselves mostly for food. The lady guards earn handsome amount as they run errands for the prisoners do petty tasks for them like bringing vegetables, or other goodies they like to eat on bribe. I have been released this year in January 2017. There at jail I had no work to do.

DP Act has become a nuisance. People like us are falsely framed. I am citing a case day before yesterday, Karchana love-couple train accident. There in jail the new comers are engaged in weeding, planting saplings, etc. Food is brought from the main Central Jail so we do not have to cook even. The food is okay. The food before two years was not of good quality but now it is good. "*Khana waha se aa jata. Kahan khate hai, kha pike let jata, wahi pe idhar udhar ghoomte hai.*" There are few (do /teen) girls who are very volatile and do lot of in-fights. When asked about the canteen she says we do carry some money but not much. We have nothing to do with the canteen as it is on the men's side (*mardana ke taraf hai.*) We are given everything, from toiletries to oil, bedding etc. We are supposed to clean our beddings and the place we sleep. She was in praise of the present lady deputy jailor (Ranju Shukla) who has been responsible in facilitating the provision of basic needs of the women in prisons. She has helped in putting new fans and reconstruction of the pathway connecting the men's jail to the women's jail. She is good and promotes us to get involved in education. She was also in praise of the superintendent Kedarnath who promoted the girls and women in jails to apply for higher education and promised all support. As we do not have work there so no source of income. Whatever petty amount (Rs. 50-Rs.100) we get during our meetings with family members (*mulakaat*) we keep it with us. Doctors visit us both meetings daily. They are same ones who visit in the main Central Jail. We do have lady doctors too. The doctors are not escorted by '*Sipaahi*' police in-charge. They come from Bailey hospital. Women do not do take any drugs or tobacco etc. Later in the course of the interview her son-in-law revealed that everything can be available in the barracks from needle to drugs you just have to grease the palms of the policemen and home guards. "*sab paise ka khel hai. Bas thodi shakhti hai, deekhwe k liye, par sab kuch jata hai*". "*jaha talashi lene aaye saman k hisab se paise thama do bas andar le jao". "Bas aap chup chaap andar rahiye, policewale aapko andar tak saman pahucha denge."* She named a few women who helped her. "aap yaha ayi humko kuch hoga to nahi na!!"

When asked do you face any type social exclusion, are you called on social functions?

Kamla vehemently says, why should I be out-casted? I have been falsely framed. My daughter-in-law's relatives got false report of strangulation death and got me and my son imprisoned. All the neighbours know that I was the one who forced inside the house when I was reported that my daughter –in-law was electrocuted. My society welcomed me, they asked me about my life style in jail and I am all with my family now.

When asked were you not able to prove in the court of law that you were outside the house when the incident took place? She said, when the doctors gave a murder report that took place by throttling her to death then the question of my absence or presence does not stand. I tell you when we were busy with saving our daughter-in-law's life her relatives were busy bribing the government doctors to frame a false report against us. I pleaded them to take back the case, but they resented. Had they been so concerned about her why they didn't take her with them? The son-in-law interfered here to say, "*agar inke paas paisa hota to na jane kya kya ho jata. Dhoomanganj thane se hi case rafa dafa ho jata"*. A demand of Rs. 50,000 was made, we are poor people we didn't have money that time with us. We wanted to arrange money by collecting help from our neighbours and relatives (*'chanda')* but by then they sent her to jail.

Did the local Vidhayak Pooja Pal not help you then? We called her to the *thana* (local police station). I was in the police lock up at Dhoomanganj Thana for three days. But she told us that she was somewhere out of station (*antai*) and that would not be able to come for help. *Are badi natak baaz hai Puja Pal. Boli* mai *kya kar sakti hu?*

Did Ajeet not help you?

Oh Ajeet was there that time with us. He kept us consoling that he would set the matter right. He was there with us at the funeral. Puja Pal's vehicle also escorted us. She again reiterated that the false report of the doctor made the situation worse for us.

When I went jail for the first time as an under trial I had no idea how it would be. Later when the case date approached, I had to appear in the court. Then I was on bail. I thought the matter would be solved and I would be free. But it was not true, I was convicted positively for the crime I had never committed. I was not prepared. I had gone to court from home. The judge told me now u can't carry the child along with you. Now I am out after completing my sentence.

Do you work now?

What work will I do in this age? I can't work as a labourer. Just work on a paltry sum of Rs. 1000 in a private school close by as a *dai*.

Self Observations: Kamla stays with, her own son and her daughter. Her son-in-law also lives with his three daughters and one son in the house next door. She lost her daughter while she had some delivery complications giving birth to her fifth child. Kamla seems to be quite dominant in the family matters and was quite vigilant and apprehensive with the interview consequences. The interview was quite guided in the presence of the whole family. She did not seem to be perturbed with the loss of her daughter-in-law's life. In the whole conversation she detailed the problems she faced with her daughter—in-law who always forced her husband to leave for Delhi for good. She became quite desperate and frequent quarrels used to take place in the house. Kamla insisted that these quarrels used to be only oral ones and that she never resorted to physical torture. Interestingly Kamla was jailed with her son and the poor child then only one and half month old; instead of being handed over to her daughter-in-law's family (nana-nani) was taken by her to jail. This eased her bail on mercy grounds when the health of the poor child and her survival was a matter of risk within the jail. Again when the court orders went against her and she was re-arrested she insisted to carrying the child with her but the judge resisted. This time the child was with her granny.

4.3 Case of Consequential Prompt Defensive Action

These women are mostly the first time offenders who took extreme steps to save their dignity or their lives or in some cases owned the shared charge of the crime to save their family members. Thus, two different sub categories emerge:

(i) The women who committed crime to save themselves i.e., as a reactionary response to crime or violence inflicted on them. The consequence of crime follows an act of violence at the first instance. Some of these cases show clear examples to this category of crime.

Case of Under Trial No. 8

Pratusha Verma[8] daughter of Kamlesh Verma belongs to a very poor Chamaar family. She was a resident of Chakau Chak, Pur-dar, Utraon Thana of Allahabad. She is educated and computer literate.

Pratusha Verma has been linked up with the very famous murder of advocate Vijay of Allahabad High Court. For several days the news channels welled up with news of the advocate's missing but soon they cracked the case and a young and beautiful Pratusha Verma was found to be the mastermind and cause for the murder. ***It is important to state here that advocate Vijay***

who was once linked up with Pratusha started blackmailing her and threatened to publish her porn videos on the social media.

Pratusha Verma belongs to a poor family. Due to ailment of his brother Mukul she took charge of the family and started working in a private company, Glass India Trading Company. She visited Chaka village for some business reason where she met the advocate Vijay. Soon they became friendly. This meeting gave U-turn to her life. Vijay promised her for lucrative salary and requested her to work in his office in Kydganj in Allahabad. Soon Vijay started taking advantage of the situation and initiated taking sexual favours from her. Pratusha Verma was obliged no to say no. Vijay also made her porn videos which Pratusha Verma never knew.

Pratusha Verma befriended one Chote Singh who is known to be the younger brother of BJP Vidhayak Praveen Patel from Phoolpur constituency. Vijay did not like their closeness. Pratusha Verma fell in love with Man Singh who used to come along with Chote Singh. Later she also got attracted towards Dilip who was Man Singh friend. Now, Pratusha Verma was in relationship with four youths. Pratusha Verma now distanced from Vijay who had now become revengeful. Twenty three days before the incident took place Pratusha Verma lost her brother Mukul.

Chote Singh on behalf of Pratusha Verma had a fight with Vijay and threatened killing him. Soon Man Singh and Pratusha Verma wanted to get married and settle. Chote Singh got them a room in Jhunsi where they could live happily and peacefully after marriage. But Vijay kept torturing Pratusha Verma and threatened her to expose her porn videos.

Now Pratusha Verma was left with the only option of killing Vijay. She along with the other three hatched a conspiracy to kill him. Pratusha Verma called up Vijay to her room to settle things. When Vijay arrived all the four hit him hard with bricks and *lathis.* Soon Vijay bled dead. She emptied Vijay's pockets of cash, mobile and pistol. She kept the cash and pistol and threw mobile along with the bike in deep waters of Ganges. Then Pratusha Verma called up her younger brother, 12 years Sonu, at the spot who took her back on his bicycle.

The police also arrested Sonu under section 216 IPC. Pratusha Verma and Man Singh were arrested and 3 cartridges, 1pistol, blood stained clothes and four mobiles were retrieved from Pratusha Verma. It is noteworthy to state here that a missing complaint had been lodged on the 3rd of June 2017 and on the 7th of June Vijay kidnapping case was filed against Praveen Singh Patel's younger brother Chote Singh. On the 10th of June the Vijay's decayed body was found in a well. His face was badly crushed. The post mortem report cleared that all his ribs were broken and head injuries were severe.

The Utraon police had to resort to lathi – charge to control the volatile mob. Villagers and Vijay's people were furious and demanded strict action against Chote Singh. The post mortem was conducted under strict vigilance by a team of three doctors and the entire procedure was videographed.

On the 13th of June 2017 Pratusha Verma was brought to Central Jail of Naini. She was booked along with her brother and fiancée who were lodged in the main prison. Pratusha Verma is tested 5 months pregnant.[9] Here in jail she is quiet and remains in solitude. The appointed writers keep consoling her and counsel her.

"It is very difficult to stay in this condition and ponder what would happen next is a difficult task[10]". The recent privacy judgment of a nine-judge Bench of the Supreme Court has observed that the A 10-Year-Old Rape Victim Will Have To Carry Pregnancy To Term After Court Rejects Abortion Plea[11] In this controversial decision, a 10-year-old rape survivor was denied permission to terminate the pregnancy resulting from the rape by the district court in Chandigarh on Tuesday. The child was allegedly raped continuously over a period of time by her maternal uncle. She is the daughter of a government employee father and a domestic worker mother. In 2006, the Ministry of Health and Family Welfare initiated consultations to propose changes to the MTP Act. In 2014, the Medical Termination of Pregnancy (MTP) (Amendment) Bill was proposed, which sought to raise the legal limit for termination from 20 weeks to 24 weeks, citing major technological breakthroughs in the field and the need to empower women.

Pratusha's brother and fiancée come to visit her every Saturday. Her behaviour is not normal. ***She has made several suicidal attempts. Therefore, she is never left alone and regularly counseled. She says mostly under trials remain lawful and don't dare to commit offence. They know "hamara case fasa hua hai. It's a psychological control. Hum fas jayenge agar koi adhikaari likh dega mere khilaf".*** Among the undertrials middle class women in jails mostly remain under control and are busy in their own tussle on issues of their lawyers, their dates of hearing etc. Ninety per cent women are in pain in jails because of the prime reason that they are away from their families. Pratusha Verma is educated and wishes to pursue her higher education from jail. Pratusha Verma's parents come to visit her and are managing to fight her case.

4.4 The Two Wrongs at a Time: Wrong Time and Wrong Place

These women prisoners are better to be termed as victims rather than criminals. These women who were illiterate and had least idea of the consequences were falsely framed as scapegoats. None of these women had drug or alcohol problems, nor had they experienced noxious home environments. They also had no previous arrest or conviction history. Cases of Anita, Asha, Jyoti, Prabha and Salma, Shakuntala, Shivakanti, Suman Srivastava and Urmila fall in this category. Interestingly this cohort also comprises also of women who were educated and well placed. Suman

Srivastava was Superintendent of Nari Niketan, Khuldabad in Allahabad, Shivakanti is a political figure and member of Samajwadi Party, Anita is an educated housewife were all victims of wrong situations where circumstances turned against them[12].

On the other hand there were also women like Prabha, Salma, Jyoti who were at wrong place in wrong hands. Let us review the cases of Prabha and Salma together and Jyoti individually.

Case of Convicts No. 6 &7

Prabha Devi and Salma both are Hindus from SC community hailing from Raktau Bihar. Prabha Devi is Salma's maternal aunt. Prabha Devi used to be a family agricultural worker and remained within her family. Her husband was a home guard and also a farmer. They had come with their family for a holy bath in Ganges in Prayaag. They were sitting with their luggage at the station waiting for the train to arrive. Someone played foul and placed a bag with drugs beside them. The police who were intimated about the drug consignment prior to this caught them and booked them under Narcotics and Drugs Psychotropic Substances Act, 1985 that prohibits a person to produce/ manufacture/ cultivate/ possess/sell/ transport/ store/ and /or consume any narcotic drug or psychotropic substance. She has been booked for a term of 10 years. Her son was also caught but was released.

"My case was put for legal advocacy and was also bailed out in seven years. But the lawyer had been charging hefty amount and my people at home (husband) are making ends meet to pay it. But now I think instead of wasting money to get bail bond, it is better that I utilize my time here in jail".

Prabha is a genuine case of prison reformation. She says "None can reform you; neither at home nor in jail unless you from within are inspired to do so". It is worth mention here that Prabha has done her BPP) correspondence course from IGNOU and carries a positive attitude for life. Her result is awaited. To waive off the fine imposed on her or an alternate of one and half years extended imprisonment; she chooses the latter. She is waiting for her results and plans to do yet another course for a year period. She seems to have accepted her fate and her punishment as a reflection of her some past mistakes. She carries no grudge for anyone. She says, ***"Agar jail mein bhi ghar ki tarah rahenge, mil jul ke, saaf safai se, aam karke, padhai karke; to yeh bhi ghar ban jayega".*** If we live in this jail like in our own home, doing all chores, amicably with all and do our studies then it is no less than home. This attitude relieves you from the pinching home sickness and urge to meet your own children.

It is worth mention here that Prabha carries a positive attitude. But she also has hopes for her release. She is studying and her time is utilized. This attitude may not be possible in case of 'lifers' who have to spend all their life in jail.

It is worth mention here that Prabha was illiterate when she was jailed. She joined the preliminary classes for them and learned the basics. Soon she gained interest in studies and made it a way to combat her solitude and pave path for better future after release. She has given her exams for BPP course from IGNOU.

Family members of Prabha do keep in touch with her but their visits are not frequent. They come once in three years. She justifies it as her relatives live in Bihar. Prabha's prison term for ten years is completed. But the '*zurmana*' of One lakh equivalent to one year extended imprisonment remains.

Prabha is a Nambardarin[13]. Her bail was done in seven years but no release happened as she refused her release. I am inside and no Mulakaat come for me. How do I tell about the progress of my case? I do not know how much has been spent on the case till now. "*Woh log itna padhe likh hai to judge bane hai. Jo kiye honge to soch hi samjh k kiye honge. Ab hum aur ka batayen. Uki nazar mein hum aaropi lage honge to hum saza pa rahe hai. To skohum na kahenge to hum jayenge kah*?"

Similar case is of Salma who has a 14 years old son. Salma laments, "My son was hardly 6 years old when I was booked under NDPS act and put in jail my husband remarried. My mother is taking care of my child. My husband never came to see me. I had come for pilgrimage on Chaat to Allahabad with my maternal uncle's family". Salma is interested in doing all work else than studies. Here in jail she is a *Nambardarin*. Salma misses her son very much. She cries, "My mother came before 3 years so I do not know what my son is doing now, if he is studying now or not. I do not have to say anything about the police or judiciary. I just know that I am here but not why. She cries and tells me, "I do not want to remember those days please do not ask...."

5. Plight of Women Living in Prisons

Revelations from our field research show that prison experiences of women in the frame of the criminal justice system provides a fertile region for analysis for functioning/non-functioning/mal-functioning of the legal institutions as custodians of law of the land on one hand and social mores. It also needs to be mentioned here that these statutes and laws bear no essence contemporary changes and situations and are based on the penal Code of 1860. The Penal Code though is one of the most important statutes in the Criminal Administration that lays a comprehensive, codified criminal law yet it needs to be scrutinized given the contemporary needs of the society. If we consider the changes, amendments and generation of new laws there has been plethora of laws on defining newer crimes and their punishments. Much needs to be done on considering the alterations required in penalties moving harsh and lengthy punitive sentences. This sluggish movement of changes in criminal justice system and its procedures with respect to the conditions and issues of the women prisoners could be attributed to the fact that prisoners face the double wrath of being labeled as 'bad woman' or 'woman from prison' that fails to draw sympathies of the society towards her problems of prison life and second the very positioning of a woman behind the bars makes her vulnerable and silent acceptor of the tortures and trauma in guise of punishment.

6. Summating the State of Marginalized Women Prisoners in the Legal Frame of the State

The determining society understood by the so called elite and privileged, those who define like the legislators, executives, lawyers and judges, to some extent police personnel above some level, they constitute a system that has accepted that the bottom-line people need to be jail because they are unruly and commit crimes as we understand them. That continues since the British times. For example, suppose the British had the idea that if some tribes were listed as criminals, now the vulnerable, illiterate, underprivileged, ignorant those who do not understand law or those who commit something without understanding the implications, they are to be put in jail. So this shows a kind of dual social frame, a determining society constituted by 5 % people while the determined society may constitute 70 per cent of people, in-between there are 10-15 per cent people comprising the so called middle section like teachers and doctors etc., who are not like Abhimanyu and Ekalavya and are also not like Duryodhana and Dushshashan. Police are state representatives. Press is not a part of the state unless it is sold.

So when we say cause and consequence, let us take the cause as a process, i.e., many conditions are concealed within a cause. That we understand as consequence could be at a point of time say at age 18 and it then it could be at 25 or 35 depending on the changes in situations and conditions that shape the consequences. Therefore often it is not a single consequence rather there could be multiple consequences over a time. The legal frames and rules that was actually brought out to empower women actually disempowered women branding them as criminals. The Dowry Prohibition Act stands a testimony to substantiate by cause effect relation.

Notes

1. Dr. (Mrs.) Tinku Paul, Superintendent, Directorate of Legal Affairs, SHUATS, Prayagraj, 211007.
2. The research paper is an outcome of Post Doctoral research initiative by the author. Fellowship was provided by the Indian Council for Social Science Research Institute, New Delhi.
3. General opinion as shared during interview with common people including women.
4. It had directed trial court judges to visit jails to identify undertrials who had undergone half the maximum sentence and had asked judicial officers to complete the task within two months.

5. http://www.youthkiawaaz.com/2015/09/mahendra-gagrai-released-from-jail-after-25-years/ by Tinku Paul.
6. Suman Srivastava is now released and has changed her residence from Agra (her homet own) or her Work town (Allahabad) to Gurgaon where her daughter is married. Again it is a case of social shame and inhibitions these women prisoners face.
7. Apart from this she also provides sexual pleasure to a dominating inmate who is also ill-famous lady don, Mundi Pasi. She is used by her in all possible ways. There is no issue of her giving consent because there remains no option of no when you have to stay in one barrack under one roof and for un-predicted number of days.
8. Name changed because her case is very sensitive and has been long in newspapers. Given the volatile nature of the case it was directed by the prison administration to keep her identity anonymous.
9. http://epaper.jagran.com/mdetail/03-nov-2017-edition-Allahabad-City-page_2-1012-649 2-79. html.
10. Right to reproductive choice of a woman is part of her fundamental right to privacy. Presently, women are forced to undertake the cumbersome process of approaching different courts, from district courts to high courts and finally the Supreme Court, for permission to medically terminate their pregnancies which are over 20 weeks old. The frequent number of such cases which come to the Supreme Court ranges from child rape victims to destitute women to women with substantial fetus abnormalities.
11. http://www.huffingtonpost.in/2017/07/19/a-10-year-old-rape-victim-will-have-to-carry-pergnancy-to-term-a_a_23036863/.
12. We are trying not to be judgmental and prove anyone guilty or fault free. We are categorizing these women inmates based on the information provided, behaviour in jail and most importantly their case backgrounds in tandem with their socio-legal and educational status.
13. Most of the women who are Nambardarins are the ones who rarely have any family visits. Therefore, being a Nambardarin provides her with an opportunity to economically suffice her basic needs. Though, all the amenities are provided by the jail administration completely once a woman becomes a convict in the court of law to become property of the government to be taken care of by the prison administration yet daily wages earned by her helps her to meet if there are any additional needs.

Chapter - 5

The Feminine Marginalized: An Indian Eco-Philosophical Analysis

***Prof. John Peter Vallabadoss*[1]**

Introduction

Marginalization of the Other has been always a result of centralization of a privileged one, the Self. Binary play of the opposites often ends up preferring one to the other. Women, body, land, nature and matter, have been treated as the negligible Other. All that is connected with 'femininity' as change, becoming, movement, active, dynamic, energetic, physical and material, have been rendered secondary. Discrimination of 'becoming and change' as untruth and non-reality, emerges from ontological positioning of 'unchanging and constant being' as truth and reality. From Heraclitus in Greek tradition to Buddha in Indian tradition, we have witnessed the constant struggle of establishing which is true, Being or Becoming. The ideological marginalization of 'change and becoming,' and its connection with the feminine reality, is caused by domination of idea of 'Being-permanence' associated with Man's self. 'Becoming-change-impermanence' as the Other, non-self, is linked to identity of 'women'. Notion of 'Being-Self' dominates the world of thinking, where marginalization of 'Becoming-feminity' emerges and spreads to impose it on socio-economic-cultural patterns of thought and activities. The paper analyses how in Indian classical system of philosophy like dualistic Sa└ m└ khya, a philosophical foundation of oppression is traceable and how re-reading it hermeneutically for the sake of emancipation of that which is marginalized, enables us to break the stereotyping and the patriarchal ideology. Moving from classical ideological system of duality to contemporary crisis of ecology, we find a similar marginalisation and suppression of nature, land, soil and fertile ground. Eco-feminist reading of the crisis allows to see the grim reality of how 'feminity,' has been ontologically marginalized, systematically side-lined and forcefully pushed to the periphery.

1. Duality and Marginalisation

The Samkhyan account of reality is purely dualistic, recognizing two ultimate realities, *prakròti* and *purusòa* - matter and self. The dualism leads to binary aspects of reality, and consequently the distinction is pictured with differentiation between the two. Acceptance of duality of *prakròti* and *purusòa* compels the thinkers to give an account of two completely different aspects and to assign characters mutually exclusive and absolutely separated. The material, physical, active and dynamic *prakròti* has to be spoken off against the spiritual, non-material, passive, conscious *purusòa.*[2] At the core of such differentiation, the scope for marginalization is vivid. The sentient *purusòa,* the self is alienated from the non-sentient, *prakròti,* the non-self. Being devoid of any consciousness, *prakròti* is labelled only as the experienced whereas the self is regarded as the experiencer, the privileged. The radical distinction between the two, as pure subject and as mere object, is absolute and indissoluble; one cannot be or become the other. The difference between *prakròti* and *purusòa* is inferred and is so indubitable and incontrovertible an experience that one cannot deny.[3]The quite contradiction would turn out to be in principle the possibility of preferring the self to the non-self, as it is subjected to change. The preference of passivity and absolutely unchanging is to be questioned in our analysis of marginalization. The self as unchanging is considered better than the ever-changing and active *prakrti.* The self which is wholly passive and devoid of will and knowledge is projected only as pure enjoyer (*bhoktrò*) and not an agent (*kartrò*).Sa└ m└ khyan understanding of *prakròti* as the non-self and devoid of consciousness, seems the philosophical basis of marginalisation.

Samkhya metaphysics concerns the relation between *prakròti* and *purusòa,* which we re-read to analyse the marginalization and to visualise the scope for emancipation. The unconscious *prakròti* in a state of dynamic equilibrium prior to evolution, cannot itself initiate evolution but requires contact with *purusòa.* The interaction between absolutely different entities is compared to harmonious cooperation between a lame and a blind to find their way out of a jungle.[4] However unsatisfactory the analogy given, the argument is lacking to explain the interaction between two absolutely independent and self-existent realities. Inconsistency and absurdity continue to haunt Sa└ m└ khya in absolutizing the concepts of dual reality. In understanding this difficulty one could push forward an idea of Ma└ dhyamika applied to Sa└ m└ khya that both *prakròti* and *purusòa* are not totally independent and wholly unrelated existents.[5] They could be relative, dependent, conditioned and mutually enriching existents. Further, Sa└ m└ khyan epistemology clearly states that *prakròti* and *purusòa* complement each other, the former providing the object of knowledge, and the latter the principle of consciousness. Neither *prakròti* nor *purusòa* is in itself capable of producing knowledge.

2. *Prakrti:* Reality of Becoming

Change is life. Life is characterized by movement. The Sa└ m└ khya points out that *prakròti* as a principle is the finest and subtlest stuff underlying all physical existence and is the first and ultimate cause of all objects, gross and subtle. Being both the material and the efficient cause of the physical world, *prakròti* itself is uncaused, eternal, and all-pervading. *Prakròti* is composed of three *gunòa* └ *s* - *sattva*, *rajas*, and *tamas*, which are finer than atoms and modified into all physical, biological and psychic entities.[6]Further analysing the constituent parts of *prakròti,* we come across the attributes of *sattva* as the component whose essence is purity, fineness, subtlety, lightness, brightness, and pleasure. Despite its close association with ego, consciousness, mind, and intelligence, *sattva* is understood only as a necessary but not a sufficient condition for consciousness, for consciousness is exclusively the *purusòa. Prakròti* is denied of luminosity and intelligence even though it has *sattva.* The quality of *rajas* which represents the principle of activity and motion, is again connected with restlessness, irrational, impulsiveness and pain. Negation of power of action, *sìakti,* is vividly clear here. *Tamas* manifesting itself as heaviness as well as opposition and resistance to motion and activity, is labelled as the cause of ignorance, coarseness, stupidity, laziness, lack of sensitivity, and indifference.

The *gunas* are not mere qualities or attributes but are substantial elements constituting *prakrrti,* remaining in equilibrium.[7]The *gunas* constituting *prakròti* enables it a dynamic complex, not a static entity and an organic unity. In a state of dynamic equilibrium there is a perfect balance among the *gunas*, even though each of them are different. Samkhya emphasises that *prakròti* is capable of keeping such unity, perfect balance amidst constant change, transformation and dynamism. Change and activity are its very essence. Consequently, every object in the world, being an effect of *prakròti,* is also in a state of constant change. Nothing is perceived as unchanging and static. Everything is really a dynamic entity in perpetual change.

Evolution into the multiplicity of objects and dissolution of the same back into primordial *prakròti*, according to Samkhya, is a process of cosmic cycles. Evolution is caused by imbalance and disequilibrium among the *gunas*, resulting in twenty-three different kinds of objects.[8] In the whole of process and result of evolution we interestingly notice that in the first kind of evolutes are the intellect (*buddhi*), ego (*ahamkara*) and mind (*manas*) which are often thought and taught to be apart from matter. Samkhya holds that these are not non-material, but evolutes from the primordial matter, *prakròti.*[9]That intellect, ego and mind are all products of matter, confirms the strong metaphysical statement of Samkhya that it is the source of all, except for the self, *purusòa. Prakròti,* the primordial matter is the mother of all in the world. Feminity has such potentiality, and supplies the energy for their sustainability.

The dissolution of the world has two kinds of disintegration: the first reduction of gross objects into their constituent gross elements, *bhu ˪ tas* and the secondly into the subtle elements, *tanmatras.* They take place as reversible transformation resulting in the undifferentiated, homogeneous *prakròti* in dynamic equilibrium. The dissolution is not total termination but assimilation into the source. The motherly nature of *prakròti* does not allow the cessation of its broods completely. The absolute and indissoluble nature of *prakròti,* retains all of its offspring. *Prakròti* is said to be only manifesting itself as various objects of experience of the *purusòa,* the self. Even though possessing all qualities and becoming everything, *prakròti* is subjected or reduced to the value of manifesting in various objects of the world only for the service of the self.

3. *Parinama* – Real Transformational Change

Life as movement is in constant change and is not structured, consolidated in a static position. The evolution of the world has been effected by the association or contact (*samyoga*) of the *purusòa* with *prakròti*, which disturbs the original equilibrium of the *prakròti* and moves it to action of manifesting fully, *parinama,* into the world of objects.[10] Samkhyan theory of causation, *satkaryavada,* shows an improvement over the Nya ˪ yayika theory of *arambavada*[11] and the Advaitic *vivartavada.*[12] Nothing arises out of nothing. The theory holds that the effect is real and is implicitly present in the cause and therefore the nature of both cause and effect is identical and not two different realities. The cause transforms itself into effect and both are real. The real manifestation of the cause into the effect is acclaimed as an expression of the same phenomenon in two different aspects of reality. The potentiality of the cause is transformed into actuality in the effect. Causation in a such view is a process of becoming with gradual changes, and is true and real. Becoming is the reality and the Samkhyan affirmation that the effect is real or *sat,* proceeds to declare that the change is real and it is truth.

In contrast to *satkaryavada,* Advaitins put forward the theory of *vivartavada* where the transformation of the cause is not accepted.[13] The effect is merely an apparent manifestation of the cause which remains unaffected. Questioning the nature of the cause after the transformation, Advaitins criticize Samkhyans saying that transformation implies a complete change and changing at every state of existence implies non-comprehension of knowledge of the cause. For the Advaita Vedanta, thus *parinama*, evolution is not real as change is not true. The manifestation is only imagined because of its *avidya.* Understanding their viewpoint of holding the ontological certitude of changing as unreal and the only reality, Brahman as transforming itself apparently into the effect, the world, we clearly see their focal point of declaring the being is true and becoming is unreal.[14] For Advaitins, thus, reality cannot actually transform itself into the world. The Brahman which is part-less, one and *aparinami,* cannot transform itself or become something, whereas *prakròti* is said to be transforming and changing.[15]The relation between Brahman and the world is thus one sided emerging from the Brahman not the other way, world to the Brahman. World then has only a dependent existence, reliant on the absolute, certain and eternal existence of Brahman, one without a second. Causation for Advaitins is real only from the empirical stand point and from the ontological viewpoint it is self-discrepant. The discussion on cause and effect, source and destination are all applied only to beings empirically. Ontologically the pure, all exclusive Brahman is the only reality.Sa└ m└ khya in contrast affirms that *parinama* is real manifestation and explains the standpoint of reality of change and becoming.

4. Liberation: Detachment from *Prakrti*?

Even though *purusa,* the passive witness (*saksòin*) is beyond pleasure and pain, bliss and sorrow, the experience of suffering is attributed to identification of the self with the objects of its experience. An attachment to the objects of the world causes its state of bondage and unfreedom. Ignorant of its true being and attachment to the non-self, *purusòa* continues in bondage and becomes entangled in the cycle of births and deaths. Although *purusòa* (the self) is in itself free and immortal, yet such is the influence of *avidya* (ignorance) that it confuses itself with the body, the senses and the mind (*manas*). It is the lack of discrimination (*aviveka*) between the self and the not-self that is responsible for all sorrows and sufferings.[16]

The curious position of Samkhya claiming that the imperfections are due to its entanglement with *prakròti,* is contrasted with the theory of evolution that association of the two enables the emergence of the world of objects. Such observation of the paradoxical and inconsistent position is further explained that the self in its ignorance becomes victim of bondage through its involvement with *prakròti* and the realisation of such entanglement and false identification has to be removed. Liberation of the self consists in the knowledge of its eternal and absolute independence from *prakrti.* The goal of *purusòa* is liberation from the imperfections and limitations that arise out of its involvement with *prakròti.* The final and total liberation, *kaivalya,* from all manifestations, gross and subtle, of the *prakròti* is such a state of absolute freedom and final isolation of the self from *prakròti.*

Liberation consists in realizing its true being as *purusòa,* eternal, immortal, free, and utterly independent of *prakròti.* Liberating knowledge, *vivekajnana* is the discriminatory awareness that the self is neither the ego, the mind, the intellect nor any other aspect of *prakròti.* The absolute distinction is achieved by such knowledge of discrimination between the self and the non-self. Sa└ m└ khyan idea of liberation does not consist in the attainment of moral or intellectual perfection but in the knowledge of the total and eternal independence of the self from the non-self. Realizing the distinction between the self and the not-self leads the self to be unaffected by joys and sorrows of life and thus become a dispassionate observer of the show of events in the world, reaching the state of liberation, *mukti*, *apavarga*, *kaivalya* etc.[17]

Closely associated with Samkhya system, Yoga philosophy aims at the discipline of theory and practice for the realization of truth by unifying and integrating.[18] Basically accepting Samkhyan dualism, Yoga teaches to attain *kaivalya,* liberation by subduing passions and having control and mastery of *buddhi, ahamkara,* and *manas,* through *astanga-yoga,* eight-limbed stages. The final stage, *samadhi* has a state of fusion of the subject and the object and coinciding of the object into the pure consciousness. In the case of one whose modifications of the mind have been almost annihilated, fusion or entire absorption in one another of the cognizer, cognition, and cognized is brought about, as in the case of a transparent jewel (resting on a coloured surface)."[19] The yogi, by sinking deeper and deeper into his own consciousness, realizes the state of pure subjectivity, of the highest consciousness, of transcendental subjectivity, of self-discovering its own nature. The state of absolute freedom from bondage and ignorance is the goal and is achieved by realization of its true nature as the immortal and all-pervading *purusòa,* utterly separate from *prakròti.*

5. Towards Existential and Ecological Emancipation

The century old blaming of the feminists about exploitation of women is about domestic chores in surface level revolts in familial, socio-economic, political spheres. The arguments characteristic of stereotyping domestic works only to women form the basis for oppression and slavery of women. While rejecting such typecasting of women confining them to as domestic domain we need to reaffirm the positive aspect of such charisma of being a woman. Every crisis in food and agrarian sector generates and perpetuates the oppression and marginalisation of feminity. At the root of dire ecological crisis, the producers or the farmers are the worst affected part of the society. Their soil is made infertile and they are alienated. Deprived of the fertility, and denial of productive ability rendered them useless.[20] Eventually, their ontological and existential status are erased. Height of marginalization of women is achieved in a barren arid terrain. Desertification happens in industrial farming. Alienation by desertification is resulted by separations which are made in food production and distribution. Women are excluded; non-human species are exterminated by pesticides; agricultural activity is defined as food production only for humans. Fertility of the soil is projected as an ability to produce in plenty and is expected to produce only healthy and huge produces. Contrary to nature of the land and soil, patriarchal mode of economy envisions food production and consumption only for humans. The interlink and inter connections among various species of plants and insects are reduced merely to help in better production.

The new economic policies, globalisation, free trading and corporate farming have endangered the fertility of the soil and destroyed the nourishing aspect of nature and of women.[21] When nature was left alone it produced in abundance with varieties of plants on which many species lived upon. The feminine aspect of the soil involving itself in such activity of producing and nourishing many has been respected and none went hungry. The dramatic changes in economic policies of mass production, where subsidies were given out for chemical fertilisers for killing the insects, eventually poisoned the productive soil with its synthetic chemicals contrary to natural minerals that would sustain and regenerate itself. The result of such perverse way of thinking of producing and profiting left many with malnutrition, hunger and even suicide. The nourishing nature was turned out to be non-productive dead element. We have inherited such perverted thinking from a highly patriarchal form of thought which wants only the immediate result of producing and does not care for next generational aspect of sustainability.[22]

6. Reaffirming Nourishing Character

The nourishing character of a woman as mother and life partner has a deeper connection to the feminine reality. In the area of food preparation and consumption, the reality of conservation of nourishing character of nature and women has various positive approximations. To counter the capitalist patriarchy, reaffirmation of the nourishing character of women and nature is inevitable. For, the oppressive market economy has given an assumption that nature is dead.[23] Such declaration helps establish man's empire over nature, in other words women. All species are dared to be exterminated only for man to live. Others are dispossessed only for some to own up exclusive rights of property. In Bacon's words it is the birth of masculine time,[24]an epoch that shaped a way of thinking that would only be in a masculine mould.Such a thinking robbed off completely women all of their thinking. The uncontrollable process of a mechanistic view of the world with its blinding aspect of interconnectedness has no regard for food-cycle or even seasonal cycles. The linear thinking is to be blamed for such negation of cyclic truth of nature and women.[25]The resurgence of a holistic thought is to be brought about as an adequate answer to such monolithic, oppressive thinking of suppression of feminity.

Women are correcting it with assertion that nature is not dead but much alive and dynamic, life giving and life nourishing. By re-declaring and re-affirming the dynamic, life giving nature of the land, women are able to revolt against the man's empire over nature. Important point is that mechanistic world view gave birth to "monoculture of the mind"[26]Death of diversity and multi-crops-culture has been the consequence of much acclaimed green revolution and monoculture industrial farming. Transforming negatively the country's production, from a land of abundance of pulses, cereals, millets to a land of imports. The impact is not only on the manner of production but also in considering nature as passive and weak. Prevention of multiplications of seeds has been systematically done by mono-cultural lobbies through genetic engineering, terminator seeds, patenting. The oppressive measures of making farmers buy seeds every time for cultivation extended up to claiming illegality of conservation of seeds.[27] Women are the most affected part of the farming society that felt the burden of such mono-cultural farming. They were not only subjected to hunger and malnutrition but also of debts and indebtedness to the corporates of food industry for their survival.

Sensing the slow and gradual genocide and eventual 'ecocidal'[28]situation women have to conserve biodiversity and multi-organisms in the land that would become counter-culture to deadly acts of large farm productions. Industrial farming has resulted not only the climate change, pollution of all kinds but also marginalised the very existence of feminity of land and women. The natural fertility and creative productivity are controlled by patriarchal industrial farming. Marginalisation is vivid and clear in contemporary farm activity, which needs to be changed not only to emancipation of biodiversity but for naturalising feminity. More than conscious denial of certain natural character of nature and women, the act of forgetting the potential power makes it denial from within which makes it easier for external forces to marginalise and oppress further more. Re-energising the land and women from the dormant state would make a change. Drastic changes are needed to deny linear line of production to revolutionising the cyclic pattern of production and consumption. It is more than an economic activity, supply and demand, and more than the corporate jargon of 'create demand and supply.'[29] Thinking contrary to such mere economic oppressive pattern, we insist on mutual nourishing that enables sustainability of food cycle.

7. Reclaiming Dynamic Femininity

Samkhyan realism holds that both *prakròti,* matter, and *purusa,* self or spirit are equally real. The distinction is fundamentally that of the subject and the object, and radically different from each other. The dualistic metaphysics of Samkhya, founded on the undeniably bipolar character reflects the existential everyday experience. The hermeneutical reading of nature of *prakròti* widely allows to reclaim the original rendering of its character as changing, active and powerful. Even the binary models and duality in concrete expressions have discrimination of one in favour of the other, the complementarity between the two cannot be ruled out. The powerful dynamism of *prakròti* is often side-lined with the other characters of being unintelligent, therefore useless. To counter the marginalization, equal positioning of ability and power allows us to acknowledge the feminine principle. Comprehension of the whole of reality, not merely the physicality permits us to move forward. Reclaiming needs affirmation of change as reality, dynamism as life, and *prakròti* having its own emotive rationality. The dualistic notion of reality divided into spirit and matter enabled the patriarchal philosophy, religion, science and society to use their power over the feminity personified in nature and women. The stereotypical perception of the feminine as weak, deceitful and seductive, could be overturned with emphasis on her being as vibrant, nurturing and life giving. Becoming is the reality and the Samkhyan affirmation that the effect is real or *sat,* proceeds to declare that the change is real and it is truth.

Indian tradition hails the feminine as *sìakti* – force, power and strength. The non-recognition of the power, leads to marginalization. As in a war tactics, one can beat the enemy, either by giving a tough fight or by making him/her feel weak or believe the myth of being a weak person. Marginalization is a mitigation of power. Femininity is associated with activity, creativity and sanctity of life, but it is considered just as passive and mere resource for manipulation and exploitation.[30] Reclaiming is by being aware of the potentiality and power of *prakròti* as in eco-feminist activism where women and especially the agrarian, peasant, rural women have become the protector of biodiversity and become the change makers. As the very foundation of every economic activity is the biodiversity of the nature which has the potential power of generating and regenerating. Nature has such a power which is only equal to women. The world has witnessed a significant change and attitudinal shift in both women's and society's thoughts about women's equality and emancipation. The sensitisation of women is marked by celebrating tearing apart the stereotyping them in familial confinements and by breaking the centuries old clichés on women. Reclaiming dynamism in the feminine enables accelerating gender parity in the socio-economic-political sphere, providing the deserved dignity and equivalent status.

By reaffirming nourishing character of land and women we reinitiate the cyclic link of biodiversity. Playing the role of a mother as nourishing, care taking, life giving, self-sacrificing, the femininity enshrines the sacredness of interconnectedness and bonding. The home-maker secures the home, the '*eco,*' the cosmos.[31]Eating is not only a physical activity or a social, familial activity. Eating is an agricultural, ecological and ethical. The way food is grown, if it does not allow connectivity and links among different species, it is ecologically unethical and unjust. By choice of food, be it organic, home grown, millets, seasonal, etc., we could make a difference. Each of us can be the change. If one chooses to eat indigenous varieties of grains, genetically modified seeds along with their patent rights are neglected. The linear line of industrial production and consumption is challenged. The consumer will have the right of choice and will empower the farmer who would in turn produce in line with biodiversity. Eating then becomes a political act too, anti-establishment rebellion, anti-market economical revolt and becomes an emancipatory act of affirming nature and women. Re-establishing the diversity of beings, we could save the producers from falling prey to market economy. Eradicating marginalization begins here.

Concluding Remarks

The foregone reflection on marginalising the 'feminity' of women and nature, has traversed from Indian philosophical milieu to eco-feminism, throwing light on how the life-giving and life-sustaining feminine, has been systematically side-lined, neglected and suppressed. The Samkhya school of thought, known for its theory of causation and evolution, advocates dualism of two ultimate realities, unconscious, active and mutable *prakròti* and conscious, passive and unchanging *purusòa.* Sa˪ m˪ khyan understanding of *prakròti* as the non-self, ever changing and devoid of consciousness, seems the philosophical basis of marginalisation, or at least been used for such endeavour. *Prakròti,* constituted of three qualities or nature, *gunòas – sattva, rajas* and *tamas,* is said to be only manifesting itself as various objects of experience of the *purusòa,* the self. Even though possessing all qualities and becoming everything, *prakròti* is subjected or reduced to the value of manifesting in various objects of the world only for the service of the self. Analysis of marginalization leads us to hermeneutical aspiration of emancipation. Despite the distinctions and differentiations, equality is inherent in Samkhyan dualism and the disparities are not to be emphasised for preference of one to the other. The change and becoming nature of *prakròti* accepted as one of the realities opens up the horizon of philosophical debate of asserting dynamism in life as real. Emancipation is by reassertion of the qualities such as nourishing, life giving, evolving and changing, as something worthwhile and true.

The developmental model of modernity leads to exploitation of the forces of nature and living and creative process. The women and soil have become victims of environmental degradation. Marginalisation is vivid and clear in contemporary farm activity, especially in mono-cultural industrial farming with aggressive model of control of germination of seeds, genetic manipulation and genetic engineering. Marginalization in production, economics, politics, society, rights over ownership, segregation of public spaces, social interaction, gender, female illiteracy, fertility, women are put at a disadvantage position. Eco-philosophical rumblings take us to the core of environmental degradation, where women become the agents of change and activism. In protection and regeneration of land and nature, eco-feminism asserts itself against operation of binary mode of preferring one to the other, against consideration of the feminine as weak, dead, mere productive, devoid of sentience. The feminine principle, *prakròti* from which all life evolves, is always a living and creative process. Reclaiming of the feminine characters of dynamism, change and becoming as positive, life-living and nourishing, as true and real, is envisioned as empowerment of the feminine. The very nature of the feminine through which construed the marginalization, could be the site of emancipation.

Notes

1. Dr. John Peter Vallabadoss., Dean of Studies at St. Joseph's Capuchin Philosophical College, Kotagiri, Tamil Nadu. He has been Treasurer and Secretary of Association of Christian Philosophers of India. He has been a Consultant in Philosophy at Indira Gandhi National Open University (IGNOU), for a couple

of years developing MA philosophy programme. He has convened three National Seminars. To his credit he has published two books and edited 4 books and published 42 research articles till date. Presently, he is pursuing his Post-Doctoral Research in Paris.

2. *Samkhya Kârikâ of Îsvarakrsna,* verse 3. John Davies, *Hindu Philosophy: The SankhyaKarika of Iswara Krishna,* London: Trubner's Oriental Series, 1881 reprint (London: Routledge, 2013), 17.
3. Samkhyaargument for the existence of the self is remarkably similar to the Cartesian dictum, 'I think, therefore I am.' Difference is that for Descartes thinking is the attribute of the self, for the Sa └ m └ khya,thinking belongs to the internal organ (*ahamkara*).
4. Chandradhar Sharma, *A Critical Survey of Indian Philosophy* (Delhi: Motilal banarsidass Publishers, 2003), 158.
5. M. Hiriyanna, *Outlines of Indian Philosophy*, reprint (Delhi: Motilal Banarsidass, 1994), 207.
6. *Ibid.*, 402.
7. Chandradhar Sharma, *A Critical Survey of Indian Philosophy,* 166.
8. The evolution of *prakrti*is due to instability brought about by the dominance or preponderance of one or the other of the three *gunas*. The evolutes are intellect (*mahat/buddhi*), ego (*ahamkara*), mind (*manas*), five sense-organs (*jnnanendriyas*), five motor-organs (*karmendriyas*), five subtle elements (*tanmatras*), five gross elements (*bhutas*). Refer, SuryanarayanaSastri, *Samkhya Karika of Iswara Krishna*. Madras: MadrasUniversity, 1933.
9. Chandradhar Sharma, *A Critical Survey of Indian Philosophy*, 193.
10. *Ibid.*, 151.
11. The Nyaya system holds a view contrary to Samkhyans *atkaryavada,* that everything emerges newly from the cause. The effect is not pre-existent in the cause, i.e. *asatkaryavada.* Refer, Bimal Krishna Matilal, *Nyaya-Vaisesika* (Wlesbaden: Otto Harrassowitz,1977), 58.
12. Advaita Vedanta understands the effect from the cause only as illusory or apparent. There is not real manifestation or transformation from the cause. It helps them hold the unchanging character of Brahman, the truth. All that emerges from the cause is only an apparent manifestation. Hence, the system even is not in favour of creation theory, *sìròsòtiva └ da.* Refer, V. N. Sheshagiri Rao, *Vacaspati's Contribution to Advaita.* Mysore: Samvit Publishers, 1984.
13. M. Hiriyanna, *Outlines of Indian Philosophy*, reprint (Delhi: Motilal Banarsidass, 1994), 339.
14. Our thesis of marginalization of that which is changing, the feminine, is explicitly declared by absolute idealist like Advaita Vedanta.
15. By the way, Ramanuja's *Visìisòtadvaita* Vedanta holds that the world is part of Brahman, negating the view of Advaita Vedanta. Refer, D. Nesy, *Essays on Vedanta* (University of Kerala: Department of Philosophy, 2006), 8.
16. S. Radhakrishnan, *Indian Philosophy*, Vol. 2(Oxford: University Press, 2008), 302.

17. M. Hiriyanna, *Outlines of Indian Philosophy*, 131.
18. S. Radhakrishnan, *Indian Philosophy,* Vol.2, 316.
19. *Yoga-sutra* 1.41. trans., I.K. Taimni, *The Science of Yoga* (Chennai: Theosophical Publishing House, 1961), 91.
20. Emmadi Naveen Kumar, *Agrarian Crisis: Farmers' Suicides in Warangal District* (Newcastle: Cambridge Scholars Publishing, 2012), 22-26.
21. Premananda Panda, "Land Distribution among Scheduled Castes and Scheduled Tribes," in *Contract Farming and Tenancy Reforms: Entangled without Tether,* Ed., R.S. Deshpande(Mussoorie: Centre for Rural Studies, 2007), 225.
22. Maria Mies&Vandana Shiva, *Ecofeminism* (London: Zed Books, 1993), 35-40.
23. William Lazonick, *Business Organization and the Myth of the Market Economy* (Cambridge: University Press, 1994), 272.
24. Jan Golinski, "The Care of the Self and the Masculine Birth of Science," in *History of Science,* Vol.40 (2002), 125.
25. One cannot get it right in addressing the pollution, because they have broken the cycle. The cycle of our nutrition that should go back to the land is today going as pollution to the rivers. If only we have planned it right, with sanitation, we would have no problem of soil infertility.
26. Refer, Vandana Shiva, *Monocultures of the Mind: Perspectives on Biodiversity and Biotechnology* (London: Zed Books, 1993),
27. Refer, Vandana Shiva, *Biopiracy: The Plunder of Nature and Knowledge.* Reprint, Berkeley: North Atlantic Books, 2016.
28. Ruth Thomas-Pellicer, "Dystopian Contemporary Positions: Sustainable Development as a Manifest Instance of the Epistemological Disposition," in *Cosmos and History: The Journal of Natural and Social Philosophy,* Vol.12. No.1 (2016), 310.
29. Sujan Patel, "7 Marketing Tips to Create a Demand for your New Product," https://www.forbes.com/sites/sujanpatel/2016/10/22/create-a-demand-for-a-new-product/#8e6742d7e2dd, accessed 24 May, 2019.
30. Refer, Kancha Ilaiah. *Post-Hindu India: A Discourse on Dalit-Bahujan, Socio-Spiritual and Scientific Revolution.* New Delhi: Sage Publications, 2009. The passivity of the self, as superior is derived from Brahmanical scheme of thought emerging from undisturbed, passivity (*sithaprajnÞatvam*). The activity is considered as less important, as it is construed by 'leisurely class.' But tranquillity of Samkhyan discourse renders, in that there is no life; it is dead.
31. Mark A. Schroll, ed., *Ecology, Cosmos and Consciousness* (Mochnant, UK: Psychoid Books, 2018), 324.

Chapter - 6

Digital Empowerment for Gender Neutralisation

***Dr Yazali Josephine*[1]**

Introduction

The girl – child throughout history has been subjected to varying degrees of deprivations and Subjugation. She has been stifled mentally, psychologically and physically by the dictates of Male – dominated cultures and traditions that cut across virtually all races of the world. The fact is that she has been so second rated that .The World Bank (2001) stated that"…in no region do women enjoy equal legal, Social, and economic rights. Women have fewer resources than men, and more limited economic resources.

The paper also discusses a set of broader societal forces/issues at play, such as demographic shifts,increasing inequalities, the role of women in the labour market, globalisation, the varying quality of education, rapid digitisation, and the subnational variation in development and growth between geographies in India. Finally, the paper outlines a framework for studying an inclusive future of work in India, which will be applied in subsequent research.

Issues Increasing Inequalities

India must contend with high and increasing income and wealth inequality. The top one percent of earners in India have seen their incomes increase tenfold between 1980 and 2014, while the earnings of those at the median of the income distribution have barely doubled during the same period. With automation and technological adoption comes the risk of exacerbating income inequality in a number of ways. This presents a risk of greater inequality of opportunities and outcomes, including wages for India's women as digital literacy becomes increasingly important for accessing job opportunities and employability. The relatively faster growth of capital-intensive industries in recent decades will likely lead to greater concentrations of income among equipment, machine, firm and technology owners, rather than labourers.

The demographic dividend in India is often touted as a growth opportunity. Aiyer and Mody , for example, attribute a substantial part of India's growth acceleration over the last three decades to India's changing age structure. They further argue that India's dividend may add two percentage points to GDP growth in the coming two decades.There is scepticism, however, about India's ability to capitalise on its demographic dividend, which will depend on the quality of India's labour.

Women and Work

Not only is this low, it has also declined. With respect to corporate employment,approximately 50 percent of women drop out of employment between junior- and middle-level positions, compared to an average drop-out rate of 29 percent across Asia.Women also tend to be overrepresented in lower-wage and lower-skilled occupations as compared to their male counterparts. Sociocultural factors are drivers of low female participation in the paid labour market.

It is expected that women are primary caregivers at home. To that end, women handle the vast majority of unpaid work in India, with 66 percent of women's work being unpaid,compared to 12 percent for men.

The place of ICT in women empowerment in the Indian economy

Technological innovation and Information Communication Technologies (ICTs) represent a way for developing world nations to foster economic development, improve levels of education and training, as well as address gender issues within society.Information and Communication Technology (ICT) is a general-purpose technology and as such has a pervasive impact on the economy. It introduces a new paradigm for the configuration of Globalization, ICT and the economic activities radically changing the approach to technology for development (UNCTAD, 2007). The term Information Technology (IT), as a component of ICT, refers to the gadgets with which information is generated and disseminated. Aspects of our lives, be it health, education, etc, and it is a pathway to achieving the Millennium Development Goals (MDG), ICT has proven to be increasingly fundamental for social and economic development.

Discussions on technological change and its effects on employment are hardly new. Increased mechanisation and technological advances in the 19th and 20th centuries resulted in increased efficiency in production as well as higher wages and incomes. While the demand for labour and related skills changed as technologies evolved, the overall demand for labour did not diminish nor did technology replace workers as new products, industries and sectors emerged. Recent studies, however, suggest that the advent of advanced technologies have the potential to displace labour.

The world is currently experiencing rapid and widespread advances in automation, based heavily on artificial intelligence (AI) and robotics, and the use of Big Data and machine learning. Examples of recent innovations include driverless cars, service robots caring for the elderly, smart factories, Internet of Things and 3D printing. Machines driven by computer power, robotics and AI are now increasingly able to perform tasks previously restricted to humans.

Access to basic ICT infrastructure is a key to increasing the flow of information and improving communications and by extension increasing possibilities and opportunities. It has proven to a great leveller between the developed and the developing countries of the world. A good example in this case is India. India's economy today is basically IT driven and it has attained, through this means, the position of the 4th biggest economy in the world by the end of 2020 One major reason that could account for this phenomenal growth is the empowerment of its citizens, especially women, through diverse ICT programs and training.

Case studies

An example is the "Nabanna" project which is putting a web-based information system to strategic use for the benefit of poor women of Baduria, a rural region in North-24 Parganas district in the Indian state of West Bengal. The project was a collaboration exercise among Change Initiatives, an NGO concerned about the lack of penetration of ICTs among the rural poor people, United Nations Educational, Scientific and Cultural Organization (UNESCO), National Informatics Centre, researchers of the London School of Economics and Queensland University of Technology, and the Baduria Municipality. It found that absence of information and an information-sharing mechanism among poor women thwarted their ability to fulfill basic needs, restricted their awareness and blocked their desire to break barriers that limit their participation in society.

2. Empowering Women Kerala, India

Gender-related disparities in Kerala stem from India's pre-colonial tribal caste system. The caste system was legally abolished in 1947. Women's empowerment includes their access to education, basic health and nutrition, and opportunities for meaningful employment.

Technology plays a vital role in developing programs for empowering women. It is the leading driver to providing equal access to women, where access was once limited.

Using existing political strategy mechanisms and community-based programs to improve social dimensional integration of poor women to foster enhanced education, improved health and wellness, and increase commercial demand provides an operational basis for improving the achievement of the women in Kerala India.

3. Other organizations like **Empowering Women In Technology** (EWIT) have developed a forum to drive the growth of the tech industry and are beginning to have an impact on narrowing the skills gap between women and men in the industry. According to economic reports, there are 871 working women cooperatives and over 14,000 joint stock companies started by women in 2017.

4. Resource Enhancement Academy for Career Heights

REACH, Resource Enhancement Academy for Career Heights, a finishing school initiative of the Kerala State Women's Development Corporation was launched on 29th December 2009 with a view to bridge the gap between acquired skills and required skills, for professionally qualified women called **Kudumbasree.Kudumbasree** program allows poor women access to IT sector jobs, like data entry and word processing. 75 percent of the workforce is data entry. Technology jobs open a new sector of the economy to women with lower level skills. It provides an *alternative* to customary manufacturing and agriculture-based jobs. Providing an opportunity to for women to move up the success ladder is vital. The higher wages makes them supporting members of their household.

5. [2]Accenture and READ India Empower Women in Rural Karnataka

To improve the employability and livelihood of more than 150 underprivileged women and young girls, Accenture and READ India are launching a rural community development center in Bagepalli in Karnataka. The initiative will provide life and work-skills training in areas such as self-confidence, gender sensitization, sewing and stitching, computer skills, local crafts and reading and writing.The new center will include a multimedia and communications room, an IT area for ICT-based learning, a library and places where women can attend classes, participate in trainings and receive medical examinations. Sarva Dharma Samanvaya Trust, which has been running a school for children at Bagepalli since 2001, is providing the space for the center. More than 850 village households lie within a five kilometer radius of it; several of the villages offer limited professional and vocational options, and they lack basic healthcare, sanitation and education facilities.The launch of the center reflects Accenture's global corporate citizenship initiative, Skills to Succeed, which is equipping more than 3 million people around the world by 2020 with the skills to get a job or build a business.

Digital empowerment for Gender Neutralisation

India has seen rapid digitisation in the past five years, primarily through mobile phone usage. Mobile phone subscriptions per 100 people increased from 0.3 in 2000 to 87 percent in 2016. Of the 462 million active internet users, 443 million are active mobile internet users. It is important to note, however, that despite rapid expansion, access and usage remains uneven and digital divides are pervasive. Women, for example, have much lower access to internet than men with 70 percent of internet users being male. Unless this digital gender divide is bridged, India's aggressive push towards digitisation will further entrench the political, economic and social marginalisation of women. The gender gap in mobile ownership – estimated at about 114 million – reinforces the fact of unequal access, but also paints an incomplete and misleading picture. In Madhya Pradesh, as in many parts of rural and semi-rural India, this capacity is directly shaped by gender biased belief and value systems that impose restrictions on the education and free mobility of women. Census 2011 data indicates that 65.46% of women are literate as compared to over 80% of men.

A study by the Internet Democracy Project argues that in India, mobile phones make it possible to develop new ideas of the self, to explore and exercise autonomy, choice and agency. While digital economy allows opportunities for 'flexi-work' and diminishes the reliance on physical workspaces, digital literacy must not aid in reinforcing the traditional gendered segregation of private and public. Unless accompanied by broader shifts in social and cultural belief systems, it can lead to further restrictions on the mobility and autonomy of women. While the focus on bridging the gender gap in digital access and skills is crucial for this to happen, it cannot make an effective dent on women's inclusion prospects without the removal of implicit and explicit discriminatory barriers. The South African experience re-affirms that interventions aimed at access alone are insufficient. As per a 2016 study by the Finmark Trust, South Africa is the only country in the Southern African Development Community in which the digital gender divide is narrow and women are more financially included than men with a positive gender gap of 6% in bank account ownership. Yet, women are more likely to have dormant accounts and have less access to the credit and savings market. In urban India, gender-based digital exclusion is less pronounced as connectivity and literacy rates are relatively higher and social norms are less rigid. New opportunities are being created on the back of the boom in the IT sector and the expansion of the digital economy. Structural discrimination against women makes them particularly vulnerable and reinforces the need to develop alternative social protection mechanisms. It is estimated that the chances of women benefitting from opportunities accrued by the information society will be one third less than for men. Although it's already apparent that in the digital age, 'online' and 'offline' will be intertwined, policy communities and conversations continue to be fragmented. Otherwise, the digital age will only marginalise the marginalised, and exacerbate existing hierarchies between genders.

Conclusion

India needs an inclusive future of work.[3]Recent headlines suggest that the rise of modern technologies will drastically alter the jobs landscape in India, potentially displacing large portions of the workforce. While disruptions are inevitable, it is uncertain as to what extent automation and technology will impact employment, job roles and skilling requirements. What is certain, however, is the need to create new and relevant employment opportunities for India's growing youth population and women. Approximately 62 percent of the Indian population are of working age (15–59 years), 65 percent of whom are under the age of 35.The result is an estimated 12 million people entering the workforce every year. While the Government of India has made strides in improving business environments for both established companies and start-ups, and is working on improving the skilling landscape, the task to increase the number of jobs and the magnitude of an appropriately skilled workforce is formidable. India faces the twin challenge of automation and digitisation resulting in a potential reduction of jobs, at the same time as the number of people entering the job market continues to rise. Recent headlines suggest that the rise of modern technologies will drastically alter the jobs landscape in India, potentially displacing large portions of the workforce. While disruptions are inevitable, it is uncertain as to what extent automation and technology will impact employment, job roles and skilling requirements on the marginalised and women. What is certain, however, it is the need to create new and relevant employment opportunities for India's growing youth population and women.

Notes

1. Former Professor in Economics of Education at NUEPA ,Currently as a founder member and Director of Peoples Development Academy , New Delhi.
2. The CSR Journal-September 14, 2018.
3. https://www.orfonline.org/research/43609-conceptualising-an-inclusive-future-of-work-in-india/.

Chapter - 7

Gender Justice: Challenges and Responses

***Dr. Inigo Joachim*[1]**

We live in troubled times in India. Violence seems to have become the new culture in the country. There is no safety and security for women. We are not talking about only the issues of women among marginalized communities but our concern here is just "Women". *Gender issues are not merely of women's issues. They are human issues, moral issues and spiritual issues.*

From acid attacks to raping and burning them alive, women are being pushed to the margins of society. The reason is gender inequality and gender injustice. Sexual immorality is on the increase all over the world. Adultery is fast becoming the norm and men of God are also joining the club. The rate at which immorality is increasing is alarming!As St. Paul says in his letters, *"sexual immorality is a serious crime"*:I Cor: 5: 1; Gal: 5: 19; Col: 3:5; Eph: 5: 3.

Our socio-cultural system is such that it gives *special priority to a male child and birth of a girl is considered a curse even in this ultra modern world.* This kind of misconception had been the basis for all forms of social injustices and discriminations that women have to face. Women have been victims of violence – be it at the domestic level or in the public sphere or even in the Church. Since the legal provisions were male oriented until the recent past, females and their roles were defined conveniently in a way favorable to the males. It is necessary to address its root cause.

What is wrong with the Indian male?

We cannot easily forget Delhi rape-case of *Nirbhaya on Dec, 16, 2012.* Women are becoming vulnerable in India. We, as images of God, deserve to live in dignity. We should fight against the culture of silence in this matter.

Who benefit by the subjugation of women?

1. Male members: How?In order to get her service, to be comfortable and to get property by way of dowry she should be kept as a second class citizen Will the males give up their privilege? No.

a. Women's productive or labour power

Men control women's productivity both within the household and also outside as paid workers. Within the household women provide all kinds of free service to their children, husbands and other members of the family, throughout their lives.

b. Women's reproductive power

Men also control women's reproductive power. In many societies women do not have the freedom to decide how many children they want, when to have them, whether girl or boy,

2. Capitalists

Different salaries are paid for men and womenfor the same type of work: Teachers, doctors, engineers etc., are skilled labour and they both get same salary. But they are only 40% while 60% of labourers are unskilled and unorganized. Women are more in this category and this means more profit for the capitalists. Will they liberate and empower women?

3. Business people: How?

*Women are deceived through advertisements that focus on beautifying women.*A kind of illusion is created in the minds of women regarding beauty. The media like the T.V and the cinema play their role successfully as important tools in the hands of the upper caste men to propagate gender ideology. Messages about male superiority and female inferiority are repeated constantly.

4. Politicians

The majority of those who go to election booths are women. The politicians benefit by ignorant women. With all the awareness created by the mass media, there are still remote villages ignorant of the reality. Because of illiteracy, information technology has not reached them. Ever since learning and education became formal and institutionalized, men have assumed control over whole areas of knowledge: philosophy, theology, law, literature and science.

Almost all political institutions in society, at all levels, are male dominated, from villagecouncils to Parliament. There are only a handful of women in political parties and they decide the fate of our countries. Parties may change, but the Parliament will never give a 50% representation for women.

India has had a woman Prime Minister; it has had a woman President; the chief of the ruling Alliance in the country for a time was a woman (Sonia Gandhi). Many women were chief Ministers in different states and the Chief Minister of West Bengal today is a woman. Yet even today women find themselves marginalized in the policy-making bodies of the Government. The

Report in the TOI in January 2018 was shocking when it said: *"Every hour that ticks by, India inflicts more brutality on women with 2 rapes, 2 kidnappings, 4 molestations and 7 incidents of cruelty from husbands and relatives."*

A recent survey conducted by the *Thomson Reuters Foundation* (TRF) has labeled India as a country not made for women. It says that India is the most dangerous country for women in the world in terms of human trafficking, sexual violence, child marriage, genital mutilation and acid attacks. This report should force the government to rethink and introspect. Out of 192 countries, India ranked:

: First (the worst) for sexual violence

: Fourth worst in accessibility to health facilities for women

: Third worst for non-sexual violence and discrimination

The national capital, Delhi, has retained the 'rape capital' tag since 2012 Nirbhaya case. After this infamous case, many stringent laws were enacted but subsequent incidents have proved that the males have not stopped their horrific rapes. Despite so many stringent laws and regulations, if women do not feel safe, where is the problem?

There are no quick fixes and magic solutions, but at least popular perceptions about women as 'second class citizens' should be changed. The crime reports should act as eye-openers, not as resigned eye-closers. We can live in a denial mode. But reality will continue to prick our conscience, if it is not dead.

5. Religious Leaders

I was at the Synod in Rome on "Consecrated Life" in 1994. In one of the interventions, *a Bishop said: "In the Church, 75% of the consecrated people are women. If there are no women, there is no Consecrated life and no Church. Hence, the future of the Church depends upon the response we would be giving to women religious. If they don't feel our support, eventually the Church will lose women too in this century."*

When I read some of the encyclicals and other documents of the Popes, I see that they are very much in favour of gender sensitivity and the dignity of women. The Bishops at the Asian Synod were most concerned that "the Church should be a participatory church in which no one feels excluded", acknowledging that "the contribution of women have often been undervalued or ignored" (*EA*. 34).

I Cor 14: 31 says: All can prophesy. We have to get rid of brethren theology. Acts: 2: 17-18: Holy Spirit has been poured on men and women. In Jn: 4: 39, they all believed because of one Samaritan woman's testimony. Jesus and Paul had women associates in their mission.

At the same time, we cannot deny women's negative experiences. All religious Leaders are responsible for the oppression of women. All major institutionalized religions have been created, developed and controlled by upper class and upper caste men. Women are allowed to interpret religious and legal texts.

The Situation Today

Why is the situation not different today in the church? Even after 2000 years of their existence, half of the followers of Jesus are not counted. They are neither visible nor audible in the Church. In India women constitute nearly 82% of the religious. The Synod of Bishops on "Consecrated Life" recommended very strongly that competent women religious must be given responsible tasks in the Church and that they should be included in the process of planning and decision making at all levels.

In the *book "Called to Question", John Chittister says: We never ever prayed to "God our Mother". God, the source of creation, God the eternal womb, was never, ever recognized as a Mother God. We could call God "rock, fire, light, wind, door, key and father", but never, ever "MOTHER".It was a moment of soul-shaking revelation. Where were women in these images of God? And if they weren't there, what kind of God was this? I had given my life to a God who did not see me, did not include me, and did not touch my nature with God's own.*

When Moses asks God's name in the Scriptures: Who shall I tell them sent me? What is your name? God did not say, "I am your father", but "I AM WHO AM" (Ex. 3: 13-14). This means I am pure being. God is Father as well as God is my Mother.Therefore, nobody is going to empower women or speak about equality. We have to prepare women and women religious through on-going formation.

What about the sex scandals - pedophilia - that have erupted in the Church and causing so much pain in the life of the victims? Why have Priests and Bishops committed such terrible crimes by sexually exploiting minors and women while celebrating Mass and praying their breviary? How come they were not stopped by the awareness of the suffering they inflicted, and by facing the fact that they were destroying their future? Why do their tears not make them repent? Why do some priests refuse to celebrate the Eucharist in some places because they have some personal problems with the women religious? How can they play with the Sacraments? The power of the pulpit is sacred power. How can the pulpit – a sacred place - be used to air their personal grievances and attack others?

We have become victims to certain stereotyped cultural myths of our times. What we have to do is to de-mythify them.

The "#Me too" movement was started a decade ago by activist Tarana Burke for victims of sexual violence. The church needs to learn from feminists and the #MeToo movement. They have taught us about the danger of sex between adults who are not in positions of equal power.

For the church, this would clearly be the case of a bishop or priest having sex with a seminarian or a bishop having sex with a priest, a nun or lay woman. The relationship here is even greater than that between an employer and employee. A bishop / priest is supposed to be a father to his priests and seminarians. *The church needs a zero-tolerance policy toward such abuse.*

Some practical responses: Let us light a Candle!

1. Hence the first step for gender justice is to inculcate *God consciousness* in all of us.
2. The gospels present *Mother Mary* not as docile and weak but as a daring and empowered woman. We need to present this model of Mother Mary to others and enhance the self-assertion of women.
3. A transition is needed from making *women just 'devotees' of Jesus to 'disciples'* of Jesus to continue the mission of Jesus.
4. We need to introduce *Gender-sensitization programmes and Feminist Theology* in seminary formation, on-going formation of Priests as well as in the religious formation of women.
5. They can be trained for *family counseling* and lay-leaders training.
6. Women should be involved in the *Ministry of the Proclamation of Good News*,
7. Many nuns are working in schools run by diocesan management. They are *poorly paid* and they have no freedom to take any decision. Pope Francis rightly said: "Women are not cheap labour force in the church".
8. The dioceses and parishes can *hand over the management* of certain centres to religious women where ordination is not necessary rather than keeping them as employees. This will enable priests available for their pastoral ministry.
9. We have to popularize inclusive language in liturgy, Prayer of the Church, catechesis and homilies and should judiciously use more pro-feminist and liberative passages
10. The priests *should not play with the sacramental life* like refusing to celebrate Mass due to some personal grudges. Dialogue and discussions killing ego and "I am right" attitude could solve lots of issues.
11. The *women religious should also need empowerment* if they are to lead a dignified life and become effective catalysts in the

empowerment of underprivileged women. *They should have confidence in their own abilities.*

12. We see that *bisexuality ratio* has grown over time and so have discrimination. This community deserves the dignity and respect that most people take for granted.
14. Finally: *This is the Age of Information.* I feel *both men and women should be given a radical on-going formation* to understand the signs of the times. Both men and women in the church are called to be prophets, the conscience of the society. *Then only both could be courageous, creative and compassionate missionaries* in God's Kingdom as true followers of Jesus.

To conclude

The call of Jesus in Mark Gospel 5: 41, "Little girl, get up", is a clarion call for women's freedom in the Church and society.

Into that heaven of freedom my Mother and Father, let my sisters and brothers awake!

Notes

1. Inigo Joachim, SSA, Barasat, Kolkata was twice the Superior General of St. Anne's Congregation, Chennai from 1990 – 1996 and 1996 - 2002.She has been working at Tihar Prisonsfor a number of years in counselling the inmates and also providing free Legal Aid with the help of a few committed advocates of Supreme Court.She was the only delegate elected by South Asian women religious to be at the Synod of Bishops in Rome in 1994 on "Vita Consecrata". A prolific writer, scholar, social activist and champion of justice and peace for the marginalized communities especially women.

Chapter - 8

The Role of Elected Women Representatives in Panchayat Raj Institution in India: A Study on Capacity Building and Empowerment Perspective

Dr. J. Rani Ratna Prabha and Sudam Tandi[1]

Introduction

The role of women in Panchayat Raj Institution ushered in 73rd Constitutional Amendment Act, 1993 where the 33 percent of reservation for women was implemented in all three-tier panchayats in India. Later some states like Kerala, Karnataka,Odisha, Assam, Andhra Pradesh, Bihar, Chhattisgarh, Gujarat, Himachal Pradesh, and Jharkhand adopted 50 percent reservation in PRI. As a result, Women participation in PRI in terms of representation has been ensured at least 33 percent in all states. It has resulted in participation of 1.26 million women, who constitute 44.52 percent of the total number of elected representatives in Panchayat Raj Institution.(Alok, 2011 cited in Sudipta Biswas,2016). Representation of women in unreserved seats is a most important indicator to measure the success of reservation introduced through the 73rd constitutional amendment. Therefore, MoPR Study (2008) shows that there are about 6 percent EWRs who are elected from unreserved seats (SoPR, 2008-09, cited in Sudipta Biswas, 2016) Indeed, it is their spouse or other patriarchal counterparts are the real decision makers and the women elected representatives who hail from different caste groups like Scheduled Caste, Scheduled Tribe, another backward caste. They have various sorts of experiences and difficulties in discharging their duties and also face discrimination at various levels of functioning. Therefore, the study focuses on the role of Dalit women and tribal women at the gram panchayat level at different places in India.

Rationality of reservation in Panchayati Raj Institutions (PRI)

The quota for women in Panchayati Raj Institutions intended to give voice to Scheduled Castes and Scheduled tribes women to influence policies at local governance. The political theorist Anne Phillips (1995) has made a distinction between the 'politics of ideas' and the 'politics of presence'. The former has the political vision and manifesto of different political parties, but it does not necessarily present the needs and interest of disadvantaged groups. But the 'politics of presence', can provide such group with guaranteed representation in public institutions- such as quota in lawmaking bodies through which they may effectively represent their own need and interest. In general, the diversified people representation in legislative bodies is essential to make an effective policy framework. (Norris,1997:230, quoted in panchayat thematic report, 2007-2008 IRMA,pp-187)

Since centuries the women in India have been deliberately denied both social and economic opportunities at different spheres like religion, caste, and socio-cultural practices. Untouchability is a major developmental obstacle for Dalit women as they are facing problems like illiteracy, maternal mortality and devastated identities in the society and even in their families. Women participation in the Panchayati (since the passing of the 73rd amendment in 1993), has varied based on the local socio-political structure. Various studies have illuminated that woman leaders in panchayats face difficulties in fulfilling their responsibilities and constraints that were not addressed properly.

The functioning of the three-tier of gram panchayat significantly depends on the devolution of resources, transfer of subjects, and the passing down of administrative control over civil servants and implementing the schemes at the gram panchayat level. As per mandate of the constitutional amendment, states have to devolve the power and the fund to local government and some state hesitant to deliver the power to the panchayat" (Vyasulu 2004:3282 cited in Narayana,2005) In this situation, the question automatically arise about, how the elected women leaders would take the responsibilities in the functioning of the gram panchayat? Therefore, the capacity building training is treated as a favourable solution to administer the gram panchayat for all elected representatives. In order to strengthen Panchayats, it is worthwhile to improve in governance capability building and training is a very essential aspect of strengthening Panchayats. In fact, elected representatives and Panchayat functionaries need to understand their role and responsibilities and have the skills to perform the role effectively. So the government has been provided capacity building, reaching out to all stakeholders of Panchayats, is necessary to ensure that Panchayats become effective. As several new ERs have to start functioning for the first time, it is necessary to train this target group within the first six months of Panchayat elections. In Panchayats across the country, Elected Women Representatives (EWRs) constitute 42.3 percent, SCs women are 13.7 percent while STs Women constitute 14.6 percent of all

ERs. Indeed, a large number of women ERs face multiple deprivations of caste, class and gender in families as well as the political sphere. Thus, capacity building training of these historically marginalized ERs is extremely essential, so as to help realize the Constitutional vision of inclusive and participatory democratic governance at the grassroots level. (Ministry of Panchayat Raj, India,2014) The capacity building training address the issue like socio-cultural exclusion and discrimination and help to strengthen the leaders among them, mobilisation of Gram Sabha for women for participation, inuencing public opinion, building alliances for advocacy and action partnerships with civil society organizations and overall development of the village.

The objective of the study

There are two objectives of the paper focusing on the significant role of women elected representatives in Gram panchayats in India and also made an attempt to find out the impact of 73rd Constitutional Amendment Act on women empowerment.

Table no-1: Status of Representation of Women in PRIs

There are 13.45 lakhs Elected Women Representatives (EWRs) in PRIs which constitute 46.14% of total Elected Representatives (ERs). The State-wise details are given below:-

S. No.	States/UTs	Elected Representatives	Elected Women Representatives	Elected Women Representatives (%)	Women Sarpanchs
1	Andhra Pradesh	156049	78025	50.00	6584
2	Arunachal Pradesh	9356	3094	33.07	
3	Assam	26844	13422	50.00	1093
4	Bihar	136325	70400	51.64	
5	Chhattisgarh	158776	87549	55.14	5822
6	Dadra & Nagar Haveli	136	47	34.56	11
7	Daman & Diu	97	28	28.87	
8	Goa	1559	514	32.97	79
9	Gujarat	132726	43670	32.90	4600
10	Haryana	68152	24876	36.50	2565
11	Himachal Pradesh	27832	13947	50.11	1631
12	Jammu and Kashmir	33282	11169	33.56	
13	Jharkhand	51327	30373	59.18	2284
14	Karnataka	95307	50892	53.40	3479
15	Kerala	19089	9897	51.85	494
16	Madhya Pradesh	396819	198409	50.00	11864
17	Maharashtra	203203	101466	49.93	13960
18	Manipur	1784	868	48.65	64
19	Odisha	100791	49697	49.31	
20	Punjab	97180	33609	34.58	
21	Rajasthan	121008	70531	58.29	5121
22	Sikkim	1099	549	49.95	88
23	Tamil Nadu	119399	39975	33.48	4289
24	Telangana	103468	46702	45.14	4600
25	Tripura	10939	3930	35.93	285
26	Uttar Pradesh	718667	297235	41.36	19992
27	Uttarakhand	61451	35537	57.83	4007
28	West Bengal	59296	29579	49.88	1657
	Total	**2911961**	**1345990**	**46.14**	**94569**

Source: https://www.indiastat.com and www.panchayat.gov.in/Representation/20WomenRIs

Note: Above details are based on information provided by States/UTs as on November 24, 2016

Methodology

The present paper is based on the inference from secondary data which was published in a government report, subject to various journals and different websites in relation to the selected topic. Further, the secondary source has given some inputs regarding the role of elected women representatives and their decision making and leadership. The social parameters are very important to understand the structural changes also changing over time with the association in capacity building and empowerment. The following table is depicting the information regarding the status of women representation in PRIs

The above table shows that there is 46.14 percent of women elected representatives in India and 94569 women sarpanches in the panchayat raj institution in 2016. Moreover, some state had no data on women sarpanches in the three-tier panchayat. 59.18 percent of elected women representative is the highest percentage in Jharkhand. Moreover, 28.87 percent of elected women is in Daman Diu which the lowest percentage among other states. Gujarat is considered a developed state or called Gujarat model where only 32.90 percent elected women in PRI which indicates also the lowest percentage among other states. There is more than 50 percent of elected representatives in 10 states like Andhra Pradesh, Assam, Odisha, Chhattisgarh, Bihar, Jharkhand, Karnataka, Kerala, Rajasthan and Himachal Pradesh.

Myths were created about women's disinterest and passivity in politics as many studies depicted that they own only nominal power and the real power is vested in the hands of their relatives or spouse etc. But in reality, after coming into power some women proved as effective administrators and worked effectively without intervention of their kith and kin Women entry into local politics from socially and economically weaker sections always helps them to not only hold the power but also empower them to enter in to mainstream politics of the state and nation. (Buch 1999, quoted in Nirmala Buch,2009) Nirmala Buch (2009) argued that participation in local politics women would get respect at workplace but there is no guarantee for their social respect. Through the above observations one can say that women's representation in politics from the marginalised communities have some value at work but still, marginality and humiliation are the part of their social life.

Findings of the paper

The elected women representative's constraint in the gram panchayat work in different states has given below.

Dalit elected women representative and decision making in Haryana

Pal, Mahi (2004) was elicited information about Dalit women elected representatives who participated in Haryana Institution of Rural Development in collaboration with National Commission of Women organized one day state level workshop for understanding the problems being faced by them in carrying out their public/officials duties and for eliciting suggestions from them so as to what sort of supporting system is required for their effective functioning. The methodology of the study was 188 Dalit elected representatives (ERs) of PRIs from all 19 districts of Haryana participated in the workshop. The researcher asked the question about their problem facing day to day in the activities of the panchayat. It was the reported outcome of the workshop.

Four major issues were taken for discussion in the paper that is they are the performance of the business of panchayats and powers; management of common property resources like land; special schemes for the welfare and development of Dalits; and Identification of the problems/hurdles in the way of their functioning. In order to make the programme resourceful the workshop adopted a systematic approach. As a part of discussion, differential issues has been given to each group for discussion and draw some broad conclusions out of it. Surprisingly the important finding from all the groups was that the women leaders have a lack of awareness about power, function, and development scheme.

The only subject in this gram sabha meeting was the construction of roads and house, ponds but the important issues like adverse sex ratio, anaemia among women and children, sanitation and another welfare scheme were not comes under any discussion as the patriarchal society is not interested to know or discuss about it in the open platform. The study found that they were not known the major functions, and powers pertaining to the 16 departments. Consequently, for all the activities of the panchayat, they were dependence on the gram sachiv. They were not much aware of the provision of gram panchayat act, social justice, amenities of the subcommittee and a local committee of punches for effective handling function of gram panchayat.

Common property resource is encroached by the dominant caste in the village. They (elected women) raised the voice against the encroacher but did not succeed. They neither get a chance to build the road on this land, though they approached the higher authorities, still, the struggle is continuing. Pal, M noted that the Dalit women representatives of panchayats had to face opposition from members of the panchayats and village people belonging to higher castes, particularly men, who troubled their various activities of GP. From the discussion, a sarpanch from Panchkula district revealed that gram sachiv and the vice-chairman of the panchayat samiti were hindering the process of development initiated by her GP and she alleged that they were demanding money to release the grant. They alleged that they were forced to sign the proceeding. It is worthwhile to mention that caste domination people were creating a major problem in the state, even though some Dalit women leader assertively spoke at the meeting.

Controlled of male on women sarpanch's activities in Gram Panchayat in Rajasthan

In Rajasthan SCMSPRI,(2011) conducted a study total 150 elected sarpanch taken in the sample study included both male and female sarpanch from the five district Shri Ganganagar, Alwar, Ajmer, Jodhpur, Udaipur. The study illustrates how a large number of women representatives did not reply to questions and left their husbands/relatives to answer on their behalf. On the questions of problems and hurdles in achieving their targets, 23 out of 50 Sarpanch were of the opinion that because of lack of administrative cooperation, inadequate budget provision, and lack of coordination, they could not achieve their goal. Their primary goal was to develop the infrastructure, social and economic development at the village, but they could not fulfil. Despite their low education qualification, they know that the various developmental work needs for holistic development. There are factors like socio-cultural inhibitions, fear of making mistakes, and speak less in meetings makes them less assertive in gram panchayat.

Similarly, in Tamil Nadu, a gram panchayat was controlled the sarpanch pati which in the study that L Thara Bhai (2009) highlighted in Madurai District of Vikramangalam village where the women president is from a backward caste and numerically dominant caste. In this paper depict that despite her education, she was controlled by her husband. The villagers reply that all function was carried out by her husband and she signs, whenever necessary. Her husband is an illiterate person but he was looking after the day to day affairs of the panchayat. However, the upper castes people took all decision regarding the functioning of the gram panchayat. (L Thara Bhai, 2009 pp-263-284).

Regarding the similar finding, Planning commission of India (2010) conducted a study in the States of Madhya Pradesh, Orissa, Chhattisgarh, Gujarat, Jharkhand, and Maharashtra. It was observed from the focus group discussion that in almost all the cases while SC and ST members were elected in the key posts of Panchayats in 6 states, they were not involved in the decision-making process in gram panchayat. It was found that they are generally not invited for panchayats meetings. As such often development initiatives in the village were sanctioned without their knowledge. Though in some of the Panchayats upper castes were in minority, they influenced all the important works. The study remarks that these facts are a sad commentary on the functioning of Indian democracy at the grassroots level.

Hinders of the Elected Women Members in their Performance in Bihar

Anuradha Ranjan Kumari, S.K. Dubey and U.S. Gautam (2016) conducted a study total 75 women representatives randomly selected from Pusa and Kalyanpur block of Samastipur district in Bihar on what hinders the elected women village panchayat members in their role performance. This paper illuminates what is the hinder that the elected women were confronting at the gram panchayat. Therefore, the study identified the problem was facing in Bihar that lack of unity among the villagers, caste-based co-operation in the village, conflicts in the village, lack of education among Panchayat members, lack of resources for development works, lack of knowledge of the members about the development project, carelessness among villagers for development works, bribery and misappropriation of fund non-availability of persons well versed with the rural projects. Among the problems of these, the lack of resource in the development and lack of knowledge of the members about the development project is major problem women leader were facing.

The Constraints of Tribal and Non-Tribal Women Sarpanch in Chhatishgarh

Jyoti Kumari, et al (2017) conducted a study in Bilaspur district of Chhattisgarh state during the year 2015-2016. Out of 645-gram panchayat of Bilaspur district, 336-gram panchayat was having women sarpanch, from which one-third panchayats that are 112 (56 tribal and 56 non-tribal) were taken randomly from respective lists.

The study finds the economic constraints are lack of funds from govt. for development work, lack of honorarium to women sarpanch working at village level and no work is initiated without giving bribes. In this paper, shown that 53 percent of the non-tribal women sarpanch was problems with bribing for work accomplished whereas 67 percent of tribal women sarpanch faced the same problem. By interpreting the difference between tribal and non-tribal women, the tribal women sarpanch were facing seriously in term of functioning of Gram Panchayat than non- tribal.

Technical constraints are lack of regular training to women sarpanches, lack of knowledge regarding PRI and development programme, lack of timely information regarding different rural development programmes. Regarding the administrative constraints are delay in sanctions of permission for development work from the upper level was highest among the major constraints faced by tribal women sarpanch, gram sabha restricts the village, lack of administrative and financial power to women sarpanches, lack of co-operation from society/other institutes and lack of discipline in gents members at gram panchayat and lack of good staff in village panchayat office. This study shows that tribal women sarpanch were confronting more constraints than non-tribal women sarpanch.

The Success story of Women elected representative at the Gram Panchayat functioning

PRIA (2003) study in the Manaklaav Gram Panchayat in Rajasthan, during the Gram Panchayat elections, the seat for the Sarpanch was reserved for a

Scheduled Caste (SC) woman, therefor Dalit women became a sarpanch after spend 3 lakh rupees in the village. Initially, her husband and in law were taken all decision in the affaire of the gram panchayat. Subsequently, she has, however, gained confidence and now not only does she attend Panchayat meetings but also gives her opinion in Panchayat related matters. She had received training from one organization called UNNATI thereby develop the self-confident and gaining knowledge on PRIs. She was never influenced by the higher caste communities. During her tenure, she constructed the work such as drains, Kharanja, five Anganwadi, Rajiv Gandhi Pathshalas and a Sabha Bhawan has been constructed. In this study, it observed that Dalit women became assertive and worked very effectively at the gram panchayat.

Furthermore, the depiction of Dalit women struggles in PRIA (2003) studies at Saddha Gram Panchayat of Himmatnagar district and Taluka in Gujarat about how Dalit sarpanch struggle to achieve social justice. Despite the low education, she undertakes number development activities such as constructed a road, a water pipeline, a water tank, a community hall, installed an electric motor and so on. Besides, she helps the SCs and STs and physically handicap families to draw funds from various government schemes. The popularity prevailed in her panchayat, but the members of the Panchayat and upper caste became jealous of her popularity. Their main objection against she was "how could a mere woman, that too a Dalit, take entire credit for rejuvenating the village"? The Panchayat members continued their relentless efforts to humiliate and mentally torture her. They alleged that since she belonged to a Scheduled Caste, she was using the Atrocity Act to harass people. As she did not become the puppet of the upper caste, they passed a no-confidence motion against her. The election was held again, was re-elected by a thumping majority, thus proving her immense popularity. The case study says being a Dalit and women, it is very difficult for the Dalit women sarpanch to undertake the activities in the gram panchayat, though the Dalits women have the potential to rule the village. The following are the findings where women sarpanch more effectively involved in the development process than the male leader in GP in the planning process in Karnataka

In Ainapur and Kanmadi panchayat a higher percentage of women planned for the following activities when compared to men: levelling of lands/proper weeding, proper irrigation facilities, seeds and fertilizers at subsidized rates, and good quality seeds/fertilizers/medicines. While men were more focus on the check dam, an adaptation of new technology was higher than that of women. Similarly, in Almel and Rampur P.A. Panchayats with related agriculture, it was noticed that the percentage of women who have planned for providing employment and setting up of industries, agriculture-based work, usage of good quality seeds and fertilizers and adaptation of new technology is much higher than the percentage of men who have planned. It remarks that the women leader were more actively plan in agriculture field which gains more income for the standard living of families.

In education, women leaders have planned the awareness of good teaching facilities in school education and better facilities in Anganwadi centre. In health areas, both male and female planned equally for better medical facilities. Furthermore, in water and sanitation development both were equally participating and planned for better development. With regard to poverty alleviation programme, female leaders were more concerned with providing houses to the poor, food and clothing, and employment opportunities.

Women sarpanchs have more awareness of gender budgeting and setting up of industrial units by using untied funds was found more in number. Moreover, women have more concern towards social issues like reducing child labour, PDS and transport facilities. In this study, it shows that the participation of male and female in gram panchayat meeting and gram sabha was equally good. Therefore, women leader were never less than a male counterpart in the functioning of the gram panchayat activities.

Capacity building and empowerment of elected women representative in Rajasthan and Madhya Pradesh

The Institute of Social Development with the support of the planning commission of India (2008) carried out a study Empowerment of Women through Participation in Panchayati Raj in the states of Rajasthan and Madhya Pradesh. The study chooses Jodhpur and Jaipur which belong to the non-tribal area as well as high and low literacy. Similarly, Udaipur and Dungarpur is a tribal dominated district of Rajasthan. Similarly, in Madhya Pradesh, Bhopal and sehore district is non-tribal areas, whereas Khargaon and Jhabua district is the tribal area. The respondent was 285 respondents which include 97 present women members of the selected panchayats,62 outgoing women members of selected panchayats, 66 male members of selected panchayats, both present and outgoing, and 60 women candidates who contested last two panchayat elections but were unsuccessful.

Training improves the behaviour of the person so that he/she "becomes more useful and productive for himself/herself as well as for the organization of which he/she is a part", asserts Jeff Harris. The training aims at a lasting improvement "on the job, not for knowing more but for behaving differently", observe Linton and Pareek (1990 cited in ISD,2008). After the post-training period, the women elected leader, during panchayat meetings, the involvement of women has significantly improved. Listing of people below the poverty line and preparation of village development plans emerged as areas where improvement was most marked, organizing community programme has improved, mobilizing the resource and preparing budget conspicuously developed by intervening the training programme. One important area was developed among elected women is that feeling more capable to address public meetings thereby increased the leaders among them. Despite widespread illiteracy and low education of elected women, the experience of working with PRIs tends to help women members to become aware of their structure and functions gram panchayat

It is worthwhile to mentioned that it was noticeable improve of awareness level of elected women on the subject that tenure PRIs reservation of seats for women in panchayats, reservation of seats for scheduled castes and scheduled tribes, quorum of gram panchayat, quorum of gram sabha, minimum number of gram sabha meetings in a year, interval of gram panchayat meetings, minimum number of standing committees of gram panchayat.

Involvement of elected women in Capacity Building training and changed the scenario

UNDP started a project Capacity Building of Elected Women Representatives and Functionaries of Panchayati Raj Institutions by the Ministry of Panchayati Raj (MoPR), Government of India and United Nations Development Programme (UNDP) India, from 2003 -2008. One district each of the10 selected states (Bihar, Chhattisgarh, Jharkhand, Haryana, Madhya Pradesh, Maharashtra, Odisha, Rajasthan, Uttarakhand, and Uttar Pradesh) was chosen. The primary objective of the project is to build capacities of elected women representatives (EWRs) for effective functioning and setting of women's agenda. The paper elaborate on how elected women representatives developed assertiveness after participates in capacity building training in Odisha and Maharashtra.

In Odisha, Angul District and Anugul, Banarpal, Talcher, Kaniha, Pallahara, Chhendipada, Athamallik and Kishorenagar were blocks and undertook the study areas. A forum was initiative with help of Institute Social Economic Development called the 'Mahila Manch Panchayat Nirvachan Abhiyan and it is an informal association of EWR, SHG members and Anganwadi workers. Due to this forum, women leader can participate in Palli sabha meeting, prior to that they were prohibited to participate. Moreover, forum members became members of Parent-Teachers Associations, which has led to a perceptible improvement in the quality of education in these villages and elected women leader raised their voice in gram sabha/Palli Sabha regarding the issue education, sanitation, problem of alcohol in their village. Through the forum, the computer training programme was provided to them. Subsequently, women PRI members have become more articulate and assertive in the gram panchayat meetings.

In Maharastra, five-gram panchayats 43 women leaders were selected from each of the three blocks Gadchiroli, Kurkheda, and Armori. A local NGO, Aamhi Aamchya Arogya Sathi (AAAS) provided training to the elected women leaders in Gadchiroli which is a tribal region and Naxal controlled areas. After the project of AAAS's intervention provided the network of SHG and EWRs were included in the training programmes, therefore, the capacity building and enabling them to speak out in public. The training programme was organized for EWRs as well as a villager for gender sensitize to enable them to work in cooperation with the women. On account of the training, the EWRs raised the voice in gram sabha meeting for SCs and STs who were eligible for inclusion in poverty alleviation schemes like IAY, and the Maharashtra Rural Employment Guarantee Scheme (MREGS).

Conclusion

Some studies indicated that elected women representatives had successfully controlled the functioning of the gram panchayat. On the other side, some study revealed that gram panchayat activities were controlled by the male counterpart. In Haryana, the land resource was captured by the upper caste people and the Dalit women sarpanch are unable to run the functioning the gram panchayat. Due to the intervening of the training programme to the elected women representative in Rajasthan and Madhya Pradesh, they can organize the meeting and developing leadership in different programmes, even though they had not so higher education qualification. Due to not participate in any training programme of SCs and STs Women sarpanch in Odisha in Khurdha district, the Pati Sarpanch and other colleague were running the gram panchayat on behalf of them. In addition to that, caste and gender discrimination should be in policy framework to address constraints which elected women are threatening in the functioning of the panchayat thereby the women empowerment is possible.

References

Anuradha Ranjan Kumari, S.K. Dubey and U.S. Gautam (2016), What Hinders the Elected Women Village Panchayat Members in their Role Performance? Journal of Community Mobilization and Sustainable Development Vol. 11(1), 61-65, January-June, 2016 www.reserchgate. net. in.

Jyoti Kumari, M. L. Sharma, and Akanksha Pandey,2017, Constraints And Suggestions Regarding Role Expectation And Role Performance Of Tribal and Non-tribal women Sarpanch Towards Rural Development In Bilaspur District (C.G.), India, Plant Archives Vol. 17 No. 2, 2017 pp. 1184-1188 https://www.scopus.com/results/.

L.Thara Bhai (2009), gender, caste and politic in rural Tamil Nadu, BS Baviskar and George Mathew(Eds), inclusion and exclusion in local governance, sage publication.

Narayana (2005) Local Governance without Capacity Building: Ten Years of Panchayati Raj, Economic and Political Weekly, Vol. 40, No. 26 (Jun. 25 - Jul. 1, 2005), pp. 2822-2832 Stable URL: https://www.jstor.org/stable/4416821 Accessed: 30-01-2019 08:19 UTC.

Nirmala Buch (2009) Reservation for Women in Panchayats: A Sop in Disguise?, EPW, Vol. 44, Issue No. 40, 03 Oct 2009, pp-8-10.

Ministry of Panchayat Raj, National Capability Building Framework- 2014, Government of India.

Pal, M (2004) Caste and patriarchy in the panchayat, EPW, VOL.39 No.32 (Aug .7-13.2004).pp. 3581-3583 www.jstore.org.

Planning commission,(2010) research study at a glance (2006-2007), Strengthening The Capacity of Elected Women in Preparation of Village Level Planning in Women-Led Panchayats, planning commission report, retrieved from http://planningcommission.gov.in/reports/sereport/.

Planning Commission, Government of India, New Delhi (2010) Impact of Bottom-up Planning under PRIs and Women participation therein in the States of Madhya Pradesh, Orissa, Chhattisgarh, Gujarat, Jharkhand, and Maharashtra.

Promod Kumar Ray (2016) empowering women and gender sensitive in local governance: A study of Khurdha District of Odisha. Smita Nayak(eds),wither women:a shift from endowment to empowerment, Edu Pedia publication,New Delhi www.books.google.co.in.

PRIA, (2003), Dalit leader in the panchayat, published by PRAI, www.pria.org.

Sudipta Biswas,2016, Empowerment of Women through Panchayati Raj Institutions: A Critical Analysis, Vol. 4, Issue 1, Asian Journal of Multidisciplinary Studies pp-208-215.

Shiv Charan Mathur social policy research institute, 2011, Analysing the Strengths and Weaknesses of Women Elected Representatives in Panchayati Raj Institutions in Rajasthan", supported by Rosa-Luxemburg-Stiftung (RLS), Berlin, Germany. www.panchayatgyan.gov.in/documents.

The Institute of Social Development,(2008), a study Empowerment of Women through Participation in Panchayati Raj Institutions: Some Structural Impediments and a Training Strategy in the states of Rajasthan and Madhya Pradesh with the support of planning commission, http://www.nipccd-earchive.wcd.nic.in.

The State of Panchayats: 2007-2008, an independent assessment, volume one: Thematic report, IRMA, Anand, and Gujarat.

UNDP and minister of panchayat raj, India,(2008-2009) From Reservation to Participation Capacity Building of Elected Women Representatives and Functionaries of Panchayati Raj Institutions project Report.

Notes

1. Dr. J. Rani Ratna Prabha, Assistance Professor, Centre for the Study of Social Exclusion and Inclusive Policy, School of Social Science, University of Hyderabad, Email id:-ranihcu@yahoo.com, MOB-9440486381.

   Sudam Tandi, Ph.D. Research Scholar, Centre for the Study of Social Exclusion and Inclusive Policy, School of Social Science, University of Hyderabad, Email id:-sudamtandimsw@gmail.com MOB-8249844080.

Chapter - 9

Social Exclusion and Education of Marginalized Girls

Dr. Wesly Kumar V S J[1] and Dr. S. Ramudu[2]

Introduction

Even though the education plays an important role in achieving a greater degree of social justice, the educational institutions are not equipped the Dalit children to the best of their ability for securing a meaningful place in society. In India, a large number of children are still excluded from the educational system and hence cannot participate meaningfully in the economic, social, political and cultural life of their communities. The current educational policies might have failed to address the needs of children who are vulnerable to marginalization and exclusion. With this backdrop, the paper presents the inequalities, reasons and barriers in participation of marginalized girls in school from the perspective of Social Exclusion. So far the education of marginal sections of the society has been considered in terms of poverty which is a single economic factor. It is argued here that exclusion of education can happen by several factors.

First, the paper briefly discusses what we mean by social exclusion, and it is followed various dimensions of education of girls from the framework of social exclusion. And finally, the paper presents an empirical situation of slums of Hyderabad.

Meaning of Social Exclusion

According to Oxford dictionary, exclusion means to shut out whether by thrusting out or preventing admission or to debar someone from some activity or place. The concept of social exclusion was used in France to articulate the deprivations manifested by high unemployment with reference to persistent and systematic multiple deprivations (De Hann, 2001).But the United Kingdom has identified the social exclusion as more than poverty. Both poverty and social exclusion can be transmitted from one generation to another generation

(Social Exclusion Unit, 1998). The Europeans in general have conceived social exclusion as a distinct concept which is different from poverty; people who are socially excluded need not to be poor but all the poor are socially excluded (De Hann,1997). Sen (1998) observes that the roots of the social exclusion are spread in deprivation; it is an ideal measurement to understand the poverty as capabilities deprivation. He makes a distinction between the situations where some people are kept outside and some people are included. He describes those situations as unfavorable exclusion and unfavorable inclusion. **In** the unfavorable exclusion people are kept outside whereas in case of unfavorable inclusion people are with unequal treatment though within the system but that carries the adverse effects as in case of unfavorable exclusion (Sen, 2000). Buvinic (2005) has meant the social exclusion as the inability of an individual to participate in the political, economic and social functioning of a society, and the denial of equal access to opportunities imposed by certain groups in society upon others.

Finally, we can say social exclusion is the denial of ownership, access and control over resources; it is the denial of opportunity for education, health care, housing, amenities and basic needs; right of human dignity; social interaction and access to social spaces; and the denial of constitutional and human rights. Social exclusion is a form of discriminatory practice. In the societies, exclusion takes the form of segregation of a group of people from social, economic and educational domains. It exists in various spheres and forms. Social exclusion is lack of access to resources and inability of utilization. Lack of access to education and employment is an example for social exclusion. People who are socially excluded are vulnerable individuals of underprivileged who are at higher risk of facing multi-dimensional exclusion. The causes of social exclusion have been attributed to the economic and social changes and weaknesses in government policies and services also. Thus, social exclusion is connected with equity, discrimination and deprivation (Piron and Curran, 2005). The literature indicates that social exclusion is a multidimensional process of progressive social rupture, detaching groups and individuals from social relations and institutions and preventing them from full participation in the normal, normatively prescribed activities of the society in which they live.

Girls and Education

Socially excluded groups are found in countries of all regions, but accurate international figures on the numbers of girls from socially excluded groups who are out of school are generally unavailable. Lewis and Lockheed (2006) estimated that 70 per cent of all girls who were out of primary school are from socially excluded groups. This share has undoubtedly increased, given the continued progress in girls' education observed over the past decade. The most recent data available report that 39 million girls were out of primary school in 2006, for a minimum of 27 million girls from socially excluded groups who were not attending primary school in that year (UNESCO Institute for Statistics, 2008). A few household surveys in developing countries provide more specific information. These show that, girls from socially excluded groups are less likely to have ever enrolled in school or to be currently attending school, and they complete fewer years of school than either boys from socially excluded groups or children from "majority" groups. When these gender gaps within socially excluded groups are combined with the gaps arising from social exclusion alone, the differences in school participation between socially excluded girls and majority children can be stark (Arunatilake ,2006; Nguyen, 2006; UNESCO Institute for Statistics, 2005).

In India, girls lag behind the boys in education largely for the reason of interdependency between gender and culture. The lower castes suffer disproportionately in education relative to the mainstream population and to boys. Lewis and Lockheed (2006) estimate that these excluded girls make up more than 70 percent of the millions of out-of-school girls in the developing world. The importance of ethnic and linguistic divisions, their determinants, and the impact on girls' schooling is the subject of this volume of studies. Recent global assessments of education have noted that rural children, low-income children, and children from ethnic minorities are at risk. Some of these assessments have provided estimates of out-of-school children by gender, location, and income (World Bank 2005b; UIS 2005; Wils, Carrol, and Barrow 2005; Lloyd 2005; Birdsall, Levine, and Ibrahim 2005).

Social exclusion arises from three main sources of stigma: (a) past trauma at the hands of a dominant or majority population, such as a recent history of slavery or dispossession of a homeland; (b) membership in ethnic groups that are differentiated by colour, language and religion; and (c) membership of groups that are assigned lower social status in their country, such as that accorded to lower castes in countries with caste systems (Horowitz, 1985; Meerman, 2005). *Child labour is identified as a key hindrance to children attending school.* For some social and religious groups, formal sector job opportunities are limited by discriminatory employment practices. Compounding this, the marginalization of specific groups in relation to livelihoods goes even further: in India, some low caste communities face physical and well as social segregation from mainstream society, limiting informal economic opportunities too – as well as discrimination in education systems. a report concluded that high unemployment rates among low caste communities reduced motivation to send children to school because of the little economic benefit expected from schooling (Sachar Committee Report, 2006).Discrimination in the labour market contributes to low labour market aspirations for children from these communities and reduces the perceived benefits of schooling.In India, poor or absent water and sanitation facilities have a more significant negative effect on schooling for children from marginalized communities. (NEG Fire Seminar, 2011 as cited in the India OOSCI Study).

Some studies have shown that corporal punishment contributes to dropping out (Reddy and Sinha, 2010). Humiliation, harassment and abuse by upper caste teachers towards children of Dalits have been shown to undermine their motivation to stay in schools (Nambissan, 2000). And alsoteacher prejudice towards weak learners has been shown to motivate students, who are often from marginalized communities (PROBE, 1999).

According to the ILO, India has the highest number of working children in the world, an estimated 29 million children between the age of 5 and 14 go to work, even though the Child labour is illegal in India. Girls often work in informal sector such as domestic work or paid house help, which are not counted in official statistics. Most of these children belong to the poorest, most marginalized communities, including Dalits.

A Profile of Dalits

From the Table 1, it may be observed that the Dalits are being excluded in various forms of in their everyday life. Out of the total population, Dalits represents 16.48 percent and only about 54 percent are literate. The female literacy rate is only 41.9 percent. Despite many safeguards and Acts, about 80 percent are dropped from schools. Thus, the Dalits are excluded from education. About 76 percent of Dalits are still depends on agricultural and allied activities.

Table 1: Dalits of India – A Profile

S. No	*Area*	*Representation of Dalits*
1	Population	16.5
2	Literacy – Total	54.7
3	Male	66.6
4	Female	41.9
5	Dropout from schools	79.9
6	Cultivators	25.4
7	Agricultural labour	49.0
8	Agricultural and allied activities	76.2
9	Below the poverty line	56.0
10	Manual scavenging	100.00
11	Discriminated against	100.00

Source: Prakash Louis (2008) in 'Towards inclusion and equity'[3]

The literacy rate of Dalits is 54.7 as against the rate of general population of 68.81 percent. Thus, they are far behind of others. Figures of the government during 2011 show that there were 5,816,673 elementary school teachers. As of March 2012 there were 2,127,000 secondary school teachers. Education has also been made free for children for 6 to 14 years of age or up to class VIII under the Right of Children to Free and Compulsory Education Act 2009 (Brijesh 2014). This primary education scheme has also shown a high Gross Enrollment Ratio of 93–95% for the last three years in some states. Significant improvement in staffing and enrollment of girls has also been made as a part of this scheme. The current scheme for universalization of *Education for All* is one of the largest education initiatives in the world. Studies have shown that the representation of Dalits in education is lower than their proportionate representation in the population. (Wankhede, 2001). Paranjape's (2007) analysis of Maharashtra shows that the distribution of education is extremely skewed among the backward sections of the society. The inequality in education is higher among girls than boys and the caste based inequality is sharper in rural areas. The urban boys show the least disparity whereas rural girls show the highest disparity in educational attainment.

The Table 2 demonstrates that the Dalits have attained comparatively better literacy rate. In the last four decades. Literacy rate of the Dalits has improved considerably from 10.27 in 1961 to 72.99 in 2011. This trend indicates positive movement among Dalits marking the proportional to the rhetoric of special provisions made for the weaker sections. Despite the provisions, the growth of Dalits education was very slow compared to the literacy level of general population. The socio-economic conditions were also responsible for educational growth. The government of India had confessed that the officials of educational departments were displaying a hostile attitude towards the education of the Dalits. However, the consciousness of the education is being generated among the Dalits (Yagati, 2003). The data show the variation in the literacy rates among Dalits and general population. In the general population, female literacy rate is poor and the position of Dalits female is worse (Government of India: YEAR) When we compare the literacy levels of Dalits and other castes, still, this community is lagging behind in educational achievements which highlight the significance of their deprivation.

Table 2 : Gender Wise Literacy Trend Among Dalits (S.c's) And Total Population

Year	*All*			*Scheduled Castes*		
	Male	*Female*	*Total*	*Male*	*Female*	*Total*
1961	34.44	12.95	24.02	16.96	3.29	10.3
1971	39.45	39.45	29.46	22.36	6.44	14. 7
1981	65.60	65.50	43.67	31.12	10.93	21.4
1991	64.13	64.13	52.21	49.91	23.76	37.4
2001	75.30	53.70	64.84	66.64	41.90	54.7
2011	80.90	64.60	73.00	75.20	56.50	66.1

Source: National commission for S.C's and ST's, 5th report, 1998-99, vol- I; Census Report, 2001; Report of National literacy mission at http://www.nlm.nic.incensusmp.nic.in/censusmp/All-PDF/6Literacy21.12.;

Exclusion and inequality in Education

The educational inequalities arise for the following reasons: poverty, home environment, and habitat. The poor cannot afford to meet the expenses of education. The poor exposure of the children leads to poor performance. Wide inequalities arise from difference in home environments. A child from a rural household or a slum does not have the same opportunity as a child from an upper class home with educated parents and in the places where there is no educational institution, the children do not get the opportunity as those who have educational institutions in their vicinity. Children in rural areas studying in poorly equipped schools have to compete with the children of urban schools which are well equipped (Rao, 1990).

The forms of inequality from ancient to modern times are based on caste, gender and political-economic and other inequalities that were accepted as natural things. Many people supported the Indian tradition defending the traditional social hierarchy till a resistance till Dr. Ambedkar came to resist in a big way. Even though it is impossible to root out the inequality from the society, particularly from a dynamic modern society, it is possible to eliminate or reduce poverty, hunger, homelessness and illiteracy, and it is possible to make education available universally to all (Beteille, 2001).The roots of educational deprivation of Dalits are traced back to their position as Untouchables in the caste structure.

According to the Sixth All India Educa-tional Survey of NCERT (1998), Dalits mainly avail government schooling. Of the Dalits' children in primary schools, 91.3 percent in rural areas and 64.6 percent in urban areas were in schools managed by state government and local bodies. Many of these schools are plagued by various problems such as lack of basic infrastructure, classrooms, teachers, and teaching aids. Dilapidated buildings, leaking roofs and mud floors appear quite common in schools and provide a depressing atmosphere for children. Teaching aids, apart from black-boards, are relatively absent. There is a problem of absenteeism of students and teachers etc. The government of Andhra Pradesh has identified the government schools across the state that do not have toilet and drinking water facilities on the directions of the Supreme Court. Half of the 80,000 government schools lack these basic facilities. Though the other half has toilets, they do not function due to lack of water and maintenance[3]. The Dalit children do not have access to quality education. They also face discrimination and discouragement from higher caste community members who perceive education for Dalits as both a waste and a threat. Their hostility to-wards Dalits' education is linked to the perception that Dalits are not meant to be educated, are incapable of being educated, or if educated, would pose a threat to village hierarchies and power relations (Vasavi, 1997).

Dalits children's right to education free from discrimination is undermined by the treatment they receive in school. Teachers maintain and impart discriminatory attitudes in their classrooms, forcing children to sit in the back of the room, segregating Dalits children from non-Dalits during lunchtime, forbidding non-Dalit children from sitting next to Dalit children or touching their plates, intentionally limiting Dalits student participation in class, subjecting them to verbal abuse and grading them low marks. There are instances of Dalit students being made to sit and eat separately. Even Dalit teachers are segregated from non-Dalit teachers in accessing food and water during lunchtime (Human Righta Watch 2017).

The Dalits and their children are continued to suffer from various forms of social disabilities as well as economic deprivation, and also lack of education. The drop-out rate among Dalits students indicate the status of their educational development. The enrolment of children of Dalits has increased considerably at the primary stage because of the educational policies but the participation is less in proportion to their share in population at the primary level. Though dropouts are declining the gender disparities are still existing. The Dalits in slum are vulnerable due to associated influences of low socio-economic status, lower parental literacy rates and others.

Gender and social exclusion among the Dalit

Though there is a positive development with respect to girls' education, the overall difference in the enrolment ratio between boys and girls remains at around 10 percent (see Table 3). The situation is bad at the upper primary stage as less than 60% of girls are enrolled at this stage, and it is worse for children of the scheduled castes living in rural areas, especially if they are girls. A similar problem of inequity in coverage and participation can be observed with respect to different social groups traditionally identified as underprivileged. For some religious minorities also it is quite disappointing. The recent Sachar Committee Report (GoI2006a) has pointed out that same situation of children from the marginalised communities.

The traditional sexual division of domestic labor is not favorable for a girls' education. She is supposed to be essentially as the home maker, which requires informal training of cooking, washing clothes, cleaning the house and taking care of young children. The girl child is a helping hand for the mother. So whenever mother falls sick, the grown up girl will have to become the substitute and carry out most of the mother's work. Even when a sibling falls sick she will remain at home to take care of the sibling which will allow the mother to continue her work so that there is no loss of income. The girl child also collects water from the tanker that supplies water to the slum whenever there is no water supply through taps. In traditional thinking the onset of puberty brings along with it a sense of responsibility on the part of parents and the child. The parents are reminded of their duty of arranging marriage, and before that she should be properly trained in all domestic works. It is also their responsibility that she should remain virgin until marriage. The onus is on the part of the girl also to avoid boys. Since the school and education come on the way of avoiding boys the parent think about marriage, and in their opinion as the girl has to leave the natal home and join the conjugal family one day there is no need higher education for her. The traditional life combined together with ill- health and domestic demands often causes the girl to absent from school frequently and finally quit the school one day. The parents also do not mind if the child loses interest in studies and drops out from school, in the above social and cultural backdrop the higher dropout rate among the girls is quite understandable.

Table 3: Gross Enrollment Ratio (Ger)

Year	*General enrollment ratio of SC's*		
	Boys	*Girls*	*Total*
2001-02	95.7	74.6	85.5
2002-03	87.1	74.4	81.1
2003-04	88.95	77.15	83.35
2005-05	106.5	90.3	98.8
2005-06	109.5	93.7	101.9

Source: GoI (2007a, 2008), Govinda, R (2010)

The research studies explored the reasons for children's drop out without completing primary school. Two clear reasons are evident. For a substantial number, particularly between ages 6 and 11 years, education is not considered necessary, and many, especially urban boys, need to provide some income for the household. It is also evident from the NSS data that very few children in the younger age group reported lack of a school nearby as a reason for leaving school without completing 5 years of education; a negligibly small percentage of children in rural and urban areas dropped out for the reason ofschools at long distance. Further, more boys than girls in the 10–14 age groupdropout for providing income to household. For girls 6–11 and for boys 10–14 age is the time for gettingengagedin domestic chores. Thus, participation in wage labour or domestic work continues to prevent children from attending school. It isalso understandable that as children grow older, they have better chances of participating in the labour force, which prevents them from attending school.A large proportion of girls aged 10–14 had to leave school for other reasons, whichincluded socio-cultural factors such as early marriage.

Several Dalit children are prone to dropout[4] due to many factors such as irregular attendance, low learning levels and repetition etc. They are not moving for further up in education due to frequent absenteeism from school andpoor performance in studies which cause repetition of the class. This kind of problems is called 'silent exclusion' (Lewin, 2007). The private schools are better than government schools with regard to dropout rates. The dropping out is a concern for the government when children silently get excluded from the school. One of the reasons for dropping out of the Dalit children is their low socio-economic background. Another important reason for dropout is the passive learning experiences in schools. Disinterest in studies in combination with others leads to dropping out from schools. Poor performance, irregular attendance, grade repetition and overage also affect the schooling of children (Das, 2008).

In the schools and colleges Dalit children are victims of silent exclusion. They are labeled as 'students of no interest in studies'. With frequent ill health, and domestic problem in addition to the branding them up as 'students of no interest in studies' the students engages in frequent absenteeism, and eventually dropout of school after attending sometime. Many children who get excluded from the studies belong to first generation learners as their parents are illiterates. The children of illiterate parents face tremendous challenges in schooling and in learning at an acceptable level as they receive no support or little support after school hours. Many face the threat of silent exclusion from the school system (Govinda and Bandyopadhyay, 2008).

Dalits Girls in the Slums of Hyderabad

An empirical study[5] conducted in the slums of Hyderabad (Wesly, 2017) as part of Ph.D., work has revealed that in 11 out of 26 (42.3 percent) households the children are dropped out from the school and the remaining from the college. Out of the 11 who dropped out from the school 6 (54.5 percent) are from primary school level and 3 (27.3 percent) at high school level and 2 (18.2 percent) at upper primary school level. Though the number of those dropped out is not significant at primarily level it does indicate higher proportion of dropped outs after high school which strongly correlates with the economic reasons and failure to cope up with high demand of time for studies. It is also because lack of self-motivation and the lack of parental initiation due to their preoccupation with earning their livelihood. Further, the migration of the parents and late admission of children into school add to the noxious phenomena. The dropout in high school is mainly due to domestic problems, onset of puberty and discrimination in school. Teachers think that the poverty, lack of initiatives by the government and the parents are important factors for dropout of children from schools.Of all the reasons poverty seems to be the main reason for dropping out of school. In fact lack of initiative from the parents is in a way linked to poverty. The social exclusion after admission in school, relates to attendance of the child and dropout from school. The discrimination shall be examined in terms of seating arrangement, and caste background which are reflections of social exclusion.

About 26 (17.3 percent) parents have cited various reasons for the dropout of their children from the school. These include, children are not keen to attend the school; busy in household work; unable to pay the fee; attained puberty and ill treatment of fellow students and teachers. The girl students tend to dropout due to the demands of the parents for the reasons stated below. The household work and attaining puberty are the two dominant reasons for a girl child to quit the school.

Eight out of 19 (42.1 percent) of the teachers observe that there are educational disparities between male and female Dalit children. They feel that the girl children are being excluded from the education as many of the parents in slums prefer the girls to stay at home to take care of siblings and to attend household work. Besides this there is another important reason for discouraging the girl child's education apart from the cultural notion of girl child being the homemaker. It is covering long distance by bus and avoiding eve teaching and sexual harassment. Sending a girl child to a primary school is not a problem for the school which is located close to the slum and the child is not generally subjected to sexual harassment. When a girl child matures the parents find that they are in a problematic situation. They can neither provide protection to her nor control her or other's behavior. The girl herself finds it difficult to defend when by boys particularly of upper castes or male teachers tease her or behave in an inappropriate manner. For instance, Leelavathi, a 10th class student says that most of the girls do not prefer to take mid-day meal before the boys because some of the boys make comments on girls.

The case studies collected from the field presented below amply explain the reasons for the drop out from the school.

Case No1: Mamatha was studying in the government high school at Shivarampally. She discontinued her studies while studying 7th class because her mother asked her not to go to school due to the troubles created by boys. Her neighbor Padma discontinued studies since there is no proper transport facility to the high school situated at Shivarampally. Most of the parents do not prefer to send the girls by the public transport facility, as the same are packed and over crowed and in those situations they are subject to harassment by boys who travel in these buses.

Case No 2: Lakshmi who lives in Premavathipet Harijanawada walks for about 25 minutes to reach the school which is about three kilometers from her residence. She was 15 years and while studying 9th class she encountered some boys when coming back from the school. They followed her and teased her making unwelcome gestures and comments. She was scared and screamed for help. An old woman, a passerby, helped her. On hearing this, her mother did not allow her to continue in school, even though she was good in studies. She may continue through the open school but she has no idea bout it. Her father wants her to study at least up to the intermediate level but due to the incident her parents forced her to stop the studies.

Case No:3: Divya, a 9th class student living at Gopanapally says that her mother attends the works of construction and her father sells vegetables on a pushing cart. She says that uniform and books have not been provided by the school in spite of her repeated requests. She could not attend the school sometimes due to ill- health. Despite all these problems, she could get 50 percent of marks in her examinations. She is interested to pursue further studies, but her parents wanted to stop her education after 10th class because of eve teasing and sexual harassment by boys.

Recommendations

The Government alone cannot take the sole responsibility. Parents too have to play a major role. They should always encourage a girl for higher education even if they are illiterate. They should be made to understand that if we educate a boy, we educate one person. If we educate a girl, we educate a family – and a whole nation. By sending a girl to school, she is far more likely to ensure that her children also receive education. As many investing in a girl's education is investing in a nation. So, the government should intervene and help parents educating girl child.

Families and communities must be important partners with schools in developing curriculum and managing children's education. Basic education should be free or cost very little. Wherever it is possible, there should be stipends and scholarships to compensate families for the loss of girls' household labour. Also, school hours should be flexible so that children can help at home and still attend classes.

Many parents worry about girls travelling long distances on their own. Many parents also prefer to have daughters taught by women. Girls do best when they receive early childhood care, which enhances their self-esteem and prepares them for school.

In relation to the schools, the following measures need to be undertaken: The authorities must acknowledge the existence of caste discrimination and fight against the discrimination and exclusion, and they should address the issue of caste relations and human rights. Teachers must be sensitized on caste discrimination during training programs; enabling pedagogies must be evolved; and specific academic support to Dalits. Hence, there should be no caste-based discrimination on the school premises. Anyone, children be provided including the teachers, violating it should be given severe punishment.

The appointment of female teachers, and hostel facilities for slum children will help improve access and retention of girls in school.

Providing better education to the Dalit girls will automatically ensure a social status for them.

Parental support towards girls helps them better learning. However, poor Dalit parents are unable to provide the support needed, such as: books, educational study aids like a study desk or table for the student's use, and also arranging tuitions after school hours. To compensate for the effects of poverty on home learning resources, there is a need to arrange compensatory programmes. These programmes for socially excluded children are helps them for complement overall schooling investments.

After-school tuitions at school for marginalized girls helps to raise school enrolment, reduce repetition and drop-outs, and boostexamination results. After school tutoring programmes need to be implemented with caution to avoid these negative consequences.

Conclusion

The framework of social exclusion enables to closely examine the education of girls in multi-dimensional perspective. The girls are in general excluded category of individuals in education among the groups that face the social exclusion everywhere in the world and India is not an exception. In general the Indian scenario reveals that the literacy of women is lower than the men and it is true in case of Dalits who have been excluded category for ages. Not only that the rates of enrolment among the scheduled caste girls is less than the boys their drop out rate is also high. It is so because of cultural reasons apart from economic reasons. They have to remain at home to attend the domestic chorus, and parents are more concerned their marriage and training them towards that end. Most disappointing aspect is their vulnerability of being sexually harassment in the school and outside the school which encourages to them to drop out of school. Unless the government addresses these issues, the situation of girls' education may not improve.

References

Arunatilake, Nisha (2006), Education participation in Sri Lanka—why all are not in school, *International Journal of Educational Research* 45.3 (2006): 137-152.

Beteille, A. (2001) 'Equality and universality', *Economic and Political Weekly*, Sep 22:3619-25.

Birdsall N., R. Levine, and A. Ibrahim, eds. (2005), Towards Universal Primary Education: Investments, Incentives and Institutions. Sterling: Stylus Publishing.

Brijesh (2014) http://mhrd.gov.in/rte

Buvinic, Mayra. (2005) 'Social inclusion in Latin America', Baltimore: Social exclusion and economic development, John Hopkins University Press.

Das S 2008), Role of parental education in schooling and child labour decision: Urban India in the last decade, *Social Indicators Research* 89.2 (2008): 305-322.

Deccan Chronicle 2012 Oct 29, 2012.

De Hann, Arjan. (1997) 'Poverty and social exclusion, A comparision of debates on deprivation', working paper, Brighton: University of Sussex.

De Haan, Arjan. (2001) 'Social Exclusion: Enriching the Understanding of Deprivation', paper for the World Development Report, Forum on 'Inclusion, Justice, and Poverty Reduction'.

Govinda, R. and Bandyopadhyay, M. (2008) 'Access to Elementary Education in India', *Country Analytical Review*, UK: Consortium for Research on Educational Access, Transitions and Equity (CREATE).

Govinda, R. (2010) Educational Access in Madhya Pradesh and Chhattisgarh, Country Research Summary. CREATE, Delhi / Brighton: NUEPA / University of Sussex.

Government of India (2006)

Government of India (2007a) Selected Educational Statistics, New Delhi: Ministry of Human Resource Development.

Government of India (2008)

Government of India (YEAR) National commission for S.C's and ST's, 5th report, 1998-99, vol- I; Census Report, 2001; Report of National literacy mission at http://www.nlm.nic. incensusmp. nic.in/censusmp/All-PDF/6Literacy21.12.

Government of India

Horowitz, D. (1985), Ethnic Groups in Conflict. Berkeley: University of California.

Human Rights Watch (2017).

Lewin, K. (2007) 'Improving Access, Equity and Transitions in Education: Creating a Research Agenda', CREATE Pathways to Access Research, Monograph No. 1 Brighton, University of Sussex (http://www.create-rpc.org/pdf documents/India Policy Brief 3.pdf).

Lewis, Maureen A., and Marlaine E. Lockheed (2006), Inexcusable *absence: why 60 million girls still aren't in school and what to do about it*. Washington: Center for Global Development.

Louis, Prakash (2008) in 'Towards inclusion and equity'www.infochangeindia.org, accessed on 10th February 2013.

Lloyd, C.B. (2005), Growing Up Global: The Changing Transitions to Adulthood in Developing Countries. Report of the National Research Council and Institute of Medicine Panel on Transitions to Adulthood in Developing Countries. Washington, D.C.: National Academies Press.

Meerman, J. (2005), "Oppressed People: Economic Mobility of the Socially Excluded, Journal of Socioeconomics 34 (4): 543–67.

Nambissan, G. (2000), Identity, Exclusion and the Education of Tribal Communities, in Wazir, Rekha (ed.). Gender Gaps in Literacy and Education, New Delhi: Sage Publications.

NEG Fire Seminar (2011) as cited in the India OOSCI Study.Nguyen (2006), The Value of Completing a Vocational Education and Training Qualification; Australia: National Centre for Vocational Education Research.

Paranjape, M.S.(2007) 'Uneven Distribution of Education in Maharashtra: Rural-Urban, Gender and Caste Inequalities', *Economic and Political Weekly*, pp.213-216.

Piron and Curran, Z. (2005) 'Public policy response to exclusion; evidence from Brazil, South Africa and India', London: Oversees Development Institute.

PROBE (1999) Public Report on Basic Education in India, The Probe Team, Centre for Development Economics, Oxford University Press, Delhi

Purohit, Brijesh, C. (2014) 'Efficiency of social sector expenditure in India', Routledge, NY.

Piron and Curran, Z. (2005) 'Public policy response to exclusion; evidence from Brazil, South Africa and India', London: Oversees Development Institute.

Rao, R.N. (1990) 'Social Organisation in an Indian Slum: Study of a Caste Slum', New Delhi: Mittal Publications.

Reddy, A. N., & Sinha, S. (2010). School dropouts or pushouts? Overcoming barriers for the Right to Education, UK: university of Sussex.

Sen, A (1998)

Sen, A. (2000) 'Social exclusion; concept, application and scrutiny environment and social development', Manila: Asian Development Bank .

Social Exclusion Unit (1998), http://www.open.gov.uk/co/seu, accessed on 2nd February 2014.

UNESCO Institute for Statistics, 2005.

UNESCO Institute for Statistics, 2008.

UNICEF evaluation report (2018), The Out-of-School Children Initiative (OOSCI),Unicef,https://www.unicef.org, accessed on 12th December 2018.

Vasavi. (1997) 'Blue print for rural primary education: how viable?', *Economic and Political Weekly,* vol- 32(50).

Wankhede, G.G. (2001) 'Educational inequalities among scheduled castes in Maharashtra', *Economic and Political Weekly*, pp. 1553-1558.

Wesly Kumar (2017)

Wils, A., B. Carrol, and K. Barrow (2005) "Educating the World's Children: Patterns of Growth and Inequality, Washington: Education Policy and Data Center.

World Bank (2005) Pakistan Country Gender Assessment. Bridging the Gender Gap: Opportunities and Challenges. Environment and Social Development Sector Report, Washington. (Not in The Text).

Yagati, C. R. (2003) 'Dalit studies: a bibliographical handbook', New Delhi: Kanishka Publishers.

Notes

1. Dr. Wesly Kumar is Assistant professor at School of Social Sciences, University of Hyderabad.
2. Dr. S. Ramudu is Assistant Registrar at University of Hyderabad.
3. Deccan Chronicle, Oct 29, 2012.
4. In Indian education we can find drop-out and stagnation particularly among the Dalit students. Studies reveal that not even 40 percent of primary school children are completing their primary education. About 80 percent of the children are dropped out before they complete the high school. The reasons for the stagnation and drop out several include failure in an examination, denial of promotion to the next class etc. The incidence of drop-out and stagnation is more acute among the Dalit children than others.
5. Data were collected from Premavathipeta, Shivarampally and Gopanpally slums of Hyderabad. For details see (Wesly, 2017).

Chapter - 10

The # Me too Movement that Never is: Political Economy of the Eclipse of the Sexual Exploitation of the Dalit and Tribal Women

Dr. Jose Maliekal[1]

0.0 Introduction

In this Paper, entitled, "The # Me too Movement that Never is: Political Economy of the Eclipse of the Sexual Exploitation of the Dalit and Tribal Women", against the background of five Case Studies of sexual exploitation of Minor girls from the Dalit and Tribal background, attempt is being made, to bring into relief, the widespread reality of sexual exploitation of the females of the Subaltern sections of the society. This rampant sexual exploitation of the Dalit females do not often surface in the mainstream media, not receiving as much attention as the much-sensationalized cases of the sexual exploitation of the women of the Middle-Class. The political economy, latent in this eclipse of the sexual exploitation of the Subaltern women, makes the access by the exploited women, to anything like, the "# Me Too Movement", a near-impossibility, though, ironically, it is true that preceding the # Me Too Movement in India, there has been a Dalit Women's resistance, which, for four decades, has challenged the routine forms of sexual exploitation and violence. From the Mathura case[2] to the Bhanwari Devi Case[3], the Indian Feminist Movement has been defined by the struggles of the Dalit-Bahujan and Adivasi sisters.[4]

In the West too, the # Me too Movement has to recognize the grass-roots work done by the lower-class women of colour, in resisting sexual harassment and exploitation. Race and caste divides aggravate the experiences of sexual harassment, while privilege in terms of the two make a difference in averting, seeking help and recovering from abuse. If in India, the #Me Too Movement has to make sense to the masses, we have to find a way to relate the movement to the subalterns. The stuff of true solidarity should be everyone recognizing the pain, the struggle and resilience of women, who are Dalit, Adivasi, Muslim, disabled, queer, poor and non-English speaking, and saying # Her too.[5]

1.0 Political Economy of the Eclipse of Sexual Exploitation

Against this call for the need of extending the circle of solidarity of the # Me Too Movement to the Subalterns, as already stated, we listen to the stories of atrocities perpetrated on five minor girls, belonging to the Dalit and Tribal communities, towards examining the factors of Political Economy[6], that make their sexual exploitation, something that is considered as commonplace and of everydayness. Dalit women suffer from the 'triple burden' of gender bias, caste discrimination, and economic deprivation.[7]

1.1 The Story of Rani[8]

Rani (Name Changed), a minor aged about 17 years, belongs to a Scheduled Caste community. When she was studying in 7th class in her village, and working as a wage-earner, co-habited, with a young man, her neighbour and she became pregnant. After the thatched hut in which they were staying collapsed, the parents left the village and went to the house of their relatives. Rani was taken to Multi Specialty Hospital, in the nearby town, for a forcible abortion. She was discharged without the abortion, being performed, as the NGOs and the media intervened. Thereafter, her parents took her to another Nursing home, where she gave birth to a female child, which was killed by the doctors and its body made to disappear. Neither the victim nor her parents showed any interest in reporting the matter to the police. The Women's Desk of PARA Organisation enquired into the matter and reported the matter to SHO, Kothapeta. A case was registered and investigated. Rani was taken to a Safety Home. The accused was punished under u/s 376 (1) and 3 (1) (xii) of SC & ST (POA) act, 1989. Now the case is listed before the High Court by the accused, who is on bail currently.

As it is evident from the story of Rani, and the stories that follow, the interface between caste, patriarchy, and gender is a theme that needs a thorough theoretical and empirical study, for the purpose of understanding the nature and causes of the caste and gender exploitation of Dalit women.[9]

1.2 Katyayani: Victim of Rape and Murder

Kathyayani (Name Changed), aged 16 is from a Scheduled Caste Community. She had been complaining to her parents that a certain young man of had been stalking her, every day. The parents warned him seriously regarding the complaint given by her and she was stopped from work in the fields, for fear of being molested by the young man. Later, one of the female agricultural labourers, known to her parents, persuaded them to send her for work, in the fields. While she was working in the fields, a young man of the village raped her along with his friends. Not able to withstand the shame, she consumed pesticide and committed suicide. Though she was taken to the hospital, she expired there. The main witnesses in the case turned hostile and so the case was dismissed. Currently the case is being appealed.

1.3 Anasuya (Name Changed) : School Dropout and Victim of Gang Rape

Anasuya (Name changed), a 14 years old girl, belonging to a Scheduled Tribe, who was studying in 9 class, had dropped out of school, due to extreme poverty and started working with her parents, as agricultural labourer. Her mother tried to put some sense into her mind regarding her studies. She was hurt with her words and left home and went to her friend's house and stayed there for ten days. While trying to return home, at night found herself alone, waiting for the bus. She trusted the two young men, who promised to take her back home, safely, and was pillion-riding. The men took her to one of their houses and gang-raped her, along with a host of their friends, keeping her under duress for a week. When she was suffering from severe fever and was sleeping in a wayside shed, an elderly lady saw her and with the help of the locals, took her to the police station. But Anasuya did not reveal anything about the rape. So the police called for her mother and they sent her home. After a week, a news reporter came to know of everything and filed a complaint in the Police Station. Thereupon, the police called Anasuya and her mother and filed a case of the sexual abuse of Anasuya. The SI and CI investigated the case and arrested all 17 members who had raped her. She was sent for medical tests and the case was filed under section164. She was given a compensation of Rs 25,000.00 and was sent to a safety home in Hyderabad.

What causes slow progress in Human Development Indicators of Dalit Women? Although one will recognize that there are common factors (gender and poverty) that cause high deprivation for all women, including Dalit women, Dalit women additionally suffer from social exclusion and discrimination because o their lower position in the caste hierarchy. This additional factor in the case of Dalit women makes them vulnerable to more poverty and deprivation than their counterparts from the general population. Thus, it is this 'exclusion-induced deprivation' that differentiates Dalit women from other women.[10]

1.4 Indira: Victim of Rape and Suicide

Indira (Name changed), a student of 9th Standard, belonging to the Scheduled Caste Community, while sleeping on the verandah of her house, her neighbour dragged her into her house and raped her. This incident was witnessed by her sister, who locked the perpetrator inside the house and went to the fields, where her parents were working and reported everything that had happened. Meanwhile, the accused broke the tiles of the roof and ran way. The parents of Indira were ready to register a complaint of rape in the police station. The village elders stopped them from going to the Police Station, on the promise that they would do justice to the victim. The Village President and some village elders called the perpetrator for a Panchayat and he was questioned regarding the rape. He lied that Indira herself called him and he had gone there. In connivance with six village elders, the perpetrator gave a written statement stating that he had gone to her house to steel, evading the subject of rape and the elders concurred with the version of the perpetrator by endorsing the statement. On coming to know the verdict of the Panchayath, the victim felt humiliated and shamed, that justice had not been meted out to her. She committed suicide by pouring kerosene on herself and burning herself. Though she was rushed to the hospital, she succumbed to the third degree burns, she had suffered. On complaint, a case was registered in the police station, against the perpetrator.

The story of Indira is an example for the fact that, along with class and over and above it, caste also plays a role in the lives of Dalit women. Upper-caste feminists have often refused to recognize caste as a form of social privilege and capital that enables social mobility and choice. Rather than seeing caste as having its own independent identity, many feminists have seen caste as class-like; that is, as a socioeconomic category, instead of an aspect of religious conceptions of self and society that reproduce structural inequality.[11]

1.5 Bhavani: Victim of Prolonged Rape and Sexual Blackmail

Bhavani (Name changed), aged 17 years, belonging to a Scheduled Tribe, used to stay with her maternal grandfather. Due to extreme poverty she dropped out of school and was engaged in work, for some months at her place. After some time, she migrated to Rajamundry and started working in a garment company, for a salary of Rs. 1,500.00. She was accommodated at a rented place. During that time, an Advocate befriended her, with the promise of a better job and a better future. She was taken by him, to a deserted place, where she was given a soft drink and She went into a stupor. When she became conscious, she found that she was almost naked and the Advocate showed her the photos taken on the cell phone, in which she was seen as being sexually abused by him and the another person.

The Advocate, since then, has been blackmailing her, to indulge in sex with him. He used to threaten her saying that he would go public with the photos, he had in his possession. He used to threaten to kill her or throw acid on her, if she ever revealed this to anyone. He further introduced her to his friend. He too abused her sexually her. Afterwards, the Advocate took her to Visakhapatnam, abused her sexually and then offered to send her to Bangalore, telling her that, she could earn lot of money there, in the brothels. His friend, who is the second perpetrator gave her a cheque of Rs. 3, 00,000.000 and told her to cash it only on his further instructions. Unable to put up with all this torture, she left for home and called the Advocate, who threatened to find her out and kill her if she did not return to Rajahmundry. She returned to Rajahmundry and confided all these matters to an auto-driver, who took her to the police- station and registered a complaint against the accused.

Beside the low literacy rate, another problem Dalit women face is the high dropout rate from school. The percentage of dropouts at the primary, middle, and secondary levels in 2009-10 was quite high compared with the upper-caste girls. The Ministry of Human Development estimates show that at the class 1–8 stage, the drop-out rate was 51.6%. Because of the high drop-out rate at the primary and middle stages, enrolment at the higher stages of school and college level is extremely low. NSSO (National Sample Survey Office) data further indicate that the gross enrolment ratio (GER) of upper-caste women is more than four times compared with that of Dalit women at the postsecondary level. For instance, in 2009–10, the GER was 2.8 percent for Dalit women as compared to 12.5 percent for women from the upper-caste groups. The enrolment in higher education is also characterized by gender inequalities within the Dalit group. The GER in higher education for Dalit women is lower (2.8 percent) as compared to Dalit men (5.4 percent).[12]

1.6 Need for Addressing Exclusion-Induced Deprivation

The Protection of Civil Rights (PCR) Act and Scheduled Caste and Scheduled Tribe Prevention of Atrocities (POA) Act addresses the threat of violence and atrocities against the Dalits. The objective of these acts is to clearly emphasize the intention of the government to deliver social justice and to enable SCs to live with dignity, without fear of violence and atrocities. Although the acts incorporate strong compensatory and punitive measures, violence and atrocities continue against Dalits. The increase in the number of crimes and atrocities against Dalit women has raised a serious issue regarding empowerment of Dalits as a whole and especially of Dalit women, whose bodies become the sites of sexual violence committed publicly whenever they or the men of their community are seen as transgressing the caste hierarchy.[13]

The official statistics often capture only the tip of the iceberg, providing information on the most heinous crimes such as rape; other forms of humiliation such as sexual harassment and derogatory remarks are not captured in the official statistics. However, there are some primary studies that do provide us with this information. A primary-level study across 500 villages on the forms and nature of violence indicated that across the states studied, harassment of Dalit women takes the following forms: non-Dalits frequently use abusive and derogatory language when addressing Dalit women; non-Dalits refer to Dalit women as prostitutes or use caste names; in their workplace or in the market, non-Dalit supervisors or traders will often make sexual innuendoes to Dalit women. Another study of the narratives of 500 Dalit women across four states on the forms and manifestations of violence found that the most frequent forms of violence that are perpetrated against the majority of Dalit women are verbal abuse (62.4 percent), physical assault (54.8 percent), sexual harassment and assault (46.8 percent), domestic violence (43.0 percent), and rape (23.2 percent), in descending order.[14]

Apart from the experience of the problems related to gender exploitation of their labour, and economic deprivation as their poor non-SC/ST sisters do, Dalit women additionally suffer from caste and untouchability-based discrimination. It is this **'exclusion-induced deprivation'** that differentiates Dalit women's problem from those of other women, and it also makes their problems more intense and complicated than those faced by other women. For Dalit women, the genesis of this exclusion-induced deprivation lies in the fact that they are considered to be impure, polluting, untouchable, unapproachable, and 'unseeable'. In other words, not fit for social and physical association with others. This has enormous implications on the human right and human dignity of Dalit women.[15]

Therefore, the multiple challenges that Dalit women face require multiple solutions. First, policies should be in place against gender discrimination and poverty for all women, which will also help Dalit women; second, there should be complementary policy measures and legal safeguards against social exclusion and discrimination for women who belong to excluded groups. This would indeed demand group-specific gender policies, in addition to the general policy of women's empowerment, to address the voices of women from excluded groups. This would enable the State to conceptualize inclusive policies to address the problems of Dalit women more effectively. Further, the women's movement in India need to place at the centre of their theorization the fact that patriarchy in this society operates in conjunction with the caste system. This would make them more sensitive to the injustices suffered by Dalit women, which all too often are invisible to the government, the police and the judiciary.[16]

2.0 The # Me too Movement that Never is…

The phrase 'Me Too' originated with Tarana Burke, an African American civil rights activist, to raise awareness of the magnitude of sexual harassment and assault among women of colour. Yet the recent upsurge in its use, and the face of the Hollywood movement, has been spearheaded by Western (and mostly white) celebrities. Their campaigning has undoubtedly exposed the severity of sexual harassment in the film industry, but it has raised some troubling questions about the influence of race on perceptions of violence and the granting of support to its victims.[17]

Yet for many women, including those living in stigmatized Dalit ('Untouchable') communities in postcolonial India, this sort of platform remains largely unavailable. Their low status in the caste system and position within economically impoverished communities exacerbates their vulnerability to severe discrimination. As we have seen in our Case Studies above, the small distance separating women from their attackers and from the violent repercussions of men surrounding them, further restricts their ability to seek support and refuge.[18]

The denial of basic resources such as water requires Dalit women to leave their homes to provide for their families in a way that upper caste women avoid. Without access to toilet facilities, they are forced to defecate openly, and often at night, away from their homes. The distance this demands leaves them vulnerable to humiliation and harassment from upper caste individuals and groups.

Physical and sexual violence against Dalit women is so common place that it receives very little attention. In contrast, cases involving the rape of higher caste and middle class women, such as the Jyoti Singh case in 2012, are given significant attention in international media coverage. This disparity begs a comparison between the influence of racial and caste prejudice in responses to gendered violence.[19]

The complications of reporting sexual violence when it occurs at the intersection of several spheres of loyalty was emphasized in Burke's original *MeToo* campaign. African American women were much less likely to report violence committed against them when they risked incriminating men within their already-vulnerable homes and communities. The position of Dalit women presents a similar problem and one that requires a unique human rights discourse. The rise of international online movements such as #MeToo present a promising shift for women working in established industries. Yet for those trapped at the bottom of caste, class, and gender hierarchies, in economically impoverished communities in postcolonial India, the sentiment of the movement is lost. The violence faced by Dalit women is a relentless, everyday occurrence deeply embedded within the socio-religious framework that dominates Indian society.[20]

"For generations in India, Dalits have been actively stopped from speaking. It's a marvelous nexus—the actively casteist population doesn't even consider us human enough, and the population that pretends to be anti-caste forcefully silences us. Every time we try to make a point about our different experiences, liberal Savarnas shut us up with scoldings of "We don't believe in caste! There is no different experience! You are just trying to get attention!" Every time we try to raise our voices within a movement, we are told we're trying to be "divisive" and that "This is not the right time."[21]

"This is what our mothers and grandmothers have taught us: It is never the right time in India to care about our oppressions. There are movements and protests that benefit Savarnas, and whatever little we can glean from them we will receive, but we are not allowed to mention what we didn't get. We are never welcome to start anything, because we don't represent you, we are just the silent numbers you can oppress, ignore or "uplift" for your causes."[22]

The one person Savarna traditionally cannot stand is the Dalit who can speak. That person is therefore no longer a "real Dalit." So all the Dalits who are well-educated, articulate, have enough social safety—the only ones of us who have the power and skills to raise their voice and criticize the Savarna hegemony—are effectively delegitimised from speaking for our community. Raya or Meena or Christina or Thenmozhi or Sujatha or I are not the "right" kind of Dalit for liberal Savarna tastes. The "right" kind of Dalit is the body that was pulled down from the tree or fished out of the sewer, because that one is no longer squeaking.[23]

"I want to know: What does this country tell Dalit women when casteists get away with leading its liberal feminist discourse? What does the country tell us when we receive discriminations no matter what, but are not allowed to mention it unless we present some ridiculous piece of paper called a "caste certificate", in a country where over half the population doesn't have birth certificates or voter ID cards, and the bureaucracy that delivers these papers is a huge mess of corruption and red tape? What does the country tell us when Savarna women and the Savarna media erase the movement one of us created—single-handedly, bearing great personal risk to themselves, and not only for Dalit women—to build another movement of their own? Does it tell us that the country cares about our narratives or our safety?"[24]

The most important feature of the #Metoo movement is that it is built on trust. A woman who has much less power than her abuser and often no documentation that would hold up in a court comes out to the public with her narrative, trusting that people would believe her experience. That when it comes to her-word-against-his situations, people would believe the woman's word. If people don't extend that belief the entire process backfires on the woman, who risks losing personal and professional safety, possibly for life.[25]

"We Dalits, and especially Dalit women, are not accustomed to receiving that kind of belief from Savarna social systems, or even our own Savarna friends. You have always told us that our experiences were false, mistaken, divisive, bids for attention. One doesn't have to be an activist or scholar to know this. Our mothers and grandmothers have warned us, because they received these betrayals again and again, and they've only been allowed to exist next to you in your societies because they silenced themselves. We have been present for your fights, and then you let us down and told us to shut up when your own purpose was served. You have never protected us from abusers, often even thrown us at abusers to protect yourselves. We do not trust you."[26]

"I also have a #Metoo story, but Savarna India will not hear it today. I will not confide in you the horror, pain and trauma with which I am still living every day, only to watch you form a protective ring around one of your own and call me a liar. I will not present my "caste certificate" and the detailed histories of my parents, relatives and ancestors for the entertainment of your sordid "liberal feminists" and their supporters. I will not throw into your ring my education, professional credibility, romantic history, every single achievement for which I had to struggle twice as hard against your reluctance and ridicule, so that you can label me an attention seeker once again. If you want to genuinely include Dalit women in your movements, Savarna India, you have to do better."[27]

3. 0 Intersectionality in Feminism: Need of the Hour

The question raised by Mini Mondal from her autobiographical experience as a Dalit, according to me is a systemic one, and not merely, a systematic one, needing mere, " Nut and Bolt" adjustment in the system, which is advantageous to the Savarnas, as well as co-optive of the Dalits, as recent trends, after the mood and mode of majoritarian, *Dvija* nationalism is in the air. The rise of international online movements such as #MeToo present a promising shift for women working in established industries. Yet for those trapped at the bottom of caste, class, and gender hierarchies, in economically impoverished communities in postcolonial India, the sentiment of the movement is lost. The violence faced by Dalit women is a relentless, everyday occurrence deeply embedded within the socio-religious framework that dominates Indian society.[28]

Raising awareness of the historical context behind contemporary discrimination is vital. However, more needs to be done to make international women's movements and the contemporary human rights discourse inclusive for those facing violence and persecution under vastly different circumstances. Utilizing a discourse of human rights legislation, academics are beginning to draw comparative histories that categorize caste and race under 'descent-based discrimination'. This presents a vital development in widening understanding of caste issues by placing them within a global context.[29]

The question of Mini Mondal, to the oppressive and majoritarian system and the particular set of conditions of political economy, which breed it, and similar questions, calls for a vital dialogue about the importance of intersectionality in the feminist movement and of making space for women from vulnerable minorities who face discrimination on multiple axes.[30]

Intersectionality stands for "the complex, cumulative manner in which the effects of different forms of discrimination combine, overlap, or intersect". To break that down, it essentially means that discrimination does not exist in a bubble – different kinds of prejudice can be amplified in different ways when put together. The whole purpose of intersectional feminism is to listen to different kinds of feminists – not just ones like yourself. Making one's feminism intersectional makes perfect sense. One's life experiences are based on how one's multiple identities intermingle. And there are compounding forms of discrimination experienced by the Dalit women, who work, under a exclusion-induced deprivation. There are many examples.[31] I hope that the intensification of the call for greater and growing intersectionality, will further be stimulated, by the decentering of the Savrana Feminists, by the Dalitbahujan feminists, like Mini Modal and her relentless questioning(s).[32]

4.0 Conclusion

Dwelling on this need of the hour, for intersectionality in feminism(s), and celebrating the Dalit Movement, which, as stated earlier, the movement, which triggered women's movements, against exploitation of women, at various levels, I would, as I conclude re-enter my research universe of the lifeworld(s) of the Konaseema Madigas. I would like the Madiga women, who has left a fragment of their own version of #Me Too, to sing it afresh for us:[33]

> They call us, Madiga, Madiga, but my eldest son-in-law is a Madiga
> They say Âramjyôthi, Âramjyôthi but Âramjyôthi is my eldest daughter.
> When the bride and the groom pass this way, they worship Aramjyothi
> The peddakapu, peddakapu is coming, give the big stick, give the big stick
> Madiga, the ignorant one, where did your husband go?
> Why Sir, what may be the reason of your sudden calling?

This is a fragment from the filed-songs, which celebrate their identity and protest. After celebrating the Arundhati, their daughter, who is married to Vasishta, who, in their reckoning is a Brahmin, they are warning each other, against the incursion, in the evening, of the Kapu elder in the Madiga enclave, in the absence of their husbands, for sexually exploiting them, and they are collectively resisting his advance, by exhorting one another to arm themselves with big sticks, to resist/protest against the predator Big Madiga. A# Me too Mome/vement indeed!

Notes

1. Dr. Jose D. Maliekal SDB, Principal, St John's Regional Seminary, Kondadaba, Kothavalasa (P.O.) Vizianagaram Dist — 535 183 A.P. India.
2. Srila Roy, "#MeToo Is A Crucial Moment to Revisit the History of Indian Feminism," *Economic and Political Weekly* 53, no. 42, 20 October (2018): ISSN (Online) - 2349-8846..... The custodial rape of a 14-year-old Adivasi woman named Mathura epitomised, for these feminists, the manner in which sexual violence could not be separated from the logic and workings of the patriarchal state. The Mathura rape case was also significant for inaugurating a slew of successful legal reforms around violence against women and orienting Indian feminism itself towards legal strategies.
3. Akshaya Vijayalakshmi, "Extending the Boundaries of #MeToo: Sexual Harassment in the Lives of Marginalized Women, "*Economic and Political Weekly* 53, No. 42, 20 Oct (2018): ISSN (Online) - 2349-8846….It was Bhanwari Devi's battle for justice against the people who gang-raped her that got us the legal guidelines to protect women against and prevent sexual harassment at the workplace.

4. Shreya Atrey, "Taking # Me too to the Subaltern," *The Hindu*, October 16, 2018, 9.
5. *Ibid.*
6. See Jose Maliekal, *Standstill Utopias: Dalits Encountering Christianity* (Delhi: ISPCK, 2017), 1-2, for the pluriform approach of Political Economy, as followed by an economist like Amartya Sen, who approaches issues like hunger, poverty and famine, from a human and multi-dimensional approach, from a " Positional Objectivity of the Poor", as different from the approach of mainstream economics, which is solely worried about the production of wealth.
7. Nidhi Sadana Sabharwal and Wandana Sonalkar, " Dalit Women in India: At the Crossroads of Gender, Class, and Caste," 44, http://publikationen.ub.uni-frankfurt.de/frontdoor/index/index/docId/40543, as accessed on January 29, 2019.
8. This story and other case studies, narrated here have been culled from the Case Diaries of Women's Desk, PARA (People's Action for Rural Awakening), District level Public Hearing on Sex Abuse of Women, East Godavari District, on 15 October, 2009, at Ravulapalem.
9. Sabharwal and Sonalkar, "Dalit Women in India," 46. See also Ranajit Guha, "Chandra's Death," in *Subaltern Studies - V*, ed. Ranajit Guha (Delhi: Oxford University Press, 1998 - Paper Back, 3rd Impression), 135 -165, where the author describes the death of the woman, Chandra, and the causes leading to it, under the patriarchal orderings of time, space and relationships.
10. *Ibid.*, 60 - 61.
11. *Ibid.*, 49.
12. *Ibid*, 55.
13. *Ibid.*, 66.
14. *Ibid.*, 67-68.
15. *Ibid*, 70.
16. *Ibid.*, 71.
17. Francis Hargraves, "The #MeToo Movement, Intersectionality, And Its Implications For DalitWomen", https://shiloh-project.group.shef.ac.uk/the-metoo-movement-intersectionality-and-its-implications-for-dalit-women/, as accessed on 26 January, 2019.
18. *Ibid.*
19. *Ibid.*
20. *Ibid.*
21. Mini Mondal, "A Dalit woman's thoughts on #MeTooIndia" in *Indian Express*, Saturday, 22 December, 2018.
22. *Ibid.*
23. *Ibid.*
24. *Ibid.*
25. *Ibid.*
26. *Ibid.*
27. *Ibid.*

28. Francis Hargraves, "The #MeToo Movement, Intersectionality, And Its Implications For Dalit Women."
29. *Ibid.*
30. *Ibid.*
31. International Women's Development Agency (IWDA), " What does Intersectional Feminism Actually Mean," https://iwda.org.au/what-does-intersectional-feminism-actually-mean/, as accessed on January, 31, 2019.
32. Srila Roy, "#MeToo Is A Crucial Moment to Revisit the History of Indian Feminism".
33. Jose Maliekal, *Standstill Utopias*, 159.

Chapter - 11

Feminism Matter(s) in Science – Reflections on the Marginalization of Women in the World of Science

Prof. S. Stephen Jayard[1]

Introduction

To speak of women being marginalized in the world of science it may sound unbelievable to many; yes, women are not treated at par with men in the world of science; the side-lining of women takes place not only in the matters of administration and policy-making or giving them opportunities to pursue significant researches but also at the attitudinal levels, and of course such discrimination is often very subtle. Science, though it is the most rational and objective enterprise, cannot escape the issues of discriminating women, because science is also very much a social enterprise. So a closer look at science reveals the sad, and even ugly, side of discrimination against women in science.

Gender inequality has been everywhere for centuries in different societies in different dimensions. Whether or not a society is literate or illiterate, progressive or non-progressive, religious or non-religious – every society (except perhaps a few matriarchal societies!) has invariably been practising some sorts of discrimination against women, though the degree and category might differ. Thanks to the hard and sustained efforts by several social movements, women's organizations and scholars with liberal mind-set, today, we see great a drive to establish equality among the genders and eradicate any type of discrimination against women. Even science, which is said to be objective and impersonal in its investigations and researches, has also been affected by the 'virus' of women-discrimination, at various levels. Feminist critics, for the past few decades, have started critiquing science, not only to increase the quantum of hard core women scientists in the field, but also to challenge some of the fundamental assumptions of science. 'Feminism and Science', a vast and complex area of investigation, is nowadays catching up very fast. Taking cues from philosophy and history of science of the latter part of the 20th century, feminist studies of science reveal the sad fact that science is a tool in the politically powerful and dominant class of white males of the so-called superior race.

Drawing insights from some feminist critics, this paper seeks to see how far feminist considerations can benefit, if at all, the growth of science. It begins with some analysis of seeing knowledge, including scientific knowledge, as *a social construct*, and then moves on to look for the role and relevance, if any, of *feminist epistemology* in understanding science. It can also be shown, with the recent researches in the field of cognitive and neurosciences, that the full involvement of women in science, who are said to be the repositories of greater intuitive power, will lead to the enrichment of science. We try to show that science can be 'better', with some insights from Philosophy of Science (that science is an interpretative enterprise) and neuro-cognitive sciences.

It is quite encouraging to see that academic institutes of higher learning, both at the national and international levels, have established Women's Studies / Research Centres. Nonetheless all these good efforts very often stop only at the institutional level and don't percolate among the common masses to move towards a society that is liberated from such gender discrimination and prejudices. To achieve this goal, as the paper concludes, what is urgently needed is to have the attitudinal changes, both in men and women.

The Learned's Unhealthy Attitude towards Women

It would not be out of place to make a mention about the unhealthy treatment of women in the past millennia. It is unfortunate that even philosophers and influential people in society, have become a prey to the tendency of this cancerous caricature of women. When these influential people are not convinced of the worth and dignity of women, such attitudes becomes harmful and dangerous for individual women and the society at large. Western science is largely the product of European-Greek joint venture, which glorified reason and objectivity and identified them with males. Most of them were sexist or misogynist. For instance, even the examples used in logic have been biased. For instance, *Aristotelian syllogism*, 'Man is mortal, Socrates is a man, Therefore Socrates is mortal' – this argument cannot strictly be used for women. For to say, 'Man is mortal, Catherine is _____. What can we say?... We cannot say, 'Catherine is a man'. Is it that only men can represent humanity? Should one conclude that women are immortal? Why should one subsume women under the title 'men', why not the other way about?[2] Further, *Aristotle* was convinced that "The female is an impotent male, incapable of making semen because of the coldness of her nature. We therefore should look upon the female state as if it were a deformity..."; *Martin Luther* (1483-1546) declares: "Girls begin to talk and to stand on their feet sooner than boys because weeds always grow up more quickly than good crops". There was an angry reaction to this, “If they can put a man on the moon... why can’t they put them all there?”[3]. During the Middle Ages education was restricted only to men in the cathedral schools, which were later developed as universities. Women were not encouraged to study more because many were convinced as St. Thomas Aquinas, a Christian scholar, was: “She [a woman] is mentally incapable of holding a position of authority.”[4]

From the 15th to 18th century, when modern science evolved, socio cultural views of women did not allow women to participate in education. *Francis Bacon* argued that women disrupted the developments of men. *Hegel* acknowledges that women can learn, “but they are not made for activities which demand a universal faculty such as the more advanced sciences, philosophy...”.[5] *Rousseau*, in his novel *Emile*, wrote: “I would a thousand times rather have a homely girl.. than a learned lady... A female wit is a scourge to her husband, her children, her friends, her servants, to everybody”; and *Immanuel Kant* wrote that women such as the Marquise du Chatelet, who “carries on fundamental conversations about mechanics... might just as well have a beard”.[6] Thus, women were ill-treated and deliberately side-lined in the androcentric world and their literature does not give due recognition to their achievements. We need to work to bring out these forgotten women and their wonderful achievements, including their struggles in being women and scientists as well; otherwise, as Harding cautions us, “We do a disservice to our daughters and our sons - as well as to the historical record - in ignoring and undervaluing women’s work”.[7]

Part I
Sociology of (Scientific) Knowledge

Sociology of knowledge, as a theory of the social or existential conditioning of thought,[8] has its roots in the works of Marx and Durkheim. Karl Manheim and others develop it further to give it a status of a separate and serious discipline to show how knowledge is a social product. But slowly in the later part of the 20th century, because “the natural sciences including physics and mathematics, are no longer seen as possessing a special epistemological warrant”[9], sociologists included scientific knowledge also for social analysis. Robert Merton and his followers are said to be the founders of sociology of science.[10] In the mid1970s various feminists came together under the banner of ‘feminist theory’, to consolidate their work in various disciplines like anthropology, sociology, history, literature and psychoanalysis, but not yet ready to include natural sciences. Only by the late 1970s feminists began to turn their attention on scientific theories and practices. Both these trends, namely, *the sociology of knowledge* and *the sociology of science*, are together known as ‘*Constructivism*’. Sociology of science focuses on several theoretical considerations, such as, a) the ethnomethodological study of scientific practice, b) the discourse analysis of scientists’ talk, writing and pictures, c) the ethnography of scientific work, d) the relativist programme in scientific studies, and f) the sociology of knowledge in 'strong' and 'weak' programme.[11] It emphasizes the role of social factors and social conditions in the determination of scientific knowledge. It critically analyses how scientific knowledge is created, maintained, propagated in and through the established institutions and text books.

Philosophy and history of science challenged the 'standard' empiricist view of scientific knowledge in the latter part of the 20th century and it came out with important theses, like under-determination of scientific theories by the evidence and theory-ladenness of observation. Duhem, Poincare, Einstein and Quine[12] have pointed out that there is no unique and conclusive relationship between a set of observations and a theory (hypothesis) derived from it; usually a scientific theory involved a main hypothesis and several auxiliary hypotheses and by making some drastic changes in the latter ones, the main hypothesis can be upheld, in spite of any evidence. Similarly, theory-ladenness of observation, as argued by Kuhn and Feyerabend, and later further developed by Bohm, Hanson and Toulmin, clearly shows that a) observations can never be 'pure', rather they are teemed with auxiliary assumptions, psychological and linguistic aspects, without which observations are not possible, and b) it is partly the theoretical background at a given time enables the scientific community to accept a piece of observation as the relevant and proper evidence.[13] Thus theory choice in science is not ruled only by strict logical and rational considerations because the available evidence or supporting observations themselves, upon which the choice is made, are impregnated with theoretical assumptions.

History of science pays keen attention to the evaluation of scientific materials to ascertain the authenticity of the text and the author.[14] It is interesting to note that scientists themselves don't seem to be coherent and systematic in their own writings or discourses. There are even contradicting versions, in their own words, regarding their own discoveries of inventions; for instance, it has been traditionally believed that Michelson-Morley experiment had a great influence upon Einstein's theory of relativity. For, in 1922 Einstein had openly acknowledged that the experiment was the first step in the developments leading to the theory of relativity; and in 1931, in a function, where Michaelson himself was the guest of honour, Einstein thanked and congratulated him for the epoch-making experiment, without which the theory would *not* have been materialized. However, in the interviews held in 1950 and 1952, Einstein declared firmly that he came to know about the experiment through the writings of H. A. Lorentz only after he arrived at the theory of relativity in 1905. Thus, it is not easy to get the picture of science from the discourses of scientists.

Such contributions from philosophy and history of science fuelled sociologists of scientific knowledge like Bloor, Mulkay and Hesse,[15] to further sharpen their critical appraisal of science. They demand a thorough social analysis for natural sciences. They argue that even scientific facts, not just beliefs, are socially constructed. As Andre Kukla points out that "if the social history of science had been sufficiently different, we wouldn't... have the beliefs that we do have about quarks", but according to Latour and others, "if social history had been appropriately different, *there wouldn't be any quarks*"[16]. For the latter it is true to say that social elements fabricate the content of science and its facts.

Part II
Feminism and Science

Feminism and science, a very complex discipline, is a border case that "sits not on one border, but on multiple borders – indeed, on the borders between feminist theory and all the scientific and meta-scientific disciplines... By its very existence, it calls into question the borders of all these disciplines".[17] In this field most of the feminists raise several pertinent questions, though overlapping in some cases: a) Who does science? b) How does culture shape science, and vice versa? c) Can we redefine and reform science to include feminist perspectives? d) How can feminist perspectives on science and technology improve the day-to-day lives of women (and men)? All feminist critiques challenge, among many others, the underlying assumptions, including male bias, of scientific theories.

Keller was a pioneer to bring the term 'gender' into the field of science. Keller wonders why Philosophy and Sociology of science resisted to take up this important analysis. In fact her paper on "Gender and Science" appeared in a psychoanalytic journal, not in a history of science journal. She, as a feminist and scientist, a philosopher and historian of science, is aware that generally scientists are nervous or irritated by the issues feminists raise in critiquing science. Sandra Harding, another influential feminist science, focuses on five main areas: a) the analyses of women's situation in science, b) the sexist misuse and abuse of the sciences and their technologies, c) sexist and androcentric bias in the results of biological and social science research, d) the sexual meanings of nature and inquiry, and e) andocentric theories of scientific knowledge.[18]

Feminist critics of science highlight gender bias in the world of science: for instance, in the world of *Medical Sciences*, more time, energy and money are spent on the female contraceptive techniques than on male ones; problems that are specifically feminine (like menstrual cramps) don't seem to be given due consideration in developing medications. When a research is done on animals, usually only the male species is chosen; though they give the reason that the female ones may have biological cycles (e.g. female rats have a four-day cycle), which would complicate the research processes, yet the "Implicit assumption is, of course, that the male rat represents the species."[19] Even Darwin is said to suffer, may be unconsciously, from androcentric bias as he claims that only male species have shaped the course of evolution over the millennia. Women as gatherers play only a passive role while men, as hunters, decide the course of evolution at every point.

The gender bias in *Molecular Biology*: Usually the sperm cell is described to be 'active, forceful, and self-propelled'; it 'penetrates' through the egg where it 'delivers' its genetic material to 'activate' the fertilized egg to develop further. Whereas, the egg is understood to be 'transported' or just 'drifting' through the fallopian tube until it is 'fertilized' by the sperm.[20] But the recent studies have changed the mere passive role of the egg in the whole process of fertilization and the egg can be no more seen as 'a sleeping beauty'. The researches by Gerald and Helen Schatten show: "The egg is central to this drama [of fertilization]... the egg is not merely a large yolk-filled sphere into which the sperm burrows to endow new life. Rather, ... sperm and egg are mutually active partners".[21] Further researches show that both the sperm and egg cells produce the proteins that are necessary for penetration, and both find each other and get fused.[22] Electron microscope reveals that the sperm doesn't just burrow through the egg, but the egg directs the growth of small, finger-like projections of the cell surface to hold onto the sperm and gradually draws it in. Though it was discovered in 1895 in the case of sea urchin fertilization, it was ignored until recently.

Feminist critiques attempt to evaluate the metaphors, and thereby the mindsets of the scientists that create them, to show how they are sexist-oriented in their approaches. For instance, *Francis Bacon* employed rape-metaphors, in encouraging others to explore and investigate nature; for, nature was seen as feminine power that has to be restrained and controlled. *Paul Feyerabend* has compared his own analysis of science to "an attractive and yielding courtesan who tries to anticipate every wish of her lover"; Physicist *Richard Feynman*, in his acceptance speech of the Noble Prize, portrayed the idea that inspired to work and to be awarded with the honour of Noble Prize as "an old lady, who has very little that is attractive left in her... But [she] has given birth to some very good children. And I thank the Swedish Academy of Sciences for complimenting one of them".[23] Merchant points out how new discoveries in science affect the worldview of people. For instance, when the Copernican theory (15th – 17th centuries) moved the earth to the periphery from the centre, as a by-product, women were also moved to the periphery. The earth, hitherto seen as the central embodiment of the maternal instincts, was suddenly thrown far away into the dark space to be just one among the many planets, while the sun, the sign of masculinity, was brought to occupy the centre stage. The metaphor used to express this abuse of nature is: 'nature is raped'.[24] Sandra Harding argues: "As nature came to seem more like a woman, whom it is appropriate to rape and torture than like a nurturing mother, did rape and torture come to seem a more natural relation of men to women?"[25] Women are treated as baby-producing factories; if they are not able to produce them they become unwanted. So women are not seen as some significant individuals, who are capable of contributing to any growth of culture or society, except manufacturing babies.[26]

The role of women in science clearly seems to be overshadowed by male chauvinism. Harding brings out the real struggles of women who have achieved a significant status in science. She examines the lives of the double pioneers – as scientists and as women, and even triply so, if they were women of colour. Even if they emerge against all odds, their work is not duly recognized and even deliberately subdued. For instance, even as late as 1970s, James Watson devalued and ridiculed the work of Rosalind Franklin in the uphill task of mapping the DNA structure. In fact it was her pioneering work that led Watson and Sir Francis Crick to bag the Noble Prize. But to Franklin's luck she had a friend, Anne Sayre, who knew the real story; she came out boldly to challenge Watson's account and she put that in black and white in her book.[27] His ill-treatment of Franklin was not an expression of one individual's sexist and chauvinistic attitude but it reflects nature of science as a cultural institution that is infested with male supremacy, which does not realize that, "Today, Noble Prizes could not be won without the work of women as lab technicians and postdoctoral lab assistants, not to mention data analysts and computer programmers."[28]

Part III
Feminist Epistemology

Feminist (scientific) epistemology and philosophy of science show keen interests in analyzing the role of women in acquiring knowledge. Since 1980s feminists have focused on this issue to find out how gender plays a role in the production scientific knowledge and beliefs.[29] They are convinced that the present knowledge enterprise keeps women in a disadvantageous position, by (a) avoiding them in inquiry, (b) devaluing their epistemic authority, (c) belittling their 'feminine' cognitive styles and modes of knowledge, (d) producing theories to project them as inferior, deviant, or significant only in the ways they serve male interests, (e) producing social theories that render women's activities and interests, or gendered power relations, invisible, and (f) producing knowledge (science and technology) that is not useful for people in subordinate positions, or that legitimizes social (gender) hierarchies. Thus, they also argue that if women are also actively involved the resulting knowledge will be qualitatively superior to knowledge that is produced by men alone.

Situatedness of (Gendered) Knowledge

Knowledge is the production of knowers, who are 'situated'. There are several factors to show that knowledge is a 'situated' knowledge; for instance: *Embodiment* - the physical locations of the knowers in space and time, either closer to or far away from the object determines the quality and the quantity of information obtained; *First-person vs third-person knowledge* - knowers look at things in relation to their emotions, attitudes, interests and values (a rainy day is a spoiler for the travelers, while it is a blessing for farmers!); *Personal knowledge of others, the technical know-how and Skills, Cognitive styles of investigating a problem, one's background beliefs and worldviews, the net-work of relations with other investigators* etc. Such characteristics of the situatedness of knowledge affect the quality of knowledge, their attitudes towards their beliefs (open or dogmatic), their views towards justification, the confidence and authority with which they make those knowledge-claims, and their assessment as to which is important or unimportant claim. Elaborating on this feminist epistemologists go on further to stress that the social location of the knower - including social identities in terms of gender, race, language and sexual orientation, caste and ethnicity, political and religious identities - shapes what and how one knows.

Authors like Haslanger[30] make a distinction between *sex and gender*: while the former refers to the biological characteristics of men and women, the latter refers to the role, norms and meanings, which society has assigned to them due to their sexual differences. Gender roles (men for military, and women for domestic duties), gender norms, traits and behaviours (men being assertive and women being passive), gendered performance and identity – all are assigned by society. The social situatedness of the knowers and their gender identity and roles assigned by families and culture produce, what the feminist epistemologists call, 'gendered knowledge'. From childhood onwards gender consciousness is instilled in a large measure: boys are given more physical freedom, aggressive play, large motor skills, informal and relaxed posture while sitting or standing, unmindfulness of clothing, neatness or appearance; while girls are expected to have physical constraint, subdued play, formal and modest posture, much attention to clothing, neatness and appearance. Once they imbibe these norms they get reinforced as they grow, and their bodies become 'gendered', not just differently sexed.[31] Given the social and cultural conditioning and the notion of gendered knowledge, the background beliefs and worldviews also become gendered.[32]

Critique of Feminist Epistemology

There are strong-worded criticisms against feminist science and its epistemology. Levin finds writings on feminist epistemology "merely embarrassing".[33] Even some feminists like Stephen Jay Gould deny any value in the claim of women contributing to science or exclusively feminist science. Pinnick wonders, if what Harding says is correct that marginalization provides epistemic privilege, "what happens when and if feminists achieve their goals. The standpoint case for feminist science hinges on the claim that feminists, by virtue of being a repressed political minority, acquire a special insight into the nature of natural processes. But even worse, by this very argument, should feminists achieve political equality, they would thereby lose any claim to epistemic privilege, and feminist science would accordingly lose its claim to superiority over non-feminist science".[34]

Feminist epistemology does not argue that simple propositional knowledge about matters that are in principle equally accessible to everyone, like '3 + 3 = 6' or 'fire burns finger'. Rather, it argues that phenomenological knowledge, knowledge of persons, technical know-how, knowledge about morality and emotions, knowledge about interests and attitudes – are affected by gender. Because feminist epistemology stresses upon the situatedness of knowledge, it does not mean that it embraces epistemological relativism. It only questions the *general assumption that the gender and the social situation of the knower don't play any role in acquiring knowledge.* For instance, Keller does not deny objectivity in science; she rather argues to revise the very notion of objectivity; as recent Philosophy of Science reveals that we need to understand this notion in terms of "a dialectical process so as to allow for the possibility of distinguishing the objective effort from the objectivist illusion".[35] Many philosophers, like Popper and Piaget[36], clearly show that as long as the conscious mind that is involved in the inquiry is ignored, the world of science would be in a *perpetual perplexity* over the distinctions between objective and subjective, the essential and the phenomena. Keller claims that "it is time to integrate gender issues... and perhaps even to acknowledge how the inclusion of gender can transform the very questions we ask".[37] Science can never be neutral for political reasons as well. Science and technology are very often the tools in the powerful and dominant class in the society. So if the scientists are neutral that implies that they indirectly support they are in support of the prevailing distribution of interests and power. Therefore, women, as political beings, need to focus on the political content of science in order to improve science.

Part IV
Feminists' Contributions towards "Better" Science

Though we can excuse all the great minds, whom we saw earlier, for their damaging views towards women as their ignorance, humanity has to pay a big price though! Here we consider two possibilities of improving science: by removing the gender bias in the interpreting the results of the experiment; and by learning from the recent neurosciences regarding the differences between male and female brains.

Inevitability of Interpretation in Science

The results of any experiment or discovery have to be interpreted to make it useful or intelligible to the scientific community or society at large. Without this interpretation the results may not be of any importance to science or technology. But this interpretation largely depends on the creative ability and intellectual calibre, and even the values and the belief systems of the scientists. Androcentric minds will easily read into the results to affirm male superiority.

Emily Martin analyses the interpretation of the relative worth of eggs and sperms in human reproduction to show how gender bias influences such interpretation. Literature celebrates sperm production while portrays egg production *as inferior*, because sperms are produced from puberty and lasts throughout their lifetime, while egg production stops at birth. Most of the seven million egg germ cells (oogonia) degenerate in the ovary; when they become eggs, there is a further degeneration and only about two million eggs remain in the ovaries. Degeneration continues and only about 300, 000 eggs remain at puberty. In the fertile period of about 40 years (till menopause) only about 400 eggs are released from the alternative ovaries. Now this is seen as *wasteful* because eggs are formed only to die in the ovaries. However, sperm production is not seen as wasteful, though every second an average male produces more than 1000 and in a day about 100 million sperms are produced; if the reproductive life is for 60 years, he would produce over two trillion sperms. If a woman has two or three children, she wastes only about 200 eggs, while a man wastes one trillion sperms for every child, but still that is not considered wasteful.[38] If such biases are removed one can be sure to have an improved science.

Insights from the Cognitive and Neurosciences

Recent researches in cognitive and neurosciences reveal that male and female brains are somewhat different. Some feminists might not be comfortable to learn about this difference, as they insist upon equality with males. But they need to realize that *the difference in its functions does not necessarily imply inferiority or deficiency*; in fact, the functions of female brains seem to be much better than male brains. Therefore feminists have a strong reason to celebrate these differences!

Men and women respond differently to acute stress: women activate the left hemisphere's amygdale and remember the emotional details; men use the right amygdale and get the gist. The differences in the brains "start with how they got that way in the first place".[39] The sperm of the man has X and Y chromosomes; and it is he who decides the sex of the baby, not the woman, who has two X chromosomes. (Henry VIII, it is said, killed one of his wives for not begetting him a boy, though it was actually he who should have been executed for not passing on Y chromosome!).

David C. Page, a professor at MIT has found out a great amount of inequality among the two chromosomes: the most of the developmental work is done by X chromosome; in fact, Y chromosome sheds its associated genes at the rate of about *five every one million years*, committing suicide in a slow motion; it now has only *100 genes*, while X Chromosome has about *1500 genes*, which necessarily participate in the embryonic construction projects! The female embryo has two X chromosomes; one functions more like a 'back up'; it silences one of them, known as 'X deactivation' – but there are two X chromosomes, one from Dad and one from Mom – which one to be silenced?... The research shows it is only a random event (no reason or pattern is found) that some cells in the embryo chose Dad's, while some others chose Mom's. But in male embryo there is only one X chromosome, and so it cannot afford to deactivate it, as it needs all 1500 X genes to survive. So regarding X chromosome, all boys are Mom's boys, unisexed! Whereas girls are more genetically complex – and the gender based differences start right from here. In 2005 by the human genome project it was discovered that "an unusually a large percentage of the *X chromosome genes...* may be involved in establishing higher cognitive functions... Researchers call the *X chromosome a cognitive 'hot spot'*".[40]

Genetically women are far better equipped than men to face the world:[41] Mental retardation is more common in males than in females; males are affected by schizophrenia 50 % more than females; males exhibit more antisocial behaviour; most alcoholics and drug addicts are male; language and reading disorder occur approximately twice as often in little boys than girls. Women also recover faster from the stroke-induced verbal impairment than men. Girls are better in memory tasks, verbal fluency and articulation, better communicative abilities, like eye contact etc. Now researches show that the advantage for women is due to the fact that "women use both hemispheres, right and left, when speaking and processing verbal information. Men primarily use one. Women tend to have thick cables connecting their two hemispheres. Men's are thinner"[42]. Women are accused of being more emotional than men, but actually it is not the case. If men perceived the same number of data points, they might have the same number of reactions as well. Finally, John Medina is convinced that if only all these differences "are both noted and celebrated, as opposed to ignored and marginalized. Had this been done earlier, we might have more women in science and engineering now!"[43] Such significant differences would likely enrich science if both work together. Many agree without much dispute that actively involving more divergent groups in science will surely produce better science and one may hardly expect from this that this would create black science, lesbian science, gay science or women science!

Concluding Remarks: Need for an Attitudinal Change

It is highly likely that including women and other marginalized groups in science will improve it. But this is not possible unless there is a drastic change in the socio cultural atmosphere of society. Londa Schiebinger argues that the claim of value-neutrality of science and dominant class keep women and other people of 'difference' away from science. She focuses *not just different ways of doing science* by men and women, but explores *different forms of knowledge production*. Therefore, just increasing the number of women-scientists will not solve the issue of feminist science, rather we need to change scientific knowledge itself. Science is embedded in society and culture. The meaning of the terms or metaphors used in science, like 'a passive egg' or 'an aggressive sperm' is seen in and through the lens of society and culture.[44] Women must be empowered. We need to take drastic steps, like acquiring courage and willingness to enforce the Law of gender equality, educating women to make them economically independent and providing them equal opportunities for job and development, having an attitudinal change in both men and women towards women, correcting the misinterpretations of Sacred Scriptures to remove women oppression, to purify several superstitious practices that victimize women in the name of religious rituals and so on. Unless there is a change in the oppressing attitude towards women, by both men and women, there would not be any real improvement in the lives of women. Just to increase the number of opportunities for education and jobs, will not improve the condition or the status of women in our society. Women's empowerment must be holistic. True, many Social Organizations and Women movements do take efforts to make women aware of the social inequalities and discriminations, but quite often they fail to strike at the root causes of such issues. The world is paying a big price for sidelining women in all walks of life down the centuries. The subordination of women has resulted in the ecological crisis, technological haughtiness and value degradation. The whole world is now geared to eradicate poverty, environmental protection and a sustained economic growth. This is possible and will have a lasting effect only if women, the nearly half of the population, are really taken into confidence, including the world of science. [45] As Max Planck opined that only new generations of thinkers can see new facts and work for further developments, as the old generations are blinded to change and want to maintain their status quo. T. H. Huxley, an English biologist, has even advised that scientists need to be strangled on their sixtieth birthday so that their age may not go against new truths.[46]

As long as rationality in science has to be seen in a wider context, to include non-scientific factors [as Russell points out, "Complete rationality is no doubt an unattainable ideal"[47]]. as long as science faces the problem of theory choice, underdetermination of theory and theory-ladenness of observation; as long as science is a social enterprise that includes social and non-rational factors; as long as our society is sexist and male-biased; as long as the brain capacities of male and female are shown to be different... the concerns of ***feminist scientists will ever be legitimate***!

So, one may *safely conclude* that the contribution of women would certainly add to the developments of science. About what exactly those developments and their quantity and quality will be, we cannot now predict, because we have not allowed women to play that role so far. Inclusion of more female brains in pioneering researches will, I think, enlighten us more on that development.

Notes

1. Professor in Jnana-Deepa Vidyapeeth, Pune. India. He has published seven books, including *Towards a Theory of Rationality in Science – A Plea to Reasonableness* (2012) and *A Book That Cannot Be Titled* (2018).
2. Minnich Earmarck, *Transforming Knowledge* (Temple University Press, Philadelphia, 1990), 39.
3. Quoted from: John Medina, *Brain Rules - 12 Basic Principles for Surviving and Thriving at Work, Home and School* (Seattle, USA: Pear Press, 2008), 248-9.
4. See: http://en.wikipedia.org/wiki/Women in science; accessed on 4 April, 2017.
5. G. W. Friedrich Hegel, translated by Knox, *The Philosophy of Right* (Oxford University, 1973), 263.
6. Sarah Blaffer Hardy, "Empathy, Polyandry, and the Myth of the Coy Female," in Ruth Bleier, ed., *Feminist Approaches to Science* (New York: Teachers College Press, 1991), 141.
7. Sandra Harding, *Whose Science? Whose Knowledge? – Thinking from Women's Lives* (Ithaca, New York: Cornell University Press, 1991), 24.
8. K. Manheim, *Ideology and Utopia: An Introduction to the Sociology of Knowledge* (New York: Harcourt Brace ad World, 1954. [First published in German, 1929-31].
9. Trevor Pinch, "The Sociology of Scientific Community," In Companion of the History of Modern Science, (ed.) R. C. Olby, G. N. Cantor *et al.* (London & New York: Routledge, 1990), 87-99, 87.
10. Robert K. Merton, *The Sociology of Science: Theoretical and Empirical Investigations* (Chicago/London: Chicago University Press, 1973).
11. Karin D. Knorr-Cetina and Michael Mulkay, ed., *Science Observed – Perspectives on the Social Study of Science* (London: Sage Publications, 1983), 1.
12. For more on this, see: A. Grunbaum, "The Duhemian Argument", *Philosophy of Science*, 27 (1), 1960, 75-87.
13. Karin D. Knorr-Cetina and Michael Mulkay, ed., 1983, 4.
14. For 'Linguistic turn' in Sociology of Science, see: M. Lynch, *Art and Artefacts in Laboratory Science* (London: Routledge & Kegan Paul), 1982; K. D. Knorr-Cetina, *The Manufacture of Knowledge: An Essay on the Constructivist and Contextual Nature of Science* (Oxford: Pergamon Press, 1981); and *Social Studies of Science*, 12 (1982).
15. David Bloor, *Knowledge and Social Imagery* (London: Routledge & Kegan Paul, 1976); M. Mulkay, Science and the Sociology of Knowledge (London: George Allen and Unwin, 1979); and M. Hesse, *Revolutions and Reconstructions in the Philosophy of Science* (Brigthon, Sussex: Harvester Press, 1980).
16. Andre Kukla, *Social Constructivism and the Philosophy of Science* (Routledge, London & NY, 2000), p. 9.
17. Evelyn Fox Keller, "Gender and Science: Origin, History and Politics", in *Osiris*, 2nd series, *Constructing Knowledge in the History of Science*, The University of Chicago Press 10 (1995), 27-38, 27.

18. Sandra Harding, *Whose Science?*...1991, 21. Also see: "Feminist Science Criticism", in Robert Klee, (ed.), *Scientific Inquiry – Readings in the Philosophy of Science* (Oxford: Oxford University Press, 1999); "How Women's Movement Benefits Science: Two Views", *Women's Studies International Forum*, 12 (1989), 271-283; "Rethinking Standpoint Epistemology: What is 'Strong Objectivity'?", *the Centennial Review* 36(1992), 437-470.
19. Evelyn Fox Keller, "Feminism and Science", in Richard Boyd et al., (eds), *The Philosophy of Science* (Massachusetts: Massachusetts Institute of Technology, 1995), 280.
20. Emily Martin, "The Egg and the Sperm: How Science has Constructed a Romance Based on Stereotypical Male-Female Roles," in *Signs: Journal of Women in Culture and Society*, 16 (1991), 485-501, 489-490.
21. Gerald Schattern and Helen Schattern, "The Energetic Egg," in *The Sciences*, 23(1983), 28-43, 29.
22. Bruce Albert, et al., *Molecular Biology of the Cell* (New York/London: Garland Press, 1994), 868.
23. See, Sandra Harding, 1991, 44-45.
24. Carolyn Merchant and Marilyn Strathern (eds.), *Nature, Culture and Gender* (Cambridge: Cambridge University Press, 1980).
25. Sandra Harding, "Feminist Science Criticism", 1999, 278.
26. Emily Martin, *The Women in the Body* (Boston: Boston Press, 1987).
27. Anne Sayer, *Rosalind and DNA: A Vivid View of What It Is Like to Be a Gifted Woman in an Especially Male Profession* (New York: Norton, 1975); a rebuttal to Watson's claims in *The Double Helix* (New York: New American Library, 1969).
28. Sandra Harding, "Feminist Science Criticism", 1999, 26.
29. Frederick Shmitt (ed.), *Socializing Epistemology: The Social Dimension of Knowledge* (Lanham, MD: Rowman and Littlefield, 1994); in Jonathan Dancy, Ernest Sosa and Matthias Steup (eds.), in *The Blackwell Companion to Epistemology*, (Oxford, Blackwell, 2010).
30. Sally Haslanger, "On Being Objective and Being Objectified", in Antony Louise and Charlotte Witt, (eds.), *A Mind of One's Own* (Boulder: West view Press, 1993 and 2002).
31. Susan Bordo, *The Flight to Objectivity: Essays on Cartesianism and Culture* (Albany: State University of New York Press, 1987); I. M. Young, *Throwing Like a Girl and Other Essays in Feminist Political Theory* (Bloomington: Indiana University Press, 1990).
32. Helen Longino, *Science as Social Knowledge* (Princeton, N.J.: Princeton University Press, 1990); and Miriam Solomon, *Social Empiricism* (Cambridge, Mass.: MIT Press, 2001).
33. Margarita Levin, "Caring New World", *American Scholar* 57 (1988), 100-106, 106.
34. Cassandra Pinnick, "Problems with Feminist Epistemology", in Robert Klee, ed., *Scientific Inquiry – Readings in the Philosophy of Science* (New York: Oxford University Press, 1999), 303.

35. Evelyn Fox Keller, "Feminism and Science", 1995, 282.
36. Karl Popper, *The Logic of Scientific Discovery* (London: Routledge, 2002); Jean Piaget, *The Child's Conception of the World* (Totowa, NJ: Littlefield, Adams & Co, 1972).
37. Evelyn Fox Keller, "Gender and Science: Origin, History and Politics", 1995, 37.
38. Emily Martin, "The Egg and the Sperm: How Science has Constructed a Romance Based on Stereotypical Male-Female Roles," in *Signs: Journal of Women in Culture and Society*, 16, 3(1991), 485-501, 488-9.
39. John Medina, *Brain Rules* (Seattle, USA: 2008), 244.
40. John Medina, 2008, 247.
41. *Ibid*, 247-59.
42. Ibid., 252.
43. Ibid., 259
44. Londa Schiebinger, *Has Feminism Changed Science?* (Cambridge: Harvard University Press, 1999).
45. For more discussion on this, see my paper: "A Woman: 'Double You, O Man!' – Issues and Perspectives in the Empowerment of Women", in *Vikasini – The Journal of Women's Empowerment*, 24:1 (2009), 27-39.
46. Quoted in Huxley, *Life and Letter of Thomas Henry Huxley*, vol 2, (New York: Appleton, 1901), 117.
47. Bertrand Russell, *Sceptical Essays* (London and New York: Rutledge, 1988),

Chapter - 12

Politicization of the Feminine in Identity Politics and Divinization of the Subaltern Feminine as Counter-Narrative

Prof. James Ponniah[1]

Introduction

Identity construct in our aspirational contemporary society is increasingly becoming a necessary project that involves an oeuvre of agential acts and practices, both discursive and material, internal and external, personal and collective. Just as of other identities, the boundaries of gender identity too are neither pre-given nor immutable. They are rather created, invented and reconfigured at varying times and space. Perhaps gender identity is the most vulnerable identity category that is most negotiated, resisted and subverted at the fulcrum of multiple identities. Similarly, in the Indian context, caste identity is another identity that is actively engaged within the negotiation of other identities such as class, religion and ethnicity wherein low-caste or Dalit identity remains the most vulnerable category. Since identity today is getting increasingly entangled with questions of power, gender and Dalit identities have become what Patricia Uberoi would call 'tropes' in power relations of race, class, caste and religion.[2] It means that in the evolution of other identities such as class, religion, race, nation and ethnicity, the feminine and Dalit identities get necessarily implicated. Thus unlike other projects of identity construct, construction of subaltern identities such as Dalit and women identities entail a two-fold task: to undo the past by confronting and negating the schemes of domination and exploitation, and to envisage an alternative future by producing a strategic present. In this context, this paper seeks to explore how feminist identity is constructed by two different political agents in India, the Hindu right and the subaltern Dalits. It will interrogate the ways in which the two political stake-holders converge and diverge not only in their adoption of sources, methods and strategies and in their projection of the ideals but also in their interrogation/appropriation of the masculine. In this regard, the paper will bring into discussion the processes of idealization/divinization of two prototype figures—Rani Lakshmibai for the Hindu right and Jhalkaribai for the subaltern Dalits, and the surplus of meaning they carry for the project of projecting women like Sadhvi Rithambhara and Uma Bharati (for the former) and Mayawati (for the latter) as perfect leadership models.

I

Hindu Right, Women and Production of the Feminine

Just as the Indian National Congress involved women to intensify its struggle for Indian Independence from the British, the Hindu Maha Saba and the RSS too sought the support of women to advance its agenda and broaden its support base. One of the first Hindu right wing women organizations, namely, Rashtriya Sevika Samiti was born after 12 years of RSS' formation as a parallel organization which took root among the upper and middle class women. Similarly, Durga Vahini (Carrier of Durga), a female counterpart of the Bajrang Dal (male youth affiliate of VHP) was born in 1991 during Ramjanmabhoomi movement, which recruits young women from low-income earning and lower-class families. In both of these organizations women were to serve as foot-soldiers to realize the goals and agenda set by the male counterparts. Multiple strategies were adopted to make it happen. They were not only schooled in the values and ideals of these organizations, but the very concepts of the woman and the feminine were also framed in certain ways that helped the cause of the Hindutva groups. If the rise of the Hindu right is one of the visible, if not infamous, landmarks in the political history of independent India, its growth is partly due to the appropriation of the feminine and the involvement of women in India. Right from the inception, women not only became central to the construct of India as a Hindu nation, but they were also imagined and constructed in certain ways. Multiple strategies and tactics were employed to achieve this. They included equating women with nation, making women as potent actors as well as signifiers of nationalism, projecting women as victims and victors at the same time, portraying the divine figures both in the milder and the fiercer forms as prototypes, engaging in the externalization of enemy, framing war heroes like Rani Lakshmibai of Jhansi as both motherly and manly, and foregrounding celibacy and sexual renunciation as an ideal way of life for right wing activists.

1. Creating Homology Between Women And Nation

The Hindu nationalistic discourse, right from its nascent stage, established more direct and mutually constitutive relationship between nation and women. Just as Hindu nationalists sought to feminize the nation by creating a powerful symbol of Bharathmata, they also projected women as living symbols of mother

India. In Hindu nationalists' worldview, the honour of the nation (Hindu Nation) and the honour of the Hindu women were equated. They developed the idea of Hindu women in the images of "Hindu goddesses like Gauri— the benevolent mother, Durga—the tiger borne mother, Kali—the ferocious mother and not the least a Cow—the Gaumata (the Mother Cow)."[3] Their framing of the Nation and Hindu women in terms of Bharatmata and Gaumata necessitated the presence of virile men (the Men with the capital M as Golwalkar once expressed) whose duty was to protect them against the dangers from outsiders such as Muslims and the white men. The cow as a mother and a symbol of the nation became the rallying point for nationalism way back in the 19th and 20th centuries. The protection of mother cow (Gaumata) was one of the earliest issues involving the use of femininity for religious nationalism. This movement which originated in the 1880s evoked mass mobilization in the 1920s. The cow protection societies were formed to press upon the British government to ban cow slaughter. The movement turned militant when the colonial government ignored their demands while Hindu nationalists physically tried to stop cow slaughter deliberately violating the law. "Due to agitation and ensuing riots, a rift was created between the Hindus and the Muslims besides the Hindus and the Christians."[4] Hindu worship of cow was justified and valorized on the reasoning that just as infants depend on their mother for sustenance, full-grown humans depend upon the cow for the whole of their lives. An awareness that almost all the products of a cow such as milk, ghee, butter, cow-dung including its urine remain useful for the humans both as individuals and as a society was spread among the Hindus. Thus, "the construction of the cow as a mother goddess nurturing her child,"[5] became strong in Hinduism and the cow became "one of the many images of a female body in the psyche of the nationalist Hindus."[6] Thus the cow came to represent "the Hindu community at large or for that matter the Hindu *mathribhoomi* and the patriarchal social system is morally bound to protect her. Rationally therefore, the cow has assumed a symbolic image of the nation."[7]

As quoted earlier, Hindutva created the feminine not only as benign and nurturing as seen in the images of Gauri and Gaumata but also as fierce and violent as symbolized in the image of Durga. This dual view of the feminine was also materialized in the birth of two important Hindu right wing women organizations, namely, Rashtriya Sevika Samiti and Durga Vahini. The former born after 12 years of RSS' formation as a parallel organization took root among the upper and middle class women and called upon them to be caring, loving and committed women in Hindu households wherein their primary function is to rear children according to the Hindu worldview and thus remain custodians of Hindu culture at home. The mission of the organization is to "retain their basic characteristics of motherhood and thus carefully guard their children from corrupting Western influences and instill in them the right sanskars (virtues) such as devotion to duty, spirit of personal endeavor, love of motherland and readiness for service to the society."[8] Contrary to Rashtriya

Sevika Samiti, Durga Vahini (Carrier of Durga), a female counter part of the Bajrang Dal (male youth affiliate of VHP) originating during Ramjanmabhoomi movement in 1990's recruited young women from low-income earning and lower-class families. Militant in its outlook, it calls upon Hindu women to fight against dowry, child marriage and atrocities on women, and to confront the Muslim people whom they view as an enemy. "Durga Vahini's appropriation of goddess Durga for carrying out the militant activism as well as violence has aided in feminine empowerment within the broad parameters of Hindu nationalism."[9] Thus, "women in the Hindu nationalist discourse hence are portrayed both in the milder form and in the fiercer"[10] as they "have always remained the potent actors as well as signifiers of the nationalism,"[11] in Hindutva (Hinduness) project.

2. Projecting Women as both Victims and Victors

Right-wing women leaders not only played on the imagery of women as self-sacrificing, long-suffering, non-violent victims in communal conflict but also inverted it in powerful ways through their speeches and demeanour.[12] The construction of this powerful self-imagery of women as victors has brought the female Hindutva icons like Rithambhra and Uma Bharti as the vanguard of Ayodhya movement. While depicting these Hindutva icons as living symbols of fearful and formidable feminine power, they also likened the Ayodhya crisis to the partition holocaust. While pitching the victimization of Hindu women as denigration of Hindu community on the one hand and providing new forms of responses to this situation, on the other hand, in the likes of militant leaders like Rithambhra and Uma Bharti, they formed a strategic component of victim-victor narrative. They espoused the woman both as a flag bearer of family honour (and of the nation) and the *matrishakti*, i.e., victim and victor at the same time.

In this connection, we need to take note of the aggressive role played by the women wings such as Durga Vahini (the women's wing of the VHP) during the Ayodhya issue. They played a very proactive role during Ramajanmabhoomi movement which witnessed aggressive participation of 55,000 women out of a total of two lakh kar sevaks at Ayodhya. For instance, Durga Vahini called upon Hindu women to become *viranganas* (heroines) and *ranchandis* (warrior women) while the Ayodya issue was referred to as *agni pariksha* (trial by fire). The project of recasting of the Hindu women by the Hindu right organizations like Hindu Mahasabha and VHP is closely linked to the project of vilification of the religious other in the order of Muslims first and Christians next. This project gained its traction in early 20th century when the new portrait of Hindu women was created to protect them against the Muslim who was "characterized primarily by his 'excesses' - 'sexual excess' and 'martial excess'."[13] Fearful of the sexually hyperactive Muslim men, "the Arya Samaj, the Hindu Mahasabha and the Rashtriya Swayamsevak Sangh set themselves to the task of creating a mythology beginning from Allaudin Khilji (13 cent

Muslim ruler who conquered many Hindu Kingdoms) to the present about the forceful abduction of Hindu women, their rape, pillage and conversion."[14] Exposed to Muslim men were the Hindu widows, in particular, whose lonely life and repressed sexuality made them vulnerable. Hence practices such as widow remarriage or *niyoga* for widows (sexual union outside marriage for the sake of child-bearing) were promoted by Arya Samaj while at the same time desire "for brave and fearless Hindu children who could protect their women and religion against the Muslims produced women as breeders while their bodies were seen as vessels or reservoirs of future Hindu warriors."[15]

3. Externalization of Enemy

One of the ways in which the right wing Hindu organizations have managed to garner women's support is to identify and name an outside enemy who is a constant threat to the insiders, especially the weak and the vulnerable sections. This strategy of "the externalization of enemy," as Kalpagm observes "has provided a convenient way of directing the attack away from the enemy within, and has served as a persuasive way of mobilizing Hindu women to attack the other, the villainized Muslims and the British."[16] In doing so, the Hindu fundamentalist feminist groups have appropriated "some concepts of western radical feminist thought in an inverted way for achieving the goals of fundamentalism and in this way they are creating a 'feminist space' within fundamentalist agenda."[17] It is done by attributing to the men of other religious communities the same vices which radical feminists attributed to men in general. "For instance, radical feminist thinking perceives all male as potential rapists, while fundamentalist women's organizations preach the idea that all male belonging to other religious communities as potential rapist."[18] In doing so, they have made a very selective feministic critique of the patriarchal mindset in India which actually discriminates women invariably in all places either subtly or blatantly. Hindutva's critique of Muslim men in India today which targets just Muslim men is lopsided. Because, while it projects Muslim masculinity as an external threat, it conveniently overlooks Hindu women's experience of internal oppression that comes from Hindu men. Besides, its projection of 'Hindu women' as a separate category of victims leads to disunity among Indian feminists who aim at unsettling the larger nexus between religion, caste and class in India, which underscores women oppression in India. While Indian feminism seeks to evolve a pan-Indian framework of women liberation that exposes the role of all religions equally in women oppression in India, Hindutva project unfortunately indicts only a few religions while valorizing and favouring the complex Hindu religion.

4. Valorization of the Female Figure though Ambivalently

In order to take on the external enemy, these organizations employ a whole range of images and symbols from Hindu India to highlight qualities and virtues expected of a Hindu woman. "They range from the warrior queens like Rani

Lakshmibai, Durgavati and Vishbala to the able women administrators like Ahilyabai and Rani Chennama to the bhakti poetess Mirabai"[19] without ever deserting classical figures like Sita and Savitri. Some of them even valorize unorthodox figures like - Kaikeyi and Mandodari. While they were traditionally and popularly reviled as greedy and villainous, they too are praised for their role in the myth. For instance, Kaikeyi is admired for her skills in the battlefield, which saved her husband' s life and earned her boons through which she could exercise her power over him. Mandodari too is highlighted as a virtuous wife of Ravan, "whose words of wisdom went unheeded by her husband and led to his ruin."[20]

These women also heavily draw upon ancient lineage of mother goddesses to empower themselves. The most important goddess of theirs is Bharat Mata as mentioned earlier.

> The daily salutation dedicated to Mother India is emblematic of the conception of the Goddess, the nation and the awakened Hindu woman, the *sevika*. The prayer may be sung individually but maximum benefit is believed to accrue when sung in a collectivity, when the 'I' is drowned in the 'we'. Backbone of their prayer is Savarkar's notions 'of the sacred geography of the nation, the citizenship of which rests on the devotion to the 'sacred land' (*punyabhoomi*). Motherland is the origin of all divinities and is boundlessly affectionate - a quality of all mothers, is auspicious and the very embodiment of power.[21]

As her daughters, *sevikas* are the embodiment of the virtues of their primordial mother such as chastity, selflessness, fearlessness and unity. "As power she is Durga and as auspiciousness she is Parvati. In fact, Bharat Mata, Durga, Parvati and the physical mother all elide easily into each other. Durga, created from the combined energies of all Gods wields weapons and battles alone, unaided she slays the buffalo demon Mahisha to claim the title of 'Mahishasur Mardini'."[22] It is her horrific form and destructive principle that is most evoked by the Durga Vahini in its theme songs.

They also create a few new feminine divinities. For instance, Kelkar, the first president of the Samiti created a goddess, Devi Ashtabhuja, the eight armed goddess. "She represents an assimilation of Mahalakhsmi's wealth, Mahasaraswati's intellect and Mahadurga's power. (She) is above all a model of virtues to be emulated by the *sevikas*, each of her hands representing one virtue - chastity, power, dedication and so on. These images of goddesses as placid, bounteous to tempestuous and out-of-control allows women a wide array of role choices."[23] All these roles, though different, must be viewed as "one single and harmonious whole, which may manifest different characteristics or forms at different times."[24] According to these organizations, a *sevika* must place herself on this continuum that is created between the binaries and opposites such as fecundity and destruction, good and evil, caring and violence, calm and fierce while she needs to operationalize and enact qualities and virtues as demanded of the context. One of the important prototypes, a historical figure that is extolled in this connection is Lakshmibai of Jhansi. While the Rani of Jhansi is celebrated as an icon across the political spectrum in India, these organizations have a special admiration for her. No doubt there is masculinization of her femininity. For instance, various accounts of the Rani, in praise of her brave and warrior-like qualities, highlight her boy-like childhood days whence as a young woman she was "raised not as a proper Brahmin girl but among the boys at the court of the last Peshawa at Bithur. She learned not the domestic and feminine arts but riding, swordsmanship, and literacy in Persian. Her playmates were not other Brahmin girls but boys, some of whom grew into rebel leaders-Nana Sahib, Tatya Tope, and Rao Sahib. Through this extraordinary childhood she was groomed for the exceptional political and military role she played following the death of her maharaja husband."[25] Rani Lakshmibai was projected as an ideal model because she fiercely fought the British and defended mother India. Hindu women were called upon to emulate her. For instance, Sangathan Ka Bigu , one of the propagandist books, gave an open call to Hindu women to carry a knife for self-defense: "Every sister who joins the army of this revolution called the Sangathan should have a sharp knife with her which she can use whenever she needs. The knife should be made like household knife which can be used immediately. It is a prime religious duty of all the women who enter the army of Sangathan to be able to defend their chastity and honour."[26]

While such descriptions and characteristics were espoused by right wing women's groups, additionally they consider her also as "the model for women and guardian of Hindu women's virtue and honor."[27] In this context, Badri Narayan writes, "celebrations around Rani Lakshmibai focused on her feminine qualities, which are much admired by upper castes, such as sacrifice, self-effacement, sense of honour and beauty. Even today these qualities are emulated by upper-caste women and looked upon as ideals to be acquired."[28] Thus the portrait of Rani depicted and propagated by right wing feminist groups is rather ambivalent, she is both ferocious and kind, masculine and feminine.

5. Adopting Renunciation and Celibacy as Ideals

While for the right wing women movements figures like Rani Lakshmibai and others remain as distant models, contemporary personalities like Sadhvi Rithambhara and Uma Bharati have emerged as powerful icons and immediate models worthy of emulation. Their power comes from the fact that they are religious renouncers around whom an aura of selflessness, sacrifice and dedicated service has been created. Though renunciation is traditionally looked at as an individual's conscious decision to quit the mundane world in pursuit of one's religious ideal of *moksa*, these models perceive renunciation differently, namely, as a way of detached but selfless involvement in politics to "to purge the social order of its current immorality."[29] They want to project that they have emptied themselves "of the values of *artha* and *kama* that is, profit and pleasure, which tie a householder to the mundane worldly affairs."[30] In this regard, Sadhvi Rithambara once said, "Do you think we want votes? We *sants* can become the emperors of the universe simply by virtue of our claim to the omniscience of Vyas. We do not want political power in Delhi. We want our Ram. We want our Ramjanmabhoomi."[31] Their appropriation of the spiritual for the political reminds us of Gandhi's approach of building his political movement based on spiritual power of *ahmisa* and *satyagraha*. But there is a huge difference between the two as the former make use of the spiritual for divisive and sectarian politicization of religion while Gandhi used it for the liberation of the nation as a whole. These women have deliberately embraced the mantle of celibacy and sexual renunciation, as for women "the only legitimate route to political activism outside the familial roles of wife, mother and daughter was that of the renouncer,"[32] observes Uma Bharathi. By adopting celibacy, though they seem to be breaking out of the patriarchal boundaries and role assigned to women, they nevertheless become militant advocates of the male's social and political order as they remain diehard votaries of 'Ram Rajya' not 'Sita-Rajya' or Jhansi-Rani Rajya

Thus, strategies that the right wing groups followed to appropriate the feminine are : equating women with nation, making women the potent actors as well as signifiers of nationalism, projecting women as victims and victors at the same time, portraying the divine figures both in the milder and the fiercer forms as prototypes, engaging in the externalization of the enemy, casting war heroes like Rani Lakshmibai of Jhansi as both motherly and manly; and foregrounding celibacy and sexual renunciation as the ideal way of life for right wing activists. Just as Hindutva groups drew upon the feminine to achieve their communal goals, the marginal groups too instrumentalized the feminine for their end. In the following section, we will turn our attention to how Dalits of India make use of the feminine world to advance their emancipatory project.

II

Dalit Movements and Subaltern Appropriation of the Feminine

If right wing organizations such as Rashtriya Sevika Samiti and Durga Vahini were to draw upon the historical incident of First Independence war of 1857 and included historical figures like Rani of Jhansi in their campaign to build Hindu Rashstra, the subaltern Dalit political outfits like BSP also tapped into the same historic moment and created an alternative narrative to suit their political agenda. In the latter's narrative, the focus was on the unsung and forgotten female heroes, from low caste backgrounds, whose role in the freedom struggle is less known and never recorded in nationalistic discourses. Borrowing from folk songs, folk drama, oral traditions and contemporary vernacular literatures, these narratives focus on women *viranganas* (courageous woman) such as Jhalkaribai, Udadevi and Mahaviridevi and project them as models of and forerunners to Dalit political leaders like Mayawati.

One such *virangana* was Jhalkaribai, a Dalit hero forgotten in the annals of both the British and national historiography. But now she is remembered and celebrated in the emerging narratives of 1857 war of Indian independence, and her narrative too is produced, popularized and employed for political mobilization by Dalit groups. Their version of her story reads as follows: "There was a *dasi* (maid servant) named Jhalkaribai in the palace of Rani Lakshmibai of Jhansi. She was a low-caste woman. When the British besieged the fort of Jhansi and started firing from all sides, Jhalkaribai suggested that the Rani should leave the palace after securing her child (who was the heir apparent) to her back. She, on her part, would hoodwink the British by assuming the appearance of the Rani. The Rani accepted this advice and made good her escape with the child. The ruse worked and for a long time the British were uncertain about the true identity of Jhalkaribai who was posing as Rani Jhansi. It was much later that they learnt that the 'Rani' was in fact the maid Jhalkaribai. But by then it was too late and the Rani had already covered a considerable distance."[33]

This counter narrative is in the popular memory of the people of Bundelkhand region and it is recounted in several versions through folklores, folk stories and folk drama performances. According to Narayan who has researched on Dalit Virangas, "most of the Dalit communities believe that Jhalkaribai was an incarnation of a goddess who had descended upon earth to serve the country."[34] According to Raj Kumar Koree, a singer in the Jababi Kirtan Mandali, she was Goddess Durga. It was non-Dalit novelist Brindavan Lal Varma who first took the trouble to depict Jhalkaribai as she had existed in the memory of these castes before 1950 and made available the story of Jhalkaribai to the literate and educated people through his novel. Subsequently Dalit writers took her story to the common masses in the form of folk songs, poetry, drama and biography. As Narayan observes, "The dissemination of the story of Jhalkaribai has a powerful ideological motivation—a new form of awareness and a new attempt at defining identity and aspirations. One of the basic purposes of this kind of recovery of the past is to acquire legitimacy and a reconstructed identity in the new socio-political and cultural context."[35] In order to reconstruct their identity, Dalit groups had to resort to various strategies as we see below just as they appropriated the feminine to promote their political agenda.

Emancipatory Strategies of the Dalits

1. Removal of the Past Stigma

To uncover how Dalits attempted to overcome their past stigma, let us once again turn to Jhalkaribai, the Dalit heroine. Jhalkaribai hails from Kori community, a weaver caste by profession who along with Chamars, Doms and Bhangis traditionally hold very low position in the caste hierarchy. Hence heroine figures like Jhalkaribai not only inherit stigma but also their contribution gets easily ignored and remains largely unacknowledged. Local versions of Jababi Kirthan (a popular cultural performance in this region) on Lakshmibai performed by the Suresh Singh Bundela Kirthan Party does not even mention her name, which is fiercely contested by Jababi Kirthan performed by Raj Kumar Koree. The story of Jhalkaribai and her brave deeds is a common subject of most Kirthan mandalis (devotional song groups) performed by the latter. One such kirthan goes like this:

"Jai Jhalkari Durga, Kali
Jai, Jai Ma
Angrezon ka garba tune
chur, chur kiya"

(Translated)

(Hail Jhalkari Durga, Kali
Hail, Hail Mother
The pride of the British
You shattered to smithereens.)"[36]

While efforts like these can be viewed as contemporary subaltern attempt to remove the social stigma imposed on the Dalits of India, some high castes do resist such attempts as we see in the case of Ram Narayan Shukul, a Brahmin, who states "Jhalkaribai koi khas nahi thi' (Jhalkaribai was not very important). She was just a Korin and a maid servant of Rani Lakshmibai. The two resembled each other physically. When the Rani came out of the fort with her army to face the British, Jhalkaribai dressed herself as the Rani and confused the British about her true identity."[37]

2. Construction and Glorification of the Mythical Past

To restore the forgotten past of the low caste women, many plays and dramas have been written and staged since 1990. One such effort was Mata Prasad's drama (1990) on Jhalkaribai whose contents can be summarized as follows:

> Jhalkaribai was the wife of Puran Kori. The Koree jat (caste) had participated in the war against the British along with Lakshmibai. The main gate of the palace, where Jhalkaribai's husband was posted, was guarded by soldiers of the Kori caste. Jhalkaribai was as courageous as Lakshmibai and was her closest friend on account of which the upper-caste employees in the palace despised her and conspired against her. Jhalkaribai was an expert at wrestling and other physical exercises. She was trained by the Rani herself in horse-riding and shooting and was the chief of the Durgavahini, a women's battalion of the Rani's army. It was

Jhalkaribai who advised the Rani to go out of the fort with her adopted son, Damodar, and conceived the plan of confusing the British. As a consequence, without caring for her life, she went up to Dantia fighting bravely against the British army. But, here, she was arrested and imprisoned for a long time till she was subsequently released.[38]

In this narrative a Kori is not merely portrayed as a loyal servant but a friend of the queen who grew in stature as a warrior figure and came to almost act in lieu of the queen herself. This narrative goes one step further and explains why such a great Dalit woman military leader has been deliberately discarded in mainline discourses. While it places Jhalkaribai on the same pedestal as Rani Lakshmibai by extolling her for her excellence in martial arts and showing how the Rani treated her as *bahin* (sister) and planning military strategies with her etc.. it goes on to highlight the treachery of Thakur Dulhaju because of which she was eventually arrested. "In this version, she is projected as a patriot greater than any person belonging to a higher caste (ibid.). The upper stratum of society finds such an interpretation unacceptable because, on the one hand, Jhalkaribai is depicted as an equally significant strategist as Lakshmibai while, on the other hand, a Thakur is characterized as a traitor. Here a depressed caste is, by the logic of facts, represented as being more patriotic."[39]

Having suffered inequality, hierarchy and domination in their day-to-day life-world down the centuries, the subaltern groups today feel strongly compelled to confront the social stigma associated with them. They now revisit their symbolic resources, reconstruct their historical past and restore their lost self-dignity. This necessarily calls for both discursive and non-discursive acts and practices that may be construed as competing narratives but inevitable, nevertheless, for identity reconstruct.

3. Divinization of the Feminine

Aspiring for a better identity that would fetch self-respect, self-confidence and a new social status is commonly found among different social groups and more commonly among the deprived communities in a compelling and forceful manner. They articulate their aspirations for a new identity through symbols, myths, art, performances often centered around heroes who may be real or imaginary, historical or mythical. In the process of weaving an alternative narrative around them, the aspirational subaltern groups tend to attribute qualities, characteristics and potentialities to these heroes in such a way that they are raised from the human to the divine plane. Virangas like Jhalkaribai are elevated to the divine plane because they have displayed extraordinary valour, chivalry, bravery, smartness and intelligence which seem to embody some aspects of the supernatural. Most of the Dalit communities believe that Jhalkaribai was an incarnation of a goddess who had descended upon earth to serve the country. For Raj Kumar Koree, a singer in the Jababi Kirtan Mandali,

She is Goddess Durga herself.[40] Dalits of Bundelkhand celebrate their memory through festivals and performances They organize a function every year at Jhansi in the Fort of Rani Lakshmibai to commemorate the memory of Jhalkaribai. A tower near Unnao Gate and Anjani Toria is named after Jhalkaribai. A Polytechnic Institute is founded in her honour. Veerangana Memorial Trust has been established to ensure the transmission of the story of Jhalkaribai. The BSP organizes the Veerangana Jhalkaribai Mahotsav every year at the block and district levels in the Bundelkhand region. The Dalit community has constructed a grand statue of Jhalkaribai near the fort, which was unveiled by Mayawati when she was the chief minister of Uttar Pradesh.

The elevation of such figures to the plane of divinity can serve at least two purposes. Humans, raised to the superhuman level, automatically become inspirational models for the people at the bottom of society. These heroes, though born like them into low-caste society, have gained greater heights today. Now their followers can be motivated to pursue their proven ways. Secondly, by casting them as incarnations of the goddesses like Durga, they project their elevation to the realm of divinity as *an act of the supernatural* which is beyond human control and contestation. They belong to a new order of existence in the pantheon of gods and goddesses like Rani Lakshmibai. Now the high castes have to view the Dalit heroes as divinities of that elevated order which is beyond the framework of caste hierarchy and thus may have to accept their positions of power willy-nilly. Though high castes may or may not give credence to the legitimacy of their divinity, it is not likely that they would subvert or puncture their divine status that easily.

4. Adoption of Three-fold Medium

To achieve this goal of superhumanization and deification of the local heroes, they employ a three-fold articulation, namely. orality, visualization and ritualisation. In the first place, the subaltern people in India, having been kept away from the formal system of education in India for millennia, were forced to sustain their worldviews only in oral forms. Dalit communities in this region too, being mostly poor and illiterate, have a long tradition of communication and transmission of ideas—be it religious, cultural or political—through folk media such as folk theaters, dramas, *bhajan mandals* etc. In this context, Narayan notes, “The political ends are communicated orally, a mode popular in the region and practiced from very early times.”[41] Secondly, the Dalits of the region also adopt different forms of visualization as vehicles of their emancipatory project. Hoardings, posters, drawings, stamps, pamphlets and other kinds of literature that showcase the caste’s identity of these heroes are in intense circulation amongst the people of the region. “The statue of Jhalkaribai in Jhansi, built under BSP patronage during the regime of Mayawati, is made to resemble Rani Lakshmibai, but of a much larger size.”[42] Thirdly they have also adopted the strategy of ritualisation. Ritualisation is another phenomenon observable in the ‘cultification’ of hero figures like

Jhalkaribai. It invariably occurs through the organization and routinization of festivals and functions in honour of these divinities.

5. Unambiguous Masculinization of the Feminine

There is definitely a valorization of the masculine in Dalit's articulation of their identity politics as Narayan observes.[43] Even heroines like Jhalkaribai are deliberately projected as *veers* (chivalrous men) in the narratives and visuals. While their womanly aspects were downplayed if not removed, it is their muscular, chivalrous and manly qualities that are highlighted, acclaimed and valorized. Attribution of these qualities to these figures which developed gradually but systematically since 1980 in Uttar Pradesh has a political agenda. The BSP, a famous Dalit political organization in UP, deliberately engaged in this campaign to make it fit and facilitate the popularity of its upcoming woman political leader, namely Mayawati. Drawing upon the indigenous cultural resources of folk songs and dramas, they not only restored the memories of heroines like Jhalkaribai, Udadevi and Mahaviridevi preserved in oral and vernacular literary traditions, but they also popularized their name and fame, and extolled their contribution to the national freedom struggle which was totally ignored in the mainline narratives. Just as post-Mandal period in India witnessed the emergence of critical consciousness of various low caste communities across the nation, BSP tapped these resources and ingeniously employed them to frame a new narrative about Dalits' past and their hero figures. Such a narrative they believed would facilitate and legitimize the elevation of Dalit women leaders like Mayawati who will be received by the common Dalit folk as an heir to the legacy of the war martyrs. "In popular parlance they emerged as veer (chivalrous man) to glorify Mayawati's masculine qualities. Mayawati is addressed as Behenji (sister) by her followers, but for them the word is more an honorific term of address than a sign of her femininity. Mayawati's strategy also was to project herself as a brave and courageous person. Her style of speaking, epistemology of political language, everyday relations with bureaucrats and politicians is masculine and aggressive and free of feminine softness. Her attitude deconstructs the stereotypical notions about women."[44]

Contrary to this, the BJP portrayed their heroines like Rani Lakshmibai in an ambiguous and ambivalent manner. They were shown to be both male and female. Hindutva outfits emphasized the latter over the former. They were projected more as women with qualities of self-sacrifice and self-effacement. "These qualities have been glorified in religious texts and also in mainstream literature penned by authors like Maithilisharan Gupt (*abala nari teri yehi kahani, achal mein hai doodh aur ankhon mein hai pani*, vulnerable women, this is your story; in your breast there is milk, in your eyes there is water)"[45] On the contrary, BSP was very clear in choosing, eulogizing and valorizing the courageous, warrior-like Dalit heroines from the 1857 movement as they would suit the image of Mayawati. "By linking herself with these heroes,

Mayawati wanted to give herself a place in the nationalist narrative and project her warrior-like characteristics so as to successfully engage"[46] in politics. "Warrior-like Dalit heroes with masculine images were chosen as icons"[47] by her very deliberately and strategically so that she could take on, challenge and reign as the leader and CM of the largest state in India to deal with the bureaucracy and government officers many of whom came from high caste background.

Exploring Convergences and Divergences: Concluding Remarks

This paper offers an analysis of the interesting ways in which the two political stake-holders, namely, the right wing political formations like RSS and BJP on the one hand and the Dalit parties like BSP on the other hand have drawn upon various frameworks and resources, and adopted multiple methods and strategies to advance their respective political agenda. Placing their initiative and attempts side by side provides some areas of convergence and divergence.

As regards frameworks and sources, right wing groups, as expected, heavily depend upon Vedic vision and ideology and make use of Sanskritic textual sources such as Vedas, Itihasas, Puranas and Sastras. Even when they borrowed data from folk oral traditions and utilized folk platforms such as folk theatres like Nautankis (musical theatres) and *bhajan madnals* etc.. they would always circumscribe their portrait of women warrior figures and models within the ideological boundaries provided by Vedic and Manudharma vision of a Hindu woman. Different from them were the BSP initiatives who heavily depend not on Sanskritic sources but on 'the *mool nivasi* (indigenous people) concepts,'[48] vernacular publications, local folk theaters and Jababi Kirtan. As regards strategies and methods, right wing groups' approach included : equating women with the nation, making women as the potent actors as well as signifiers of nationalism, projecting women as victim and victor at the same time, portraying the divine figures both in the milder and the fiercer forms as prototypes, engaging in the externalization of the enemy, framing war heroines like Rani Lakshmibai as both motherly and manly; and foregrounding celibacy and sexual renunciation as an ideal way of life for right wing activists. BSP also differed from the right wing in its methods in that they employed strategies such as removal of the past stigma, construction and glorification of the mythical past, adoption of a three-fold medium and unambiguous masculinization of the feminine. One strategy in which both seem to converge is that of divinization of the feminine. However, as mentioned in the paper, they differ in their presentation of the characteristics of female divine. While the right wing seems to necessarily include the benign and conforming characteristics of the divinities and provide ambivalent models of the divine, the BSP is clear in its unambiguous masculinization of the feminine as was shown in the paper. While the goal of the rightwing Hindu groups is to make

India a Hindu nation that excludes a respectable place for the minorities, the subaltern groups in post-independent India continually attempt to float counter-narratives which seek to provide new sites of visibility and self-dignity to the historically oppressed marginal communities in India.

References

Basu, Amrita. "Feminism Inverted: The Gendered Imagery and Real Women in Hindu Nationalism." In *Women and right-wing movements: Indian experiences*, ed. Tanika Sarkar and Urvashi Butalia, 159-180. London and New Jersey: Zed Books, 1995.

Ghosal, Sarbani Guha. "Major Trends of Feminism in India." *The Indian Journal of Political Science* 66, no. 4 (Oct.-Dec., 2005): 793-812.

Gupta, Charu. "Articulating Hindu Masculinity and Femininity: Shuddhi and Sanghathan Movements in the United Provinces in the 1920s." *Economic and Political Weekly* 33, no 13 (1998): 727-735.

Kalpagm. "The Women's Movement in India Today-New Agendas and Old Problems." *Feminist Studies 26*, no. 3 (Autumn, 2000): 645-660.

Lebra-Chapman, Joyce. *The Rani of Jhansi A Study in Female Heroism in India*. Honolulu: University of Hawaii Press, 1896.

Narayan, Badri. *Women Heroes And Dalit Assertion In North India*. New Delhi: Sage Publications, 2006.

Sethi, Manisha. "Avenging Angels and Nurturing Mothers: Women in Hindu Nationalism." *Economic and Political Weekly* 37, no. 16 (Apr. 20-26, 2002): 1545-1552.

Singh, K. Chanderdeep. "In the Service of Nationalism: Women in the Hindu Nationalist Paradigm." *Fudan Journal of. Humanities and Social Sciences* 9, (2016): 493–515.

Vidrohi, M.R. *Dalit Dastavej*. Delhi: Satyam Prakashan, 2004.

Notes

1. James Ponniah, PhD, Assistant Professor, Department of Christian Studies, School of Philosophy and Religious Thought, University of Madras, Mobile: +91-9952913141, Email: jamesponniah@gmail.com.
2. As cited in Manisha Sethi, "Avenging Angels and Nurturing Mothers: Women in Hindu Nationalism," *Economic and Political Weekly* 37, no. 16 (Apr. 20-26, 2002): 1545.
3 K. Chanderdeep Singh "In the Service of Nationalism: Women in the Hindu Nationalist Paradigm," *Fudan Journal of. Humanities and Social Sciences* 9, (2016): 497.
4. Ibid., 498.
5. Ibid., 499.
6. Ibid.
7. Ibid.
8. Ibid., 505.

9. Ibid., 506.
10. Ibid., 506.
11. Ibid., 494.
12. Amrita Basu, "Feminism Inverted: The Gendered Imagery and Real Women in Hindu Nationalism," In *Women and right-wing movements: Indian experiences*, eds. Tanika Sarkar and Urvashi Butalia (London and New Jersey: Zed Books, 1995), 159-180.
13. Manisha Sethi, "Avenging Angels and Nurturing Mothers: Women in Hindu Nationalism," *Economic and Political Weekly* 37, no. 16 (Apr. 20-26, 2002): 1547.
14. Ibid.
15. Ibid.
16. Kalpagm, "The Women's Movement in India Today-New Agendas and Old Problems," *Feminist Studies 26*, no. 3 (Autumn, 2000): 659.
17. Sarbani Guha Ghosal, "Major Trends of Feminism in India," *The Indian Journal of Political Science 66*, no. 4 (Oct.-Dec., 2005): 805.
18. Ibid.
19. Manisha Sethi, "Avenging Angels and Nurturing Mothers," 1550.
20. Ibid.
21. Ibid.
22. Ibid.
23. Ibid., 1551.
24. Ibid.
25. Joyce Lebra-Chapman, *The Rani of Jhansi A Study in Female Heroism in India* (Honolulu: University of Hawaii Press, 1896), 154-155.
26. Charu Gupta, 'Articulating Hindu Masculinity and Femininity: Shuddhi and Sanghathan Movements in the United Provinces in the 1920s,'" *Economic and Political Weekly* 33. no.13 (1998): 732.
27. Ibid., 153.
28. Badri Narayan, *Women Heroes And Dalit Assertion In North India* (New Delhi: Sage Publications, 2006), 114.
29. Manisha Sethi, "Avenging Angels and Nurturing Mothers," 1551.
30. Ibid.
31. Ibid.
32. Ibid.
33. Vidrohi, M.R. *Dalit Dastavej* (Delhi: Satyam Prakashan , 2004), 56.
34. Badri Narayan, *Women Heroes,* 117.
35. Ibid., 124.
36. Ibid., 118.
37. Ibid.
38. Ibid., 123.
39. Ibid.

40. Ibid., 117.
41. Ibid., 131.
42. Ibid.
43. Ibid., 150-168.
44. Ibid., 106.
45. Ibid.
46. Ibid.
47. Ibid.
48. Ibid., 109.

Chapter - 13

Challenges of Education of Tribal Women in India

Thomas K. J[1]

Introduction

According to Prof. Harbion of Princeton University the basis of wealth of a nation depends upon the human resources[2]. The skills and knowledge of the people should be developed to utilise them for the development of the national economy. Education helps in the development of skills. Education need to augment the overall development of a person. It is a continuous process that leads to enlightenment and wisdom. Margaret Mead defines education as the cultural process, the way in which each new born human infant is transformed into a full member of a specific human society[3]. For some people education is for the development and progress of the nation. A number of education Committees and Commissions were formed in India after the independence, to formulate effective education policies to improve literacy and level of education of people belonging to various sections of the society. Special encouragements were offered to boost education among the backwards class people and women of this nation.

Educational Reforms in Post-Independent India

Reforms were needed in the educational sector in India after gaining independence for the nation. The educational status of women in India needed to be improved. The University Education Commission headed by S. Radhakrishnan have suggested improvements in the education of women according to the needs of the country. Only education can empower and strengthen the life of women in India. The University Education Commission has pointed out various problems in the areas of admission, teaching and research[4]. Later on, the first Five Year Plan also considered education as the best means to achieve planned development in the country. However, it also recognised that the approach to attain the objectives of women's education should be different from that of men's education[5]. Women need opportunities for self-expression.

There was a felt need of a national authority to create more opportunities for women. The National Committee on Women's Education was appointed for this purpose by the government of India in 1958[6]. This committee recommended the expansion of elementary education for girls, appointment of more women teachers, establishment of separate schools for girls at higher secondary stage, special fund by UGC for the higher education of women and the establishment of National Council for Women's Education.

A few years later, in 1965, the Bhaktavaslam Committee[7] recommended special programmes for the .education of women and focused the need for giving greater attention to the education of girls at every stage in every sector. It also insisted that the general programmes for the improvement and expansion of education in India should make education for women an integral part of its activities. The Education Commission (1964-66) also endorsed all the recommendations of the previous committees with regard to girls' education and it further suggested that:

> Education of women should be regarded as major programme for some years to come and bold and determined effort should be made to face difficulties involved and to close the existing gap between the education of men and women in as short a time[8].

Considering all these recommendations the government of India formulated the National Policy on Education in 1968[9]. It also argued that to achieve social transformation and social justice, the education of women is of utmost importance. However, the major thrust of the national policy on education was on economic development, national integration and socialistic pattern of Indian society. Education of women did not receive sufficient emphasis through this national education policy.

Education of women and illiteracy

Though several initiatives were taken by various educational committees, 87 per cent of women in the age group of 25 years and above were illiterate in India, by the end of 1975[10]. It was observed that one girl out of every three in the age group 6-11 years was out of school at primary school level in India during this period. The problem of wastage and drop-out was very high among the girl children. The Sixth Five Year Plan gave priority for the development of women, especially for education, health and employment. All these measures by the government helped the improvement of literacy of women from 7.95 per cent to 24.82 per cent by 1981. However, there was a large gender gap in education, and the number of female illiterates increased to 241.6 million in 1981. Thus, there were 1,322 illiterate women for every 1,000 illiterate men in 1981. As per the Census of India (1961- 81), in all the states except Kerala, more than 60 per cent of the female population was illiterate, during this period.

The following Table clearly shows the gap in literacy for women from 1971 to 2011. During this period the gap in literacy is reduced from 23.98 per cent to 16.68 per cent. The data clearly show that women are not having equal access to education and literacy in India.

Table. 1. Male/Female Literacy in India from 1971 to 2011

Year	*Per cent of Literacy in total*	*Per cent of Male Literacy*	*Per cent of Female Literacy*	*Gap in Literacy*
1971	34.45	45.96	21.98	23.98
1981	43.57	56.37	29.75	26.62
1991	52.21	64.13	39.29	24.84
2001	63.38	70.85	54.16	21.69
2011	74.04	82.14	65.46	16.68

Source: Government of India, Ministry of HRD, Deptt. Of Education.

The dropout rate among girls is much higher than the boys in most of the states. Social and economic factors play a major role in the dropout rate of girls. The number of illiterate aged seven and above in India as per the provisional population totals of Census 2011 is 272,950,015 which constitutes 26 per cent of the total population. The effective literacy rate for India according to Census 2011 turns out to be 74.04 per cent. For the males the literacy rate is 82.14 and for the females the effective literacy rate is 65.46. Thus, there is a gap of 16.68 percentage point between male literacy and female literacy rate in India in 2011, which was 24.85 in 1991. The State of Kerala holds the first position in the country in female literacy with 91.98 per cent and Rajasthan has recorded the lowest female literacy rate of 52.66 per cent.

Equal opportunity for education is guaranteed in the Indian Constitution. But there are several negative factors that affect the education of women in this country. The traditional view still commands that women should be educated to become better wives and mothers only. Education has not become an instrument of women's equality and development in this country. Even the Radhakrishan Commission report supported the traditional view of education for women. Thus, there is persistence of this ambivalence between traditional and modern attitude towards the objectives of women's education in India.

Even the school curriculum does not provide equal space for the contributions made by women. It always projects the contributions of women inferior to that of men. There are always the traditional prejudices of inequality shown to women in every sphere of education. Sometimes the curriculum is stereotyped, sexist and biased. In spite of the recommendations of the Committee on the Status of Women in India to improve the policies for women's socioeconomic development and awareness of women's issues, there still exists a patriarchal influence on the educational system in India. Some of the cultural and religious traditions in India refuses to provide the rights of women in India. New values need to be promoted for equal rights of participation of men and women. Social and economic justice need to be provided for women through quality education and employment. Education has to become a powerful tool to remove all kinds of obstructive attitudes in people and should develop more of humanistic and positive outlook, where women receive the desirable status in the society.

A section on education for equity has been incorporated in the National Policy on Education 1986[11]. It was meant for removing the disparities between men and women in the field of educational opportunities. Many suggestions are made in this policy towards positive interventions to empower women and to promote women's studies and formulation of new redesigned curricula and text books to further the development of women. A well thought about Programme of Action was prepared by the government of India as a follow up of the national policy on education 1986. It was committed to eradicate illiteracy among woman belonging to the 15-35 age group by 1995. This action programme helped to some extend to increase the enrolment and retention of girls in schools. Some efforts were made to promote the vocational skills among the girls which would enhance the employment opportunities for them. This would help the women to participate in the process of nation building. Though many adult education centres were started to eradicate illiteracy, they became non-functional within a short period. Thus, the educational status of women continued to be very low.

Education and empowerment of women in India

Empowerment can be seen as a means of creating a social environment in which one can make decisions and make choice either individually or collectively for social transformation. The empowerment strengthens the innate ability by way of acquiring knowledge, power and experience[12]. It is the process of enabling or authorising individual to think, take action and control work in an autonomous way. It is also a process by which one can gain control over one's destiny and the circumstances of one's life. Empowerment allows individual to reach their full potential to improve their political and social participation, and to believe in their own capabilities. There is a growing tendency to underestimate women in the Indian traditional society. Very often they are given a secondary position in the society and are deprived of their basic rights. Most of the times, women are not able to enjoy the freedom that is provided in a free nation. Though the constitution of our nation does not discriminate between men and women, very often our society has deprived women of their basic rights. The first Prime Minister of India, Pandit Jawaharlal Nehru once said, "If you educate a man you educate an individual, however, if you educate woman you educate a whole family. Women empowered means mother India empowered". Education of women in India plays a very important role in the overall development of the country[13]. However, many women in India still do not enjoy the freedom to enrol themselves for quality education.

When a woman is educated and empowered, she is acquiring knowledge and understanding of gender relations and the ways in which these relations may be changed. She will be able to develop a sense of self-worth, a belief in one's ability to secure desired changes and the right to control one's life. She also gains the ability to generate her own choices and bargaining power. Above all, empowerment helps a woman to develop the ability to organise and influence the direction of social change, to create a more just, social and economic order, nationally and internationally. Thus, empowerment brings personal control or influence leading to actual social influences. It also safe guards political power and legal rights as an ongoing process. It also involves mutual respect, critical reflection, group participation and control over the resources of the community. Gender equality and women's empowerment are to form the core of development in every country. Women need to be involved in the process of administration and policy formulation at every level in a democratic country. However, women are very marginally represented in the political arena in India, though the 73rd and 74th constitutional amendment Acts have provided for reservation of seats for women in the local bodies. Only education can bring about reduction in the inequalities experienced by women in India even in political and social sectors.

According to Nabanita Bera, the major barrier for women empowerment in India are: gender discrimination, female infanticide, atrocities on women, child marriage, dowry system, patriarchal order, lack of health care and safety, professional inequality, harassment at work place, lack of proper educational programmes for women and inequality in sharing the burden of house hold work. Thus, women empowerment and gender equality in India is an alarming issue. However, the National Mission for Empowerment of Women 2010, has emphasised to facilitate the process of integrating all programmes for welfare and upliftment of women undertaken by the ministries and departments[14]. Still the ground realities show that majority of women, especially women from the backward social back ground, are not able to experience the freedom that empowerment provides.

Education of Tribal Woman in India

The tribal communities all over India have undergone various forms of deprivation. Most important among them is the alienation of land and other resources. Tribal women have been experiencing the impact of socio-economic changes that takes place in the main stream of national life. They have been forced to adhere to the new norms which may even take away their freedom and control over the traditional productive system, house, family and children. It is a fact that large number of tribal women have missed education at different stages of their life. There is a great need to provide them with sufficient opportunities to empower them to face the challenges of the modern life. Education of tribal woman should focus on developing their leadership qualities. It should help them to achieve economic self-reliance and even social transformation. Education can improve the level of aspirations among tribal women. Adequate educational opportunities should be provided to them to motivate them and participate in the development activities of the economy and state. While stating about the importance of education for tribal development, the Working Group on Tribal Development (1980) reiterated that:

> We feel while the core economic sectors might hold primacy in planning education is the key to tribal development...education is an input not only for economic development but also for inner strength of the tribal communities so that they can meet the new challenges on terms of some degree of capacity[15].

However, ignorance of the people is pointed out as one of the constraints of tribal development. Many of the socio-economic development programmes that were undertaken in tribal areas could not make much headway due to the ignorance and illiteracy of the tribes. They are unable to take advantage of the various development schemes due to lack of education. The disparity in educational attainment among the tribal children is caused by several factors. They need to be given functional literacy rather than following the traditional literacy methods. The system of education should help them improve their skills in various areas of their daily life. The functional literacy for tribal women will enable them to have better knowledge of tribal development. It will also help them raise the standard of their living. By attaining expertise in agriculture and industry, they will be able to produce more and earn more in various capacities. However, the scenario of education among the tribal women is deplorable and they are most backward in this regard.

The main aim of education for tribal women should be to make them economically independent and organise themselves to form strong groups so as to analyse their situations and conditions of living. Education should help understand their rights and responsibilities and enable them to participate and contribute to the development of women and the entire society. The development of skills among the tribal women could help them to assume political leadership, economic self-reliance and social transformation.

The gaps in literacy rates for the Scheduled Tribes is still very high in India. Though the overall literacy rate as per Census 2011 is 73 per cent in India, for the Scheduled Tribes it is 59 percent only.The overall literacy gap amongst the various groups and STs has come down from 19.77 per cent in 1961 to 14.03 per cent in 2011.The state-wise literacy data reveal that in most of the North Eastern states like Meghalaya, Mizoram and Nagaland, STs are at par with the general population when it comes to literacy. However, in Madhya Pradesh, Maharashtra, Odisha, Tamil Nadu and West Bengal, which have sizeable ST population in remote areas, the literacy gap is as high as 18 to 26 per cent. Thus, the Census data reveal that 41 per cent of the tribal population is still illiterate in India. Even after 71 years of independence, the educational status of tribal population in general and tribal women in particular is deplorable. They are not able to enjoy equal justice and liberty on par with other citizens of India.

Conclusion

Gender disparity in education need to be eliminated at all levels. Participation of women in empowerment and decision making remains far less than that of men. In spite of constitutional guarantees, legislative provisions, judiciary mandate and administrative efforts, education of women and literacy is not on par with that of men in India. More than 41 per cent of tribal population is still illiterate in this country. And more than 25.96 per cent of Indian population is still remaining illiterate, in spite of all the efforts by various educational agencies. The prevalence of illiteracy among Indian women population is 34.54 per cent as per the Census data. Unless every woman in this country is educated, empowerment of women cannot be attained and the participation of women in the developmental activities of the nation remains an unattainable goal.

References

Bhat, Rouf Ahmad. 2015. Role of Education in the Empowerment of Women in India. *Journal of Education and Practice.* Vol.6, No.10.

Government of India. 2011. *Census of India 2011*. New: Registrar General of India.

Kambala, J.Y. 2016. Status of Women Education in India. *International Journal of Multidisciplinary Advanced Research Trends*. Vol.3, Issue.1(1) January.

Mohapatra, Harapriya. 2015. Status of women in Indian Society. *Journal of Research in Humanities and Social Science*. Vol.3, Issue.6, pp.33 – 36.

Pandey, Balaji. 1987. Post Independent Educational Development among Women in India. *Seminar Paper. "Women in Changing Society"*, Centre for Women's Development Studies, University of Hyderabad, p:1-16.

Sundaram, M. S. 2014. Women empowerment: Role of Education. *International Journal in Management and Social Science*. Vol.2, Issue.12.

Notes

1. Thomas K.J., Ph.D. Research Scholar, Centre for Study of Social Exclusion and Inclusive Policy, School of Social Sciences, University of Hyderabad. ID: tkavumkatta@gmail.com.
2. G. Sandhya Rani, N. Rajani and P. Neeraja, "An Analysis of Tribal women's Education in India", International Conference on Social Science and Humanity, IPEDR, Vol.5, Singapore, 2011. pp. 507.
3. G. Sandhya Rani, N. Rajani and P. Neeraja, "An Analysis of Tribal women's Education in India", International Conference on Social Science and Humanity, IPEDR, Vol.5, Singapore, 2011.
4. Report of the University Education Commission, Government of India, 1948-49, Vol.1, Chapter XII.

5. The First Five Year Plan, Government of India, 1951, Chapter XXXIII.
6. Report of the National Committee on Women's Education, Government of India,1959.
7. Report of the Bhaktavaslam Committee, 1965.
8. Report of the Indian Education Commission 1964-66.
9. National Policy on Education, Government of India, 1966.
10. Pandey, Balaji. 1987. "Post- Independence Educational Development among Women in India". Seminar Paper, University of Hyderabad, March, 1987.
11. National Policy on Education, 1986, Part IV, pp. 6.
12. Rouf Ahmad Bhat, "Role of Education in the Empowerment of Women in India", Journal of Education and Practice, Vol.6, No.10, 2015.
13. Suguna M. "Education and Women Empowerment in India", International Journal of Multidiscipinary Research, Vol.1, Issue.8., 2011.
14. Nabanita Bera, "Women Empowerment through Education", International Journal of Humanities & Social Science Studies, Vol.2, Issue.6, May 2016.
15. G.Sandhya Rani, N.Rajani and P. Neeraja, "An Analysis of Tribal women's Education in India", International Conference on Social Science and Humanity, IPEDR, Vol.5, Singapore, 2011.

Chapter - 14

Women among the Marginalized Communities of India: Issues and Challenges

Dr. S. Srikanta Swamy[1]

Introduction

The Institution of family has undergone many changes and the trend is towards nuclear family. Compared to quality of life, standard of living is given more importance. Hence, every family wants to increase their standard of living so that they can lead comfortable life. This has lead women to go for higher job oriented courses leading to more job opportunities. Especially in cities, men prefer to select their life partners who are working or prefer them to work. This trend is spreading everywhere and helps the family to have better accommodation, food, clothing, and good education to their child/ children. As a consequence, the home makers are forced to go for jobs and some of them are taking risks and working. Thus women workers are faced with lot of problems. In India, even today, many of the families are dominated by men, and educated women with higher educational status are not treated properly and are not involved in making decisions. However, in the employment market the demand for women employers are increasing day by day with little variations from Urban to rural.

The eleventh Five Year Plan document for the first time in the history of Indian planning recognizes women not only as equal citizens but as 'agents of sustained socio-economic growth and change' (Planning Commission 2008, p. 5).According to Wentling (2003) the twin roles of women cause tension and conflict due to social structure which is still more dominant in the lives of people. In her study on working women in Delhi, she has shown that traditional authoritarian set up of Hindu social structure continues to be the same basically and hence women face problem of role conflicts. Ali.J.S (2011) investigated the challenges facing women in career development. She found that most of the women employees were dissatisfied with career development programmers and women were discriminated against in career development opportunities.

Problems faced by working women in India

In the traditional Indian society, women had low status when compared to men. As and when the educational opportunities increased, greater percentage of women acquired higher qualifications and moved to job market, thus bringing a paradigm shift in their status. Though, economically, their status has increased, their double responsibility at home as well as in the working place has created a lot of problems. According to Chandrima Chatterjee and Gunjan Sheoran (2007 in Indian society women face double discrimination being members of specific caste, class or ethnic group apart from experiencing gendered vulnerabilities. The working women in the modern society face lot of problems such as;

Occupational stress: It is also called work related stress. According to World Health Organization "it is the response people may have when presented with work demands and pressures that are not matched to their knowledge and abilities and which challenge their ability to cope." (2003). There are other factors associated with the Occupational Stress namely:

- Discrimination at Workplace
- Sexual harassment
- No Safety for Working Women
- Lack of Family Support
- No freedom to use her own earnings
- Insufficient Maternity Leaves
- Job insecurity
- Under- employment
- Gender discrimination
- Marginalization
- Workplace Adjustment

Thus, the working women in India face lot of occupational related problems. The intervention of the Government and also the welfare measures taken by the employer has reduced some of the problems and built confidence among the working women,

Nagda (2001) conducted a community survey of 230 women in tribal areas of Rajasthan and found that among tribal women, 62 percent women were physically beaten by their husbands at least once a month. Majority (83 %) of females reported was verbally abused by their husbands, in-laws and other family members at least once a week. About 39 percent women suffered mental and physical tortures in the family. Sometimes in extreme forms of violence the victim may be killed. Further, it was reported that more than two-thirds of the tribal women were abused by their husband, having fights regularly in evening and being insulted, taunted and criticized. Despite of this the majority of wives who suffered in domestic violence are also suffering in many health hazards like reproductive tract infection/STD, depression anemia, blood pressure, somatic disorders and broken family etc.

Women among the Marginalized Community

The concept of Marginalization was first introduced by Robert Park. It refers to "a processes by which individuals or groups are kept at or pushed beyond the edges of society" (Park, 1928). Encyclopedia of Public Health defines marginalization as, "to be marginalized is to be placed in the margins and thus excluded from the privilege and power found at the centre" (2002). According to Gurung and Kollmair (2005), the concept of marginality is generally used to analyze socioeconomic, political, and cultural spheres, where disadvantaged people struggle to gain access to resources and full participation in social life. Thus, people belongs to marginalized community are deprived of social, economical and political status and are aspiring to join the main stream of the society.

In any society, marginalization can affect a community at two levels namely, the macro as well as micro. In the macro level, the marginalized community members lack access to education, employment and gender related jobs. They do not have voice in the decision making process. Whereas, at the micro-level, one can notice difference in income discrepancies, occupational status, and race, religion or gender related issues. The marginalized community exhibits, usually, low educational and economic status, and poor health conditions.

Marginalization

- also varies from culture to culture
- happens simultaneously at the micro and macro levels
- occurs at different levels, such as individual, group, community, and global
- discriminates across different social institutions, such as family, schools and neighborhood, at work places, or places of worship

Types of Marginalized Groups

(i) Socially Marginalized Groups

(ii) Economically Marginalized Groups

(iii) Politically Marginalized Groups

According to Devesh Saxena a minority group has the following characteristics:

(1) It suffers from discrimination and subordination.

(2) They have physical and/or cultural traits that set them apart, and which are disapproved of, by a dominant group.

(3) They share a sense of collective identity and common burdens.

(4) They have shared social rules about who belongs, and who does not.

(5) They have a tendency to marry within the group.

Issues

It is commonly observed that women from the marginalized community are not considered for certain jobs and occupations. They are always marginalized relative to men. Women belonging to lower classes, lower castes, illiterate, and the poorest region have different levels of marginalization than their better-off counterparts (Ramakrushudu,B 2015); In India women are expected to adhere to strict gender roles. It is observed that they are affected by more health problems when compared to men. There are many factors because of which the health conditions of women are affected such as, economic dependence, experience of violence and gender bias, Apart from this, discrimination also exists in some groups, because of other factors like educational status, urban or rural background or health conditions. In the working place, discrimination is also shown by

- Denying of academic or professional opportunities based on identity (i.e. racism, sexism, ableism)
- Use of preferred pronoun without bothering its effect on their status
- Criticizing or interfering with culture or language usage issues.
- Denying equal access to certain facilities
- Abusing cultural practices related to marriage and ceremonies.

The issues created because of marginalization causes a negative impact in terms of psychological, emotional and physical health such as; anger, anxiety, fear, depression, sadness, frustration etc.

Challenges

The following are some of the challenges related to marginalization especially with respect o women:

- Interference of social stigma
- Competing with gender related issues.
- Problem of getting good education
- Overcoming the exploitation

- Difficulty in getting facilities for maintaining good health
- Overcoming the stereotype threat
- Discomfort participating in class discussions, study groups, student organizations, intramural sports and other institutional sponsored events
- Poor academic performance on exams and/or assignments due to negative impacts on concentration and emotional well-being
- Internalization of negative messages
- Ineffective coping such as disengaging, avoidance, and substance use

Action suggested

1. Provide access to gender sensitive primary healthcare to improve the diverse health needs of women.
2. Establishment of more and more Anganwadi and ICDS centers in tribal and rural areas so that the marginalized women can be prevented from malnutrition.
3. Proper implementation of laws to prevent and to protect the marginalized groups from domestic violence, physical and sexual abuse in urban as well as rural areas and also to create awareness about free legal aid.
4. More freedom to marginalized women with respect to their sexuality, including their sexual and reproductive health, and free from coercion, lack of information, discrimination and violence.
5. Provide social security for unorganized workers through mechanisms against sexual harassment at the workplace.
6. To build a support network with campus groups or organizations so that diversity could be honored, and also encourage women to become the members of self help groups to improve their financial sustainability.
7. Establishment of Counseling Centers with professional staff to assist the women for health, education and employment
8. Provide Adult and functional education so that women from marginalized community can be socialized so that they can move freely with the main stream and encourage them to Participate in campus such as C.A.R.E Dialogues that address issues of marginalization and oppression.
9. Encourage women from marginalized community to improve their educational status through Open University (Dr. BRAOU. IGNOU. etc.)

10. Implement the constitutional provisions and the initiatives of the government effectively for the welfare of the marginalized groups by all those who are in the field.

Conclusion

In every society is heterogeneous in many aspects and diversity exists. We should not think negatively that it is a curse; instead we have to honor and celebrate this, so that it leads to better harmony and development. In spite of many efforts by both governmental as well as non-governmental agencies, expected and significant changes have not occurred.

Therefore, it is the concern and commitment of every citizen to join hands with the government and NGO's to work for the cause, so that marginalized women community comes to the main stream and participate happily in the welfare of the country.

References Cited

Ali, J.S (2011), Challenges facing women employees in career development: A focus on Kapsabet Municipality,Kenya.International Journal of Current Research, 3(8),196-203

Chatterjee,C.B.,& Sheoran,G.(2007).Vulnerable groups in India.Mumbai India:Centre for Enquiry into health and Allied themes.

Gurung, G.S and Michael Kollmair (2005),Marginality: Concepts and their limitations, IPS,Working paper No.4,University of Zurich, CH8057 Zurich

Leka,S.,Griffiths,A.,Cox,T., and World Health Organization (2003).Work Organization and Stress:Systematic Problem Approaches for Employers,Managers and Trade Union Representatives.World Health Organization.

MaryWentling,R(2003) The Career Development and Aspirations of Women in middle Management Revisited.Women in Management review,18(6),311-324.

Nagda, B.A &Zuniga,X. (2001).Design considerations in Intergroup dialogue. Intergroup dialogue:Deliberative Democracy in School,College,Community and work place,306,327.

Park, R.E.(1928).Human Migration and Marginal Man.American Journal of Socioplogy,33(6),881-893.

Planning Commission.(2008).Eleventh Five year Plan 2007-12,Volume 1 Inclusive Growth.Page-5.

Ramakrushnudu,B.(2015).Socio-economic and Cultural Status of marginalized groups in Andhra Pradesh, http://hdl.handle.net/10603/104217.

—000—

Notes

1. Prof. S.Srikanta Swamy, Academic Consultant, Research and Analysis Wing, NAAC, Former Additional Director, Centre for Research, Christ University, Bengaluru. India.

Chapter - 15

Women among Marginalized Communities of India: Issues and Challenges

***Dr. Atola Longkumer*[1]**

The dream of socio–economic empowerment of women will not be complete without empowering those who are living at India's last periphery, the ones whose day start before sunrise and continues after sunset. These are the women farmers of India, whose voices often go unheard owing to their gender, and who struggle to establish their identity at a grassroots level due to patriarchal traditions and gender socialization.[2]

I. Introduction

The topic assigned for this essay remains an urgent concern in India today. Conditions and circumstances of women across the different communities, located in disparate socio-economic spheres share a commonality: discrimination.[3] Women in India continue to be discriminated across the spectrum of social classes and economic statuses and religious spaces. Experiences of violence, exploitation, negation, exclusion, abuse, harassment, and indifference suffered by women in India are reported regularly. The variation of discrimination might be in the nature of exploitation and the degree of control within the androcentric society.

There is a paradox, however, while the reality of discrimination of women derived from gender biased attitudes persists, it needs to be recognized that women in India have progressed immensely in every aspect of society: politically, economically, socially and even in religious participation. In many levels, women in India are visible as participants in the society as leaders, workers and capable citizens. Yet, statistics, many publications, media reports and experiential narratives of women continue to hold the mirror up and the stark reality of discrimination of women in India cannot be denied.

Among women in India, the experience of discrimination and marginalization is threefold for women in the marginalized communities the *Dalits*, the *Adivasi* and the indigenous communities of Northeast India.[4]Women in the marginalized communities experience discrimination at least at three levels of visible social hierarchy: within their own communities as women, the women from other communities and the men beyond their communities. The triple discrimination is further intersected with class, caste, religion, region urban, rural and educational levels. In other words, a woman from the indigenous communities of Northeast India is discriminated in multiple levels: as a woman, generally identified as belonging to a minority religion (for example, a Christian), from a region that is considered "the other" and measured as an object of both envy and disdain depending on the vantage point of the viewer. A woman from the Northeast part of India, experiences the "othering" in multiple layers especially in the metropolitan cities, often reported as experiencing cultural bias manifested in sexual harassment.

In this essay, I shall briefly delineate the marginalized communities to serve as a broad framework, which is followed by a section that lists four areas of challenges pertaining to women in the marginalized communities. The areas include: health, education and employment, land rights, and religious rights. This will be followed by arguing for a theology of inclusive justice in the public space from a woman's perspective as derived from the Judeo-Christian sacred text.

II. Women in Marginalized Communities in India

As a democratic and secular nation state, India has provisions guaranteeing equality and dignity of every citizen in the country. However, these provisions continue to be an enormous challenge in the modern nation state that is multicultural with a plurality of religions and their vehement assertions of traditions and conventions derived from them. While a democratic and secular nation, India in the practical reality is a nation governed by socio-cultural traditions that are far from being democratic and secular. Caste and its manifestations in a variety of forms continue to define, assert and measure the worth of individuals and many communities. The deep caste divisions, while strictly a Brahminical construct and privilege derived from their sacred text – the Vedas – has come to influence and hold sway over most of the country.[5]

Despite the fact that the Indian Constitution provides equality and dignity to all its citizens, caste hierarchy remains pervasive and violently discriminating against those perceived as low-caste or those who do not even inhabit the caste social hierarchy. Caste hierarchy creates a multi-layered social-economic society in India. It can be argued that caste remains the most powerful social force even in the modern liberal economy India is today. In that, caste identity remains rigid and influential across different aspects of the society observably manifest in political power and social relationships.

As modern Indian society persists to be defined, delineated and dictated by caste and its rigid social allocations, many are rendered powerless and vulnerable. If Indian society remains demarcated along the violent caste lines, marginalized and discriminated communities are the so-called low caste people, rendered to multiple levels of powerlessness, landless and propertied to the landowner, the capitalist and the middle-class elite in different forms of labour. Marginalized communities in India, therefore, inhabit a web of multiple intersections of caste, class, regions, religions, urban, rural and gender. Dalits, Adivasi, indigenous communities of Northeast, religious minorities such as Muslims, neo-Buddhist Ambedkarites, and Christians all share the marginalized socio-political and cultural space in India. To be sure, within each larger identity group, there are internal hierarchies that continue to marginalize the most vulnerable. Moreover, economic status apparently correlates to the degree of vulnerability across the different communities. In other words, the growing economic inequality across the spectrum of Indian society, despite the recent economic growth has made many vulnerable.

The recent economic development of the country has also added another dimension to the social realities of the country. Migration occurs within the nation state, not just an international phenomenon.[6] There is a large number of movements of migrants within the country, moving out from familiar socio-cultural locations to multi-cultural most often, technologized and industrialized cosmopolitan centers in the country.[7]

Modernization and its many dimensions – capitalism, globalization, market economy, professionalization, technological progress, industrialization and privatization –continue to transform the country, ushering tremendous changes in communities with both good or bad ramifications. The consensus of many studies is the irrefutable experience of women as a consequence to these changes in the country. While there is visible progress made by women as well as their situations, these developments are specific to the welfare of women's circumstances and conditions in the society. Despite the advancements made by women in general, there are challenges and limitations. Exploitation, and insecurity of women in modern India are glaring social realities. Particularly, the conditions of women in the marginalized communities continue to question the conscience of the nation. Traditional beliefs and practices curtailing women's freedom are compounded by the modernized economy that consolidates patriarchal attitudes. For instance, *Adivasi* women serving as house maids in the metro cities are directly related to the modern economy marked by developments as the Neetha N. writes, "acquisition of land for non-agriculture uses, expansion of mining operations, exploitation/destruction of the natural flora and fauna, and the impact of these changes on *Adivasi* lives are now widely acknowledged….The most visible and affected victims of the 'modernization' process have been women in these communities."[8]

Women in general and women of the marginalized communities in particular face significant challenges for their equal participation and welfare as equal citizens. Some key areas of challenges are discussed in the following section.

III. Issues and Challenges

While progress and welfare of women is not limited to the following four areas of challenges, they are identified as critical issues that leave their impact across multiple aspects of women emancipation and empowerment. Moreover, these socio-cultural conditions also pose crucial challenge to the nation as a democratic, inclusive country with a growing economic growth.

1. Women's Health

The harrowing image of a tribal man carrying on his shoulder the dead body of his wife in 2016 is just one instance of the indignity and deprivation faced by marginalized communities in the country.[9] Lack of primary health care centers in accessible locations is only compounded by the unavailability of the health workers. Maternal mortality, scourging female infanticide, malnutrition, labourers' exposure to carcinogenic chemicals in large-scale agriculture, and disabilities, along with seasonal health issues, such as *dengue*, typhoid, malaria, and encephalitis are health challenges faced by women among the most vulnerable communities in India. In the recent years, there are reports of women from the marginalized communities who are trafficked and sold for commercial sex in metro cities of the country.[10] Increasing health programs designed are insufficient to address the need, unless disciplined implementations are ensured. Allotment of funds in the annual budget will not ensure the health of the citizens if corruption and negligence remain unchallenged.

2. Education and Employment for Women

According to an Oxfam report, "Women's labour force participation in India is one of the lowest in the world. Women comprise half of the Indian population but make up less than a quarter of the labour force. Three in four Indian women do not work in the country."[11] As employment is directly related to education and the literacy level, it is not unexpected to have the fewer women in the labour force of the country, given the dismal percentage of female literacy. To be sure, there are variations across the different states and most probably varying levels according to region and religious communities. However, women in the marginalized communities in the country could comprise the highest percentage of illiteracy and hence unemployment. The dismal level of female literacy rate among the marginalized communities, in particular among some *Adivasi* communities contributes to further exploitations of women in these communities, as they become easy victims of human traffickers.

Accessible modern education for the girl child remains a challenge for the most vulnerable communities of the country. Ensuring education and employment for women will contribute to the welfare and flourish of the communities.

3. Land Rights for Women

Women empowerment is not limited to education and employment, but women's right to land ownership and their freedom to control the resources is crucial to their welfare. Land and property ownership by women in India is complex and lacks a uniform code. The following statement from Bina Agarwal provides a general position of women and land rights among the Adivasi and Tribal communities in India:

> *"Tribal women are the second major category facing substantial disabilities in inheritance. Given the non-codification of their laws, tribal communities are governed by customs, which (except under matriliny) discriminate against women. And even the limited customary land rights many tribal women enjoyed historically have been eroding."*[12]

Agarwal provides a comprehensive analysis of land rights and women India, with ample examples from various communities. Despite the movement, debate and legal process to provide ownership of land resources, right to inheritance and freedom to control the land resources by women remains elusive in general. Marginalised women such as landless labourers, tribal and *adivasi* women are discriminated by traditional practices of patriarchy that deny the right ownership of land. Under the control of the male members of the family a woman – a widow, an unmarried daughter, and a sister – faces the perils of becoming homeless and destitute without the right to land ownership and inheritance.

4. Religious Rights for Women

Across the diverse religious communities in India, one commonality shared by women in specific communities is the exclusion from complete participation as well as leadership in the religious space. The Supreme Court's decision allowing women to enter the temple, the incident and debate around the entry to Sabarimala temple in Kerala provides a very public example of limitations imposed upon women by different religions. There is systematic discrimination of women in almost all the religions. Entry to temples, churches, mosques, *gurudwaras* and prayer halls might not be explicitly restricted, but beyond the surface women adherents do not have equal rights as leaders and teachers. To be sure, there are a number of churches that have accepted the ordination of women in the ministry and women are teachers of theology. But even among Christians, where there is relative freedom for women to participate in the religious community, women's equal participation remains distorted wherein women are second to the male leadership and authority.

The argument that religious rights for women be granted is crucial because religion whether it is good or bad will continue to be an important social reality for many people in India. The beliefs and their practices persist as influential source of identity and normative traditions for the communities. Therefore, it could be argued that the religious space pose the most rigid sphere to uphold existing discriminatory practices and interpretations in relation to women. While it is more complicated as entrenched in patriarchy, religious texts that are liberative can be discovered and brought to fore to the faithful community. Where religion is still an important socio-cultural reality of a people, there is potential to organize the space and media to negotiate women's participation as equal members of the faith community.

IV. Theology of Inclusive Justice

The discussion and list of issues and challenges faced by women among the marginalized communities in India will continue, and therefore deliberate and radical transformation of patriarchal beliefs and practices are required. From different aspects with a variety of approaches the empowerment and equal participation of women need to be sought. Policymaking, advocacy, legal measures, socio-cultural reforms and grassroots involvement are crucial approaches. Writing from a location of faith, it is critically important to question, what resources are there within the community of faith? While the Christian tradition seems ambivalent in its understanding, interpretation and practice of gender equality, the reading of the Bible, particularly from a feminist perspective challenges the community towards an inclusive life. Elizabeth Johnson states clearly the dominant androcentric interpretation of the sacred text, yet she directs the modern reader to discover the "powerful presence" of women and the inclusion of women in the history of salvation.[13] The life and work of Jesus Christ, the central figure of the Christian faith surely welcomed, befriended and included women in his ministry. The joy of good news that Christ declared as reconciled humanity and fellowship with God included women. The community of faith as disciples of Jesus Christ is called to follow faithfully in living out the good news in the community ensuring inclusive justice.

Moreover, inspired by the good news, mission workers across different historical periods have worked among the most marginalized and continue to work among the communities. And, despite criticisms and oppositions, these mission movements are contributing toward empowerment and emancipation of communities by individuals, and organized societies are serving the women in the communities through medical, literacy, and skills-development programs.

To conclude, I list the goals set by the United Nations (UN) towards gender equality and empower all women and girls. Under the Sustainable Development Goals (SDGs), Agenda 5 lists Gender Equality and the following targets are set towards achievement of gender equality:

- End all forms of discrimination against all women and girls everywhere.
- Eliminate all forms of violence against all women and girls in the public and private spheres, including trafficking and sexual and other types of exploitation.

- Eliminate all harmful practices, such as child, early and forced marriage and female genital mutilation.
- Recognize and value unpaid care and domestic work through the provision of public services, infrastructure and social protection policies and the promotion of shared responsibility within the household and the family as nationally appropriate.
- Ensure women's full and effective participation and equal opportunities for leadership at all levels of decision making in political, economic and public life.
- Ensure universal access to sexual and reproductive health and reproductive rights as agreed in accordance with the Programme of Action of the International Conference on Population and Development and the Beijing Platform for Action and the outcome documents of their review conferences.
- Undertake reforms to give women equal rights to economic resources, as well as access to ownership and control over land and other forms of property, financial services, inheritance and natural resources, in accordance with national laws.
- Enhance the use of enabling technology, in particular information and communications technology, to promote the empowerment of women.
- Adopt and strengthen sound policies and enforceable legislation for the promotion of gender equality and the empowerment of all women and girls at all levels.[14]

V. Conclusion

Women among marginalized communities in India continue to face many levels of discrimination and exploitation. A confident India with rising economic power and global presence is challenged with the conditions and experiences of the vulnerable women. An ancient civilization with a marked tradition of sacred women and with diverse local cultures with traditions that revere women, need liberating, disciplined and diligent programs to ensure the wellbeing of women among the marginalized communities in the country. In this persistent challenge, the community of faith – particularly the church – is called to advocate and empower the marginalized women. The community has both a long history and tradition of working for the uplift of the vulnerable. Above all, the re-reading of the sacred text of the community directs the community in its movement of inclusive justice.

Notes

1. Dr. Atola Longkumer a tribal woman from Nagaland writes on religions and Christian mission.
2. Report on Women Inequality in India, Oxfam, in https://www.oxfamindia.org/women-empowerment-india-farmers accessed 6 April 2019.
3. For the earliest writings on India women see, Bina Agarwal, *Gender Challenges*, 3 Volumes (New Delhi: Oxford University Press, 2015), this monumental publication in three volumes addresses the issues of equity and policy related to women in wide ranging area: forests, property, family, technology and market economy.
4. The differences among these three communities, while there are similarities, yet, culturally and religiously there are differences that need to be recognized, in order to make sense of appropriate policy and interventions.
5. Nicholas B. Dirks, *Caste of Minds: Colonialism and the Making of Modern India* (Princeton: Princeton University Press, 2001).
6. https://www.un.org/development/desa/publications/international-migration-report-2017. html.
7. http://censusindia.gov.in/Census And You/migrations.aspx.
8. Neetha N., "Urban Housekeepers from Tribal Homelands: Adivasi Women Migrants and Domestic Work in Delhi" in Meena Radhakrishna ed., *First Citizens: Studies on Adivasis, Tribals, and Indigenous People in India* (New Delhi: Oxford University Press, 2016), 228.
9. See, https://www.ndtv.com/india-news/tribal-man-walks-10-km-carrying-wifes-body-on-his-shoulder-in-odisha-1449948 accessed 6 April, 2019.
10. https://www.thehindu.com/news/araku-valleys-dark-secret/article23336755.ece accessed 3 July, 2019.
11. As quoted in Shagun Kapil "Women's labour force participation in India among the world's lowest: Oxfam" in https://www.downtoearth.org.in/news/agriculture/women-s-labour-force-participation-in-india-among-the-world-s-lowest-oxfam-63743 accessed 6 April, 2019. See also, https://www.thehindu.com/news/national/inequality-has-female-face-in-india-womens-unpaid-work-worth-31-of-gdp-oxfam/article26048261.ece accessed 6 April, 2019.
12. Bina Agarwal, *A Field of One's Own: Gender and Land Rights in South Asia* (Cambridge: Cambridge University Press, 1994).
13. Elizabeth A. Johnson, *Abounding in Kindness: Writings for the People of God* (Maryknoll, NY: Orbis Books, 2015).
14. See, https://www.un.org/development/desa/disabilities/envision2030-goal5.html accessed 6 April, 2019.

Chapter - 16

Women of Marginalized Communities: Violence and Violations

Julie George[1]

Introduction

This paper seeks to analyse the contours of violence and violations against women of marginalized communities in the backdrop of some of the widely reported cases in the media as well as certain judgements on rape and sexual abuse, in order to illustrate the ways in which the discourse of marginalization is translated in the language of dominance. The argument in this paper is that there is a clear connection between violence against women and the identities that they possess. For every woman the individual identities are made up of multiple identities, including class, caste, race, religion, age, ethnicity and economic status. These identities that women possess cumulatively result in multiple levels of discrimination.

The headlines in the newspapers catch our eyes daily, with some of the columns lamenting that the attitudes of men have changed little since the landmark 1972 Mathura case. Others claim that the tragic cases happening again and again and the nationwide outcry is an indication that little has changed since the Mathura case. In spite of the sustained collective actions such as 'women chain' in some places, 'women wall' in Kerala, and 'one billion rising', #MeToo and many such movements, the discrimination and violence against women still persists.

Misogyny and Dominance: Sexual Abuse and Rape from Mathura to Kathua

There is the emergence of a new Indian macho-ism centred on extreme aggression and sexual violence. Sexual abuse and Rape has become a common thread for control not only of women's selves and their bodies but also of every identity that they are made to represent ranging from clan, tribe, caste, religion and nation. Women's bodies have become the sites for various social and political battles especially of women from marginalized communities. The Justice Verma Committee Report points out, "Another humiliating aspect of the crime against women is that her status in the patriarchal structure of society also impedes her access to justice. The inequities of social status, caste prejudices, and economic deprivation further compound the gender injustice"[2].

The first case of brutal violence on a woman from the marginalized community that came to the forefront was that of Mathura Rape case.[3]Mathura was an Adivasi young girl of sixteen years old, who eloped with her upper caste boyfriend. She was brought to the local police station to record the statement in respect of a complaint lodged by her brother. Mathura was gang raped at the police station by two policemen.The Trial Court, refused to convict the accused. Because the Judge held that Mathura was "a shocking liar" whose testimony "is riddled with falsehood and improbabilities". The High Court reversed the order and came to the conclusion that Mathura did not consent to intercourse. The case disturbed the conscience of the nation when the Supreme Court of India in 1979 set aside the conviction of the policemen on the grounds that Mathura was "habituated to sex"; there were no proof to show that she raised an alarm when the rape took place; and there were no signs of injury or struggle on her body. The implication was that submission of a poor tribal girl to the brutal rape by the custodians of law amounted to 'consent' on the part of Mathura and the accused were acquitted.

The passage for the anti-rape movement launched in 1980 was the Supreme Court judgment in the Mathura rape case. The judges acquitted policemen who had gang raped the sixteen yearold, who was subjected to multiple layers of marginalisation such as poor, illiterate, orphan and tribal, on the ground that there were no marks of injury on her body and hence she must have consented. Rather than the violence inflicted upon her, her sexual conduct became the central context and her past sexual history, that she had eloped with her lover, was used to discredit her, and acquit the policemen.

Her case was iconic both from a social and legal perspective. It sparked public protest for the first time about a rape in India that led to the reform of sexual assault lawsand the rape law was amended for the first time. When a survivor/ victim is in the custody of the state, as was Mathura, the law mandates that a court presume a woman who says she did not consent is telling the truth. Mathura's case also led to rape trials being conducted in- camera and to a ban on identifying victims by their real names and publishing the name in the media.

Almost six years after Delhi rape case, there is yet again immense public outrage on the rape of a minor girl from Gujjar – Bakarwal community. The rape and murder of the 8 year old minor girl in Kathua which brings to light the manner in which sexual violence against women and children is used as a tool to further subjugate marginalised communities. The instance of violence against the minor girl in Kathua is not an isolated incident, but one among several others that bear evidence to the growing incidence of rape and brutality against women and girls as sites for the assertion of increasingly masculinised caste, class and religion-based patriarchies.

The endorsement of violent and exclusionary politics and laws by the governments further compounds these challenges and offers impunity to dominant groups.The government has failed in its legal and constitutional duty to secure the life and liberty of the minor girl who was marked again by multiple marginalization of age, gender, religious and tribal identity, and her vulnerable situation compounded by sustained efforts to evict her community from their land. Her rape was to instil fear, exert power and drive out the community from the region.

Despite a robust anti-rape campaign spanning over three and a half decades, the perception that all women who complain about rape are "liars" still persists, especially when it comes to marginalized communities or vulnerable women against the powerful. The law and the implementation of it which is situated within a patriarchal framework fail to question the conservative notions of women's chastity, virginity, and concept of "good and bad" women in our society.

Seeing #MeToo Narrative from the Lens of Marginalized Communities: from Banwari Devi to #MeToo

In 1992, Bhanwari Devi (Vishaka and Others Vs State of Rajasthan[4]), then a grassroots worker with the women's development project in Rajasthan, was raped by a group of men from an upper caste family, for campaigning against child marriage. The most abysmal feature of the case is that the trial court acquitted the accused observing that the rapists were middle-aged and respectable persons from upper caste who could not have raped a Dalit woman.The incident prompted women's groups to file a writ petition and in response to which the Supreme Court of India formulated clear guidelines on Sexual Harassment at Workplace popularly called the Vishakha Guidelines which has now been incorporated into a law by the Indian Parliament called Sexual Harassment of Women at Workplace (Prevention, Prohibition and Redressal) Act 2013. The woman whose legal battle played a crucial role in the making of Sexual Harassment of Women at Workplace Act, 2013, though she did not get full justice, she has become a symbol of resistance.

Bhanwari Devi, a lower-caste social worker, is a hero in the truest sense of the word. It was for the first time that a woman was not ashamed of rape and in fact, spoke openly about it. She tried to explain to people that the rape was not her fault. Although BhanwariDevi never received justice, her case brought significant victories for the women's movement in India.This was a major legal victory for the women's movement in India, though it was only in 2013 that these guidelines were made as a legislative Act.

Bawander, a movie based on her story, received national and international accolades, yet she continues to live life in solitude, ostracized by her family and community members. When her mother died, her brothers and other family members barred her from participating in the funeral. Her family also faced great challenges in various ways. It has been over 25 years, two of the accused are no more, yet Bhanwari Devi still awaits justice.

The recent social-media movement, the '#Metoo campaign' in an Indian context effectively began in the year 2017 and has since opened up issues of sexual harassment to the public gaze. This movement has made it accessible for women to speak publicly about incidents of sexual harassment. But for every woman who has spoken out about such violence, there are likely tens of thousands of others, especially in the unorganised sector such as domestic workers, migrants and other marginalized communities, who are yet to find an avenue to speak out. They are not on the social media and may not know how to make their presence known on the social media. They may not want to share fearing that they might lose their work since they are not backed by any laws or welfare measures.In the light of this, a Dalit women's collective—Dalit Women Fight released a statement regarding the movement and stated, "We have been wondering about the 'me' in #metooindia and have not been able to locate ourselves in this current."[5]

Dalit activist Mruduladevi Shashidharan spoke to SheThePeople. TV and said that she is in full solidarity of the campaign because it has allowed women to raise a voice. "We need social justice against sexual harassment. But at the same time, I condemn the lack of positioning of Dalit women in this campaign. Even in this movement, we have to ask reservation within reservation because of the prominent and dominant caste system is prevailing even inside the MeToo movement."[6]

Those arguing that it's an elite wave, are failing to understand that in a hyper-connected, media world of WhatsApp and videos are fast collapsing the distance between metros and hinterland. English-speaking women may be leading the movement today by coming out and speaking openly, but already a great stir up is building across India.

Domestic Violence: A Reality Check

Domestic violence is a matter of serious concern not only because of the physical, emotional, sexual, verbal and psychological trauma which they engender in the victim, but also because these are practices which are being tolerated by society and even by women themselves. Domestic violence at different levels has contributed to women's social exclusion and poverty, when they are left alone to protect themselves.

Domestic violence is a battle declared on women to achieve a range of direct control that include masculine supremacy, religious hierarchism, communal revenge, class, caste subjugation and political mileage. Among the women of the unorganized sector, such as women domestic workers, migrants etc., the alcoholism of their husband's are becoming a major cause for domestic violence. Most of the women from economically weaker sections tolerate the violence fearing the future of the family and children. Those who are migrants find themselves in a tricky and vulnerable situation, as recording a police complaint would reveal that they are migrants.Families may be forced to live in cities for their survival without the requisite documentation and papers. In such cases they are afraid to go to police.

The intersectionality of class, caste and gender has real-life consequences for many battered women who are seeking safety. Women, who are dependent on the husbands for survival, stay on in their abusive marriage and get beaten up by their husbands rather than be out on their own where they have no safety and in all probability five men could assault them.

The option of leaving her abusive spouse may seem irrational to a woman who depends on her spouse to provide a home for her. Women from the marginalized communities may suffer abuse not only from their partners but also from the larger society. Religion and caste are essential components of individual and collective identities of women. To understand the root cause of this situation, it is essential to examine the basic factors that contribute to their vulnerability, in other words, we need to analyse how patriarchy feeds from caste and vice-versa.

Conclusion

Most of the above mentioned cases are breakthroughs in the discourse of Indian Judiciary as it addresses the issue of denial of justice and a fair investigation to the weaker sections. It reflects how the nexus of power, which operates on the hierarchies of caste, class and gender, works to oppress the minorities in our society. The deep-rootedness of Brahmanical patriarchy and the caste system is evident from the way justice systems operate, and it also enabled the upper-caste men to manipulate the narrative in their favour and turn the people against victims.

Debates on gender and violence in India have always located the privileged, upper caste women as its central subject. Violence is the weapon used to keep women "in their place" on the basis of their identities. Women from marginalized communities are at the bottom in our society. Even within the women's movement, Dalit issues have not been taken seriously. Within the Dalit movement, women have been ignored. In such a scenario, the systematic, systemic and unrelenting violence against Dalit women is seldom highlighted in most mainstream discourses. More importantly violence against women is often seen in terms of patriarchy alone as though our society is homogenous for all women, with all of them having similar privileges and vulnerabilities. Here, the intersectionality of gender, caste and class, which is so important to understand the violence against Dalit women, goes totally unseen. Every woman who has spoken out about violence, there are likely tens of thousands of others, especially in the unorganised sector and semi-formal workspaces, who are yet to find an avenue to speak out.

Our educational institutions are steeped in named and unnamed equations of power, flowing from caste, class and gender. And if you are a Dalit woman, the difficulties multiply manifold. Says an anonymous writer. She says that she is anonymous because she does not have the patience to fight the angry *savarna* women. She further states that she is anonymous because she is a nameless Dalit. She is anonymous because, without dismantling Brahminical feminism, any fight against patriarchy will be a victory only for the brahminical feminists. The women's movements need to continue to have discourse around these issues, so that voices like her will get more space. Feminism should be intersectional. Because women are not one homogeneous unified group and our challenges are also from and impacted by caste, religion and class etc. The caste system is driven by specific forms of subjugation of women, within castes and between castes. So far there are no sustained engagements with issues concerning women of marginalized communities.

Women need to bond, in spite of all the nuances that continue to divide us. The nuances are important to further our positions, but we should not let them seep into our lives so much that we never can come together as a larger whole.

Notes

1. Julie George is a practicing Advocate, Director of Streevani (Women's Voice), Pune. India.
2. Justice J.S.Verma et al., Report of the committee on amendments to Criminal Law, 23 January,2013 p 14.
3. Tukaram vs. State of Maharashtra, A.I.R. 1979 S.C.185.
4. Vishaka & Others Vs State of Rajasthan, A.I.R.1997 S.C.3011.
5. https://www.shethepeople.tv/top-stories/issues/metoo-narrative-marginalized-communities.
6. *Ibid.*

Chapter - 17

Women in the Jewish Community of Biblical Era: Issues and Challenges

Prof. Savarirayan[1]

Introduction

In the context of the Seminar on "Women among the Marginalized Communities of India: Issue and Challenges," I intend to explore the life and the place of "Women in the Jewish Community of Biblical Era" in order to draw a comparison between these two communities with high religious values at stake. Jewish community has been a very special one as they boast of giving Jesus Christ and the world's largest religion, Christianity to the world while the Indian society will boast of giving many religions such as Hinduism, Jainism and Buddhism besides many other religious sects and great leaders such as Mahatma Gandhi and so on. This paper will delve on and unfold the life of a non-Jewish woman in the Jewish Community and the life of a Jewish woman in her own community in the Old Testament times. This paper begins with biblical-historical perusal of Jewish Community before Jesus, during his ministry and post resurrection era. The creation of Eve as the first woman and mother of all living beings will set the tone for our further discussions.

Appendix: A Biblical-Historical Perusal of Jewish Community

TaNaK (Torah, N^{e}bi'im and K^{e}thubim = the Law, the Prophets and the Wisdom Writings), written in Hebrew, the language of the Jews, is the collection of 39 holy books considered normative by the people of Israel. It duly takes the form of the Holy Bible, with seven more books, written in Greek and added later to TaNaK, with its two sections (Old Testament and New Testament), rules the lives of 2.10 billion[2] Christians in the world, guides and leads the adherents of the world's largest religion.

According to the Holy Bible, the history of the Jewish people begins with the call of Patriarch Abraham (2200 BCE[3]), the primogenitor of the people of Israel, Isaac and Jacob. God called Abraham (cf. Gen 12:1-4) with a promise to make his descendants like the stars of the sky and the sand of the seashore (cf. Gen 22:17; Heb 11:12).

The Jewish community, known also as the people of Israel, considered itself a superior one. The Lord himself instructed Moses to tell Pharaoh that "... Israel is my firstborn son" (Exod 4:22). The Lord God considered Israel as His "treasured possession out of all the peoples ... a priestly kingdom and a holy nation" (Exod 19:5-6). The people of Israel strongly believed that they are a holy people, specially chosen from out of all the peoples on earth as a treasured possession (cf. Deut 7:6; Ps 135:4).

When we pass on from the Old Testament to the New Testament, we find Saint Peter echoing the sentiments of the Old Testament writers and readers (cf. Exod 19:5-6). Peter writes in his First Letter, "But you are a chosen race, a royal priesthood, a holy nation, God's own people" and this is that God Who ... called you out of darkness into his marvelous light" (1 Pet 2:9).

Is the Jewish Community a Marginalized One?

The direct answer to the question is both in the affirmative and negative. In the first place, we shall begin our discussion as to why it cannot be called a marginalized community? Although they were a nomadic community through the times of the Patriarchs Abraham, Isaac and Jacob, they became a kind of settled people during their sojourn in Egypt. A twist in their story comes with the death of the Pharaoh who appointed Joseph the governor, the Hebrews became slaves. They are ill-treated. They become marginalized for almost 430 long years (cf. Exod 12:40). By killing the male children and getting the women married to the Egyptian men, the Pharaohs tried in vain to relegate the Jewish society. Working on the liberative mandate given by their God, they obtain freedom through the efforts of Moses and his brother Aaron. Forty years of journey through the fertile crescent under the leadership of Moses and Joshua comes to fruition on the day they enter to occupy Canaan.

The time of the Judges ushered into a new Era in the settled people of Israel. Samuel being the last judge and prophet and the performance of his sons as judges made the people to reject them and request God for a king "like other nations" (1 Sam 8:5). This request of the people angered Samuel, but God yielded to their request and thus began the era of Monarchy with the wealthy and courageous military leader Saul son of Kish from the tribe of Benjamin becoming the first king of Israel. His disastrous forty years of reign came to an abrupt end when he committed suicide in the battlefield against the Philistines (cf. 1 Sam 31:1-5).

The baton of leading Israel fell on David, described by the Bible as a man after God's own heart (cf. 1 Sam 13:14; Acts 13:22). During his rule, he kept all the enemies of Israel at bay. There was lots of peace and prosperity. In all probability, it was during these forty favourable of years of rule that the major part of the Jewish Sacred Scripture was given the written form (1000 BCE).

Although King Solomon began his innings as the king of Israel well, seeking wisdom instead of personal glory and had the honour of building the first ever Temple of God in Jerusalem, his marriages with Gentile women and the altars that he built for Gentile gods brought him down from his disgraceful rein. He also lost the Jewish kingdom as his sons Jeroboam and Rehoboam divided the land into Northern Kingdom (known as Israel and Samaria as its capital) and Southern Kingdom (called Judah and Jerusalem as its capital).

The chosen people of God in the Northern Kingdom came under Assyrian invasion (723/721 BCE) and were deported to Exile. About 200 years later came the Babylonians to loot the Southern Kingdom. Nebuchadnezzar took the cream of Judah to Babylonian exile (587-537 BCE). On both these occasions, the people of Israel became a landless, temple-less, priest-less, Torah-less and circumcision-less, in short, a people totally abandoned by God. An exile is an expulsion from one's own home and land. There is nothing more devastating than this. The Persians, under the inspired leadership of Cyrus the Great gave them an opportunity to return to resettle and rebuild the Temple and the walls of Jerusalem. They did rebuild the Temple of Jerusalem but then as time passed by, they fell into the hands of the Greeks (Alexander the Great in 333 BCE) and then the Romans (63 BCE). The Maccabees, the sons of the soil seized power from the Greeks and founded the Hasmonean dynasty (167-37 BCE) and functioned independently from 110 to 63 BCE, the time of the arrival of the Romans. But they themselves began to exploit the people through nepotism and other political misbehavior and it was at this time the Qumran Community came to existence. The people of Israel struggled to evict the Romans from their land. In fact, the struggle for freedom and independence continued till 1948 Arab-Israeli War. Until this moment, certainly some kind of marginalization was experienced by the Israelites in one or the other way.

Appendix 2: Why is a Study on Marginalized Women?

Woman, one of God's best creations in the universe, has been the topic of numerous discussions, novels, philosophical treatises from time immemorial. Honoured for her role as a mother who gives birth to and nurtures her child through numerous sacrifices, a woman is also seen as an object of sex, enjoyment and slavery. A study on marginalized women in the Biblical times can offer numerous insights into how we can liberate women who are marginalized even today.

It is imperative to understand that the Biblical texts that we are going to have a closer look at were all born in a particular cultural milieu and linguistic tradition of an era very far from us both in space and time. They reflect the ethos of that particular setting. And yet, one has to identify the influence of certain religious and cultural beliefs that oppress women. My humble effort in this paper would be to discover the author meaning as presented by the author and then apply that meaning to the context of India, by doing this I will also try to find out the meaningfulness of the text. The 'reader meaning' is significant to address the local issues and realities.

1. Made off Man and Made for Man: The Holy Bible teaches us that God created the first human persons. Adam (made of *adama*, the soil), the first man was fashioned by God very carefully. The Lord God then said, "It is not good that the man should be alone; I will make him a helper as his partner" (Gen 2:18). We take note of two important terms which the Lord God Himself used: 'helper' and 'partner'. The Word of God continues, "So the Lord God caused a deep sleep to fall upon the man, and he slept; then he took one of his ribs and closed up its place with flesh. And the rib that the Lord God had taken from the man he made into a woman and brought her to the man. Then the man said, "This at last is bone of my bones and flesh of my flesh; this one shall be called Woman, for out of Man this one was taken" (Gen 2:21-23). It is evident then that woman was fashioned from the rib of man. God did not want that man be alone and therefore he designed a woman to be an able companion.

Influenced by the patriarchal enclosure one may say that woman is seen in relation to man and his needs as suggested by the expression 'helpmate' but the following two texts, Gen 2:18 and 2:21-23 imply that a man must treat his wife with dignity and honour and as his equal and partner. It goes without saying that he will have to honour every woman in the world. Unfortunately what happened to the first man continues to happen even today.

1.1 Man Blames the Woman and the One Who Gave him the Woman: In spite of all the honour granted to Eve both by God and Adam, the latter let her down when it mattered the most. Upon enquiry after having consumed the forbidden fruit, Adam blames the woman and the One Who gave her to be his companion (cf. Gen 3:12). Adam failed to stand by his wife when it mattered the most and thus began the marginalization of woman.

1.2 Leviticus 12:1-8 and 27:2-13: Women and Childbirth and Value: A casual and cursory reading of these two passages lead people to misinterpret them. Lev 12:1-8 teaches us that a woman is unclean for seven days on two occasions: at the time of menstruation and at the delivery of a male child. Not only what she touches becomes unclean but whoever touches her will also become unclean (cf. Lev 12:2, 5; 15:19-24). She was also denied sexual rapport with her husband and any contact with the people of her household. She could not enter the sanctuary for thirty-three days. The circumcision of the male considerably reduced her days of impurification. Unfortunately, this was not the case with the female child as the days were doubled. The woman was impure for fourteen days at the birth of a daughter and she had to abstain from entering the sanctuary for sixty-six days. Scholars are of the opinion that these customs do not demonstrate the low status of Jewish women.[4] In fact, Prov 31:10-31 sings the praise of a capable wife/woman as "more precious than jewels"; "She is like the ships of the merchant"; "her lamp does not go out at night"; "Strength and dignity are her clothing"; "she opens her mouth with wisdom and the teaching of kindness is on her tongue". Walter summarizes that "the ancient Israelite woman wielded power in the home equal to that exercised by her husband". With this background, let us proceed further to the life of a non-Jewish woman among the chosen people of God.

2. Hagar the Egyptian Slave (cf. Gen 16 & 21[5]): Hagar and Sarai episode (chapter 16) comes to us from the Priestly Source/Strand. Some study this chapter to know the roots of the Ishmaelites, the Bedouin tribes or even the religious heritage of Islamism through Abraham. The purpose for which I am going to study this 'conflict narrative' or 'the family problem of Abraham' is to investigate Hagar as a marginalized non-Jewish woman of biblical times.[6] Hagar was an Egyptian slave woman. Since Abraham's wife Sarai could bear no children[7], as per the custom of the day she gave Hagar to Abraham and requested him to take her as his wife and give Sarai children through her. Abraham obliged Sarai and the Egyptian slave becomes the would-be-mother of his son Ishmael (cf. Gen 16:1-16). The moment Hagar conceived her child, she began to despise Sarai, her mistress and looked at her with contempt. Sarai harshly reacted to the unexpected attitude of the slave-promoted wife of Abraham and began to ill-treat Hagar and the latter ran away as she could not anymore tolerate it. We abruptly stop the story over here for a while in order to get a good grip over the story and investigate it step by step and continue with the rest of the narrative as the discussion grows.

It is true that Hagar was a slave. She was a woman with no voice and no choice. She was uprooted from her land (settled life) as she left Egypt (her homeland) and lived a nomadic life. Abraham and Sarah could do whatever they wanted to do with her. It was within their ownership deal. Abraham could have had sexual relationships with the slave woman even before and after she had become the mother of his son Ishmael. Hagar's motherhood is certainly one of the types of 'surrogate motherhood'.[8] The slavery system of the Patriarchal era could have allowed this practice. This episode perhaps reflects the patriarchal mentality of the author and his times. One cannot also hide the cultural and religious influences over human life and its situations in this story. But a few questions that we wish to face are: "Is all well with the episode? How is God portrayed in the whole incident? What is the role of God in establishing Hagar's womanhood or motherhood and her personality? Why does Sarai or even Abraham or Hagar behave this way in the narratives of the Sacred Scriptures? Would we forgive the author for propagating such an oppressive value system even if it reflects his/her time? Does Hagar remain forever in her marginalized state or does she do something towards her emancipation?

2.1 Conflict and Rivalry: Human slavery of any kind is condemnable at all times and in every culture, except for someone who considers him/herself a slave of God as the issue enters into a religious realm totally and it comes under one's personal choice. In spite of being a slave, Hagar, a woman who is marginalized, does not seem to give up her rightful position as she has become the wife of Abraham and more so even the would-be-mother of his son. All of a sudden she becomes assertive and emphasizes her right. She is perhaps fighting against the current: patriarchal, cultural and religious beliefs. And yet, due to the ill treatment of her mistress she runs away but does not hesitate to complain to the angel of the Lord upon enquiry, "I am running away from my mistress Sarai". Since Hagar's assertion meets with futility, she begins to rebel and runs away in search of freedom and meaningfulness of her life. The angel of the Lord advises her to return to her mistress because the Lord has a plan for her child.

2.2 Renewal of Conflict and Rivalry: Once Isaac was born of divine intervention (cf. Gen 21:1-7) and Sarai came to be called Sarah, she was unable to tolerate that her maid-servant's son was playing with her own son at par and therefore she requested Abraham to send her away: "Cast out this slave woman with her son; for the son of this slave woman shall not inherit along with my son Isaac"(Gen 21:10). Abraham was distressed with what Sarah said and he contemplated over the idea amidst many personal struggles (after all Ishmael was his own flesh and blood) and ethical questions (How to abandon his wife and son although she is still called a slave woman) but was advised by the Lord God Himself to send her away with some provisions for a few days (cf. Gen 21:8-21).

2.3 Hagar: A Model for the Marginalized: Hagar, in spite of being a slave-wife of Abraham, suffers the ignominy of a marginalized woman and yet she becomes a model. As Antony John Baptist rightly points out, "through her revolt (Gen 16:4), flight (Gen 16:6) and in answering the messenger of God (Gen 16:8)," courageously, in unfolding and giving voice to "her inner feelings"[9] Hagar becomes a role model for all the marginalized women who need not fear in the face of adversity and not take things lying down but try to transform them as opportunities for a new beginning.

2.4 Hagar: The First Biblical Female Liberation Activist: Bible scholars believe that Hagar had two choices before her: either to remain in the house of Abraham and Sarai and suffer all the abuses silently to win Sarai's favour or take the risk of running away into the unknown, to the desert even if it means to die. Hagar decided to do the latter with dignity. Antony John Baptist summarizes it beautifully. Hagar's "will for freedom is expressed in her flight from the 'legal' oppression, into the desert exposing her to all the dangers it involves. She preferred the unknown danger of wilderness, as free woman, to the 'comfortable life' in her mistress' house. Thus she becomes the first female in the Bible to liberate herself from an oppressive power structure"[10].

2.5 Hagar and God's Providence: The text says that Abraham could provide Hagar and Ishmael some provisions for a few days, but it is God who makes a life project for her and her son. It is God who takes the initiative. He intervenes at the right moment. It is not that God cares only for the chosen ones, but He loves all. Fretheim says, "God remains focused on Hagar. Sarai and Abram have sent Hagar away, not God. God appears on the scene on behalf of this oppressed one ..."[11] God also promises numerous descendants to Ishmael, after all he is also Abraham's son (cf. Gen 25:12-18). Thus, the providence of God continues in the life of Hagar and Ishmael.

2.6 Creation of a New Order: Antony John Baptist says that through her revolt and back-answering Hagar was trying to raise her voice claiming "equality and mutuality with Sarai".[12] It is very intriguing to see that in asserting her rights, she did not demonstrate any hatred but only stressed "a reordering of relationship"[13] and the need for a "renegotiation and reordering".[14] Antony John Baptist recalls the suggestion of Ska that "The reaction of Hagar is more to the 'mistress' who represents the social order, than to the person or woman named Sarai. It is a social conflict between a mistress and a maidservant".[15] In this process, Hagar was able to recognize her self-worth and self-esteem. It comes from her realization that "she is capable of something which her mistress was not".[16] "Making use of her opportunity and capability as mother, Hagar created a new capital and she transforms it into a liberative potential".[17]

2.7 Hagar: A Story of Assertion and Agency: From the answer of Hagar to the questions of the angel as to where she has come from (her past) and where she is going (future), scholars arrive at a possible conclusion that Hagar is concerned more about her present: "I am running away from my mistress Sarai" (Gen 16:8). The questions of the angels are answered. The answer contains both the origin and destiny of Hagar. She believes that her fleeing away has made her a free woman and that now she is able to speak her mind without any fear. She becomes a model for all those women who suffer. Thus, her story becomes a story of assertion and agency.[18]

2.8 Hagar: A Woman of many Merits: In spite of having been a rebellious slave-surrogate mother, according to Fretheim:

> Hagar is the first person in Genesis to be encountered by the angel of God, and the first woman to be given promises (see Gen 25:23). ...Hagar becomes the *only* person in the OT to name God. She engages in theological formulation, using her own experience with God and the knowledge of God gained thereby to shape new language for God. She thereby shapes contemporary language for God in view of ever-changing human experience and new experiences of God in the midst of that change. Being open to naming God in new ways based on personal experience was not a luxury, but a necessity if God would accompany people in their changing lives.[19]

2.9 Hagar: A Woman of Faith: Hagar is able to see God Himself in the messenger of God and that too being a stranger, an Egyptian. She believes that she saw God in human form. She calls God 'Elroi'. He is a God who sees. He is a God who rescues. This declaration comes from her faith that this God has promised her son a future. He is a God of hope. Antony John Baptist says that Hagar "is the first woman to see God face to face, get divine revelation and dared to name God. Thus Hagar narrative can help us to the encounter with God and can be an inspiration for our missionary models".[20]

2.10 Application to Life

2.10.1 Hagar: A Woman of Hope: Antony John Baptist says, "Hagar episode (Gen 16 and 21) addresses major issues of human life such as slavery, poverty, ethnicity, sexual and economic exploitation, surrogacy, rape, domestic violence, homelessness, motherhood, single-parenting and encountering God etc."[21]

2.10.2 Hagar: A Woman of Openness: Hagar feels that her womanhood has been taken for granted. Sarai wanted only a child from Hagar's womb with no strings attached. What changes Hagar's mind and convinces her to return is the plan of God. That would mean that God does not abandon this woman. Even in this moment of distress God is planning something more for her because Ishmael is Abraham's son and not because he is an offspring of Hagar. She excels in her openness.

2.10.3 Hagar and Sarai: Sisters in Struggle: In reading and meditating upon this episode, both Sarai and the reader would not naturally expect Hagar to verbalize her feelings and back-answer her mistress. But then this is expected of her if she had to come out of slavish mentality. Even Sarai is not devoid of struggles. We have to take note of Sarai's struggle to grope with her own incapacity to become a mother as barrenness is a social disgrace.

3. Tamar the Daughter-in-Law of Judah: The story of Tamar is very intriguing (cf. Gen 38:1-30). She was the wife of Judah's first born Er. He was a wicked man in the sight of the Lord and so he died without an heir. Judah urged his second son Onan to marry Tamar and raise up an offspring to his brother Er to fulfill the duty of a brother towards his sister-in-law. He married Tamar but refused complete sexual union to give birth to a child[22]. It was displeasing in the sight of the Lord and so he also died without a child. Judah got worried about the third son Shelah. At this juncture, Judah played a trick to save Shelah and instructed Tamar to go back to her father's house as a widow and come back when Shelah attained marriageable age. In the meantime, Judah's wife died, and Tamar realized that she was tricked, and she too played her game as she presented herself in the garb of a prostitute. It was Judah's turn to be tricked and he fell in the trap. Since he did not have enough money to pay, Tamar forced him to leave the signet, cord and the staff. Upon hearing that Tamar became pregnant, Judah wanted her to be burnt but she presented the signet, cord and the staff and made her father-in-law realize his unrighteous act and how he marginalized a daughter of Abraham although Shelah was by then a grown-up man.

3.1 Nature of the Event: This narrative proposes that Judah leaves his brothers and moves to a new place and gets married to a Canaanite woman and begins his family. We have to acknowledge that this story is highly sensitive even as a piece of literature.[23] Von Rad very beautifully summarises the event that in this family story one finds a "wonderful openness to what is human – passions, guilt, paternal anxiety, love, honour, chivalry, all churning up the narrow circle of one family in labyrinthine entanglement".[24]

3.1 The Trick of Judah to Save his Son Shelah: Judah was an anxious father. His only concern was the life of his third son after the fateful end of both the sons Er and Onan. Er was a wicked man. Onan was very shrewd as he did not want to lose his ancestral property by giving an heir to dead brother. Onan dishonoured the duty of the levirate marriage[25]. Perhaps Judah thought that the sons died because there was something wrong with Tamar. That could be one of the reasons why probably Judah took his daughter-in-law for granted. Judah cheated her to protect Shelah. Onan failed in his duty and Tamar was not able to give an heir to the family. Tamar could have known why she did not conceive through Onan.

3.2 The Trap Set by Tamar: An Attempt towards Justice: Once Tamar realized that Judah had concocted a story to protect his son Shelah, she takes the issue into her hand and conceives an idea in order to conceive a son, an heir for her first husband Er as an attempt to obtain justice. Judah becomes a victim of his passion, especially in the absence of his wife who was no more. Since the ancient convention of temple prostitution was an accepted custom Judah had no hesitation to approach the roadside prostitute. It was indeed a risky affair, but Tamar was determined and therefore turned out to be righteous at the end.[26]

3.3 The Accused Accuses the Daughter-in-Law: Tamar kept an eye on Judah's movements. At the right time she presented herself as a prostitute. She was astute in her demands and God seems to help her as Judah did not carry any money. Fortune favours the brave. Scholars say that the narrator of the story does not say that she was a harlot but only the friends of Judah say so. She became pregnant. Interestingly Tamar's identity is kept secret while Judah's identity was known to Tamar. As usual, this biblical narrative too does not draw any moral conclusions about the hero and heroine of the story. But Judah becomes a furious judge and he wants her to be burnt alive. The irony is brought out very well by Terence, "When Judah saw her as a prostitute …, he used her; when he sees her in this capacity as his daughter-in-law …, he condemns her. Clearly Judah applies a double standard".[27] But God stands by Tamar and the Evangelist St. Matthew considers it important to mention her name in the Genealogy of Jesus in his Gospel (1:3).

3.4 The Confession of Judah: One has to admire Judah the culprit on both the occasions for the way he responded to the situation. He 'responds magnanimously; his words and actions go beyond what would have been necessary. His guilt-admitting recognition that Tamar has been more righteous … than he means that Tamar has done justice to *this relationship* in a way that he has not in failing to give her to his third son".[28]

3.5 God's Intervention: God is at work. He stands by the affected and marginalized and brings to fruition the efforts of the victim. There is a divine drama at the time of delivery. Tamar gives birth to twins. Although Perez is born first but Zerah's arm comes out first and he claims the right of the first born. As in the case of Esau and Jacob, God stands by Perez and it is through him the lineage continues and thus he becomes the ancestor of David and eventually to Jesus.[29]

3.6 Application to Life

3.6.1 The Plight of Women: The story of Tamar is the story of the plight of many women in human history. For Terence, "the text offers two primary perspectives. On the one hand, the ancient author recognized Tamar as one misused by a key authority in her life. In spite of her oppression, she possesses resources to find a way into a more hopeful future. She subverts Judah's intentions and accomplishes a stunning reversal of authority. Tamar's resourcefulness occurs within the order of creation; God does not directly act".[30] On the other hand, we also get to see how Judah abuses the power of being the *pater familias* and miserably fails to live up to his stature. But we know that he repented of his failures.

3.6.2 The Need to Fight Injustice without Bloodshed: Tamar was rebellious. She took control of the situation. What she did perhaps cannot be justified. Not all the cultures will appreciate it. But Tamar is the product of her culture and time. But Judah has something to tell us. He himself confessed that "she is more in the right than I …" (Gen 38:26). When he makes this statement as the father-in-law and one of the respected sons of Jacob, the statement elevates Tamar and puts her on a pedestal. Yes! Indeed, she didn't take the route of violence. She achieved her goal through her calm, well-calculated risk and natural wisdom. Of course, these are the qualities which bring honour to a woman.

4. The Indian Society: The Indian ethos is full of paradoxes. A woman suffers as a daughter, daughter-in-law, wife and a mother and yet there are many festivals celebrated around the figures of numerous Goddesses. Most of the violent activities are committed against women. Every Indian boy wants to marry a virgin while many Indian males appear in the News Papers every day for crimes related to rapes and molestations. Indians want to promote women and their welfare but will not allow the Women's Reservation Bill of 2008 to come into force. Cows find more dignity than women as cow-slaughters are taken to severe tasks while those who dishonour women and rape them escape. Female homicides and dowry deaths go unabated.

4.1 The Role of Religions: The religions and religious beliefs suppress women besides certain amount cultural and patriarchal elements that are seen in the narrative. Tamar, the non-Jewish woman challenges both the Jewish and Indian societies by her "heroic measures' through which she "triumphs in the end. In resolutely following the intent of the law, by unorthodox and hazardous means, Tamar … takes her place alongside Rachel".[31] It is time that Indian women claim their rightful place at home and in places of work. Dehumanizing attitudes against women must disappear and boys need not be boys for wrong reasons.

4.2 The Role of the Parents and Family: The upbringing of the girl-children is an important issue. They need to be treated like boys. New avenues should be opened to them that they too may shine in all the fields. India can boast of having had a woman-Prime Minister, woman-President, woman-Lok Sabha Speaker, women-Chief Ministers, women-pilots, women-space scientists, women IAS and IPS officers. There is absolutely nothing that women cannot do what men think that they have monopoly over it. It all depends upon their upbringing and the areas they are exposed to right from their childhood. Therefore, parents and teachers have a big role to play in the emancipation and empowerment of women in Indian societies.

Conclusion

In Hagar and Tamar stories, we get to see the power of personal choice and going against conventional thinking. Times of India, in its edition of July 7, 2019 carried an article on "women show us the power of personal choice". According to the write-up, what stands out in both Zaira Wasim and Nusrat Jahan is that they were willing to listen to their inner voice even if it was a question of their religious beliefs. Both of them became the talk of the town as both, according to Shobha De, were daring to break archaic moulds to be themselves. Zaira Wasim from the movie world could not go ahead with career sporting '*imaan*'.[32] As an 18 year young, successful and beautiful girl she quit the showbiz which guaranteed more fame, money and adulation. She simply thought that she did not belong to the tinsel world while the newlywed Member of Parliament Nusrat Jahan appeared with *mangalsutra*, *sindoor* and *chooda* typical traditional symbols of a Hindu bride. What is more amazing is that she was accompanied by her husband. And the occasion was her marriage. Zaira Wasim was criticized for being a victim of radical Islam. Shobha De concludes her post "Politically Incorrect" with a statement which carries a lot of weight, "Choice is the ultimate feminist proof of owning one's identity".[33]

The men who stood by these daring women deserve our praise for their humility and willingness to let their respective wives to follow their inner voice. Unless men allow their mothers, wives and sisters to come out of all that paralyzes them, women in India cannot break the shackles. Nobel Laureate Rabindranath Tagore said, "for we women are not only the deities of the household fire, but the flame of the soul itself". A family without a woman is like a human body without a soul. As the famous Hindi saying goes, "*Shakthi ke bina, Shiv bhi shav ban jaatha hai*" (without the deity Shakti, even Lord Shiva becomes a dead body).

References

Antony John Baptist, "Together as Sisters: Hagar and Dalit Women; Exercising their Agency Unorthodox Way," in *Unsung Melodies from Margins*, ed., Antony John Baptist, Delhi, ISPCK 2014, 36 — 44.

Antony John Baptist, "Encountering the Divine: A Study of Hagar's Encounter with God in Gen 16," in Planted by the Stream: Biblical Themes for Today, ATC Publishers, Bengaluru, 2019, 3 — 17.

Kim Sangwha, "The Story from Hagar's Perspective – Genesis 16:1-16; 21:0-21," In God's Image, 12 no. 4 (1993).

Renit J. Weems, *Just a Sister Away*, San Diego," Lura Media 1988.

Ska, J. L., Abraham Cycle: Synchronic and Diachronic Analysis, Unpublished class notes, Rome: PIB, 1996.

Speiser, E. A., *Genesis: A New Translation with Introduction and Commentary*, The Anchor Bible, Vol. I, Doubleday, New York 1962.

Terence E. Fretheim, "Genesis," in The New Interpreter's Bible, Vol. I, Abingdon Press, Nashville 1994, 321— 674.

Von Rad, Gerhard., *Genesis*, Westminster John Knox Press; Revised edition, 1973.

Walter C. Kaiser, JR, "The Book of Leviticus," in The New Interpreter's Bible, Abingdon Press, Nashville 1994, 985 — 1191.

https://timesofindia.indiatimes.com/blogs/politically-incorrect/2-women-show-us-the-power-of-personal-choice/ 07.07.2019.

Notes

1. Dr. Arockiasamy Savari Rayan, SVD, Rector, Khrist Premalaya Regional Theologate, Seminary Road, Ashta Madhya Pradesh – India, Mobile: 089 82 86 1337 and 089 89 52 53 92.
2. According to a census taken in 2010.
3. This and other biblical dates taken from "Events in Biblical Chronology" found in New Revised Standard Version of the Holy Bible. Another source fixes the date of Abraham to 1800 BCE.
4. Cf. Walter C. Kaiser, JR, "The Book of Leviticus," in The New Interpreter's Bible, Abingdon Press, Nashville 1994, 1084-1086.
5. Genesis chapter 21 could originate from a mixture of JEP sources/strands.
6. Terence E. Fretheim, "Genesis," in The New Interpreter's Bible, Vol. I, Abingdon Press, Nashville 1994, 349.
7. Amazingly Sarai says that the Lord has prevented her from bearing children. The History of Salvation narrates that God commanded Adam and Eve to "be fruitful and multiply" (Gen 1:28) and God repeated the same to Abraham when He called to move towards the land that He would show (cf. Gen 12:1-4). But

nothing was happening and so Abraham tried to interpret the promise of God by adopting Eliezer of Damascus, son of a slave born in Abraham's house. God rejected this proposal. Now it is Sarai's turn to try her luck to construe God's promise.

8. Cf. Terence E. Fretheim, "Genesis," 454.
9. Antony John Baptist, "Together as Sisters: Hagar and Dalit Women; Exercising their Agency Unorthodox Way," in *Unsung Melodies from Margins*, ed., Antony John Baptist, Delhi, ISPCK 2014, 38.
10. *Ibid.*, 40.
11. Terence E. Fretheim, "Genesis," 452.
12. Antony John Baptist, "Together as Sisters," 39.
13. Sangwha Kim, "The Story from Hagar's Perspective – Genesis 16:1-16; 21:0-21," In God's Image, 12 no. 4 (1993), 24 as quoted in Antony John Baptist "Together as sisters," 39.
14. Renit J. Weems, *Just a Sister Away*, San Diego," Lura Media 1988, 5 as quoted in Antony John Baptist "Together as sisters," 39.
15. J. L. Ska, Abraham Cycle: Synchronic and Diachronic Analysis, Unpublished class notes, Rome: PIB, 1996, 89 as quoted in the footnotes in Antony John Baptist "Together as sisters," 42.
16. Antony John Baptist "Together as sisters," 39.
17. *Ibid.*, 39.
18. *Ibid.*, 38.
19. Terence E. Fretheim, "Genesis," 454.
20. A. John Baptist, "Encountering the Divine: A Study of Hagar's Encounter with God in Gen 16," in Planted by the Stream: Biblical Themes for Today, ATC Publishers, Bengaluru, 2019, 6.
21. Antony John Baptist, "Together as Sisters," 37.
22. The sin of Onanism tells the world that "Humans can thwart the will of God concerning progeny by their sexual practices (Gen 38:9-10)". Terence E. Fretheim, "Genesis," in The New Interpreter's Bible, 452.
23. Cf. E. A. Speiser, *Genesis: A New Translation with Introduction and Commentary*, The Anchor Bible, Vol. I, Doubleday, New York 1962, 299.
24. Gerhard von Rad, *Genesis*, Westminster John Knox Press; Revised edition, 1973, 361.
25. The institution of levirate requires the brother of a deceased man to marry his sister-in-law in order to provide continuity for the line of the deceased. It is an alternative to adoption
26. Cf. Terence E. Fretheim, *The Book of Genesis*, 605.
27. *Ibid.*, 605.
28. *Ibid.*, 606.
29. Cf. Terence Fretheim, *The Book of Genesis*, 606.
30. Terence Fretheim, *The Book of Genesis*, 607.
31. E. A. Speiser, *Genesis: A New Translation with Introduction and Commentary*, 300.

32. Its most simple definition is the belief in the six articles of faith, known as *arkân al-îmân*. The termiman has been delineated in both the Quran and hadith.
33. https://timesofindia.indiatimes.com/blogs/politically-incorrect/2-women-show-us-the-power-of-personal-choice/ 07.07.2019.

Chapter - 18

Jesus and the Syrophoenician Woman in Mark 7: 24-30 A Paradigm for socio-religious affirmation

Adaikalasamy, Wilson SVD[1]

Introduction

The story of Jesus and the Syrophoenician woman is undoubtedly an interesting and powerful Markan story. As I read and watched[2] several times the performance of Jesus and the Syrophoenician woman episode, I realize it is pregnant with deep meaning, theological and social significance that impels

one to action. The encounter between the Syrophoenician woman and Jesus, dramatically recaptures the socio-religious values prevalent at Jesus' time and the social status of the Gentile believer and much more the status of a Gentile woman. Therefore, I intend to study this story as presented in the Gospel of

Mark and explore the relationship between religious and ethnic identity presented in this pericope and analyze the socio-cultural complexities imbedded in it. I wish to study this episode because even today, the women in many parts of the world, particularly in my country and mission places are being subjected to multiple forms of social evils, male dominance and religious injustices. In such context, the Syrophoenician woman becomes an embodiment of socio-religious reformation and faith. She is a powerful motivating symbol towards women affirmation and equality. In this encounter, Jesus rebuffs the woman and embarrasses himself but the wisdom of the Gentile woman makes him undergo transformation and he dares to break the barriers and affirm openly that everyone is a child of God and is member of Kingdom of God. I undertake this research study employing the tools of narrative critical method and study systematically the plot, character, setting, narrative and literary style, rhetoric impact, analysis of conflicts and characters, theological significance and its implications for today's context.

Narrative Critical Method

Reading or hearing or watching the performance of a narrative can be a powerful experience and the Bible that we revere as a sacred literature is all the more compelling. Narrative Criticism is a methodology of study that analyzes the formal features of Biblical narratives and it illuminates the text. Narrative Criticism focuses on the narrative, the text as it is. How do we understanda narrative, it's meaning and how it works for our context? our faith and lives? There are five key features of narrative for analysis; they are narrator, setting, plot, character and rhetoric.[3] The systematic analyzes of these key elements of a narrative provides profound insights into the text, aids fresh understanding and unpacks personal, communal and relevant meanings persuading to action. David Rhoads and many Markan scholars employing narrative criticism approach the Gospel of Mark as a whole. The unity of the Gospel is evident in the integrity of the stories, coherence in plot and the characters are consistent from one scene to the other.[4] Since, the Gospel of Mark is a coherent narrative, it is precisely important for the study of any individual episode to be carried out as an integral part of the entire narrative. Therefore, I study the episode of the Syrophoenician woman as an integral part of the whole narrative and not as an independent narrative. Here, I take up the Narrative Critical study of 7: 24-30 and in the process, dedicate adequate importance for the narrative rhetoric[5] and its impact on the reader/hearer.

Text and Context

The Episode in the Wider Context of the Narrative World

How does the episode of the Syrophoenician woman fit into the overall narrative of the Gospel of Mark? The study event happens in 7th chapter and this would mean that the reader/hear has already entered into the story world.[6]

The narrative begins stating, "the beginning of the good news of Jesus Christ, the Son of God" (1: 1) and the Good news of Jesus Christ is "the time is fulfilled, and the kingdom of God has come near, repent and believe in the good news" (1:15). Hence, the arrival and establishment of the Kingdom of God through the person of Jesus Christ, the messiah is the main thrust of the entire narrative[7]. As Mark's story is focused on a theme/narrative purpose, each event of the narrative systematically, progressively and coherently unfolds, interconnects and illuminates the main thrust as it builds up the whole narrative. The stories that follow the announcement of Kingdom of God (1: 15): healings, parables, exorcisms[8], nature miracles, human transformation, conflicts[9], prophecies[10], persecution, death and resurrection[11] are expressions of that Kingdom and consequences of Jesus' active ministry to establish that Kingdom of God. Thus, the entire narrative of Mark is unified around this theme. Therefore, the episode of the Syrophoenician woman fits pretty well into the overall narrative of Mark, especially in relation to Kingdom of God. The episode is an expression of kingdom of God as it powerfully upholds the values of faith and equality above socio-cultural, religious, political and ethical conflict. So, the event advances the plot by embodying the values of the Kingdom of God.

Immediate Context of the Study Text

It is of paramount importance to consider the immediate context of the study pericope because no suppliant is interchangeable with the other and each one plays a unique role in the precise context in which they appear.[12] The pericope is integral to its immediate context as it is integral to whole narrative. I perceive 6: 31 – 8: 21 as the immediate context of 7: 24-30. This story comes at a most crucial place and the section is bounded by two miraculous bread feeding narratives[13]. I propose the following framework of the narrative to delimit the immediate context.

a. Jesus feeds 5, 000 Jews, walks on the water and disciples do not understand the bread (6: 31-44, 45-51, 52).
b. Jesus heals those who come to him (6:53-56).
c. Controversy with Pharisees over the eating with defiled hands (7: 1-16).
d. Jesus teaches disciples, declaring all foods clean (7: 17-23)
c. Immediately goes to Gentile territory and controversy with a Syrophoenician woman over healing (7:24-30)
b. Goes to Decapolis and heals a deaf man (7: 31-37)
a. Jesus feeds 4, 000 gentiles, Pharisees demand for a sign, disciples do not understand the bread (8: 1-10, 11-13, 14-21).[14]

It is evident that the central event of this section is teaching the disciples regarding ritual purity declaring that all foods are clean. This declaration provides an ambience for a transition in the narrative from feeding in the Jewish territory to feeding in the Gentile territory. I perceive that the episode of the Syrophoenician woman is well placed immediately after the declaration that all foods are clean to provide and initiate a concrete breakthrough to mission and establishment of kingdom of God among the gentiles. As David Rhoads says, "our episode, with its particular details, is not a generic healing which could appear anywhere else in the story. Rather, it is the turning point in an important sub-plot of the Gospel."[15] Therefore, Jesus' exorcism and healing in Gentile territory reinforces his teaching on purity and the socio-religious concept of purity is challenged by the coming of God's kingdom, which is the driving force of the whole narrative.

Type Scene

One of the means by which the narrator builds up the plot of the Gospel is by recurring type- scenes. Type-scenes are similar episodes repeated with variations throughout the narrative[16]. These episodes have a common form and they set up a conventional patternand so the reader/hearer becomes familiar with this pattern and are able to absorb any new variations introduced with each repetition of a healing story.These type-scenes contribute to the characterization, plot development and thematic amplification[17]. Healing story is one of the type-scenes and the episode of Syrophoenician woman is an example of such a type-scene.

General Outline of the Episode and the Variations Introduced

Type-scene functions in two ways: its provides a pattern of repetition for the reader and variation in a type-scene introduces new elements into the story. Hence, "repetition with variation is a dominant stylistic feature and rhetorical strategy of Mark's narrative".[18] I propose the following general outlineof the episode and new variations introduced.

a. Jesus' arrival in Tyre, a Gentile Territory, seeks to be unnoticed (v.24 setting).

b. The woman approaches – implies she has already heard about him (v.25-26a, a note on her ethnicity, repetition and absence of her name).

c. The woman's petition – knelt and she begged him (v. 26).

d. Jesus' response – a refusal (v. 27).

e. The woman retorts – the turning point of the story-shift in the plot (v. 28).

d. Jesus' second response – affirmation (v.29a).

c. The woman's petition granted – exorcism of an absent daughter. (v. 29b).

b. The woman returns home – Jesus commands her to go – she returns and finds her daughter well, no reaction from the observers. (v. 30).

a. Jesus returns from the region of Tyre (v.31a)[19].

Thus, the story of the Syrophoenician woman reflects the type-scene both in terms of repetition and introduction of variations. At this point, the reader/hearer is familiar with type-scene and so is able to identify the fresh details and grasp them.

Rhetoric Elements

Two-step Progressions

Two-step progression is a rhetoric technique whichis employed to add precision to what has been already said[20]. When the narrator introduces the Syrophoenician woman, he refers to her as 'the woman was a Greek, a Syrophoenician by birth' (ἡ δὲ γυνὴ ἦν Ἑλληνίς, Συροφοινίκισσα τῷ γένει). This repetition is a two-step progression in which the narrator repeats -'a Greek, a Syrophoenician by birth', an information in order to make sure that the reader/hearer makes note of it. The first part gives a general information while the second part provides specific detail, which is vital for the story[21].

Parallelism

The reader/hearer could observe an intricate parallelism present in this pericope. David Rhoads elucidates parallelism in this text as following: Jesus' rejection of request (v.27) is subsequently paralleled by woman's answer (v.28). The command to 'go' (v.29) corresponds to the phrase 'going away to her home' (v.30). Jesus' declaration of exorcism 'the demon has left your daughter' (v.29) corresponds to 'from the little child, the demon had gone out'(v. 30).[22]

Metaphor

Metaphor is a symbolic representative of something else and it is a figure of speech. Metaphors communicate more than what they represent and they need to be inferred. Hence, Fowler insists that, "to understand the encounter with metaphor in the experience of reading Mark's Gospel, we need to find ways to talk about the pragmatic, rhetorical effects that the Markan metaphors have on the reader."[23] Only a rhetorical or pragmatic approach can possibly enable the readers to make sense of metaphors. The metaphors employed in this narrative are *Children, bread and dogs*. The reader who is to make sense of the elliptical dialogue concerning *children, bread and dogs* must recall the parenthesis in 7: 26 – A Greek, Syrophoenician woman. Jesus is hesitant to give children's bread to dogs, it is because she is from a non-Jewish origin and the woman takes up the figures of speech Jesus uses and turn them against him.[24] Therefore, the reader can infer that *dogs represent Gentiles, children represent Jews and bread is the benefits of the kingdom* that which Jesus can do for all the people.

Suspense

Suspense is the state of being anxious or uncertain about what may happen. It is an anxiety developed from unpredictable events. The episode begins stating that Jesus enters a house in a gentile territory and wants to hid it. Why does he want to hid? The reader is anxious. The episode progresses with a surprise that a Gentile woman immediately approaches Jesus (Male, a Jew) with a request and so the surprise intensifies the anxiety and creates a suspense to the reader/ hearer to wonder how Jesus will respond. Is there a connection between Jesus wanting to hid his presence and the Gentile woman's request? - The suspense builds up. The suspense apparently appears to be resolved when Jesus rejects her request. However, this rejection in reality escalates the tension because the reader/hearer has so far known Jesus as a healer. The suspense builds up further again when the woman retorts immediately. The quick response of the woman raises the doubt for the audience regarding whether the daughter will be healed. Thus, the rhetorical device is carefully developed and employed in this episode to create suspense at every development of the story.

Riddles – Allegory: Allegorical Riddles

There are 'stories within the story', a character recounts a brief story within a story. David Rhoads opines that Markan Gospel has many of such 'stories within the story' and it is more appropriate to call them as 'riddles' and not 'parables' because Markan parables are often cryptic and obscure.

Jesus' riddles in Mark are allegories with several points of correlation and reader/hearer is to decipher allegorical riddles as 'stories within the stories' in order to understand.[25] Markan parables are allegories in which Jesus explains to other characters what is going on around them. In our study episode, Jesus uses an allegorical riddle to explain to the woman why he cannot grand her request and it is a carefully crafted allegory[26]. The Syrophoenician woman in her response, develops and extends Jesus' riddle in such way that her request may find a place in the scheme. The following framework explains the allegorical riddle and its application and how it relates to the story.[27]

Jesus' Riddle

The Allegory	*Applied within this Episode*	*Applied to the whole narrative*
Firstlet the children be satisfiedfor it is not good to take the bread for the children and throw it to the little dogs.	Now, let only the Jews (not this Gentile womanhave the benefits from God/Jesus, for it is not good to takethe benefits (here exorcism) meant for the Jews and carelessly give it to the Syrophoenician woman and her daughter	When Jesus is alive let only the Jewshave the benefits of the Kingdom of God, for it is not good to takethe benefits of the Kingdom of God meant for the Jews and carelessly give them to the Gentiles.

Woman's Riddle

The Allegory	*Applied within this Episode*	*Applied to the whole narrative*
Even the little dogs (pups) under the table eat the little crumbs of the children	Even now, I and my daughter could (should/deserve) benefit from just one (exorcism) of the many benefits for the Jews.	At this time (from now on), the Gentiles, who live in/near Israel (universality) could (should) benefit from some of the benefits of the Kingdom, for the Jews.

Conflict in the Plot

Conflict is one of the vital dimensions of the story. Conflict analysis examines the circumstances of the conflict, what or who initiates the conflict, how it escalates, what are the complications imbedded and what could be the solution.[28] Like any healing stories of Mark, the plot of the Syrophoenician woman revolves around a conflict. The conflict is the refusal – Jesus refuses to heal. The episode comes to an end when the obstacle is over come and the conflict is resolved.

Setting: Boundary Shattering Encounter

The setting provides the narrative with a 'world' where the events take place and characters act.[29] The narrative takes place in the region around the city of Tyre[30] and the setting is 'Jesus goes to Tyre, a Gentile territory and the episode concludes with Jesus' healing the daughter of a Gentile woman'. The setting of this pericope is very significant and symbolic[31]. The hostile wall between the Jews and the Gentiles had grown enormously thick due to ethnic, cultural, religious, economic and political boundaries.The reader/hearer may wonder what has Jesus to do in Tyre? What was Jesus' mission in Gentile territory? Was it to break the boundaries between the Jews and Gentiles? Or does this crossing represent Jesus' magnanimity to include Gentiles into Kingdom of God? I perceive that the episode is fundamentally about crossing the conventional boundaries and beginning new avenues.[32] The crossing-over represents the incredible shattering of socio-cultural, religious and political boundaries. Jesus is taking a deliberate turn to Gentile territory and his entry into Tyre signals clearly and strongly that Jesus has shattered these boundaries and they hold good no more. Jesus' crossing of social and geographical boundaries to come to Tyre, signals that he is making "an onslaught upon boundaries because he sees holiness as a reality which spreads cleanness."[33] He makessacred what was considered unclean and profane. Further, I am inclined to think that Jesus came to the Gentile area and willingly became an outsider, a stranger, a foreigner to identify himself with the least. Perhaps he was trying to experience the status of being an outsider, facing the challenges of discrimination.

Greco-Roman World and the Women

It is of paramount importance to understand the nuances of the Greco-Roman world of Jesus' time inorder to grasp our episode well. The Greco-Roman world of Jesus' time was a patriarchal, male dominated society. The rights, privileges and even the very existence of women was always in relation to a male[34]. In such a context, one can easily imagine the status of a Gentile and that too a Gentile woman. She was almost a non-being, who could be easily trampled upon. The beauty of this episode is Jesus restores the dignity and affirms the daughterhood of the Syrophoenician woman.

Jesus and Syrophoenician woman Encounter

The scene starts across the border and inside a house. Jesus travels to Tyre and enters a house with a desire to remain secret. There, a Syrophoenician woman, a Gentile comes to him seeking to cast out a demon from her daughter. He refuses her request abruptly, insults her and calls her dog and Jesus does it face to face. The Gentile woman as Richard Swanson says, "absorbs the insult, waits for the bitterness to subside and then presses her claim on Jesus' attention. She says, 'Even the dogs…', even the dogs, what does it cost her to say such a thing? Her daughter is more worth than anything else"[35]. Consequently, Jesus changes his mind and she finds her daughter clean. This encounter sets on fire the revolution over conservatism and socio-religious dominance: a woman faces a man; the woman is a Gentile, the man is a Jew, they confront, dialogue and arrival at a peaceful win-win solution. A beginning of communion of cultures, peoples and attitudes.

Characterization

Characterization refers to the way a narrator brings characters to life in a narrative. We infer the characteristic traits of the characters from what they say, what they do, and what others say about them and how they react and how others react to them.[36] There are basically two characters in this episode; Jesus and Syrophoenician woman and it is amazing to unravel the many traits of these two characters.

The Syrophoenician Woman: A Complex Stock Character

I am fascinated by the prominence of the woman in this episode. This outstanding prominence has a lot to communicate. Any change and social reformation requires an adequate knowledge of who Am I and what Am I? As it appears to me the Syrophoenician woman knew herself pretty well and that served as launching pad for her assertive attitudes. She is rather a complex stock character.

Jesus travels into the Gentile domain of Trye, and there he is approached by a woman seeking healing for her daughter who is afflicted by an unclean spirit (πνεῦμα ἀκάθαρτον). When the narrator introduces the woman, he refers to her as 'the woman was a Greek, a Syrophoenician by birth' (ἡ δὲ[37] γυνὴ ἦν Ἑλληνίς, Συροφοινίκισσα τῷ γένει). The repetition reveals and emphasizes her ethnic identity and resonates the existing hostility and discrimination. It is to be noted that neither the woman's nor her daughter's name is mentioned. A nameless person would mean, a person without roots, without identity and is not worthy of any social status. With this information, the reader can identify that the woman is described as an 'outsider'. I would say, she is an outsider three times: she is a Gentile, a woman and her daughter is demon possessed, hence, three times outsider, an accumulated social stigma.

The suppliant comes, kneels at his feet and begs for a favor[38]. David Rhoads writes, "the posture of the woman in begging for a healing is integral to Jesus' depiction of her as a scavenger dog."[39] While Jennifer Glancy says, "the complexity of the woman's cultural identity is in play when, like Jairus, she falls at Jesus' feet. Her body is precisely the location that makes present this complex cultural identity, just as Jairus's body is precisely the location that makes present his complex cultural identity."[40] However, I am inclined to consider her posture as an expression of an attitude of self-abasement, humility, supplication and smallness in all the ways before Jesus, a Jew.

Jesus, the known healer quickly refuses and uses rather offensive words to communicate his unwillingness to heal the sick child. Jesus' refusal is a surprise and even more surprising is the way he refuses, "Let the children be fed first, for it is not fair to take the children's food and throw it to dogs." The words 'first (πρῶτον)[41] and dogs' function to support the Jewish superiority and define the Gentiles as second-class citizens. Is the woman doglike because of her gender? Her religion? The region that she lives in? Her Greek identity? Her Syrophoenician heritage? Jesus uses a disdainful metaphor comparing the mother and daughter to dogs explicitly indicating that they are not worthy to be fed with children's bread. Jesus insults the Gentile mother and the daughter and portrays them as outsiders. The reference to dogs (κυναρίοις) occurs in biblical texts as a term of abuse for Gentiles (1 Sam 17: 43, 2 Kgs 8: 3).Several scholars have analyzed the usage of the term 'dog' and they vary in their opinions[42]. However, comparing someone, specially a woman and the child to dog is definitely insulting and dishonoring.[43]

Bold, Wise and Assertive Woman

In this striking incident, the Syrophoenician woman emerges out to be a model of bold, wise and assertive woman. Considering the socio-cultural context, it is certainly unusual for a woman to approach a man and initiate a conversation without a male mediator. But, this woman breaks many such conventional social practices by her approaching Jesus and asking him in person to heal her daughter. Jesus very bluntly rejects her plea with an insult over the refusal. If any woman in today's world were to hear such response, she would become very angry even to remain there and depart instantly preferring to endure her daughter's suffering instead of swallowing such a slur.[44] But this woman is different, she was accustomed probably since birth to be submissive and has shouldered all sorts of grief but now would not allow herself to be over-powered. She is courageous, she listens to the abrupt response and wisely takes on Jesus on the same cord, "even the dogs under the table eat the children's crumbs." She did say this because she is determined and she exemplifies boldness and understanding. Mary Ann Tolbert writes, "Her unconventional behavior, which initially draws the dominant male's wrath, by its increasing boldness, cleverness and basic moral correctness eventually subverts that wrath into agreement."[45] The reader/hearer may suffer from lack of understanding because of the strange response of Jesus but the woman displays a great understanding of the situation. She is optimistic and has an enormous tenacity. She does not say 'no, how can it be' and argue with Jesus instead affirms promptly Jesus' negative reply and turns the offensive label into her advantage. Her insightful response is the turning point of the story. Instead of confronting the insult, she turns the offensive label into a harmless one[46] and uses it to her advantage. She uses the same word that Jesus uses but in her own way. Therefore, she answers, 'sir, even the doges under the table eat the children's crumbs'. For her, probably, the dogs are also domestic animals: children do drop the food and dogs quickly eat what falls from the table. Likewise, she and her daughter would benefit from the food that falls from Jesus's table. Thus, she takes the rejection as an opportunity and indicates to Jesus what he is capable of doing. The Syrophoenician woman, an outsider as a Gentile and an outsider as a woman, achieves her goal because of her 'saying', not because of her faith alone or her reasoning alone, but because of her speaking up and speaking out; because of her action.[47] The Syrophoenician woman's clever reply seems convincing Jesus to change his mind and he grants the woman her request. In this way, she displays that she is understanding, wise, bold, persistent and assertive.

Embodiment of Faith

The type-scenes overwhelm with aspects of faith. The narrator does not often make an explicit notification that the suppliant has faith instead faith is manifested through the actions and dialogues of the characters. In this striking incident, the woman turns out be a model of strong and persistent faith. The Syrophoenician woman's desperation to find a cure for her daughter enables her to recognize the power of Jesus to heal. In Mark, faith is embodied in action.[48] Considering the traits of the stock personalities, the reader/hearer knows that the major trait of the Syrophoenician woman is faith. She comes to him, falls at his feet, and begs to drive the demon from her daughter – these are the actions of faith. Jesus recognizes and acknowledges the persistent faith of the woman in his response 'for this word, your daughter is restored.[49] The woman's perseverance is made possible due to her faith, and so faith accompanied by persistence and wisdom succeeds in changing the mind of Jesus. A faithful woman is a successful woman.

A paradigm for Social Reformation

This is a powerful story particularly amidst male dominance, marginalization and discrimination. The Syrophoenician woman is considered unclean because she is a Gentile andher daughter is with unclean spirit and this could double the stigma but that does not stop her from achieving what she needs.Apparently, she did not accept the refusal, for the sake of her daughter she broke customs, went after what she wanted, stood up, spoke up, confronted, and established her human dignity[50]. The feminist scholars celebrate and interpret the success of the Syrophoenician woman in many ways; Hisako Kinukawa notes that the Gentile woman has created an opportunity for Jesus to Change his attitude[51], Sharon Ringe emphasizes that Jesus is helped by the least expected person, a Gentile woman and a social outcast[52] and Susan Miller views her as the foremother of Gentile woman and Gentile mission.[53] Ranjini Wickramarantne Rebera extols her as a role model who rose above the obstacles, claiming inclusion and retaining her own identity.[54]

They are correct and I perceive she is a single mother, who has been stigmatized, frustrated and may have constantly experienced humiliation but she does not allow her to be aggressive. When she said 'yes' in fact, it was 'no'. She did not say 'yes' and walk away in obedience but makes a profound remark, which leads Jesus to further thought.[55] She asks Jesus to give her what she needs, what is her due and not what others have, she claims her basic fundamental equality. Her action and response were the catalyst for Jesus' change of mind. The event confirms firmly the role of this woman in leading Jesus to initiate a mission in Gentile territory. Thus, she stands out as a paradigm for social reformation, woman affirmation, assertiveness and liberation. If one Syrophoenician woman can make a difference, every woman can! Let the Syrophoenician woman resonate in every woman today!

Jesus: A Found Character

Jesus remains central to this story though the prominence is apparently gained by the Syrophoenician woman. Jesus of Mark, the reader/hearer knows pretty well, has been consistently responding favorably to the healing requests. Amidst such an ambience, it is surprising that Jesus refused the desperate Gentile woman using ungraceful language and by this he embarrassed himself. As a student of Mark, I am troubled by Jesus' blunt ungracious reply. The refusal questions and shatters my convictions about a compassionate Jesus. There are several questions that topple my mind: Why did Jesus refuse to heal the daughter of the Gentile woman? What does this imply? Was Jesus racist? Was gender an issue? Was it because she was an impure woman, a Greek? Would Jesus give a same response if it was a man asking help? What made Jesus feel obliged to heal Jairus' daughter in chapter 5 and refuse the woman now for a similar request? Was Jesus going through an inner conflict of crossing the barriers? Or Was Jesus inviting the Syrophoenician woman for a dialogue by provoking her? The woman dared to cross the social, political, economic and several symbolic barriers to reach Jesus but Jesus hesitated to extend a helping hand to the suffering mother. The reluctance is puzzling.

However, I would like to argue along with David Rhoads that Jesus undergoes a genuine change of mind. His genuine change of mind overshadows the initial reluctance[56]. Jesus begins the encounter with an assumption that the kingdom is for the Jews primarily and later for all the Gentiles and in contrast the scene ends with a willingness to share the benefits of the kingdom with the Gentiles immediately. Jesus responds to her positively and commends argument saying, 'for saying that you may go, the demon has left your daughter'. It is evident that his attitude is dramatically changed and this encounter was not only a liberative experience for the Gentile woman but for Jesus himself. Although I strongly acknowledge the role of the Syrophoenician woman as powerful and liberating one for women, I would like to emphasize equally on Jesus' openness and willingness to reconcile instantly. Jesus willingly learned from the Gentile woman. Jesus rectified his mistaken attitude of 'Jews first and others later' by offering healing to her daughter at once. It is Jesus' humility to learn from a Gentile woman and readiness for reconciliation actually leads to implementation of justice. He breaks through the boundaries of insider-outsider and challenges all who function rigidly within these confinements. Jesus now makes available the benefits of the kingdom for all beyond any limits[57]. Jesus sets an example for all to transcend such barriers and form kingdom.

Standards of Judgement

The standards of judgement manifest the moral fabric of the narrative. Standards of judgement are norms that are implicit or explicit in the narrative by which the audience evaluate the characters.[58] The whole narrative of Mark reflects the moral dualism; 'thinking the things of God' and thinking the things of people'[59]. The characters vacillate between these two values. In our episode, the Syrophoenician woman embodies the things of God in many ways: she exemplifies faith, courage, wisdom andvalues her daughter and so initiates fight against social injustices. She is ready to stoop down and became the least, a scavenger dog, for the sake of her daughter. Jesus too courageously and willingly changes his mind to share the benefits of the kingdom with the Gentiles and breaking the barriers commences all-inclusive mission, including everyone children of God - a real expression of Kingdom of God.

Rhetorical Impact in the Then Historical Context

The episode begins with an information that Jesus travels from Galilee to the region of Tyre. Tyre and Sidon are Phoenician cities, were places of wealth and power and they were also places of Jewish interaction. Hence, this passage may reflect the hostility that existed between the Galileans and the Tyrians.

Galilee served as a source of food for the Tyrians and so there existed economic conflict among the them.[60] Tyre and Galilee were also patriarchic societies rampant with socio-religious injustices and ill-treatment of women under the umbrella of social and religious customs.[61] It is of paramount importance to understand the nuances of the Greco-Roman world of Jesus' time in order to grasp our episode well. The Greco-Roman world of Jesus' time was a patriarchal, male dominated society. In such context, the Syrophoenician woman is an expression of despair and hostility and the audience of Mark then shared the same experience and so would have identified themselves and their situation with the episode pretty well. Jesus himself portrays hostility and then changes his mind; this was a challenge thrown to the audience to break the hostile feelings and embrace the universality of kingdom of God and embrace each one as brothers and sisters. The Gentile woman enabled the narrator to bring home this point vividly through her faith and perseverance. Therefore, this story defuses and neutralizeshostility of the hearers in Mark's time.

Rhetorical Impact Today

Our world is still, in spite of progress in education and human development not different from Mark's time. The social injustices, gender, cultural and religious dominance, economic diversity is rampant all over the world. In a way, every one of us go through some sort of hostility and dominance. In such context, the story of the Syrophoenician woman is one of the powerful texts that impels to break down barriers of every kind. This story shatters presumptions and limits on several fronts: the Gentile woman gets her daughter healed, disdains status[62], destroys the hostility of every nature, understands the value of life, assertive and insightful, impure yet preserved to reach God. Jesus has proved that unless the oppressor decides to change, the oppression will continue. Hence, the narrator seeks to hint at the root of human hostility and promote communion and universality of the Gospel and values of the Kingdom everywhere.

Conclusion

The longer time I spent, the more I begin to admire and appreciate the Syrophoenician woman and Jesus for their genuineness and openness. Jesus and the Syrophoenician woman, an event of boundary-breaking activity. It is an encounter that brings mutual transformation and victory to both parties. The intelligent retort of the woman wins the contest. Her assertive faith and boldness wins Jesus' favor and Jesus changes his attitude and implements justice, restores the daughter. It is a powerful text that motivated Jesus to act, breaking oppressive structures and boundaries, inviting the Gentile, the socially outcast, the materially poor, the oppressed and rejected into God's Kingdom, an inclusive community of communion of hearts.May Jesus and the Syrophoenician woman resonate in us to realize the kingdom of God here and now.

Bibliography

Books, Commentaries and Dictionary

ANDERSON, JANICE C., and MOORE, STEPHEN D., (eds.), *Mark and Method: New Approaches in Biblical Studies*, second edition (Minneapolis, Minnesota: Fortress Press 2008).

BARCLAY, WILLIAM., T*he Gospel of Mark. The Daily Study Bible Series, Rev. ed.* (Philadelphia: The Westminster Press 2000).

BETSWORTH,S., *The reign of God is such as these: A Socio-literary Analysis of Daughters in the Gospel of Mark*, (London, New York: T &T Clark 2010).

CORLEY,KATHLEEN E.,*Women and the Historical Jesus: Feminists myths of Christian Origin* (Santa Rosa CA: Pole bridge Press 2002).

DANKER, FREDERICK W., 3rd ed., *A Greek-English lexicon of the New Testament and other early Christian literature.* "Based on Walter Bauer's Griechisch-deutschesWrterbuchzu den Schriften des Neuen Testaments und der frhchristlichen [sic] Literatur, sixth edition, ed. Kurt Aland and Barbara Aland, with Viktor Reichmann and on previous English editions by W.F. Arndt, F.W. Gingrich, and F.W. Danker." 3rd ed. (Chicago: University of Chicago Press 2000).

DANOVE, PAUL L., *The Rhetoric of Characterization of God, Jesus and Jesus' Disciples in the Gospel of Mark* (New York: T & T Clark 2005).

ELLIOTT, SCOTT S., *Reconfiguring Mark's Jesus: Narrative Criticism after Poststructuralism* (Sheffield, England: Sheffield Phoenix Press 2011).

FOWLER, ROBERT M., *Let the Reader Understand Reader-Response Criticism and the Gospel of Mark* (Harrisburg, Pennsylvania: Trinity Press International 2001).

—, *Loaves and Fishes:The Function of the Feeding Stories in the Gospel of Mark* (Atlanta, Georgia: Society of Biblical Literature 1981).

IVERSON, KELLY R., and SKINNER, CHRISTOPHER W., (ed.), *Mark as Story: Retrospect and Prospect* (Atlanta, Georgia: Society of Biblical Literature 2011).

KINUKAWA, HISAKO., *Women and Jesus in Mar*k (Maryknoll, New York: Orbis Books 1994).

LEVINE, AMY-JILLand BLICKENSTAFF,MARIANNE.,(eds.),*A Feminist Companion to Mark* (Cleveland, Ohio : Pilgrim Press 2001).

MALBON,ELIZABETH S., and MCKNIGHT, EDGAR V., (ed.), *The New Literary Criticism and the New Testament* (Sheffield: Academic Press 1994).

—,*In the Company of Jesus: Characters in Mark's Gospel* (Louisville, Kentucky: Westminster John Knox Press 2000).

—,*Mark's Jesus: Characterization as Narrative Christology* (Waco, Texas: Baylor University Press 2009).

MARCUS, J., *Mark 1-8: A new translation with introduction and commentary Vol. 2* The Anchor Yale Bible, Vol. 27A. (New Haven, London: Yale University Press 2008).

MILLER, S., *Women in Mark's Gospel* (London: T & T Clark 2004).

RHOADS, D., DEWEY,J.,and MICHIE,D., *Mark As Story An Introduction to the Narrative of a Gospel,* Third Edition (Minneapolis: Fortress Press 2012).

RINGE, SHARON H. and NEWSOM CAROL A., (ed.), *Women's Bible Commentary,* (Louisville: Westminster John Knox 1998).

ROBERT, A., *The Art of Biblical Narrative* (New York: Basic 1981).

SKINNER, CHRISTOPHER W., and HAUGE, MATTHEW R.,(eds.), *Character Studies and the Gospel of Mark*, Library of New Testament Studies, 483 (London and New York : Bloomsbury T&T Clark 2014).

SWANSON, RICHARD W., *Provoking the Gospel of Mark: A Storyteller's commentary Year B* (Cleveland, OH: Pilgrim Press 2005).

WILLIAMS, JOEL F., *Other Followers of Jesus: Minor Characters as Major Figures in Mark's Gospel* (Sheffield: Academic Press 1994).

Articles

ALT, CHRISTOPHER E., "The Dynamic of Humility and Wisdom: The Syrophoenician Woman and Jesus in Mark 7: 24-31a", *Lumen et vita* 2 (2012) 1-13.

BAFFES, MELANIE S., "Jesus and the Canaanite Woman: A Story of Reversal", *Journal of Theta Alpha Kappa* 35.2 (2011) 12-23.

BURKILL, T. A.,"The Historical Development of the Story of the Syrophoenician woman", *(Mark VII: 24-37), NovumTestamentum* 9 (1967) 161-177.

—,"The Syrophoenician Woman: The Congruence of Mark 7: 24-3", *Zeitschriftfu ᴸ r die neutestamentlicheWissenschaft und die Kunde der a ᴸ lterenKirche,*57.1 - 2 (1966) 23-37.

CROSSAN, JOHN DOMINIC, "The Challenge of Multicontextual Interpretation", *Semeia* 62 (1993) 149-155.

DAHLEN, ROBERT W., "The Savior and the Dog: An Exercise in Hearing", *Word & World* 17.3 (1997) 269-277.

GLANCY,JENNIFER A., "Jesus, the Syrophoenician Woman, and Other First Century Bodies", *Biblical Interpretation* 18 (2010) 342-363.

MALBON,ELIZABETH S., "Disciples/Crowds/whoever: Markan Characters and Readers", NovumTestamentum 28, 2 (April 1986) 104-130.

—, "Echoes and Foreshadowings in Mark 4-8: Reading and Rereading", *Journal of Biblical Literature* 112.2 (Sum 1993) 211-230.

—, "Fallible Followers: Women and Men in the Gospel of Mark", *Semeia* 28 (1983) 29-48.

—, "In Search of a Context: The Function of Scripture in Mark's Narrative", *Biblical Interpretation* 14.4 (2006) 412-415.

—, "Narrative Christology and the Son of Man: What the Markan Jesus says Instead", *Biblical Interpretation* 11.3 (2003) 373-385.

—, "Reflected Christology: An Aspect of Narrative 'Christology' in the Gospel of Mark", *Perspectives in Religious Studies* 26.2 (1999) 127-145.

—, "Text and Contexts: Interpreting the Disciples in Mark", *Semeia* 62 (1993) 81-102.

NELAVALA, S., "Smart Syrophoenician Woman: A Dalit Feminist Reading of Mark 7: 24-31", *The Expository Times* 118.2 (Nov 2006) 64-69.

RHOADS, D., "Jesus and the Syrophoenician Woman in Mark A Narrative-Critical Study", *Journal of the American Academy of Religion* 62.2 (1994) 343-375.

—, "Narrative Criticism and the Gospel of Mark", *Journal of the American Academy of Religion* 50 (1982) 411-434.

SMITH, JULIEN C.H., "The Construction of Identity in Mark 7: 24-30: The Syrophoenician Woman and the Problem of Ethnicity", *Biblical Interpretation* 20 (2012) 458-481.

SWARTLEY, WILLARD M., "The Role of Women in Mark's Gospel: A Narrative Analysis", *Biblical Theology Bulletin* 27.1 (1997) 16-22.

Appendix

The Text: Mark 7: 24-30 (RSV)

24 And from there he arose and went away to the region of Tyre and Sidon. And he entered a house, and would not have any one know it; yet he could not be hid.	24 Ἐκεῖθεν δὲ ἀναστὰς ἀπῆλθεν εἰς τὰ ὅρια Τύρου. Καὶ εἰσελθὼν εἰς οἰκίαν οὐδένα ἤθελεν γνῶναι, καὶ οὐκ ἠδυνήθη λαθεῖν·
25 But immediately a woman, whose little daughter was possessed by an unclean spirit, heard of him, and came and fell down at his feet.	25 ἀλλ' εὐθὺς ἀκούσασα γυνὴ περὶ αὐτοῦ, ἧς εἶχεν τὸ θυγάτριον αὐτῆς πνεῦμα ἀκάθαρτον, ἐλθοῦσα προσέπεσεν πρὸς τοὺς πόδας αὐτοῦ·
26 Now the woman was a Greek, a Syrophoenician by birth. And she begged him to cast the demon out of her daughter.	26 ἡ δὲ γυνὴ ἦν Ἑλληνίς, Συροφοινίκισσα τῷ γένει· καὶ ἠρώτα αὐτὸν ἵνα τὸ δαιμόνιον ἐκβάλῃ ἐκ τῆς θυγατρὸς αὐτῆς.
27 And he said to her, "Let the children first be fed, for it is not right to take the children's bread and throw it to the dogs."	27 καὶ ἔλεγεν αὐτῇ· ἄφες πρῶτον χορτασθῆναι τὰ τέκνα, οὐ γάρ ἐστιν καλὸν λαβεῖν τὸν ἄρτον τῶν τέκνων καὶ τοῖς κυναρίοις βαλεῖν.
28 But she answered him, "Yes, Lord; yet even the dogs under the table eat the children's crumbs."	28 ἡ δὲ ἀπεκρίθη καὶ λέγει αὐτῷ· κύριε· καὶ τὰ κυνάρια ὑποκάτω τῆς τραπέζης ἐσθίουσιν ἀπὸ τῶν ψιχίων τῶν παιδίων.
29 And he said to her, "For this saying you may go your way; the demon has left your daughter."	29 καὶ εἶπεν αὐτῇ· διὰ τοῦτον τὸν λόγον ὕπαγε, ἐξελήλυθεν ἐκ τῆς θυγατρός σου τὸ δαιμόνιον.
30 And she went home, and found the child lying in bed, and the demon gone.	30 καὶ ἀπελθοῦσα εἰς τὸν οἶκον αὐτῆς εὗρεν τὸ παιδίον βεβλημένον ἐπὶ τὴν κλίνην καὶ τὸ δαιμόνιον ἐξεληλυθός.

Notes

1. Wilson Sagayaraj holds licentiate in Biblical Theology from Rome. Currently he is the Biblical Coordinator of the Divine Word Society in India and the Director of Divine Word Centre in Vadipatti, Madurai.
2. The performance of David Rhoads and Richard W. Swanson's team.

3. David Rhoads explains that Narrative Criticism carried out analyzes of formal features of narrative such as tone, style, narrator, setting, plot, character and rhetoric. Narrator refers to the way the story gets told, the voice of the story teller, manner of address, tone of the narrative and the techniques of storytelling. The narrator is not the author or composer but a device the composer uses to get the story told. Setting refers to the context within the story as well as the specific temporal and spatial contexts in which the event occurs. Plot describes the order and progress in the narrative, sequence of the story, turning points, break throughs and conflict resolutions. Characters are the actors in the story. There are major, minor, active and passive characters and each one's role is pivotal and significant. This methodology carries out a detailed study of their identity, place in the society, their traits and motives, action, reaction and change that takes places in the characters as the story develops. Rhetoric refers to various ways that an author employs to persuade the readers and hearers and embrace the world presented by the narrative. The study of rhetoric further indicates how the narrative may transform the audiences. For a more detailed study and information on Narrative Criticism ref. DAVID RHOADS, JOANNA DEWEY AND DONALD MICHIE, *Mark As Story An Introduction to the Narrative of a Gospel,* Third Edition (Minneapolis: Fortress Press 2012). And JANICE CAPEL ANDERSON, and STEPHEN D. MOORE, eds., *Mark and Method: New Approaches in Biblical Studies*, second edition (Minneapolis, Minnesota: Fortress Press 2008). And DAVID RHOADS, "Narrative Criticism and the Gospel of Mark", *Journal of the American Academy of Religion* 50 (1982) 411-434. For more detailed explanation of the various features of Narrative Criticism see also PAUL L. DANOVE, *The Rhetoric of Characterization of God, Jesus and Jesus' Disciples in the Gospel of Mark* (New York: T & T Clark 2005). And SCOTT S. ELLIOTT, *Reconfiguring Mark's Jesus: Narrative Criticism after Poststructuralism* (Sheffield, England: Sheffield Phoenix Press 2011). AndELIZABETH STRUTHERS MALBON, *Mark's Jesus: Characterization as Narrative Christology* (Waco, Texas: Baylor University Press 2009).

4. David Rhoads observes that Mark's narrative is remarkably whole. The plot is coherent: the stories are interrelated, conflicts are resolved and prophecies are fulfilled. The oral techniques of storytelling such as recurring designs, repetitions, riddles, overlapping patterns and interwoven motifs interconnect the narrative throughout the Gospel. There is also consistency in the thematic presentation of human condition, faith, God's reign, healings, miracles and transformation. See DAVID RHOADS, JOANNA DEWEY AND DONALD MICHIE, *Mark As Story An Introduction to the Narrative of a Gospel,* 1-8.

5. Robert M. Fowler explains the need for a shift from *story level* of the narrative (settings, events and characters within the narrative) to the *discourse level* or the rhetoric of the narrative. When the readers of the Gospel focus only on the *story level* of the narrative, they fail to dedicate an adequate importance to the rhetoric of the narrative (*discourse level*); the ways in which the language attempts to spell over the reader. Therefore, Fowler emphasizes that adequate attention be given to the rhetoric of the narrative and to what it tries to do to us or how we respond to it. The shift in focus from story to discourse, stimulates a shift from looking for a static structure in the text to the dynamic structure and temporal experience of reading the text. Reading takes place in space and time and the

rhetorical effects of narrative is also a temporal experience of reader. In the process, we discover that the meaning is no longer static instead the meaning is dynamic and needs to be excavated. The reader actively participates in the event of unearthing the dynamic meaning hidden in the text. This shift from meaning-as-content to meaning-as-event leads us to understand the workings of the language of the Gospel in new and profound ways. Thus, the language of the Gospel functions no more primarily as informative but becomes rhetorical, affective and powerful. For further explanation on the various elements and dynamics of narrative rhetoric and reader-response criticism ref. ROBERT M. FOWLER, *Let the Reader Understand Reader-Response Criticism and the Gospel of Mark* (Harrisburg, Pennsylvania: Trinity Press International 2001).

6. The reader/hearer has entered into the story world would mean: he/she is familiar with the events, the plot progression and the characters that has happened so far. The reader/hearer must be following the narrative development closely as he/she encounters each event. As the story progresses, the reader/hearer has gained certain information, might anticipate few things, might evaluate the characters and may be anxious over the suspense and secret in the narrative and characters. So he/she has travelled along the narrative until now. The reader/hearer at this point is aware of the certain aspects of the story and dynamics of certain characters and which the characters of the story do not know. Hence, the episode of Jesus and the Syrophoenician woman is not an isolated experience for the reader/hearer instead will be an integrated event within the realm of the entire narrative. Therefore, it needs to be viewed in the light of the whole narrative in order to understand the episode comprehensively.

7. David Rhoads describes that Mark's story is unified around one overall theme: The Kingdom of God has arrived and God is establishing God's rule over all the creation, over all the people, over all the nature, over all nations and bringing it to fulfillment. DAVID RHOADS, JOANNA DEWEY AND DONALD MICHIE, *Mark As Story An Introduction to the Narrative of a Gospel,* 73.

8. David Rhaods explains that "the Markan story which follows the announcement of the coming of the kingdom of God displays that kingdom. All subsequent healings, exorcisms and miracles are expressions of the kingdom of God. These works of power are a string of incredible happenings in which each event appears to the hearer to be different and more astounding; healing by touch, healing by word only, exorcising a legion of demons, calming a storm, healing someone by her touch, raising a child from the dead, providing bread in the desert and so on. In our episode, Jesus exorcises the demon and thus, the exorcism and healing are a major means for conveying the activity of kingdom of God." Each of such events reinforces the understanding of the dynamic nature of kingdom of God. DAVID RHOADS, "Jesus and the Syrophoenician Woman in Mark A Narrative-Critical Study", *Journal of the American Academy of Religion* 50 (1982) 345.

9. Conflict – is one of the vital dimensions of the story. Conflicts reveal the core values, purposes and beliefs of a narrative. Without conflict, stories would be only a sequence of events interconnected without tension, spice, suspense or struggle towards a goal. The motivating force in Mark's narrative is for Jesus, the messiah to establish the kingdom of God. From this perspective, the reader/hearer can see how a character either toils towards or blocks the goal and

consequently, the characters come in conflict with various forces. Conflicts provide an opportunity for clarification and intensity of events. Jesus, the protagonist of Mark's Gospel is engaged with conflicts on four main plotlines: 1. Conflict with demons, illness and nature, 2. Conflict with authorities, 3. Conflict with the disciples and 4. Conflict with the current socio-cultural elements. For more details on dynamics of conflicts, its importance in a narrative and conflict resolution ref. DAVID RHOADS, JOANNA DEWEY AND DONALD MICHIE, *Mark As Story An Introduction to the Narrative of a Gospel,* 73-96.

10. Jesus foretells three times his passion, death and resurrection 8: 31-33, 9: 30-32, 10: 32-34.
11. The chapters from 14 to 16 are events of persecution, death and resurrection of Jesus, the suffering messiah.
12. "The particular importance of each suppliant may be provided by the setting or by the type of ailment or by the character of the suppliant or by Jesus' manner of healing or by the reaction of the crowd or by any combination of these". For example, Bartimaeus' cry, 'Jesus, Son of David, have mercy on me' (Mk 10:47) provides the entrance to Jerusalem for Jesus (Mk 11: 11). DAVID RHOADS, "Jesus and the Syrophoenician Woman in Mark A Narrative-Critical Study", 347.
13. The two feeding stories are pivotal in this section of the narrative. In the first feeding story Jesus feeds the Jews – his own people. But in the second feeding story Jesus feeds non-Jews – Gentiles, outsiders, almost an equal number. The setting of first feeding event is on the west and the setting of 7: 31-37 and 8: 1-9 are in Gentile dominated territory on the eastern shore of the sea of Galilee. The Jewish nature of the crowd probably suggest the narrator's stated reason for Jesus' compassion because 'they were like sheep without a shepherd' (6: 34) – it is an image with strong Jewish background (Num 27: 17, 1Kgs 22: 17, Eze 34: 5). The narrator's stated reason for Jesus' compassion for the second feeding event is 'because they were with him now for three days and have nothing to eat. If he sends them away to their homes, they will faint on the way and some of them have come from a great distance' (8: 2-3) an imagery of universality. This suggests a continuation of the Gentile theme begun in 7: 24-30 and so 6: 31 – 8: 21 should be read as section that prepares and initiates the Gentile mission. For more detailed analysis on the function of the Feeding stories ref. ROBERT M. FOWLER, *Loaves and Fishes: The Function of the Feeding Stories in the Gospel of Mark* (Atlanta, Georgia: Society of Biblical Literature 1981). And see also ELIZABETH STRUTHERSMALBON, "Echoes and Fore shadowings in Mark 4-8 Reading and Rereading", *Journal of Biblical Literature* 112.2 (1993) 211-230.
14. The narrative framework that I have proposed to delimit the text is similar to the one proposed by David Rhoads. DAVID RHOADS, "Jesus and the Syrophoenician Woman in Mark A Narrative-Critical Study", 348.
15. DAVID RHOADS, "Jesus and the Syrophoenician Woman in Mark A Narrative-Critical Study", 348.
16. ROBERT ALTER, *The Art of Biblical Narrative* (New York: Basic 1981). 45-60. See also DAVID RHOADS, "Jesus and the Syrophoenician Woman in Mark A Narrative-Critical Study", 348.

17. These type scenes have common basic forms and features: setting of place or time, prior knowledge about Jesus, coming to Jesus, making a request over an obstacle or sickness, demonstration of faith, Jesus fulfills the request by touching or speaking, the healing occurs and the reaction of the crowd or audiences. Each additional repetition reinforces the basic pattern. There are many type scenes of exorcisms, healing, nature miracles, conflicts with the authorities and misunderstanding by the disciples. DAVID RHOADS, JOANNA DEWEY AND DONALD MICHIE, *Mark As Story An Introduction to the Narrative of a Gospel,* 51.
18. DAVID RHOADS, "Jesus and the Syrophoenician Woman in Mark A Narrative-Critical Study", 351.
19. I have adopted and modified the outline from Sharon Ringe's essay, "A Gentile Woman's Story, Revisited: Rereading Mark 7: 24-31A," in AMY-JILL LEVINE AND MARIANNE BLICKENSTAFF (ed), *A Feminist Companion to Mark* (Cleveland, OH: The Pilgrim Press 2004), 82. The episode of our study is 7: 24-30 and the headlines in NRSV/RSV bible break at verse 30, however verse 31a is included in the general outline of the episode because I understand that Mark encloses the pericope between the act of Jesus' arrival and departure from the region of Tyre (7: 24, 31a).
20. The two-step progression is one of the most pervasive patterns of repetition in Mark's Gospel. It occurs in sequence of sentences and phrases, clauses, pairs of sentences and the structure of episodes. It is a key to understanding many lines and events. The two-step repetitions create suspense by maintaining audience's desire to know what is to come, because audience's familiarity with this rhetoric technique creates suspense and curiosity over what the second part would reveal. DAVID RHOADS, JOANNA DEWEY AND DONALD MICHIE, *Mark As Story An Introduction to the Narrative of a Gospel,* 49-50.
21. So here, in our study episode, the narrator wants the hearer/reader to notice without fail that the woman is not only Greek speaking but a Syrophoenician, precisely a Gentile, an outsider and so not a Jew. This specifically emphasized information is very important as it creates the stage for the scene to follow.
22. DAVID RHOADS, "Jesus and the Syrophoenician Woman in Mark A Narrative-Critical Study", 353-354.
23. For detailed discussion on Metaphor, various metaphorical expression in Mark and its rhetorical effects on the reader refer ROBERT M. FOWLER, *Let the Reader Understand Reader-Response Criticism and the Gospel of Mark*, 175-184.
24. ROBERT M. FOWLER, *Let the Reader Understand Reader-Response Criticism and the Gospel of Mark*, 117.
25. Jesus, the protagonist often tells stories that illuminate the Gospel and they are generally called parables. However, these stories in Mark's Gospel are appropriately called riddles and allegories. Allegory is an extended comparison of one scene with another. The characters must decipher these riddles in order to grasp their meaning in the context. Markan allegories interpret events and people in the framework of the kingdom of God. There are occasions where Jesus explains the allegories and at times does not explain them. The hearers, who hear or read

the riddle/allegory are in a better position to understand them than the characters are. DAVID RHOADS, JOANNA DEWEY AND DONALD MICHIE, *Mark As Story An Introduction to the Narrative of a Gospel,* 56-57. See also MARY ANN TOLBERT, *Sowing the Gospel: Mark's World in the Literary-historical Perspective*, (Minneapolis: Fortress Press 1989) 122-124.

26. DAVID RHOADS, "Jesus and the Syrophoenician Woman in Mark A Narrative-Critical Study", 355.
27. I have adopted and modified the framework explaining the allegorical riddle and its application from DAVID RHOADS, "Jesus and the Syrophoenician Woman in Mark A Narrative-Critical Study", 356-357.
28. Refer foot note 8.
29. Setting is the vital element of a narrative, it includes the cosmic depiction of space and time, the cultural ethos, socio-political configurations, geographical locations and so on. In a narrative world, settings are not incidental backdrops to events but serve as many functions; creating atmosphere, providing the occasion for conflict and resolution, provide overall structure for a story. Hence, familiarity of the setting in the story is vital to comprehend the event well. Hence, settings provide the conditions and possibilities for a reader to grasp the event and for the character to chart their destinies in the story. DAVID RHOADS, JOANNA DEWEY AND DONALD MICHIE, *Mark As Story An Introduction to the Narrative of a Gospel,* 63-64.
30. The city of Tyre is located about forty miles northwest of the Sea of Galilee, Tyre was a predominantly Gentile city on the coast of present day Lebanon. As the leading city of Phoenicia during the first millennium BCE, it was a center of trade and political influence. It had farm lands essential to the agricultural production to provide for urban population around. Typical of many of the borderlands, Tyre too was ethnically mixed probably. Though Tyre was principally populated by the Gentiles, the surrounding territory included Jews as well. As a result, presence of uncomfortable ethnic collision, religious and cultural differences was strong and it led to suspicions and prejudices among the residents in and around the territory. This ethnically missed and tensed region was also a site of economic tension between the poor and the rich. Tyre was an epitome of socio-political and religious division and conflict. SHARON RINGE, "A Gentile Woman's Story, Revisited: Rereading Mark 7: 24-31A," 84-85. The Old Testament references to Tyre and Sidon are often negative and condemn the wealth and materialism of these cities (Isa 23: 8-9, Ezek 27-28, Zech9: 2-4).
31. Refer foot note 28.
32. One of the major conflicts depicted throughout the Gospel of Mark is the conflict between the differing attitudes toward physical and social boundaries. As per Mark, the leaders of Israel see these boundaries as lines to be guarded in order to protect the holiness of God's people against the evil influence of uncleanness. By contrast Jesus makes an onslaught upon these boundaries, he touches a leper, eats with sinners, is touched by a woman with a flow of blood, he declares all food clean and heals a Gentile, etc. In the narrative, Jesus crosses many culturally-established boundaries. However, the geographical and social boundary separating the Jews and Gentiles intensifies the hostility among them. So, Jesus'

entry into Tyre and interaction with the Syrophoenician woman is the point at which the fundamental social and geographical boundaries are crossed and foundation for gentile mission is laid. The subsequent feeding of 4000 Gentiles in the Decapolis is the result of this breakthrough. DAVID RHOADS, "Jesus and the Syrophoenician Woman in Mark A Narrative-Critical Study", 363-365.

33. DAVID RHOADS, "Jesus and the Syrophoenician Woman in Mark A Narrative-Critical Study", 364.

34. Greco-Roman society was not a culture that was concerned much about equal rights of women and children. They enjoyed no legal or social statues or privileges. The dominant culture and male chauvinism was rampant in the realm of society, religion, culture and politics. The woman had neither voice nor say, there were the marginal members of the society. Over above these discriminations, the Jews further distinguished between sacred and profane, free beings and slaves. For more detailed information and reconstruction on the lives of woman in Greco-Roman world and situation of a Gentile woman refer SHARON BETSWORTH, *The reign of God is such as these: a Socio-literary Analysis of Daughters in the Gospel of Mark*, (London, New York: T &T Clark 2010) 26-59. And KATHLEEN E. CORLEY, Women and the Historical Jesus: Feminists myths of Christian Origin (Santa Rosa CA: Pole bridge Press 2002) 20-25.

35. RICHARD W. SWANSON, *Provoking the Gospel of Mark: A Storyteller's commentary Year B* (Cleveland, OH: Pilgrim Press, 2005) 207.

36. We may distinguish different types of characters and predominantly there are stock, flat and round characters in the Gospel of Mark. Stock characters have basically one trait. Flat characters have several consistent traits and are predictable. Round characters have many complex and conflicting traits and often are unpredictable. In Mark, Jesus and the disciples are round characters. The authorities are flat characters and minor figures are stock characters. DAVID RHOADS, JOANNA DEWEY AND DONALD MICHIE, *Mark As Story An Introduction to the Narrative of a Gospel,* 99-104. And DAVID RHOADS, "Jesus and the Syrophoenician Woman in Mark A Narrative-Critical Study", 359.

37. Fowler explains that *de* (är - and, but) is a weak particle and often not worth translating. Since this particle is employed frequently in the Gospel, it becomes a relatively strong particle in Mark, particularly when used in an adversative fashion, setting one phrase sharply against another. Several times in the Gospel *de* signals a piece of commentary by the narrator, one such is 7:26 (and the woman was Greek...). It explains further the ethnic identity of the woman. ROBERT M. FOWLER, *Let the Reader Understand Reader-Response Criticism and the Gospel of Mark*, 116-117.

38. This description is very close to that of the woman with the hemorrhage in 5:27, 33, who "heard about Jesus" and "came and fell down before him." The similarity between the two women is they are ritually impure. The Syrophoenician is impure by being a Gentile and her daughter is possessed by unclean spirit, a double social stigma. Yet, despite her impurity, the Syrophoenician, like the woman with the hemorrhage, hopes for healing from Jesus. Mark's audience would presumably share this trust, because elsewhere in Mark, when people in need hear about Jesus and come to him, he invariably heals them (cf. 3:8; 5:27; 6:55;

10:47). JOEL MARCUS,*Mark 1-8: A new translation with introduction and commentaryVol. 2* The Anchor Yale Bible, Vol. 27A. (New Haven, London: Yale University Press 2008) 467.

39. DAVID RHOADS, "Jesus and the Syrophoenician Woman in Mark A Narrative-Critical Study", 351.
40. JENNIFER A. GLANCY, "Jesus, the Syrophoenician Woman, and Other First Century Bodies", *Biblical Interpretation* 18 (2010) 360.
41. Jesus' harsh answer implies as though the woman requests to take the 'food' meant for Jewish children and give to her own Gentile daughter. Ἄφες πρῶτονχορτασθῆναι τὰτέκνα - let the children be fed first. By this word πρῶτον, Jesus hints that the time of the Gentiles is coming and so the Jews are to be nourished first by the benefits of the Kingdom of God. On the level of the Markan narrative this salvation progression is reproduced by the order of the accounts of miraculous feedings: first five thousand Jews are satisfied (6:30–44), then four thousand Gentiles are fed (8:1–9). The use of πρῶτον may indicate that Jesus does not deny food to the Gentile girl in the long run but then her need is immediate and she is suffering currently. JOEL MARCUS, *Mark 1-8: A new translation with introduction and commentaryVol. 2, 469.*
42. The reference to dogs occurs in other biblical texts as a term of abuse for Gentiles (1Sam 17: 43, 2 Kgs 8: 13). There are only a few positive references to dogs in the Old Testament (Job 6: 2, 11: 4) The Hebrew word (ëìá) usually refers to the wild or semi-wild dogs of the streets, although occasionally the reference is to domestic pets. Deut 23: 18 uses the term 'dog' for a male prostitute, unclean persons. In rabbinic literature, 'dog' is used metaphorically for a person who is unlearned in the scripture. c.f. ADELA YABRO COLLINS, Mark A Commentary (Minneapolis, Fortress Press 2007) 366-367.

   To the Greek, the word *dog* meant a shameless and audacious woman; it was used exactly with the connotation that we use the word *dog* to-day. To the Jew it was equally a term of contempt. "Do not give dogs what is holy." (Math 7:6, Phl 3:2, Rev 22:15.)The word dog was in fact sometimes a Jewish term of contempt for the Gentiles. No matter how you look at it, the term *dog* is an insult. One of the explanations for this usage is; (*a*) He did not use the usual word; he used a diminutive word which described, not the wild dogs of the streets, but the little pet lap-dogs of the house. In Greek, diminutives are characteristically affectionate. Jesus took the sting out of the word.(*b*) Without a doubt his tone of voice made all the difference. The same word can be a deadly insult and an affectionate address, according to the tone of voice. We can call a man 'a rascal' in a voice of contempt or a voice of affection. Jesus' tone took all the poison out of the word.C.f. William Barclay, T*he Gospel of Mark. The Daily Study Bible Series, Rev. ed.* (Philadelphia: The Westminster Press2000) 178. See also ROBERT W. DAHLEN, "The Savior and the Dog: An Exercise in Hearing", *Word & World V. XVII, n.3* (1997) 269-277.

   Probably the dogs meant by Jesus are not pets. They could be dogs waiting to get scraps from the food. Jews considered dogs unclean because dogs did not fit the category of clean animals and because dogs had contact with and ate things which were unclean. It is for this impurity that Jews referred Gentiles as dogs.

Jesus also appears to be playing on the depiction of the dog as a scavenger, because the role of the woman appears to be such and she is asking for something that does not belong to her. She is scavenging for food like a dog. David Rhoads argues that the narrator may be depicting Jesus as being playful by using the term 'little dogs' as in Greek, the term êõíáñwïéò is diminutive and could mean 'pup' and so may be non-offensive. The diminutive term may be regarded as a term of 'endearment' referring to a puppy rather than a dog. However, one should be cautious about softening the harshness of Jesus' rejection. DAVID RHOADS, "Jesus and the Syrophoenician Woman in Mark A Narrative-Critical Study", 356-357.

43. Burkill writes, 'to call a woman 'a little dog' is no less abusive than to call a woman 'a dog' without qualification." T. A. BURKILL, The Historical Development of the Story of the Syrophoenician woman *(Mark VII: 24-37), Novum Testamentum* 9 (1967) 172.

44. HISAKO KINUKAWA, *Women and Jesus in Mark* (Maryknoll, New York: Orbis Books 1994) 56-58.

45. MARY ANN TOLBERT, "Mark" in CAROL A. NEWSOM& SHARON H. RINGE (ed), *Women's Bible Commentary,* (Louisville: Westminster John Knox 1998) 356. See also ELIZABETH STRUTHERS MALBON, "The Major Importance of the Minor Characters in Mark" , in ELIZABETH STRUTHERS MALBON& EDGAR V. MCKNIGHT (ed), *The New Literary Criticism and the New Testament* (Sheffield: Academic Press 1994) 65.

46. Instead of confronting the insult, she turns the offensive label into her advantage. For her to be a dog does not mean to be servile. She points out that the dogs under the table eat from the children's crumbs. The woman accepts the position of the household dog, recognizing that she can make no demand on the mercy of Jesus. Her wisdom and insightful dialogue turns Jesus's rejection into assent to her request. C.f. SHARON RINGE, "A Gentile Woman's Story, Revisited: Rereading Mark 7: 24-31A," 91 and HISAKO KINUKAWA, *Women and Jesus in Mark* (Maryknoll, New York: Orbis Books 1994) 59. And JOEL F. WILLIAMS, *Other Followers of Jesus: Minor Characters as Major Figures in Mark's Gospel* (Sheffield: Academic Press 1994) 24-25.

47. ELIZABETH STRUTHERS MALBON, "Fallible Followers: Women and Men in the Gospel of Mark", *Semeia* 28 (1983) 37.

48. The Gospel of Mark manifests faith as embedded in action. For example, four men lowering the paralytic man through the roof (2:5), touch of the hemorrhaging woman (5:34) and begging of Bartimaeus (10:52). Markan faith has little to do with the belief in Jesus and the suppliants trust in Jesus as a person and in many instances, they do not even know that Jesus is the Messiah. Hence, what is required in trust in the person of Jesus. And Jesus rewards this trust; 'Do not fear, only believe' (5: 36), 'if you able, all things can be done for the one who believes' (9:23). C.f. DAVID RHOADS, "Jesus and the Syrophoenician Woman in Mark A Narrative-Critical Study", 359-360.

49. This equivalent to saying 'your faith has healed you/your daughter.

50. She did not accept the low esteem in which the society/Jesus held her and her daughter. She did not hesitate to approach Jesus and even actively to importune him. She valued her daughter, her daughter was everything for her. In the society

that considered woman as having no value, the Syrophoenician woman highly valued her daughter. She was suffering and her life was precious to her and so against all odds she demands for healing and may not be an exaggeration to say that in the process even Jesus undergoes a Transformation. C.f. LETTY M. RUSSELL, *Feminist Interpretation of the Bible* (Oxford: Basil Blackwell 1985) 70-71.

51. HISAKO KINUKAWA, *Women and Jesus in Mark,* 60-61.
52. SHARON RINGE, "A Gentile Woman's Story, Revisited: Rereading Mark 7: 24-31A," 90-92.
53. SUSAN MILLER, *Women in Mark's Gospel* (London: T & T Clark 2004) 101-105.
54. RANJINI WICRAMARATNE REBEREA, "The Syrophoenician Woman: A South Asian Feminist Perspective"; in Amy-Jill Levine and Marianne Blickenstaff, eds., *A Feminist Companion to Mark* (Cleveland, Ohio : Pilgrim Press 2001) 110.
55. Traditionally V.28 has been interpreted to signify the woman's faith and she was subsequently exalted for her humility. But here, evidently when she said 'yes' it was actually 'no'. In her politeness, instead of saying 'but' she says 'yes'. The woman made a wise remark from her experience of being rejected. She wins over Jesus in two ways: By pretending she was accepting what Jesus said and using his argument to her own advantage and by paying no attention to whether Jesus wanted to insult her. C.f. SUREKHA NELAVALA, Smart Syrophoenician Woman: A Dalit Feminist Reading of Mark 7: 24-31 *The Expository Times* 118.2 (Nov 2006) 67-68.
56. Perhaps a holistic outlook on the Markan narrative may enable to grasp Jesus' refusal and may explain the reasons for his reluctance. In Markan portrayal, he has had no reception among Gentiles and does not therefore make himself available to them. In 5:1-20 – upon arriving the Gentile territory of Decapolis, he exorcises a legion of demon but the people plead him to go away. So, in 7:24 he enters the Gentile territory and wishes to remain secret. DAVID RHOADS, "Jesus and the Syrophoenician Woman in Mark A Narrative-Critical Study", 361-362.
57. The result of change of mind of Jesus does not end with the healing of the Gentile woman's daughter instead it is a solid beginning of a mission among the Gentiles. This is confirmed by feeding of the four thousand people in the Gentile territory (8: 1-13) Jesus took the bread, people ate and were satisfied. It is vivid that Jesus does not abandon the larger eschatological framework in this immediate and remote activities. He is always focused on mission of the kingdom of God. This episode too clearly indicates the beginning of the Gentile mission and it foreshadows the latter mission command of Jesus to his disciples that 'the good news must be first proclaimed to all the nations.DAVID RHOADS, "Jesus and the Syrophoenician Woman in Mark A Narrative-Critical Study", 361-363.
58. DAVID RHOADS, JOANNA DEWEY AND DONALD MICHIE, *Mark As Story An Introduction to the Narrative of a Gospel,* 171.
59. David Rhoads explains that Things of God are 'faith, courage, losing one's life for the good news, being least, being servant and doing good. Things of human beings are, lack of faith, fear, saving one's life, being great, lording over people

and doing harm. DAVID RHOADS, "Jesus and the Syrophoenician Woman in Mark A Narrative-Critical Study", 366. See also DAVID RHOADS, JOANNA DEWEY AND DONALD MICHIE, *Mark As Story An Introduction to the Narrative of a Gospel,* 45.

60. If the Gospel of Mark was written in Galilee, then this passage may well reflect the hostility that existed between the Galileans and Tyrians especially during or just after the Roman Jewish War. During the war, Tyrians killed and imprisoned may Jews in the city of Tyre. This also could be due to the fear of Jewish aggression against the Gentiles since long time. DAVID RHOADS, "Jesus and the Syrophoenician Woman in Mark A Narrative-Critical Study", 361. And RICHARD W. SWANSON, *Provoking the Gospel of Mark: A Storyteller's commentary Year B*, 208.

61. For information on the social conditions of women in Greco-Roman world, refer foot note 33.

62. One of the values of the kingdom is being least and not desiring to be great. It is interesting to note that about eight diminutives are used in this single episode; 'little daughter, little dogs, crumbs and little ones and demon. Probably a rhetoric technique to emphasize the motif of lest-ness. The Syrophoenician woman disdained status therefore, she did not hesitate to kneel down and beg and did not shun from becoming a little dog that eats the crumbs. C.f. DAVID RHOADS, "Jesus and the Syrophoenician Woman in Mark A Narrative-Critical Study", 366.

Chapter - 19

Can you hear me please?: Media and Empowering the Marginalised Women of India

***Dr. S. Janet Mary*[1]**

Introduction

Nearly seven years after the Nirbhaya tragedy shocked India and the world at large, a 19 year-old, who was allegedly raped in 2017 by a local MLA in Utter Pradesh's Unnao district, is battling for her life. Poor women in India are disadvantaged as supplicants before powerful men till such crimes continue with impunity and patriarchal mind-set. Therefore, the question of empowerment of marginalized women is now on the international agenda. Empowerment of women can take place at a hierarchy of different levels - individual, household, community and societal. The components of empowerment of women essentially include - access to economic resources, participation in economic decision making, opportunities for self-development, participation in socio-political decision making, scope for skill development and impact on general welfare of the family. Half of the humanity – women have been suffering from the politics of oppression, discrimination, inability, injustice, inequality and exploitation all over the world for almost centuries. Several development experts have rightly defined development as an upward movement of the entire social system towards equality, justice, fraternity and empowerment. Nobel Laureate Amartya Sen rightly advocated that the empowerment of women is one of the central issues in the process of development for many countries in the world today Mahatma Gandhi was a great statesman who liberated India from the European colonial forces led by the British through democratic and non-violent means. He had almost an instinctive to understanding of women and their problems. His concern for the empowerment of women was unquestionable. This paper investigates the status of women from the marginalized groups.

Explanation of the niche

The Government of India constituted Central Social Welfare Board in 1954 and State Government constituted regional welfare boards to facilitate the improvement of the **status of women and weaker sections of India.** These boards are responsible for coordinating the welfare and development activities undertaken by the various departments of the Central and State Governments which may be conducive to the fulfillment of the objectives of empowerment of women. The Government of India also has implemented Rural Women's Development and Empowerment Project (World Bank Scheme), Norwegian Agency for International Development Scheme (NORAD), Support to Training and Employment Programme (STEP), Training the Rural Youth for Self-Employment (TRYSEM), Integrated Child Development Scheme (ICDS) and so on for the empowerment of women. The Government of India also created Department for Women and Child Development in all States and Union Territories in order to facilitate specific programmes for the empowerment of women and children. The focus of the programmes for women has shifted further from welfare to development since 1990s. Once again the turn of the century marked a policy shift from development to empowerment of women. These departments primarily focus on the economic development and integration of women into the mainstream of economy. Government and non-governmental organizations working in the field of women and child development are also guided and assisted by these departments.

The sorry state of affairs relating to the women-empowerment programmes are systematically documented and evaluated by several commissions and research agencies in India. The Joint Women's Programme observes: "The basic vulnerability of women which was the cause of poverty was not addressed in the various schemes/projects. A majority of the projects have failed to deliver the expected results in the form of overall betterment of women's status in the society. The reasons are many: lack of identification with the spirit of the projects among the officials entrusted with the implementation, procedural hassles that most illiterate applicants found intimidating (production of letters or certificates for instance, from relevant authorities) and most important, failure to involve the beneficiary population as participants and treating them instead, as subjects/targets, with decision-making retained in the hands of officials." (1995:97).

Current scenario

In this paper a special attention will be paid to the status and the role media to empower the vulnerable women in Indian society. The National Mission for Empowerment of Women aims to generate awareness, build strategies, create gender resource centers, form women's collectives, improve their capacity, enforce laws and policies and encourage implementation of programmes for the empowerment of women. The Central Social Welfare

Board, Rashtriya Mahila Kosh and National Commission for Women are also responsible for the implementation of various programmes and provisions for the protection and development of women.

Media Intervention for the Empowerment of Women

Media have a social responsibility of educating the women and various stakeholders on the significance of empowerment of women among the marginalized communities in India. Academics have examined the relationship between women and media at regional, national and international levels. The role of media in the empowerment of women is also widely discussed by the policy makers, administrators, academics, professionals and activists. Media institutions are required to provide judicious space and time for the discussion of issues concerning the empowerment of women in the new millennium. The representation of the women, portrayal of women in the media and role of media in the empowerment of women are extensively examined by various scholars and researchers across the globe over a period of time. An attempt is made in the present paper to discuss the relationship between media and empowerment of women with reference to India.

Feminism and Media

Scholars have studied the status of Indian women during different periods such as Ancient India, Indus Civilization, Vedic Age, Age of the Latter Samhitas, Manu-Smriti, Epic Age, Buddhism and Jainism, Islamic Age, Colonial era, Christian Missionaries, Freedom Movement and Post-Independence era. Several visionaries and missionaries have fought against gender based discrimination in Indian society. Buddha, Ramanuja, Basava, Raja Ram Mohan Roy, Jyoti Ba Phule, Ishwara Chandra Vidya Sagar, Dayananda Saraswati, Govinda Ranade, Ramaswamy Periyar, Narayana Guru, Mahatma Gandhi, Ambedkar and others played a historical role in the empowerment of women in India. They vehemently fought against gender inequality, Sati system, child marriage, Devadasi system and other discriminatory and exploitative tendencies. Several Indian women like Savitribai Phule, Pandita Ramabai, Ranade Maharani Tapaswini, Bhagini Nivedita, Swarna Kumari Devi, Kamaladevi Chattopadhyaya, Manmohan Kaur, Rajani Alexander, Uma Rao, Meera Desai, Aparna Bosh, Sarojini Naidu, Shakuntala Reddy and others created new consciousness among the women, actively participated in the feminist movements and prepared grounds for gender justice in India. The Indian Women's Conference was established by the Congress in order to educate and organize women before the independence.

In a detailed study, Zoonen (1996:258) pointed out that media have always remained at the centre of feminist critique. American newspapers brought out women's section in order to highlight the issues concerning women and their welfare. Joseph Pulitzer enhanced female readership by popularizing women's pages. The media were also criticized by 25 the feminists for the treatment of women as sex objects. In 1970s the feminist press emerged in America and Europe in order to strengthen women's liberation movement. Women's studies programmes also gave rise to feminist journals, presses and bookstores. Mac Bride Commission (1982:124) examined the images of women in radio, television, film and press and reported that the coverage of issues related to women's position in society steadily increased over a period of time. UNESCO (1985:245) reported that women gained marginal position in the media studies.

In the same vein, Shaw and Zach (1987:213) noted that about 25% of women related issues appeared in the press. Gradually efforts were made by the media professionals and women activists to improve the coverage of women in the media. A new organization called Gender and Communication Group came into existence in 1981 to scientifically assess the portrayal of women in the media. A new magazine called Research on Women and Communication was brought out by Western States Communication Association in order to enhance the status of feminist communication in the media.

Professional journals also gave importance to publication of issues concerning gender and empowerment. Several books were also brought out to draw the attention of scholars toward women and media issues. The United Nations Organization and UNESCO also contributed notably for the organization of intellectual exercises all over the world toward enlisting the active participation of media institutions for the empowerment of women. The UNESCO (1985:245) further stated that the volume of the research commissioned and published on women and communication issues was slight and occasional. Pawar (2009:178) reports: "The UNESCO's activities in the field of women and communication strengthened more during the United Nations World Conference on Women.

Role of Media in the Empowerment of Women

The concept of empowerment has been widely discussed and debated all over the world. The United Nations Development Programme (2001:246) has provided a meaningful conceptual framework of empowerment of women. It reads: "Empowerment is defined as the processes by which women take control and ownership of their lives through expansion of their choices. It is the process of acquiring the ability to make strategic life choices in a context where this ability has previously been denied," (2001:246)

Several researchers have tried to define the empowerment of women in their own ways on the basis of theoretical and empirical evidences and experiences. The definition most quoted by the scholars is one provided by Baltiiwala. It reads: "Empowerment is the process by which the powerless gain greater control over the circumstances of their lives. It includes both controls over resources and over ideology. Ultimately it includes a growing intrinsic capability – greater self confidence and an inner transformation of one's consciousness that enables one to overcome external barriers." (1994:13)

Inherent in this definition are two important ideas, the first of which is that empowerment is not about power over others (a feature of domination), but power to achieve goals and ends. By conceptualizing empowerment in terms of power the definition explicitly recognizes that the process of empowerment involves not only changes in access to resources, but also an understanding of one's rights and 28 entitlements and the conscientization that 'gender roles can be changed and gender equality is possible'.

While empowerment literally means 'to invest with power', in the context of women's empowerment the term has come to denote women's increased the control over their own lives, bodies and environment. Scholars have placed emphasis on women's decision making roles, their economic self-reliance and their legal rights to equal treatment, inheritance and protection against all forms of discrimination in addition to the elimination of barriers to their access of resources such as education, finance, political power and developmental initiatives.

Role of Media in the Empowerment of Tribal Women

There are about 650 tribal groups in India. The women are considered as an incorporated entity in the male-dominated social, economic, political and cultural order. The tribal women are equal partners with men in relation to work participation in forests, fields, markets and other spheres of human life. The position of tribal women in Indian society is quite paradoxical. The tribal women have always played a dominant role in agriculture, handicraft and forest based economy in India. The Constitution of India has guaranteed equal opportunities to all sections of society including the tribal women. But they lag behind in every sphere of human life including education, employment and politics. The tribal women are subjected to discrimination in many ways. Communication media have also neglected the tribal women due to several reasons in the post-independence era in India.

Communication is rightly viewed as an instrument of development. Many scholars have studied the role of communication in the process of development in India and abroad. The essence of the ideology of 'development communication' is the creation of a new society on the basis of equality and justice. The media intervention packages and programmes are required to popularize the beneficial effects of various development projects and to enlist the active participation of the beneficiaries in the process of development. Media and development are inter-related systems. The maximum responsibility lies on the media to make the developmental activities clear and accessible to the common people.

Communication Support for Tribal Women

Empowerment Serious doubts are also expressed as to the wanton devaluation of the tribal life and its core values. Literally, the information underclass has become powerless. This is very much true especially in tribal areas where people are alienated from the mainstream of national development. The Indian Space Research organization (ISRO) carried out several progressive communication experiments in the tribal areas to enlist the active participation of tribes in the process of development.

The policy makers have also encouraged the media institutions to undertake joint projects with user agencies to facilitate satellite based operational systems to support education and development in rural and tribal areas. Communications media including television and social media are expanded in the tribal areas. The print media, electronic media and new media have increased their space, time and resources in order to reach out to the unreached tribes. Communication support for tribal development is crucial in the present times. Participatory approaches to tribal development communication are required to open up new vistas of empowerment of tribal women. The Jhabua Development Communications Project (JDCP) of Madhya Pradesh facilitated the installation of community television station and disseminated various tribal development programmes for the benefit of tribal women in the project area.

The media professionals are called upon to assume pro-active roles as catalysts of tribal women empowerment in the country. Tribal development communication management in general and tribal women empowerment oriented media intervention in particular are enduring areas of research in India. The future agenda for media organizations must deal with the expansion of communications media in the tribal areas, production of tribal development oriented media programmes, and involvement of tribes in the communication programmes and evaluation of the impact of media on tribal women. The media institutions have to work in close collaboration toward designing tribal women empowerment centered communication programme at this juncture.

Scholars have examined the role of media in tribal development over a period of time and reported that media have not done justice to their role from tribal development point of view. The contributions of media for the empowerment of tribal women are not noteworthy in letter and spirit. Systematic media intervention for tribal women empowerment helps the tribal women to change their mindset, adopt healthy lifestyles, obtain the benefits of development projects and achieve development through active participation.

The media institutions should do serious introspection about their role in the empowerment of women in India and elsewhere. The women are considered as an incorporated entity in the male-dominated social, economic, political and cultural order. The tribal women are equal partners with men in relation to work participation in forests, fields, markets and other spheres of human life. The position of tribal women in Indian society is quite paradoxical. The tribal women have always played a dominant role in agriculture, handicraft and forest based economy in India. But they lag behind in every sphere of human life including education, employment and politics. The tribal women are subjected to discrimination in many ways. Communication media have also neglected the tribal women due to several reasons in the post-independence era in India. Communication is rightly viewed as an instrument of development. Many scholars have studied the role of communication in the process of development in India and abroad. The essence of the ideology of 'development communication' is the creation of a new society on the basis of equality and justice A comprehensive policy of communication related to tribal development goals is not formulated to facilitate meaningful media intervention for tribal development over a period of time. Majumdar observes, "The transition of the tribal people from their tribal economy to national economy, from their tribal organization to national political organization, must be planned and piloted in the due consideration to the social group's concern." In the empirical studies carried out by Parkins (1972:171), Goldthrope (1984:78), Crompton and Mann (1986:46), Michall Mann (2004:134), Myers, Diana Tietiens (1987:150) and others have revealed that the topic of gender has been relatively neglected in the mainstream stratification theory and research which has brought about the oppression of tribal women. Tribal women continue to be the bearers and rearers of children. There are many factors associated with gender identities of tribal women. The tribal culture has facilitated the construction of positive gender identity for tribal women. Anthropologists like P.N.Mishra, L.K.Anantha Krishna Iyer, G.S.Ghurye, Iravati Karve and others have also provided a new dimension to research in tribal development in India. There is a rich tradition of tribal studies in Indian society. The scholars have reported that developmental projects have adversely affected the tribal women. Sinha (1978:228), Prasad (1988:182), Alam (1998:04), Damodaran (2002:49) and others have observed that tribal women in the informal sector have experienced several disadvantages and suffered from severe economic stress and oppression due to destruction of the forest in the name of development. Mahashwetadevi fought for the empowerment of tribal women in India and noted that tribal women are subjected to two-tier exploitation – as a laborer and also as instrument of sexual gratification to the new controllers of economy. She presented the politics of oppression hatched by the newly formed mafia which is responsible for the saddening state of affairs of tribal women in India. The process of tribal development did not have a positive impact on the structure of tribal society and status of tribal women. The new forces of modernization have drastically affected the indigenous systems and their culture, tradition, social practices, occupational pattern and so forth according to Bodra (2008:29). The implications of social change, modernization and development on tribal women are scientifically analyzed by the anthropologists. They have reported that the penetration of alien culture in the age of globalization has adversely affected the status of tribal women. The emergence of new market economy has increased the control of market forces over tribal communities and reduced the status of tribal women.

Communication Support for Tribal Women Empowerment Serious doubts are also expressed as to the wanton devaluation of the tribal life and its core values. Literally, the information underclass has become powerless. This is very much true especially in tribal areas where people are alienated from the mainstream of national development. Communications media including television and social media are expanded in the tribal areas. The print media, electronic media and new media have increased their space, time and resources in order to reach out to the unreached tribes. Communication support for tribal development is crucial in the present times. Participatory approaches to tribal development communication are required to open up new vistas of empowerment of tribal women. The media professionals are called upon to assume pro-active roles as catalysts of tribal women empowerment in the country. Tribal development communication management in general and tribal women empowerment oriented media intervention in particular are enduring areas of research in India. The future agenda for media organizations must deal with the expansion of communications media in the tribal areas, production of tribal development oriented media programmes, and involvement of tribes in the communication programmes and evaluation of the impact of media on tribal women. The media institutions have to 37 work in close collaboration toward designing tribal women empowerment centered communication programme at this juncture.

According to Ms. Jeya Rani[2] a journalist the mainstream media is not for the poor, not for the oppressed. It has carved its kingdom out of loyalty to the powers, to bureaucracy, to domination. It is neither for minorities nor for women and children. Most certainly not for the Dalits. Over 95% of owners of the mainstream media including print and television come from dominant caste backgrounds. About 70-80% of the topmost positions are occupied by dominant caste men. Dalits don't even constitute 1% when it comes to deciding power in the country's media.

Crimes against Dalits see a rise of 10-20% every year. In a just society, the media's space to violence against Dalits should have correspondingly increased too. But has it happened? We all know it has not.

Today, media organisations find news value even in a non-news item. But they are still not concerned about manual scavenging in this era, about cooks refusing to cook for Dalit children in schools, or about Dalits displaced for urbanization. These atrocities are never capable of hitting the headlines in front page. We have seen screaming headlines when an Indian is racially attacked elsewhere .

How could the same media turn a blind eye to the racist attacks in the name of caste happening right under its nose?

Mathew notes: "Women's education and health are yet to get the kind of serious attention they deserve from the Indian media. Empowerment of women can happen only when women become aware of their psychological enslavement and rebel against it. There are signs of this happening. We find more and more women taking up challenges, chasing their dreams, and standing up for a cause." (2008:136)

The media can facilitate the empowerment of women by sensitizing men and society in general, by voicing the silent screams of women, by creating more female icons who can rouse women's consciousness, by initiating stimulating debates on women's issues, by simply devoting more print space and television time for women, by using television to break male stereotypes, by influencing legislatures to enact laws for protection of women's rights, by employing more women communicators, by promoting literacy and women's education, by advocating active deployment of women in the police and other visible symbols of power, and by using non-sexist language and metaphors".

The future lies with women. The future has come closer, with the dawn of the digital age where the World Wide Web is a great leveler. It is a world of infinite possibilities for women as well as men, and anyone with an innovative idea and the willingness to work hard can realize their dreams here. Anyone can start a business on the internet, showcase one's talents, market anything and network with an awesome number of people- and publish newspapers without worrying about installing huge printing presses. The Internet can be liberating for women. It is their future, for there is no gender discrimination on the web. Women, therefore, need to be actively involved in decisions making regarding the development of the new communication technologies as effective instruments of empowerment of women. In addressing the issue of mobilization of media for the empowerment of women, governments, media institutions and other authorities should promote an active and visible policy of mainstreaming a gender perspective in the management of media institutions.

The media have not achieved notable success in the empowerment of women since the market forces are controlling the media. There is increasing glorification of atrocities on women but the media have not facilitated meaningful social, political, intellectual and cultural mobilization with reference to empowerment of women in India.

References Cited:

Algarsamy, Hamsadhwani "Dalit Women in Media and Politics Conference: When Dait Women speak up, Revolution Beckons. Feb. 22, 2019. Intersectional Feminism, - Desi Style (Google search).

Arun, Joe (2007). Constructing Dalit Identity, Rawat Publications, New Dlehi.

Beteille, Andre (2001) "Race and Caste", The Hindu, March 10, 2001.

Ghurye, G. S. (1963). The Scheduled Tribes, Popular Prakashan, Bombay (Now Mumbai).

Guillaumin, Collette (1995), Racism, Sexism, Power and Ideology, London and New York: Routledge, 1995.

Kadam, K. N. (ed.), (1 993). Dr. B. R. Ambedkur the Emancipator of the Oppressed, Popular Prakashan, Bombay.

Kannabiran, Kalpana (2001), CASTE, THE ACADEMY AND DALIT WOMEN [Published in The Hindu, edit page, 17 June 2001.

Kumar, Vivek (2003). Uttar Pradesh: Politics of Change, Economic and Political Weekly, vol. XXXVIII, no.37, 13-19 September, Mumbai.

Kumar, Vivek (2009), "Locating Dalit Women in the Indian Caste System, Media and Women's Movement", in Social Change, 39 (1), 64-84, March 2009, Jawaharlal Nehru University, vol 39, No. 1.

Oommen, T. K. (1990). Protest and Change: Studies in Social Movements, Sage Publications, New Delhi.

Prasad, Sushma Sahay (1988) Tribal Women Laborers – Aspects of Economic and Physical Exploitation, Delhi: Gyan Publishing House.

Ram, Nandu (2007). Caste System in South India: Genesis, Mechanism and Growth, RC9 Dalits and Backward Classes, Indian Sociological Society, New Delhi.

Rege, Sharmila (2006). Writing Caste/ Writing Gender: Narrating Dalit Women's Testimonies, Zuban, New Delhi.

Shivaraju, H.S. "Role of Media in the Empowerment of Tribal Women in Karnataka State – a Study. (source: http://hal.handle.net/10603/90687.

Vatuk, Ved Prakash (1979), "Studies in Indian Folk Tradition", New Delhi: Ramesh Jain for Manohar Publications.

Notes

1. Dr. Janet Mary, Assistant Professor in Madras Christian College, Tambaram, Chennai, India. A social activist who worked among the marginalized communities in Bihar, Maharashtra and Tamil Nadu.
2. Jeya Rani is a journalist for over 15 years from Tamil Nadu. Her Tamil original has been translated into English by Kavitha Muralidharan.

Chapter - 20

Are The Voices Heard: Status of Low Caste Women in Religions

Dr. G Lazar[1]

Introduction

Within the discipline of religious philosophy, this paper can be positioned as regards to its method and substance in the following fields of study: ritual studies, contemporary popular religious traditions, and studies on women and religion. This research paper has been guided by other disciplines as well, particularly cultural anthropology and women's studies. In what follows, I will discuss the niche of this research in the context of those voices of low caste women whose voices are unheard due to traditional social and religious belief systems. I will also situate this work within a wider academic context and assess its possible scholarly and societal contributions.

Gender Inequality

Gender inequality according to Inglehart and Norrist (2003), belongs among other things to the most prevalent forms of social inequality and exists all over the world, with different effects in different regions. These differences are primarily due to cultural legacies, historical development, geographic location, and, last but not the least, the religious norms which predominate in society. Religion plays a vital role in the cultural life of different spaces. It is deeply rooted in peoples' experiences and influences the socio-economic and political direction of societies (Stump, 2008). On a similar note, Peach (2006) asserts that for social geographic investigation, religion may now be a more important variable than traditional beliefs.

The status of women in a society is an outcome of the interpretation of religious texts and of the cultural and institutional set-up of religious communities (Klingorová, 2015). The role of religion is, obviously, complex and it varies across time and space. We work with the premise that everyone benefits from gender equality (Verveer, 2011). We consider gender equality and the emancipation of women as important factors for the economic, social, and democratic progress of the world's regions and for the development of human society. This process is influenced by institutional norms, as well as culture and tradition, which are both largely determined by religion (Uuksulainen, 2013). As the relationship between religion and culture is reciprocal, religious systems are locked in a circle of mutual influence with social norms and patterns of social organisation (Sinclair, 1986).

From Indian Perspective

According to Allen (1990, 6–7) the status of women in India can be approached from various dimensions, each of which produces a different view on the topic. Most scholars agree that the position of women has deteriorated continually through different periods of Indian history. The literal sources show that in early Vedic (1600–1000 BCE) times women were active participants in the sacrificial rites of Vedic religion along with their husbands. They were also equal owners of households and property. Rigidity regarding gender roles developed during the post-Vedic period (1000–350 BCE). The initiator was the ascetic tradition, which excluded women from official religious practices and identified them with sexuality, impurity, desire, and embeddedness in the material world – all of which had to be renounced by the liberation-seeking ascetic. This worldview afforded an opportunity for the development of a discriminatory attitude to women due to their biological functions. As the pure/impure dichotomy grew in importance, women were increasingly perceived as impure, especially during menstruation and the period following childbirth. Many restrictions and rules were formed because of the concern for women's purity (Uuksulainen, 2013).

In Hinduism, male gods are incomplete without their female consorts. But women are deemed unclean when they menstruate and, hence, kept out of kitchens and temples like Sabarimala. In Christianity even the chaste nuns are not allowed to enter the holy of holies during ritual times. In Islam shrines like the dargah of Nizamuddin Aulia and Ajmer Sharif, women are not allowed into the sanctum sanctorum where men throng freely. Even in Medina women are directed to the outer line, far away from the Prophet's grave while men are allowed within touching distance. The clergy are largely a men-only club in many world religions. Why this disparity?

Religious Rituals and Pollution of Women

The concept of religious ritual is widely utilized in the social sciences, and is also recognized in the natural sciences. It has been given numerous definitions and approaches using a range of theoretical frames of reference. Religious rituals in particular, as distinct from 'rituals' which in casual conversation are referred to as rituals, but are more like routines, habits, or any mundane, repetitive activities lacking a supernatural orientation.

The study of ritual practices of Indian women is an academic research tradition, which has been carried out by Kathleen Erndl (1987, 1997, 2000), Julia Leslie (1992, 2000), June McDaniel (2003), Mary McGee (1987, 1991, 2000), Anne Pearson (1996) and Tracy Pintchman (2007), to name but a few scholars. In this study women's rituals are seen as a way of both maintaining and challenging cultural conventions (for example, Banerjee 1989, 131–132; Gold 2003, 107–109; Raheja 1994, 5; 2003, 173; Sax 1994, 175). In line with Lina Fruzzetti (1990), Lina Gupta (1997) and Susan Wadley (1995), rituals are approached as the domain of women in the sense that they reflect the concerns, needs, fears and life histories of women in particular, if only to confirm the conventional notions of ideal wife and mother.

Riikka Uuksulainen (2013), in her studies on women and ritual notes that women's rituals are mainly transmitted orally and flourish under the shadow of the authoritarian, scripture-based ritual tradition. In institutionalized Hindu rituals, women are hardly permitted the role of a viewer, whereas in rituals of their own women themselves are the subjects; they are the actors determining the objectives of their activity (see, for example, Gold 2003; Raheja 1994, 2003c; Gupta 1997). Ritual behaviour is thus seen as playing a part in building and strengthening women's identity and even in giving women psychological support and confidence by providing them with a channel to also express such feelings that ought not to be shown. Gupta, 1997, 97-98), sees women's rituals fulfilling two purposes; they are preventive of pain and loss, and conducive to peace, prosperity, power and ultimate freedom (*moksha*). Gupta calls into question the common feminist argument that Hindu women contribute to their oppression by conforming to the religious guidelines, and that women's ritual conduct is a major hindrance on the way to female emancipation. In contrast, Gupta claims that women indeed regain and reaffirm their essential power by observing rituals. By participating in rituals, women ultimately redefine their own status.

Hélène Stork in her study on Tamil women and their mothering practices applies the concept of the mothering ritual in reference to procreation rituals in general (Stork 1992, 89–105). A mother is either the subject performing the rituals and seeking supernatural assistance in carrying out her duty, or she is the object for whose sake others perform a rite. This is not to say that fathers have no role in birth rituals. In post-natal rituals in particular fathers are traditionally active participants. They recite sacred verses and contribute to the adaptation of the child into the world.

Dalit Women Today

Dalits facing Human Rights violations is a legion. A random sampling of deadlines in mainstream Indian newspapers tells their story: "Dalit boy beaten to death for plucking flowers"; "Dalit tortured by cops for three days"; Dalit 'which' paraded naked in Bihar"; "Dalit killed in lock-up at KURNOOL?";

"Seven Dalit burnt alive in caste clash"; "Five Dalits lynched in Haryana"; "Dalit women gang-raped, paraded naked"; "Police egged on mob to lynch Dalits".

The situation of Dalit women in India needs special attention. They are one of the largest socially segregated groups anywhere in the world, and make up 2% of world's total population. Dalit women are discriminated against three time over; they are poor, they are women, and they are Dalits. Dalit women constitute half of the 200 million Dalit population, and 16.3 of the total Indian female population. The traditional taboos are the same for Dalit men and Dalit women. However, Dalit women have to deal with them more often. Dalit women are discriminated against not only by people of higher castes, but also within their own communities. Men are dominant in Dalit communities. Dalit women also have less power within the Dalit movement itself. Women are active in large numbers in the movement but most leadership positions in the organizations, local bodies and associations have until now been held men.

The discrimination that Dalit women are subjected to discrimination. The caste system declares Dalit women as 'impure' and therefore untouchable and hence socially excluded. Dalit women are thrice discriminated, treated as untouchables and as outcastes, due to their caste, face gender discrimination being women and finally economic impoverishment due to unequal wage disparity, with low or underpaid labour. Among the untouchables, the status of women is further eroded and closely linked to the concept of purity. Women are made to suffer the stigma precisely to ensure the caste purity of the family. It is only Brahmins and upper-castes who have the privilege to uphold the caste purity while the lower castes and Dalits have no such entitlements to ritual purity and self-respect. Impurities like menstruation can affect the purity of the household periodically for a limited period of time. This limited period of "untouchability" is also suffered by Brahmin and upper-caste males in case of the death of a family member (though the rituals differ from what women go through during their menstruation). This is in sharp contrast to the eternal untouchable condition that the actual untouchables suffer. This is the way in which the caste Hindus guard their household from temporary pollution apart from securing it from the pollutions caused by the entry of an untouchable.

However, there has been a systemic process of emasculation of lower caste men in several contexts in the rituals of Hindu society. Baby Kamble discussed how Potraj, a Mahar male child, wearing bangles, anklets and skirt, dances in the procession during the festival of Ashad for alms.(Kamble,2008) In some similar festivals of Telanagana region like Batukamma and Bonalu, Potraj, a Dalit man bare-chested, flagellates himself in the procession. This is an example of how an untouchable male is emasculated by the masculine upper-caste groups and even Shudra castes. To take cues from Bell Hooks, masculinity is a system of power. (Hooks,1984) Upper-caste women are part of such masculine power centres according to the caste system in relation to the lower castes and Dalits. Hence, they are part and parcel of the process of emasculation of the lower castes or Dalits. A tradition that is followed even today in Andhra Pradesh is that the upper-caste girl's clothes worn on the day of attaining puberty, clothes with blood stains are mandatorily offered to *chakali* women. This ritual relieves the upper-castes from the pollution caused by the first menstruation of the girls thus directing the pollution to *chakali* women. These *chakali* women are considered as receivers of the pollution in order to protect the purity of the upper-caste households. Untouchables and lower castes are an essential part of the society for the upper-castes to uphold their purity[2]. Gopal Guru says, "Just imagine what would happen to the touchable, if the untouchable were to refuse to become the dumping ground for somebody's moral dirt or refuse to illuminate the touchable. It perhaps would lead to the moral decomposition or atrophy of the touchables' body or they would get crushed under the accumulated weight of these impurities. (Thank god, there has been an untouchable around to carry this burden!)"(Guru, 2009).

This is what the rigid, fundamentalist Hindu promotes through continuation of caste system, imposing the Brahminical values to maintain the caste system. Dalit women, who fortunately had not fallen prey into the net cunningly women by Hinduism was more free and less dependent. She was physically strong and could work hard. Anti-women feelings were not to be found in their social life. Child marriage, strict monogamy, widowhood, dowry practice and the heinous practice of "Sati" were all unknown to them. Dalit woman has more freedom than her counterpart in the higher castes. But this freedom does not really mean anything. This is the freedom given to her by men for their own conveniences. In their vain attempt to be identified with and approved by the caste Hindus, tried to follow their practices, forced their women into subjugation; widowhood was thrust on them. They are forbidden to remarry. The freedom that the Dalit woman was enjoying was mercilessly taken away so in the present day society a Dalit woman is also considered to be unequal to her men. Today, the Dalit women who constitute the major working force.

Dalit women say that they instinctively avoid touching non-Dalit women in the workplace. They eat separately. When working in the fields, if non-Dalit landlords provide the food, Dalit males and females have to either bring their own utensils or eat in leaf plant. When serving water, non-Dalits hold the pot at a height, pouring a trickle into Dalit hands to avoid pollution. Working in the fields and homes of non-Dalits exposes Dalit women to sexual abuse and violence, which they are often powerless to resist. The dependence on non-Dalits prevents Dalit women from devising work routines that avoid non-Dalit spaces and the experience of being humiliated every day.

Anthropological Perspective

It is a historical fact that women's sexuality is controlled by patriarchy. Feminist anthropologists and historians believe patriarchy introduced the notion of women's impurity to establish male supremacy. Gradually, as patriarchy took root, women were chastised for their power of healing and prophesying, and during the medieval ages, in Europe many healers and midwives were burnt as witches. Patriarchy is already in place and everybody is caught up within that set of relations in which men have power over women and men also control the world of ideas. Beliefs which attribute spiritual power to individuals are never neutral or free of the dominant patterns of social structure. If some beliefs seem to attribute free-floating spiritual powers in a haphazard manner, closer inspection shows consistency. The only circumstances in which spiritual powers seem to flourish independently of the formal social system are when the system itself is exceptionally devoid of formal structure, when legitimate authority is always under challenge or when the rival segments of a political system resort to mediation. Then the main contenders for political power have to court for their side the holders of free-floating spiritual power. Thus it is beyond doubt that the social system is thought of as quick with creative and sustaining powers.

All religions, it would seem, are inherently patriarchal. Some feminist anthropologists are of the opinion that until the concept of property rights emerged; the world was matriarchal, based on a mother goddess, who is the earth. But property rights gave rise to inheritance rights and so fatherhood became important. With that the female divine lost her privileged position and was overshadowed by the father god.

Hindus take the mythologies connected to gods and goddesses literally. Many assume Lakshmi and Durga embody women, rather than ideas. In the mythological vocabulary, the male form is used to embody the mind and the female for to embody matter. The unenlightened dependent mind is Brahma, the enlightened independent mind is Shiva, and the enlightened dependable mind is Vishnu (REFERENCE). No body of ideas can remain a challenging one unless you change the social structure. This has a long way to go.

The Qur'an's Surah al Baqr speaks of women's menstruation in clear unambiguous terms: 'O Prophet, they ask you about menstruation so tell them it is a time of 'adhan' (hurt). It is better if they (men) stay away from women; until they finish their ayyaam (days), and cleanse themselves." These lines have been used from time immemorial to restrict women from participation in anything pertaining to religion in these days. The word 'yat-hurn' which means 'clean', pure' has been read to imply they were 'dirty' before the cleansing. That men and women have to cleanse themselves before offering prayers is a Qur'anic injunction which applies both to 'Haiz' menstruation as well as to washing off body fluids post intercourse, before Namaaz is offered. Nowhere in the Qur'an we read a single line explicitly stating that they should be excluded from any other religious practices.

In Islam, most interpreters of Qur'an give 'pollution' as meaning for the Arabic word *'adhan'*. That meaning has opened the flood gates for all gender exclusions. Men have used this word to imply '*naapaaki*' (uncleanliness), a tool to increase control over women. In all matters pertaining to religion, women are regarded as inferior because they menstruate, and the male is superior because he does not. According to Maulana Abul Kalam Azad the injunction to stay away from reading Qur'an or entering mosque is not because women become *naapaak* but because women's sexual contact during these days is '*muzir*' (harmful, or hurtful). In the same light, it may be averred that during the menstrual cycle keeping Ramadan fast may be tedious, or the act of *rukus* and *sijdah* during Namaaz could be strenuous. But patriarchy latched on to a certain vocabulary and a slew of practices were declared forbidden to women during their courses.

The practice of ritual pollution by low caste women can be viewed either from the 'emic' or the 'etic' perspective. The emic perspective is the native's interpretation or model in the context of culture, whereas the etic perspective is a representation of the outsider's view. Most of the Hindus understand the practice of ritual pollution with the emic perspective of investigation. The etic approach is from a non-religious perspective and is perceived by the emic scholars to be anti-religious. This is because, the emic group approach considers the practice from a religious point of view. Their interpretation, even if not explicitly expressed, is often inspired and motivated by religious sentiments of awe-filled appreciation and exaltation of their religious sentiments as they believe the practice to be of divine origin and propagating religious truths. Hence, they feel that the non-religious are biased and cannot interpret the practice impartially. On the other hand, the etic perspective is socio-historical and often criticizes and belittles the work of emic interpreters branding it religious and superstitious. They look for historical and scientific proofs rather than religious meaning.

As cultural anthropologists believe, an emic approach on its own would struggle with applying overarching values to a single culture. The etic approach is helpful in enabling researchers to see more than one aspect of a particular culture, and in applying these observations to other cultures. A combined approach can be of help to get a benignant understanding of the daily struggles of social-outcastes of India, while transforming the baneful religious system into a beneficial force in society.

For a fair, rational and balanced view both interpretations need to be considered and respected. Our investigation of the practice of ritual pollution by the out-caste women is one such combined emic-etic perspective.

According to Clifford Geerz, right hearing requires knowledge of the context. Only after the context is "thickly described", that is, after exploring the details of the setting of the study, the informants, their symbolic system, and how the field work is carried out, is it possible to assess the likely sense and meanings underlying the behaviour of the people studied. Geerz argues that "Nothing is more necessary to comprehending what anthropological interpretation is, than exact understanding of what it means to say that our formulations of other people's symbol systems must be actor-oriented" (Geerz 1973, 14). Geerz criticizes anthropologists who casually claim that they "are seeing things from the actor's point of view" without really going into explicating what they mean by it.

The disturbing questions are: why do these women perform rituals, and what do they wish to gain by devoting themselves to adhering to the ritual conduct? This question takes us into the heart of issues concerning the reliability of the anthropological interpretation. The question is how can we hear the voice of others? According to the well-known view of Hans-Georg Gadamer, understanding is a linguistic event, historically conditioned, during which the worlds of the interpreter and the interpreted are fused in what he calls the "fusion of horizons". Gadamer 1995, 306–307; Gothóni 2011, 21–22; Gothóni 2002, 158–159.12). Gadamer says that the process of human understanding takes place in a "hermeneutical circle", in which the details of a text or other object are understood in the light of the whole text and the whole in turn is understood in the light of the details of the text (Gadamer 1995, 265–269).

Two main, interconnecting facets on ritual practice have been advanced by feminist discourse: First, women's rituals in many respects confirm male superiority, and second, women's rituals essentially nurture the construction of women's identity and role as wife and mother. I join this debate by introducing the views of a group of low caste women, which, I assume, will be supportive of both stands.

Understanding low caste women's status requires examining and reflecting on it in the context of the general duties and ideals of the castes. According to several scholars, the value and position of a Hindu woman depend on the life orientation and dominant ideology of a caste (Allen 1990, 1; Kelkar 1995, 37; Krygier 1990, 81, 93; Young 1987, 64). Each caste and community is to fulfill a certain innate duty to maintain the right order of the whole. According to Michael Allen, the four human goals (*purusharthas*) stated in the Hindu tradition, as well as related ideologies peculiar to Hindus produce a different view of women (Allen 1990, 1–19). The pursuit of the four goals of human *life artha, dharma, ka'ma* and *moksha* was shaped in the Dharmashastra treatises and the epics of Mahabharata and Ramayana.

According to Grimes and others (Grimes 1996, 251–252; Lipner 1999, 159–160). Liberation (*moksha)* and the right order (*dharma*) are innate goals for the people of high castes whereas lower castes tend to pursue primarily material prosperity (*artha*) and pleasure (*kama)*. This rough division is obviously an over-simplification, and it could be argued that most Hindus aim at more than one of them – or even all of them – at different stages of life. However, the division provides a hypothesis for examining the position of women in terms of the four traditional human goals.

In the course of Indian history, the pursuits of liberation (*moksha*) and right order (*dharma*) have resulted in several practices that subordinate and devalue women. The ascetic ideals conceive of women mainly as a distraction and hindrance on the way to higher spirituality and liberation. Liberation itself is not attainable for most women, who are bound to nature and periodical impurity by their biology and duty to procreate. Instead, their sexuality threatens and tempts the ascetics who have renounced their bodily desires. Those aiming at keeping the right order see women as potentially harmful and polluting, but when carefully administered they are important and necessary instruments in maintaining the order. Such conventions have resulted in strict control over women who have had to carefully abide by the purity codes and orders, and thus, have been forced into a repressive position. In the course of history the purity ideals have contributed to the emergence of oppressive practices such as child marriage and widow burning. Allen thus distinguishes three positive components that provide a basis for the value of women: Women are sources of purity, power, and productivity. According to his view, positive attitude is more visible among the low caste communities, and thus the position of women both in terms of status and autonomy is relatively better the lower one descends the social and caste hierarchy (Allen 1990, 17–18).

Of course, at least two key questions remain to be asked: (1) How significant is the influence of world religions on gender inequality and the social status of women? Every religion promotes somewhat different norms, creates different institutions, and builds on different cultural and historical foundations. The influence the individual world religions have on the status of women is very differentiated (Klingorová 2013, 2015), and we should then ask: (2) Through an analysis of diversification of the selected religions, as part of this assumption, we would like to expand on the study by Seguino (2011), which primarily concerned itself with the influence of religiosity on gender inequality within a set of socioeconomic parameters of the selected states. Furthermore, we accept the statement that the level of gender inequality is also influenced by a state's level of economic development (Dollar and Gatti 1999; Seguino 2011).

Conclusions

Most world religions today maintain male social dominance within societal structures (Young, 1987). On the other hand, women are more inclined to participate in religious life (Hamplová 2013, 2011; Renzetti and Curran 1999). Empirical research on developments in the individual religions, especially in the case of Islam, indicate a negative shift in society towards a decreased status of women with the emergence of the so-called advanced religions (Holm 1994; Krejèí 2009). Also, religious norms and prejudices may reflect patriarchal values (Nešpor 2008), which are characteristic of all societies of the world religions (Seguino 2011). The role of God, or a creator of a religion, is always taken by a male and the woman is primarily valued as a mother. Her place is in the household, less so at religious ceremonies or in public positions. The real status of a woman in a religion is more complicated, however, as in some religions certain women have acquired significant posts (Holm 1994).

In the histories of religions, the voice of marginalized women is rarely heard, due to the patriarchal dispositions of societies in which these religions emerged, and which eventually stifled some of the changes in the status of women triggered by these new religions. The world religions all agree on the respect for women and their crucial role in family life, especially with emphasis on women as mothers and wives. They do not, however, advocate emancipation in the sense of total equality of high caste women with low caste women. According to Holm (1994), the most severe restrictions apply to women during their periods of menstruation and pregnancy, when, for example, they cannot enter the temple or touch the Quran.

Male and female roles in marginalized communities are therefore much differentiated and also unbalanced in the world religions. The influence of women in the rural set-up on the formation of religious norms and traditions is small, even though in certain doctrines, we can find women who succeeded in having their normative views accepted, or men who advocated equal integration of women into religious ceremonies. It needs to be stated that there exists a certain discrepancy between normative conditionality, which refers to what the given religion proclaims and practical conditionality, which involves the role of women in tribal or Dalit communities and state societies in terms of everyday life (Holm 1994). In addition, the heterogeneity of the global categories ('Islam', 'Hindu', etc.) must be emphasized, such that general conclusions must be tempered by admitting such variability in religious affiliation – otherwise we would tend to stereotype religious affiliation, which is certainly not intended here.

References

1. Das, Veena. 1997a (1977) Structure and Cognition: Aspects of Hindu Caste and Ritual. 2nd ed. Delhi: Oxford University Press. 1997b (1991) Concepts of space in ritual. – Religion in India. Ed. by T.N. Madan. Oxford in India Readings. Delhi: Oxford University Press. 156–171.
2. Dubois, J.A. 1972 (1906) Hindu Manners, Customs and Ceremonies. Ed. by H.K. Beauchamp. London: Clarendon Press.
3. Geerz, Clifford. 1973 The Interpretation of Cultures: Selected Essays. New York: Basic Books.
4. Geetha, V. 2002 Gender. Theorizing Feminism Series. Calcutta: Stree.
5. Ghadially, Rehana (ed.) 1996 (1988) Women in Indian Society. A Reader. New Delhi: Sage Publications.
6. John, Mary E. 2003 Dalit women in Western ethnography. – Gender & Caste. Issues in Contemporary Indian Feminism, Vol.1. Ed. by Anupama Rao. New Delhi: Kali for Women. 218–222.

7. Kakar, Sudhir. 1988 Feminine identity in India. – Women in Indian Society. A Reader. Ed. by Rehana Ghadially. New Delhi: Sage Publications. 44–68.
8. Kelkar, Meena A. 1995 Subordination of Women: A New Perspective. New Delhi: Discovery Publishing House.
9. King, Ursula. 1980 Women and religion: The status and image of women in some major religious traditions. – Women in Contemporary India and South Asia. Ed. by Alfred de Souza. New Delhi: Manohar Publications. 179–197.
10. Leslie, Julia (ed.). 1992 (1991) Roles and Rituals for Hindu Women. Delhi: Motilal Banarsidass Publishers.
11. Sugirtharajah, Sharada. 1994 Hinduism. – Women in Religion. Ed. by Jean Holm and John Bowker. Themes in Religious Studies Series. London: Pinter. 59–83.
12. Östör, Ákos & Fruzzetti, Lina & Barnett, Steve (eds.). 1992 Concepts of Person: Kinship, Caste, and Marriage in India. Delhi: Oxford University Press.
13. Guru, G. 2009 "Archeology of Untouchability" EPW, Vol. 44, No. 37 (Sept. 12-18, pp.49-56.
14. Hooks, B. 1984 Feminist Theory: From Margins to Centre, New York: South end press.
15. Jondhale, Surendra. 2013 "Theoretical Underpinning of Emancipation of Dalit Women" in Jogdand, P. G, (ed.) Dalit Women in India: Issues and Perspectives, New Delhi: Gyan Publishers.
16. Kamble, B. 2008 Prisons We Broke, Delhi: Orient Black Swan.
17. Spellman, E.1990 Inessential Woman: Problems of Exclusion in Feminist Thought, Boston: Bacon, Press.

Notes

1. Director – SANSKRUTI – Institute of Dravidian Culture and Research, Hyderabad, India. lazarsvd@gmail.com.
2. Sawjanya, T. (2017) "Why the Beates on Menstrual Taboo are one-sided" Sept. 21. (Complete reference).

Chapter - 21

Economic Policy: Change in the Socio-Economic Conditions of Marginalised Groups (SC/ST) in Independent India

G. Jagadeesh[1] and Thomas K. J[2].

Introduction

The major objective of planning in India right from the First Five Year Plan onwards was to accelerate economic growth with justice. Accordingly, State was assigned a crucial and active role in the process of economic development (Ahluwalia, 1991:9). To uplift socially and economically deprived sections such as Scheduled Castes (SCs) and Scheduled Tribes (STs), a variety of special development programmes were designed. Land Reform was one such programmes and was viewed as an important one as it not only promoted equity but also increased the agricultural productivity. In addition to the general programmes, a specific sector of backward classes was included in the First Five Year Plan to cater to the detailed needs of the SCs/STs/OBCs. Since desired results were obvious if not in full-length at least partially, in the Sixth Fiver Plan a 'Special Component Plan' for Scheduled Castes to facilitate and monitor the development programmes of SCs was introduced. Later, 'National Scheduled Castes and Scheduled Tribes Finance and Development Corporation' was established primarily to act as a catalytic agent of Development Schemes which would finance Pilot Employment Generation Projects. Eventually 'Integrated Rural Development Programme' (IRDP) was launched to implement Poverty Alleviation Programmes especially for SC/ST families. So also, Jawahar Rojgar Yojana Programme was conceptualised to liberate and enhance wages and employment opportunities of bonded SC/ST labourers. This Jawahar Rojgar Yojana Scheme was taken to the Rural Panchayats where SCs/STs presence was dense and exploitation and discrimination was rampant. Moreover, to effectively implement Jawahar Rojgar Yojana at Panchayat level nearly 15% of the total Annual allocation was set aside. Furthermore, all

Panchayats were directed to undertake employment schemes which would directly benefit SCs and STs. Notion of Positive Discrimination was highlighted to provide Scholarship facilities to SCs and STs so that the literacy rate among them would eventually reach 100% and social and biological poverty would disappear and the employment opportunities would be abundant.

Though the Scheduled Caste and Scheduled Tribe population which was 14.6 percent and 6.2 percent respectively of total population in 1951 and increased to 16.6 percent and 8.6 percent of total population of the country in 2011 (Table-1), even in the present digital world the shameful and depressing reality and chief problem is poverty superimposed by Social Discrimination and Segregation. Unfortunately, among some SCs and STs we also notice biological poverty.

Table-I: Trends in Proportion of Scheduled Caste and Scheduled Tribe Population

Census Year	*Total population (in million)*	*Scheduled Castes population (in million)*	*Proportion of SCs population*	*Scheduled Tribes population (in million)*	*Proportion of STs population*
1951	356	52	14.6	-	-
1961	439.2	65	14.7	30	6.9
1971	547.9	80	14.6	38	6.9
1981	665.3	106	15.7	52	7.8
1991	838.6	138	16.5	68	8.1
2001	1028.6	167	16.2	85	8.2
2011	1210.1	201	16.6	104	8.6

Source: Educational Statistics at a Glance, Government of India, Ministry of Human Resource Development bureau of Planning, Monitoring & Statistics, New Delhi, 2014.

Therefore, this paper attempts to carefully study the outcome of intended Economic Growth with Justice to the SCs and STs. Various Development Schemes initiated by the Government of India from the First Five Year Plan for the progressive Socio-Economic growth of Scheduled Castes and Scheduled Tribes would be granularly scrutinized to have the down to earth Socio-Economic conditions and status of SCs and STs in Independent India. Factors that improved the life standards and quality of SCs and STs along with causes that prevented progress would be thoroughly analysed. The study of transformative Socio-Economic change among the SCs and STs would be in terms of ***access to land, education, occupational distribution, incidence of poverty and employment in government sectors***.

After the last census in 2011 we realize that up till now Uttar Pradesh (UP) has the maximum concentration of SC population. It is followed by West Bengal, Bihar, Andhra Pradesh and Tamil Nadu in the descending order respectively. These five States together account for nearly 55 percent of SC population in India. Similarly, 68 percent of ST population dwells in several major states Chhattisgarh, Jharkhand, Odisha, Madhya Pradesh, Maharashtra, Gujarat and Rajasthan. About 24 percent of SC and 10 percent of ST population live in Urban Areas as against 35 percent of non-SC/ST population, which means approximately 76 percent of SC and 90 percent of ST population live in Rural Areas as against 65 percent of non-SC/ST population (Primary Census Abstract 2011).

Access to Land

Table II evidently points to the facts that in 1982 SC Households were 20 percent of total Rural Households and controlled only 8 percent of the total Area owned. Whereas other Households accounted for 70 percent of total Rural Households controlled 82 percent of total Area owned. Positively by 1992 the percentage of SC Rural Households increased to more than 21 percent and their share in Area owned too increased to 10 percent. Obviously, the other Rural Households reduced to 67.4 percent and Area owned to 78 percent. Interestingly by 2003 the percent of SC Rural Households scenario remained at 21.58 percent and their share of Area owned declined to 9.04 percent while the other Households which constituted 67.87 percent of total Rural Households owned 79.81 percent of total Area owned. Curiously by 2013 SC Households percent reduced to 20.06 of total Households and Area owned dropped to 8.52 percent of total Area owned but the other Households which constituted 23.23 percent controlled 32.02 percent of total Area. Both the percent of SC Households and their access to owned Area alarmingly deteriorated during 1992-2013.

In 1982, the ST Households were 9.7 percent of total Rural Households and possessed 10 percent of total Area owned. Nevertheless, the quality of land owned by ST households was inferior to that of non-STs. Therefore, the Agricultural Produce and consequent Profits were very meagre. Certainly by 1992 the percentage of ST households increased to more than 11 subsequently the Area owned too increased to 11. Regrettably by 2003, percent of ST households dropped to 10.55 successively their share in Area owned continued to be almost the same at 11.15percent. In 2013, ST households accounted for 11.89 percent of total Households accounting for 13.06 percent of total Area owned. Nonetheless the OBC Households registered 44.82 percent of total Households and possessed 45.68 percent of total Area owned in 2013.

Landlessness among the Dalits and Others

From Table II it is clear that the landlessness is more prevalent among SC and ST households. This trend was steady up to 2003. The percentage of landless SC households was 12.6 and the percentage of landless other households was 10.2 in 1982. By 1992 the landlessness among the SC households increased to 13.3 percent and the percent of landlessness among the other households remained at 10.2 percent.

The percentage of SC households was steadily on the decline: in 2003 it plummeted to11.31 percent and further nose-dived to 7.18 percent in 2013. The situation of other households was very uneven in 2003, decreased to 9.51 percent and rose to 14.2 percent in 2013. The position of ST households was slightly better in this respect. In 1982 among the ST households the percentage of landlessness was 17.1 percent and in 1992 it got reduced to 11.5 percent and was almost stable in 2003 and increased to 12.06 percent in 2013. On the other hand, 44.82 percent of Households of total households belonged to OBCs and they in turn owned roughly 45.68 percent of total Area owned in 2013. It is to be noted that this is the highest among all the social groups in terms of households and area owned. Another fascinating element is that the percentage of landlessness among the OBC households is only 6.98 percent in 2013. Perhaps at this juncture we can draw credible conclusion that the OBCs have more benefited from the positive discrimination programmes envisaged by the Five-Year Planning down the ages than the SCs and STs in terms of socio-economic growth. Such observable growth paved the required path to claim and assert political power and economic benefits. Consequentially the SCs and STs who were discriminated and exploited by the hegemonic groups in the past are now have another hegemonic social group to discriminate and exploit in the form of neo-rich OBCs. It may not be out of place to hypothesize that the OBCs have become perpetrators of discrimination and oppression (most of the honour killings, mob lynching and cow vigilantism is sponsored and carried out).

Table - II: Share of Scheduled Caste and Scheduled Tribe Households in Total area owned and landlessness among them (Rural)

ITEM	*SOCIAL GROUP*					*ALL HOUSEHOLDS*
	YEAR	*SC*	*ST*	*OBC*	*OTHERS*	
(1)	*(2)*	*(3)*	*(4)*	*5*	*(6)*	*(7)*
1. Percentage of distribution of Households	1982	19.7	9.7	-	70.6	100
	1992	21.5	11.2	-	67.4	100
	2003	21.58	10.55	-	67.87	100
	2013	20.06	11.89	44.82	23.23	100
2. Percentage of distribution of Area owned	1982	7.9	10.1	-	82.0	100
	1992	10.2	11.8	-	78.0	100
	2003	9.04	11.15	-	79.81	100
	2013	8.52	12.06	45.68	32.02	100
3. Percentage of landless house-holds owning no land less than 0.02 ha.	1982	12.6	17.1	-	10.2	11.3
	1992	13.3	11.5	-	10.5	11.3
	2003	11.31	12.81	-	9.51	10.03
	2013	7.18	9.41	6.98	14.2	7.41

Source: NSS Report No.399, (48th round, Jan – Dec.1992) 1997, P.33 & XI five year plan, Vol.I.

- NSSO Report No571(70th round, jan-Dec.2013 p. 28).

- Other refers non- SC/ST up to 2003. In 2013 other refers to Non-SC/ST/OBC

We shall now examine the sweeping changes that have occurred in the occupation of Dalits as against the general population despite the land reforms and agricultural growth in the post green revolution context.

Occupational Distribution of Dalits

The following Table III presents the changes that have taken place in the occupational distribution among SCs during 1971 to 2011. It is evident that between 1971 and 1981 there was a significant increase in the percentage of SCs turning into cultivators from 27.87 to 28.17 percent. Simultaneously SC agricultural labourer's percentage declined from 51.75 to 48.22 percent. Alongside the percentage of general workers and cultivators too declined from 26.9 to 24.94 percent. At the same time the percentage of non-farming workers among SCs increased from 20.38 to 23.61 percent. Thus, there were some noteworthy variations among the SCs with regards to occupation. Some became cultivators and good many entered into non-farming occupations indicating visible upward mobility. Such changes could be attributed to the redistribution of waste and surplus lands under 20-Point Programme in 1970s. This shiny bubble did not last long. In the course of 1981 and 1991 the percentage of SC cultivators sank to 25.44 from 28.17 percent and the percentage of SC agricultural labourers increased to 49.06 from 48.22 percent showing downward trend among SCs. Fascinatingly during 1991-2001 there was an increase in case of SC cultivators from 25.44 to 26.78 percent and parallel decline among the SC agricultural labourers' percentage from 49.06 to 46.15 percent. However, there was an increasing trend in non-farming workers percentage from all social categories, this was slightly on the higher side between 1991 and 2011.

It should be noted that the percentage of cultivators considerably declined among all social categories nonetheless it was very high among the SCs and STs. During 2001-2011 the SC cultivators declined from 26.78 to 14.8 percent and ST Cultivators from 54.32 to 34.5 percent.

Of course, in the case of occupation of the general population the percentage of Cultivators dropped from 41.58 to 38.75 percent and the percentage of agricultural labourers increased from 24.94 to 26.15 during 1981-91. Though the cultivators declined to 31.7 percent, the percentage of agricultural labourers almost remained the same during 1991 and 2001. The percentage of cultivators further declined to 24.60 in 2011 whereas the agricultural labourers increased to 30 percent. However, the percentage of non-farming workers increased from 33.48 to 35.10 in 1991 and further increased to 41.5 in 2001 and further to 45.40 in 2011 indicating the occupational shift in case of general population. The situation of STs was not so different. Among them the percentage of cultivators and agricultural

Table – III: Occupational Distribution at all India level

CATEGORY	*PERCENTAGE IN TOTAL MAIN WORKERS OF SCs.*					*PERCENTAGE IN TOTAL MAIN WORKERS OF STs.*					*PERCENTAGE IN TOTAL MAIN WORKERS OF GENERAL POPULATION*				
	1971	1981	1991	2001	2011	1971	1981	1991	2001	2011	1971	1981	1991	2001	2011
Cultivators	27.87	28.17	25.44	26.78	14.80	55.60	54.43	54.50	54.32	34.50	42.9	41.58	38.75	31.7	24.60
Agricultural labourers	51.75	48.22	49.06	46.15	45.90	33.00	32.67	32.69	29.88	44.50	26.9	24.94	26.15	26.5	30.00
Non-farming workers	20.38	23.61	25.41	27.07	39.30	9.40	12.90	12.81	15.80	21.00	30.2	33.48	35.10	41.5	45.40

Source: 1. Government of India, VII Five Year Plan, (1987 – 1992), Vol. II, P.330.

2. Census of India, 1991, Series 1, Paper – I, Union Primary Census Abstract for Scheduled Castes/Scheduled Tribes.

3.Primary Census Abstract for Total population, Scheduled Castes and Scheduled Tribes, 2011 Office of the Registrar General & Census Commissioner, India.

labourers declined marginally. On the other hand, the percentage of non-agricultural activities increased from 9.4 percent in 1971 to 15.8 percent in 2001. It further increased to 21 percent in 2011.

Thus, during 1971-2001 most of the SCs remained as agricultural labourers, of course there were some minor changes in the composition of agricultural labour. According to Professor Nancharaiah the shift was from attached agricultural labour to casual labour (Nancharaiah, 1998, pp. 105-106). This could be attributed to the onset of market forces and the introduction of green revolution. This was further accelerated by the State's Anti-Poverty Interventional Programmes in the post green revolution period. Such State's intervention was necessitated since many studies established that poverty was extensive among agricultural labour households (Rao. 2010).

Incidence of Poverty among SCs/STs

The Table IV highlights the data on incidence of poverty among various social groups across India

Table – IV: Incidence of Poverty among Social groups in percentages (Head Count Ratio)

YEAR	*Total(population)*		*Scheduled Castes*		*Scheduled Tribes*	
	Rural	Urban	Rural	Urban	Rural	Urban
1993 – 1994	37.30	32.40	48.11	49.58	51.94	41.14
2004 - 2005	28.30	25.70	36.80	39.990	47.30	33.30
2009-2010	33.8	20.9	43.5	33.0	47.1	28.8

Source: 1. Government of India, XI Five Year Plan, 2007 – 2012, Volume I, P.107.
2. Statistical Profile of Scheduled Tribes in India 2013, Ministry Of Tribal Affairs Statistics Division Government of India, p 94.

It is evident from the Table-IV that the Incidence of Poverty in general declined from 1993-94 to 2004-05. Nonetheless, the incidence of poverty among SCs and STs was much higher than the incidence of poverty among general Population in 2004-05. Also, among STs during 2004-05 and 2009-10 there was a sharp decrease in the incidence of poverty from 33.3 to 28.8 percent in urban areas and remained the same at 47 percent in the rural areas. The reversal was registered among SCs. The incidence of poverty among the rural SCs between 2004-05 and 2009-10 had increased from 36.8 to 43.5 percent. In 2009-2010 there was a marginal decline from 39.99 to 33 percent in the urban areas. Very same trend was noticed among the general population. The incidence of poverty among the rural general population increased from 28.3 to 33.8 percent between 2004-05 and 2009-10 and simultaneously decreased in urban areas from 25.7 to 20.9 percent during 2004-05 and 2009-10. By and large biological poverty seems to be on the verge of disappearance whereas social poverty still remains to be addressed.

Access to Education

The education and health index determine the progress of the Society. These are very crucial indicators to assess the status of the society. They are also vital components of Human Resource Development. Education not only improves the information, knowledge, skills of the people but also forms character and expands horizons of individuals to realise their capabilities and thus become social agents. In particular the technical and vocational education ensures and guarantees employment. Such assured and secured employment generates income, consumption and socio-economic status of the people. Government has been allocating nearly fifty percent welfare outlay for social and economic development of Dalits in and through education since the inception of First Five Year Plan. The details of literacy and educational changes that have occurred among different social groups are presented in Table V.

Table-V : Literacy Rates of SC/ST by sex from 1961 to 2011

Year	*General*			*Scheduled Castes*			*Scheduled Tribes*		
	Males	*Females*	*Persons*	*Males*	*Females*	*Persons*	*Males*	*Females*	*Persons*
1961	34.44	12.95	24.02	17	3.29	10.27	13.83	3.16	8.53
1971	39.45	18.7	29.45	22.4	6.44	14.67	17.63	4.85	11.3
1981	46.89	24.82	36.23	31.1	10.93	21.38	24.52	8.04	16.35
1991	52.74	32.17	42.84	40.24	19.03	30.07	32.5	14.5	23.63
2001	63.24	45.15	54.51	55.1	34.62	45.2	48.23	28.36	38.41
2011	80.9	64.6	73.0	75.2	56.5	66.1	68.5	49.4	59.0

Source: Educational Statistics at a Glance, Government of India, Ministry of Human Resource Development bureau of Planning, Monitoring & Statistics, New Delhi, 2014.

The above data beyond doubt substantiates the fact that there is a remarkable increase in the literacy rate of Scheduled Castes and Scheduled Tribes. In 1961 the percentage of literacy among the SCs was 10.27 and escalated to 66.1 percent in 2011. Simultaneously the literacy rate of STs in 1961 was recorded to be 8.53 percent and spiralled to 59 percent in 2011.

Though we notice quantum jump in literacy rate among SCs and STs, it is still far behind in comparison to general population. At the same time the standards of education and rate of pursuance of further education is still an unrealized dream among SCs and STs. There is also a literacy gap of 6.9 percent between the SCs and general population. In case of STs the gap is much more at 14 percent. The gap is still wider between SCs and STs. In comparison to SCs, STs are behind in literacy rate. When it comes to female literacy among SCs and STs, it is rather disheartening. The gap is very frightening and alarming even after six decades of independence.

- Educational Statistics at a Glance, Government of India, Ministry of Human Resource Development bureau of Planning, Monitoring & Statistics, New Delhi, 2014. PP-17.

Table-VI: Literacy gap of SC/ST to others in 2012-13

	Literacy Rates			*Literacy gap of SC/ST to others*	
	SC	***ST***	***Other than SC/ST***	***SC***	***ST***
1991					
Male	49.91	40.65	69.53	19.62	28.88
Female	23.76	18.19	44.81	21.05	26.62
Total	37.41	29.6	57.69	20.28	28.09
2001					
Male	66.64	59.17	78.7	12.06	19.53
Female	41.9	34.76	58.17	16.27	23.41
Total	54.69	47.1	68.81	14.12	21.71
2011					
Male	75.2	68.5	80.9	5.7	12.4
Female	56.5	49.4	64.6	8.1	15.2
Total	66.1	59.0	73.0	6.9	14.0

Source: Educational Statistics at a Glance, Government of India, Ministry of Human Resource Development bureau of Planning, Monitoring & Statistics, New Delhi, 2014.PP-22.

Table-VII
Dropout Rates, 2004-05 AND 2012-13– SC/ST (Provisional)

Category	*Class I-V*			*Class I-VIII*			*Class I-X*		
	All	*Boys*	*Girls*	*All*	*Boys*	*Girls*	*All*	*Boys*	*Girls*
General	31.47	33.74	28.57	52.32	52.92	52.92	62.69	60.98	64.94
SC	32.7	36.1	34.2	55.2	57.3	57.3	69.1	74.2	71.3
ST	42.3	42.6	42	65.9	65	67.1	79	77.8	80.7
2012-13									
General	21.2	18.3	19.8	39.2	32.9	36.3	48.1	46.7	47.4
SC	17.7	15.4	16.6	42.4	34.4	38.8	51.8	48	50.1
ST	31.9	30.7	31.3	49.8	46.4	48.2	63.2	61.4	62.4

Source: Govt. of India XI five year plan, 2007-2012, Vol.i.P.105

The school drop-out rate is one of the chief indicators to assess the status and standards of education. The dropout rates are disappointing among SCs and STs in general. The dropout rate of SC 1st to 5th standard children is 32.7 percent and 55.2 percent for the students of 1st to 8th classes. If were to record the dropout rate of 1st to 10th standard children it is 69.1 percent according to 2004-05 data mentioned in Table VII. The gap in the dropout rate between SC population and the general population is phenomenal. As per the data though the dropout rates have come down during 2012-13, still we have higher dropout rate among the SCs and STs among the 1st to 10th students.

This huge gap perhaps could be attributed to lack of finance, poor basic foundation, discrimination and poor mentoring. In fact, most of the higher education institutes are unfriendly to SCs and STs. Sometimes these SCs and STs are ragged and teased by passing derogatory comments such as; on reservation they have entered, their standards are poor, even at times their attire is laughed at, teaching faculty too is biased and non-receptive.

Access to Employment in Government Sector

From the Table-VIII it is understandable that there have been positive efforts to have significant SCs representation in government sectors during 1994-2013. However, still there is a noteworthy gap of two percent between their respective quota and the actual numbers and positions occupied by SCs even in 2013. In case of STs the gap is about 3.5 percent between their respective quota and the actual numbers and positions occupied in Class I positions according to available data. The representation is found to be better in case of Public Enterprises with reference to SCs in 2013. Very interestingly all the jobs with Social Stigma vis-à-vis Scavenging and Sweeping in Group-D category is more than filled by SCs and STs. This is a glaring example to prove that even after six decades of Independence India has not overcome caste-based professions and caste discrimination.

Conclusion

We have looked at the present socio-economic status and conditions of SCs and STs with the help of available data, facts and figures of *access to land, education, occupational distribution, incidence of poverty and employment in government sectors*. We have also critically analysed the outcome in the light of the development programmes initiated by the Government of India in the name of National Economic Policy-Five Year Plan with a specific intention of growth with justice of Scheduled Castes and Scheduled Tribes right from the First Five Year Plan.

Though various special development plans were drafted and subsequently several relevant schemes and programmes were implemented to augment the situation, the socio-economic status and conditions of SCs and STs, have not been raised to the desired state. Surely economic measures meant for SCs and STs ever since First Five-Year Plan improved the living standards in terms of *access to land, education, occupational distribution, incidence of poverty and employment in government sectors*. However, most of the SCs remain as landless agricultural labourers without proper and decent wages. On papers the Land Reforms are very glossy and promising. In reality the ownership and title deeds stand as a mirage. These days even the Assigned Lands are on platter handed over to corporates, whereas OBCs lands are registered and protected. Though lands of STs are protected by the Constitution and Scheduled Acts, in the name of dams and multipurpose projects the Lands are grabbed and SCs and STs are neither financially compensated nor settled in other places with equivalent land. Most of the SCs and STs are small farmers. With the onset of corporate agriculture, the marginal and small farmers are under threat. Despite Land Reforms we still notice substantial gap in the levels of

Table-VIII

Percentage of SC/STs Representation in Central Government Services in 1994, 1999, and 2004 (as on 1.1.200)

	1994			*1999*			*2004*			*2013*		
Group	Total	SCs	%	Total	SCs	%	Total	SCs	%	Total	SCs	%
A	59016	6046	10.25	93520	10558	11.29	80011	9744	12.2	69157	9043	13.08
B	103198	12442	12.06	104963	13306	12.68	135409	19602	14.5	153584	24906	16.22
C	2381613	374758	15.73	2396426	378115	15.78	2040970	344865	16.9	2555461	438724	17.17
D	1023285	209423	20.47	949353	189761	19.99	802116	147212	18.4	111878	33536	29.98
Total	3567112	602670	16.9	3544262	591740	16.7	3058506	521423	17.05	2890080	506209	17.52
Group	Total	STs	%	Total	STs	%	Total	STs	%	Total	STs	%
A	59016	1727	2.92	93520	3172	3.39	80011	3311	4.1	-	-	-
B	103198	2902	2.81	104963	3512	2.35	135409	6,274	4.6	-	-	-
C	2381613	128228	5.38	2396426	145482	6.07	2040970	136630	6.7	-	-	-
D	1023285	62945	6.15	949353	66487	7	802116	53776	6.7	-	-	-
Total	3567112	195802	5.49	3544262	218653	6.17	3058506	199991	6.54	-	-	-

Source: 1. Government of India ,XI Five Year Plan, 2007 – 2012, Volume I, P.114.

2. National Commission for SCs, annual report, 2013-14, p-93.

development between SC/ST and Non-SC/ST population. In the implementation of Land Reforms there are many loop holes and anomalies, hence the desired and intended fruits have not been reaped by SCs and STs. Political will also seems to be doubtful in this regard. Another frightening element is that today we are heading towards powerless politics and powerful economics. Digital revolution has totally anesthetized the middle class who have by and large been think tanks and activists in the past. Here after more than exploitation of the SCs, STs and the marginalized, irrelevance of SCs, STs and marginalized might be a concern. digitalization is slowly and steadily doing away with human labour in almost all the sectors. In fact, our India has now three worlds vis-à-vis world of poor SCs and STs, world of neo-rich BCs and OBCs and world of rich politicians and corporates. Therefore, digital world would sweep under carpet the concerns of SCs and STs slowly and steadily without notice. Hence, concurrently Government and NGOs have to initiate special measures like strict implementation of land reforms, redistribution of surplus land, wastelands among scheduled caste agricultural labourers and marginal farmers as an emergency priority and provide opportunities to cultivate coping mechanism to have smooth transition into digital world. Which means access to education shall not be confined only to literate them to sign digitally but also to equip them with information, knowledge and skills to be all the time relevant as digitalization of every aspect of human life is going to be reality sooner or later. At the same time the State should also provide necessary credit to enable SCs and STs to augment the productivity of their economic assets and also extend financial assistance to improve the educational levels while increasing the share of education in GDP from 4 percent to at least 7 percent.

Another important component that has to be seriously considered and immediately executed without fail is to have members who uphold the dignity and have respect for the identity of SCs and STs in the implementing team and authority. Preferably the implementing authority shall be enlightened and liberated SCs and STs. Otherwise so many Five-Year Plans will come and go still the socio-economic status and conditions of SCs and STs will remain as they are.

Reference Cited

Ahluwalia I.J. (1991): Productivity and growth in Indian manufacturing, Oxford University Press, Delhi.

Government of India (2011) Registrar General and Census Commissioner. Primary Census Abstract for Scheduled Castes and Scheduled Tribes. New Delhi: Ministry of Home Affair.

Gummadi, Nancharaiah (1988) Land and Caste, Himalaya publishing house, Bombay.

Rao C. H. (2005) Agriculture, Food Security, Poverty, and Environment, Oxford university press, New Delhi.

Notes

1. Dr G Jagadeesh, Research Officer, IV State Finance Commission, Tadepalli, Government Of Andhra Pradesh, mail ID: jagadeesh.hcu@gmail.com.
2. Thomas K.J., Ph.D. Research Scholar, Centre for Study of Social Exclusion and Inclusive Policy, School of Social Sciences, University of Hyderabad. ID: tkavumkatta@gmail.com.

Index

E

F

S